WINE PAIRING FOR THE PEOPLE

Wine Pairing for the People

THE COMMUNION OF WINE, FOOD, AND CULTURE FROM AFRICA AND BEYOND

Cha McCoy

with Layla Schlack

Foreword by Stephen Satterfield
Illustrations by Joelle Avelino
Photographs by Clay Williams

HARVEST
An Imprint of WILLIAM MORROW

Without limiting the exclusive rights of any author, contributor or the publisher of this publication, any unauthorized use of this publication to train generative artificial intelligence (AI) technologies is expressly prohibited. HarperCollins also exercise their rights under Article 4(3) of the Digital Single Market Directive 2019/790 and expressly reserve this publication from the text and data mining exception.

WINE PAIRING FOR THE PEOPLE. Copyright © 2025 by Chacine McCoy. Foreword © 2025 by Stephen Satterfield. All rights reserved. Printed in Malaysia. No part of this book may be used or reproduced in any manner whatsoever without written permission except in the case of brief quotations embodied in critical articles and reviews. For information, address HarperCollins Publishers, 195 Broadway, New York, NY 10007. In Europe, HarperCollins Publishers, Macken House, 39/40 Mayor Street Upper, Dublin 1, D01 C9W8, Ireland.

HarperCollins books may be purchased for educational, business, or sales promotional use. For information, please email the Special Markets Department at SPsales@harpercollins.com.

hc.com

FIRST EDITION

Designed by MELISSA LOTFY

Illustrations by JOELLE AVELINO

Photography by CLAY WILLIAMS

Library of Congress Cataloging-in-Publication Data has been applied for.

ISBN 978-0-06-332967-6

25 26 27 28 29 PCA 10 9 8 7 6 5 4 3 2 1

To my mother, Gwen, who taught me how to walk it,
and my father, Tony, who taught me how to talk it.

#TheChampayneLife

Contents

Foreword by Stephen Satterfield viii
A Letter from Layla Schlack x
Introduction xiii

AFRICA 1

Morocco 4

Senegal, Ghana, and Nigeria 10

Ethiopia and Somalia 18

Kenya and Tanzania 28

Angola, Mozambique, São Tomé and Príncipe, and Cape Verde 34

South Africa 42

THE WINE LIST: AFRICA 52

THE CARIBBEAN 55

Puerto Rico 58

Cuba 67

Dominican Republic and Jamaica 72

Barbados 82

THE WINE LIST: THE CARIBBEAN 88

LATIN AMERICA 91

Mexico 94

Chile 104

Argentina 118

Brazil 125

THE WINE LIST: LATIN AMERICA 136

UNITED STATES OF AMERICA 139

Soul Food 142

Lowcountry 153

Barbecue 159

Creole 169

THE WINE LIST: UNITED STATES OF AMERICA 176

ASIA 179

China 182

Japan 192

South Korea 199

Southeast Asia 204

Turkey 212

Georgia 218

United Arab Emirates 227

India 230

THE WINE LIST: ASIA 236

Acknowledgments 240

Bibliography 242

Index 244

Foreword

Stephen Satterfield

It seems I have never once missed an opportunity to talk about becoming a sommelier by age twenty-one—not in a talk or interview and now, not even in a foreword for a friend's book. It isn't so much a source of pride as it is an important fact to know about me, one that has colored my life more than any other hobby, occupation, or curiosity. I don't know if other sommeliers feel this way, but I suspect they do. When you begin on a professional path at a young age, while still a teenager, it is bound to leave a deeper impression than later, less committal endeavors. It is the combination of youth and indoctrination that makes it so much a part of one's identity. So long after I left the wine profession, I saw (and still see) myself as a sommelier.

Beyond what I'd learned in the trade, the experience of being in such a homogeneous space—even outside the United States—helped me understand the world beyond my own borders. I did not want to be bullied out of the wine industry, but I also didn't want it to be so boring! For a group of professionals trained to have good taste, we left much to be desired. We were a flavorless bunch of grapes—that is what happens when everybody in the group is the same.

In a righteous and indignant state, imbued with the hubris and exuberance of youth, I was looking for a cause to throw myself into. I soon found it in South African wine. Reading about the history of the Western Cape, the reflection of racial segregation—the US South and South African apartheid—was clearly evident in the stories of the Brutus Sisters and the band leader, Vivian Kleynhans, who is featured later in these pages. It was the energy of women like Vivian and the talented winemaker and Chardonnay artist Carmen Stevens that brought me back to South Africa time and again.

Had I known Cha McCoy back in those days, perhaps I would not have needed to go to Africa to find myself and my voice in wine. I would have been too busy listening to Cha's stories! Luckily, in *Wine Pairing for the People*, we are treated to just that—and with an international, cosmopolitan lens. Back in the day, all of the wine books were pretty much the same. All of the rules were so rote and rigid that it was almost as if the same author had ghostwritten an entire category. Even a cursory glance here makes it clear that, mercifully, those days are a distant memory.

For instance, consider the Calulu de Pieixe—an Angolan and São Toméan dish of dried fish stew cooked with red palm oil, greens, garlic, bell peppers, and eggplant. The thought of this dish paired with a chilled glass of Vinho Verde Tinto is nothing short of transportive. This combination, informed by Cha's time living in Portugal and Italy, her travels across the African continent, and her upbringing in Harlem, lends the text a refreshing quality that feels, at long last, truly different.

FOREWORD

Wine Pairing for the People lives up to its name and serves as an impressive showcase of Cha's scholarship as a sommelier, entrepreneur, and now author. This book is unlike any other wine book because, simply put, Cha is the author. I have come to know her as adventurous, enlightening, and hilarious—a beloved colleague and friend. Part of the charm and allure of being in Cha's company is her way of telling a story as if she were sittin' on the porch, delivering it with the energy, thoroughness, and animation you'd expect from a Harlem native. Growing up, Cam'ron and Mase made Harlem seem as if it were still at the center of Black culture, just as it was when Art Kane captured *A Great Day in Harlem*. After reading about the food in Little Senegal, I could be convinced that it's still true.

Lastly, I offer you a fair warning regarding the section featuring São Toméan dishes. It may incite severe wanderlust, provoking strong and recurrent urges to drop all of your responsibilities—laptop, book, and board. I encourage you to keep the book close, somewhere in your kitchen where you can return to it regularly. What brings me the most joy is knowing that for the mini-mes, the young people, and the twentysomethings just starting out in wine—those dreaming of the inspired places their craft could take them—they need look no further than Cha as a North Star.

Congratulations to you, my friend, on this tremendous achievement, and to you, the reader, for your excellent discernment. Salute!

A Letter from Layla Schlack

I came into the wine world almost by accident, with a background editing food and travel magazines. Prior to taking a job at *Wine Enthusiast*, which brought me into the industry and introduced me to Cha, I was an adventurous wine drinker who was frequently asked by friends or family to pick a bottle to pair with dinner, but I had never made any formal study of wine. That's all to say that my relationship with wine, from the beginning, has been about exploration. I come from a place of playing with the ways different pairings can alter my experience of a meal or a wine. In this area, I've never thought much about rules.

When I started working in wine in 2016, it was still pretty common for beer or a sweet wine to be recommended alongside anything spicy and/or fried. More nuanced conversations about highlighting certain elements of a dish with certain wines tended to be reserved for European cuisines. There were exceptions, of course, but that was my observation. As someone who wasn't quite acclimated to the wine world yet, I didn't fully understand it. Why get so detailed, down to the vintage and cru of a wine, to pair a French dish, only to say, "Try an off-dry Gewürztraminer" for any and every Thai dish? (This is not a dig at off-dry Gewürztraminers! It's just not the only option.) Unburdened by history and formal training, I was positive that interesting, nuanced pairings must exist for everything.

Those were also the days when people would bicker on Twitter about whether a taco that cost more than two dollars could really be authentic. At that time, the perceived value of a food had a direct relationship to how thoughtfully it was paired, and it wasn't lost on me that usually the cuisines of Black and brown people around the world were assigned a lower monetary value by white media and restaurant financers. Now, we still have a ways to go as far as treating all of the world's cuisines as equally complex and interesting, but increasingly, all sorts of foods are served in fine-dining settings with exciting wine lists. A movement is under way to document these pairings and the stories behind them, to add them to that canon that for so long focused on only one continent.

One of my favorite parts of this book was diving into history and the idea of cultural terroir. When we look at how something like peri peri moved through the world, where the spices and cooking techniques originated and who popularized the dish to a broader audience, I think it brings a new perspective to the idea that what grows together goes together. So much of what we eat and pair is being served in a different context than where it originated, and I'm excited to be part of a growing number of books that face that fact head-on.

All the best,
Layla

Introduction

I fell in love with wine while living in Italy. While there, the wine and food themselves weren't the only things that were fascinating to me—I was drawn to a lifestyle where food, wine, and socializing around the table come together as a focus of daily life.

Enamored by wine, I started my wine journey by working in wine retail and going after my sommelier certification. As my passion for travel persisted, so did my thirst for knowledge about wine. I started organizing trips to wine country to further understand the agricultural component as well as the science of wine making, while drinking well, and to experience this thing called *terroir*, firsthand.

With my growing wine knowledge, I was eager to share with others and take my wine career to the next level. However, I found it difficult to find a job as a sommelier without the formal wine pedigree that was required for this title. After many attempts to get an interview for a sommelier position in New York City, I decided to take matters into my own hands and build an experience in which I can introduce connoisseurs and enthusiasts to new styles of wine. And it turns out, they were eager to learn and explore.

INTRODUCTION

The great Shirley Chisholm once said, "If they don't give you a seat at the table, bring in a folding chair." In my case, I brought two folding tables and started my own wine dinner series called The Communion. I wanted to create a communal experience where wine was equally important as the food and not the afterthought, and where socializing and building community was a focal point. These pop-ups were more than a wine tasting—they became a cultural exchange from the curated menu of wine and food served to the guests at the table. It was important to me to feature wines from around the world with foods from around the world. Focusing on producers who cared about quality over quantity, sustinablity, and low-intervention practices in the vineyards and the winery was going to be my differentiator, engaging all levels of wine lovers.

My first pop-up was in 2017, and over five years, I went from my Harlem apartment to international cities such as London, Rome, Madrid, and Quebec City. And since then, I have expanded these dinners within the United States to San Francisco, Charleston, Harlem, Brooklyn, and Syracuse, where I opened my first brick-and-mortar, The Communion Wine & Spirits boutique shop. Each destination had a different wine and food theme, but all with the same goal of making wine feel more accessible and part of everyday life for everyone. This quickly became my motivation and mission and the focus of my events around the world.

Through my wine dinner pop-up series, The Communion, my engagements as a wine educator, my travels, and now this book, I'm driven to prove that wine has a place on every table. The cuisines of Africa and its diaspora, as well as Asia, are just as worthy of delicious pours. I became motivated to share how Senegalese, Jamaican, and Chinese cuisines, to name a few, also had the potential for and deserved the experience of wine and food pairings, despite the fact that my formal wine training said otherwise, except for Riesling.

INTRODUCTION

Vinous curriculums often focus on the principle that "what grows together, goes together," and on the notion that fine dining is limited to Western European cuisines. These educational materials classify spicy and funky foods, among others, as a challenge to pair, rather than an adventure. However, that didn't match my experience. I knew that good food well made goes with wine of the same caliber, regardless of whether they had a history together. More to the point, as a sommelier, formal education and training is passed on to customers and clients. I couldn't send that message or reinforce the idea that greatness means conforming to Eurocentrism. As a Black woman sommelier who had to fight my way into the room, I wanted this book to make space for those of us who felt othered in this industry, and that our food, our hair, our style, our music did not long belong here. I hope this book inspires you to challenge the social norms of the wine industry, especially if it silences your identity.

The unapologetically seasoned, spiced, and sometimes spicy foods of the world outside Europe are long overdue for wine pairings that match their complexity, vibrancy, and cultural relevance. And if you're still craving beef bourguignon by the end of this book, hopefully you'll approach wine pairing with The Communion way of thinking.

This book is for those wine lovers like myself, who did not grow up with wine at the family dinner table or with the language for it. And who, perhaps, like me, after discovering your favorite wine (mine was Sauvignon Blanc), you felt like you missed an eternity of enjoying one of life's simple pleasures. Maybe you want to get to know wine more intimately or to expand your palate, and you just don't know where to start. Don't worry, I got you: I was you and this book is for you.

Cheers,
Cha McCoy

How to Use This Book

First, we start with the basics: In this introductory section, you'll find a glossary of wine terms, tips for how to taste wine and identify flavors, and my favorite down-for-whatever wines that will pair with most foods and situations. So if you're new to wine, don't worry. I'm not going to throw you into the deep end.

The majority of the book is organized by country, except when we get to the United States, where I break down the pairings by different styles of regional cooking. Each chapter serves as a guide to pairing its respective cuisine, so you will learn about the history and culture that goes into a dish, the spices and aromas that define a locale, which wines to pair with which dishes, and why they work together. At the end of each section, you'll find the Wine List, sort of a cheat sheet that tells you what wine I recommend for each signature dish covered in each country or region. So if you just want to know what bottle to bring to a Lowcountry boil or serve with a Moroccan tagine, I've got you covered. You can find what you need quickly summarized at the end and keep moving.

You can also read this book cover to cover and get an education on the history of the dishes and the different principles around how geography plays a role when pairing wine and food. For some readers, this will be more valuable than me telling you what to drink on a specific occasion. My approach is informed by my own experiences, travels, and preferences, so in that sense, it's different from a lot of the classic wine guides. Some of the principles are the same, and some are ways of thinking that I had to develop when my instructors and textbooks didn't help when, say, I was consulting for my restaurant clients the best wine to go with Jamaican oxtails or jollof rice.

Because travel has been such a key part of my wine journey, I hope this book provides an element of armchair travel too. Come join me at an Angolan café in Lisbon or in the vineyards in Chile. Immersing yourselves in these cultures and destinations will deepen your understanding of why the pairings work and why the dishes in these pages deserve great wines to go with them.

In some chapters, you'll find a cocktail recipe or information about other, non-wine beverages that are signature to a country or cuisine. And for those countries that do make wine, you'll learn about the history of their wine industries, the people making the wine today, and how these bottlings work with local dishes. That is to say, no two chapters are exactly the same, but I can promise that you can flip open to any page of this book and find digestible wine information that will wet your palate. Grab a bottle and have fun choosing your own adventure.

Understanding How to Taste Wine Like a Pro

For anyone who's newer to wine or hasn't really interacted with industry pros, I know it can be intimidating to watch people swirling their glass and sniffing before sipping, then begin waxing poetic about what notes they found in the glass. Think of this section as a quick guide to get you comfortable with the wine world so that you can focus on what's in your glass and how well it goes with what's on your plate.

INTRODUCTION

THEORY ON TASTING

When sommeliers, critics, and other wine professionals taste wine, they do it in a very methodical way in order to deduce its quality. What's considered good depends on factors such as balance, complexity, intensity, and for certain styles of wines, how well it might age or has aged.

Good wine is one that you like, and what's good to me may not be good to you. That's fine. You should drink what you love. Still, deductive tasting, as it's called, will help you develop the vocabulary to explain why you like what you like and prepare you to translate that to a sommelier. This process is known as the five *S*'s:

See: Hold your glass of wine against a white background and examine it. What's the color? How opaque is it? Does this red wine have a brownish tint or pink rim to it?

Swirl: Give it some air. This is different from the oxidation that can happen in the bottle; it's a way to activate the aromas and flavors in the wine, to open them up. You are now decanting the wine in the glass.

Sniff: Give the wine a good sniff. Some pros will try one nostril, then the other, and then both. Others have a preferred side. Try different ways and see what you get. This is an important step, as our sense of smell is responsible for 80 percent of what we taste.

Sip: This is the moment you've been waiting for. Swish the wine around in your mouth a bit, maybe suck in some air. Pay attention to the structure of the wine: How do the acidity, tannins (if there are any), body, and alcohol balance each other out? What is the mouthfeel?

This is also when you match up what you sniffed with what you're tasting. I've always divided scents and tastes into four categories. From these macro categories, I can get down into more detail, which you can see in the Flavor Wheel (page xviii):

Fruity (cherry, cranberry, apple, peach) and **floral** (rose, white blossoms, citrus blossoms)	**Mineral** (salinity, slate, rocks) and **vegetal** (bell pepper, jalapeño, grass)
Spice (baking spice, wood, tobacco)	**Chemical** (petrol, kerosene, tar)

Savor: After you've swallowed your sip, pay attention to the finish. How long does it last? Do new flavors or sensations reveal themselves? I also like to take this moment to think about how I feel about the wine. Do I like it? Do I want to drink it again? Does the wine need food? It's one thing to buy wines that are highly rated or award winning, but if you're sitting in that savor moment and don't love what you just drank, that's not the right wine for you.

AROMAS AND FLAVORS

Everyone's seen a TV show or movie with someone making fun of some wine snob for saying a wine tastes like leather-bound books or the forest floor. But being able to identify what you taste and smell from a wine is a valuable tool when you're pairing because it will help you think about flavor combinations you like.

Here is something called a flavor wheel. The idea is, you can scan it to help you identify what it is you're tasting and smelling. I didn't invent it, but mine's a little different from other ones out there, because these are notes I use. It's influenced by my palate and my frames of reference. The things we taste and smell on a regular basis shape the descriptors we reach

The Flavor Wheel

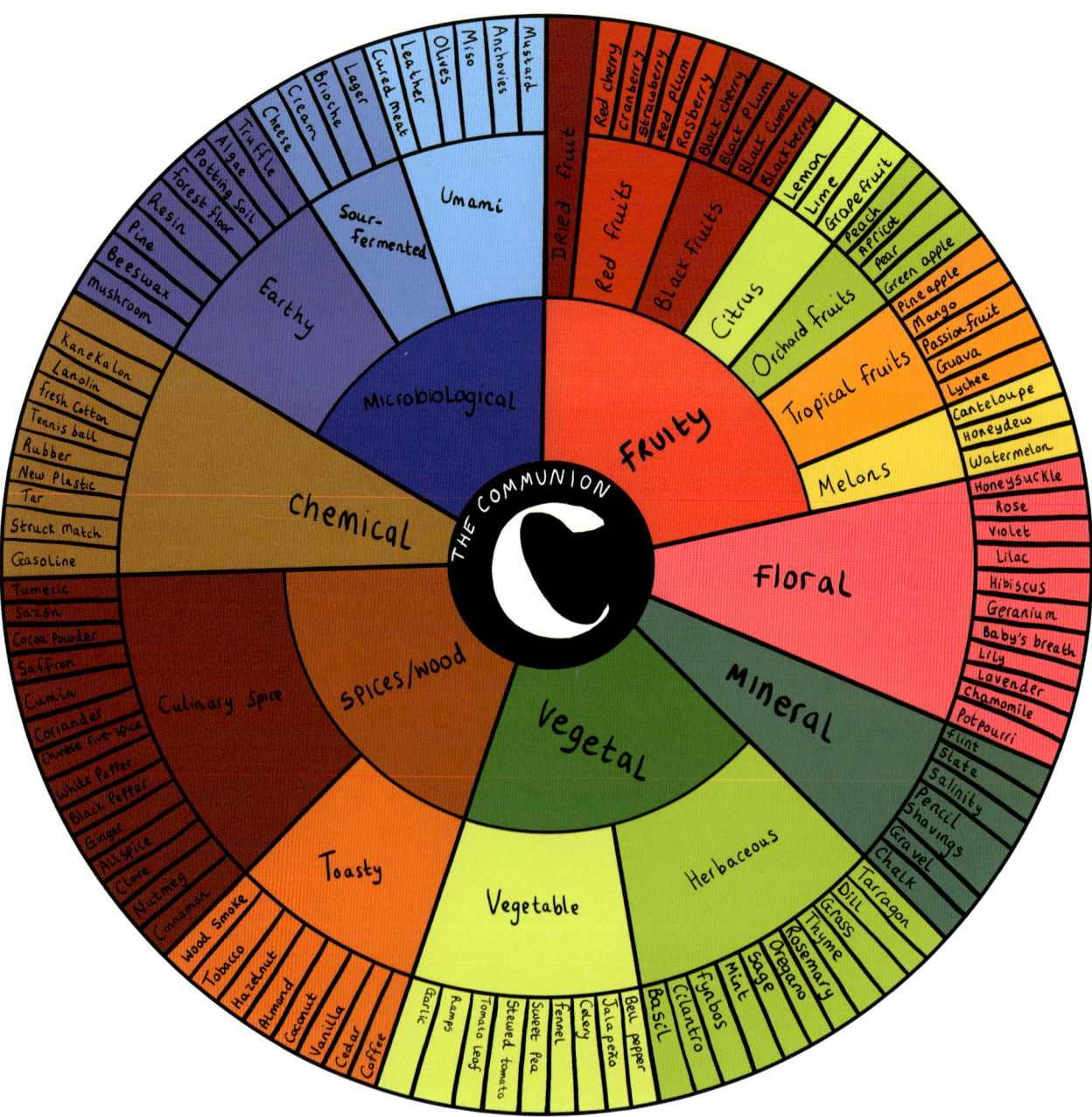

for when we're tasting wine. So use this wheel as a guide to help you put words to what you're experiencing in a glass and keep building on it.

THEORY ON TERROIR

Terroir is the way wine reflects the environment in which the grapes were grown. Terroir influences the flavors and structure of the wine, and it also provides the special, magic quality that makes drinking wine a transporting experience. In some cases, I'll look for similar elements of terroir between wine and food. A lot of seafood goes well with wine from coastal regions, for one. When you're talking about terroir, here are the main components to consider:

Aspect and elevation: Put more bluntly, this is site selection. Whether vineyards are on a hill, a mountain, in a valley, or on flat land, location will affect how the wine tastes. So does the direction the vineyards face, whether it's east, with morning sun, or west, with afternoon sun. Angling a vineyard toward ocean breezes or sheltering mountains can also have an impact.

Climate and weather: In theory, climate is the long-term patterns of weather, defined by things like average temperatures and rainfall during a given season based on location. For example, Paso Robles, California, is mostly known for having a warm, sunny climate (minus a few cooler pockets), with cool nights and a bit of rain and fog coming over the mountains from the Pacific Ocean. That's its climate. Typically, most of its rain falls in the winter. That's where weather and climate meet. A lot of those patterns are changing, and in some regions, there no longer seems to be much of any pattern, but for now we still consider climate distinct from but closely related to weather. The latter is the conditions in a given year, and it's the primary factor in why one vintage is different from another.

Soil and geology: Whether the soil the grapes grow in is sandy, clay-based, volcanic, gravel, or any number of other variations, geology determines both how water drains away from the vines, and the mineral nutrients available to them. The presence of rocks and how much soil sits on top of the rock is another factor here.

Culture and tradition: Not all wine books or educators will include this as a factor of terroir, but I think it's an important one. Some regions have historical methods and standards for wine growing and wine making that influence even those wines that break free of those traditions. In other regions, wine is a relatively new product, but culture or conditions might be similar to a region with a history of wine making, so that will inevitably influence the wine.

Pairing for the People

There are two major ways to approach pairing a dish: marrying similar flavors, or layering in a contrasting flavor. Simply put, the flavor pairing will either be a complement to each other or a contrast. There are many ways to match food with beverages, but the key to a great pairing is finding balance. The main elements to consider in the dish in order to identify a potential pairing are the same ones a chef or a mixologist has to approach when creating a new recipe: acid, fat, salt, spice (heat), and sweetness. Once you understand where your dish ranks on each of these measures, you are able to cultivate the palate experience you want with the wine.

INTRODUCTION

The first thing to match is flavor, which is pretty straightforward: You can look at the flavor categories on page xviii and think about what flavors will be in your dish. If you're taking this approach, it's important to think about acidity and sweetness too: Tart, tangy dishes like a salad with a vinaigrette will want a wine with a good amount of acidity, while desserts will call for a sweet wine, to give two examples. You can also match based on texture and weight. For example, some wines have sort of an oily or waxy texture, and those will pair well with greasier foods. For denser, richer foods like steak, you want a rich, full-bodied wine.

I do want to talk about the idea that "what grows together, goes together," which is so common in wine. In the chapters that include wine regions, I'll get into more detail about that. But even for countries that don't grow wine grapes or have a wine-making culture, there can still be a nugget of truth to this theory. For example, sometimes the cuisine of a seaside area will pair well with a wine whose grapes are grown in a maritime region, because both will have that oceanic salinity to them. The same can be true for mountains or deserts.

If you want to create a yin-and-yang effect with your pairing, think of contrasting flavors that work well together, like sweet and salty, or sweet and spicy. I sometimes think of this approach as using the wine as a sauce or a condiment, like the wine can stand in for a squeeze of lemon on your fish. It's harder to pair for texture this way—a light-bodied wine like Alvarinho won't lighten a rich, saucy dish like barbecue ribs; it will be overpowered. But there's one important exception: Sparkling wine goes with just about anything. For richer or oily dishes, its acidity and light texture can act as a palate cleanser between bites.

Wine Rules for Serving

Regardless of what food and wine you're serving, you want to have decent wineglasses that make it easy to swirl and aerate wine and that concentrate aromas toward your nose. They don't have to be fancy, but preferably you'll use clear glass and with a stem. You don't necessarily need a different shape for every style of wine; there are plenty of good universal glasses on the market these days. Be sure to have a corkscrew to open the wine. It sounds obvious, but it never hurts to remind yourself before company shows up.

You also want to serve your wines at the right temperature, and that's different depending on the style. A good rule of thumb is that the lighter the body, the more chilled the wine should be. Here's a quick guide:

Style	Temperature	Chill Time
Sparkling	40–45°F	2 hours
White	45–55°F	1½ hours
Rosé	50–55°F	1½ hours
Red	55–65°F	45 minutes–1 hour
Fortified	55–60°F	45 minutes–1 hour

DOWN FOR WHATEVER WINES

If you're hosting a potluck or aren't quite sure what your guests like, stock up on wines that are easy, approachable, and will pair well with many cuisines.

Red	White	Sparkling
Gamay	Chenin Blanc	Blanc de Blancs
Pinot Noir	Viognier	
Garnacha	Chardonnay	

INTRODUCTION

Wine Terms Defined

Acidity: The tartaric, malic, citric, and succinic acids in wine that create a mouthwatering sensation and balance tannic and sweet characteristics.

Age: The amount of time wine spends maturing in the bottle before it's opened. Wine is also aged before bottling, but that's generally not what's being referred to when we talk about the age of a wine.

Alcohol, ABV: Most dry wines fall in a range of 10–15 percent alcohol by volume (abv); the alcohol level correlates with how ripe the grapes were when they were picked and will affect the wine's flavors and body.

Appellation: A legally defined region where wine is grown.

Balance: How the acidity, tannins, sweetness (if present), and alcohol work together with the flavor notes and aromas.

Body: The weight of the wine on your tongue.

Botrytis/noble rot: A beneficial yeast that infects grapes late in the harvest season; these grapes are often used to make sweet wines.

Bright: High in acidity.

Dry: Not sweet.

Fermentation: The process of yeast converting grapes' sugar into wine's alcohol.

Finish: The persistence of flavor after you've swallowed a sip.

Lees: Spent yeast left in the wine for weeks, months, or years that imparts a bready or toasty flavor.

Malolactic fermentation: A secondary fermentation in which tart malic acid is converted into lactic acid, which gives the wine a buttery or creamy sensation.

Mouthfeel: The wine's texture, such as silky, creamy, velvety, or coarse.

Oxidation: The chemical reaction that occurs when wine is exposed to oxygen. Often, this is a flaw that reduces the wine's vibrancy, but sometimes it's a choice by the winemaker to achieve certain characteristics.

Pyrazines: chemical compounds found in grape skins that can give wine a green bell pepper flavor.

Residual sugar: Sugar left in the wine after the fermentation process that makes a wine sweet to varying degrees.

Tannins: A biomolecular compound present in grape skins and oak, among other things, that gives wine a drying sensation.

Terroir: The factors such as climate, weather, soil, aspect, and elevation that create a wine unique to a specific time and place.

Texture: How the wine feels in your mouth.

Variety/varietal: Variety is the type of grape used, such as Chardonnay or Cabernet Sauvignon, while varietal is an adjective used to describe characteristics of or wines made from one specific grape.

Vintage: The year in which a wine's grapes are picked. Not all wines will have a vintage, because some blend multiple vintages.

Vitis vinifera: The Mediterranean grape species from which a lot of the world's wine is made.

Africa

Morocco	4
Senegal, Ghana, and Nigeria	10
Ethiopia and Somalia	18
Kenya and Tanzania	28
Angola, Mozambique, São Tomé and Príncipe, and Cape Verde	34
South Africa	42

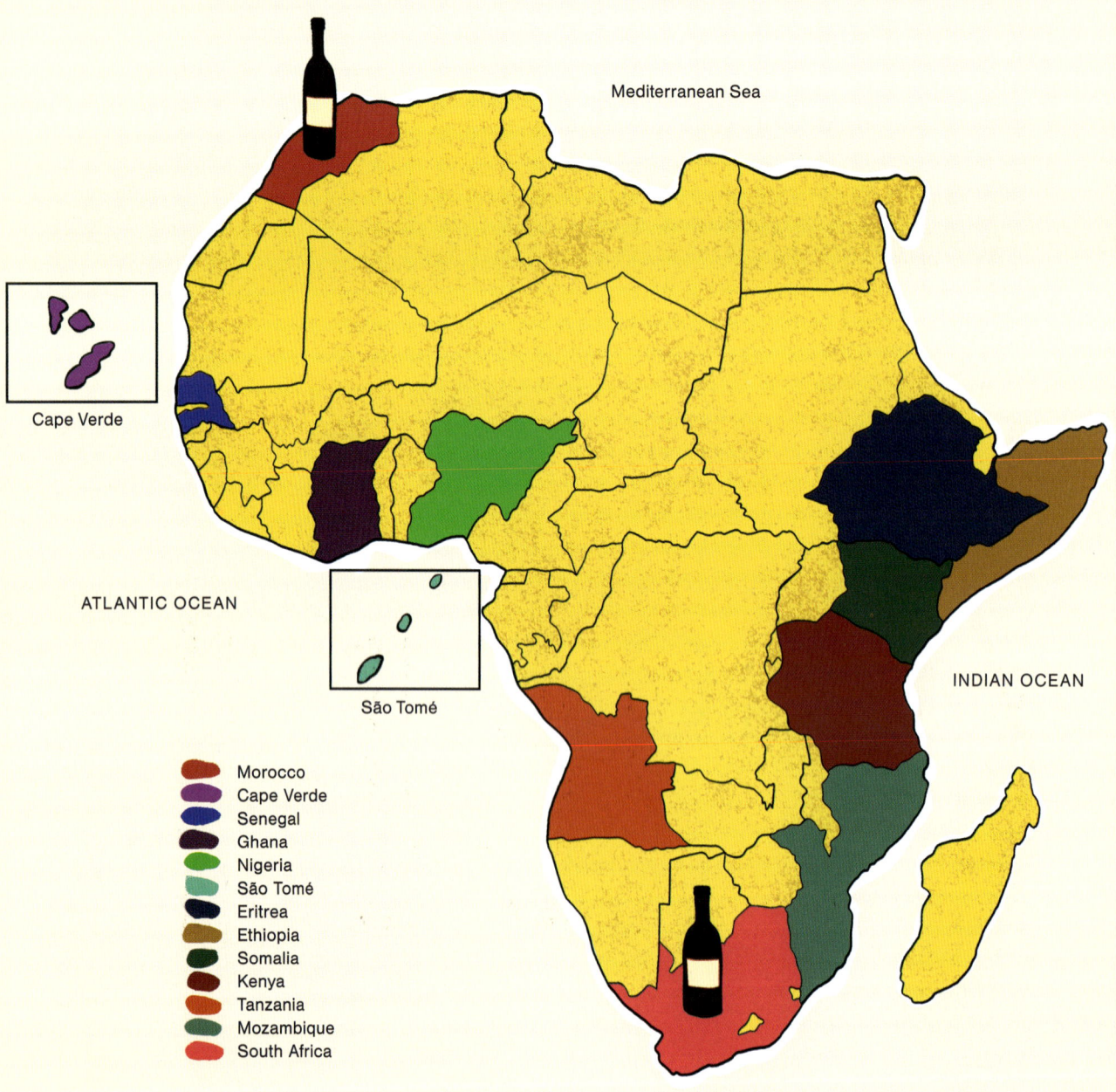

This book had to start with Africa, because everything starts with the Motherland. From the souks of Marrakech down to the top of Table Mountain, the Continent has also been a vital part of my own journey as a traveler, inspiration as a wine professional, and identity as an African American.

I don't t cover every African country here, and some have been combined. That's not meant to diminish the thousands of unique cultures, languages, cuisines, or terroirs that aren't included or that are grouped together. I just wanted to focus on the areas that have made an impact on my journey so far, and to highlight the spices, dishes, and cuisines from the main travel destinations and the accessible cuisines from the continent that you can find globally. Maybe this section will spark your own journeys of learning, traveling, and tasting. I am excited to continue to discover more of Africa in the future, and I hope this inspires you too.

In this section, you'll learn about everything from South African wine making and its connection to Portuguese colonialism, to my personal connection to East Africa through DNA testing. I go beyond travel and wine, into a journey of self-discovery. And I have my own motive here too: I think that exploring these cuisines through the lens of fine wine will provide more opportunities for chefs on and from the Continent to break into the fine-dining world. Opening the door for more fine dining African experiences in the Western market would create real financial gain.

WINE PAIRING FOR THE PEOPLE

Morocco

Coordinates: 31.7917° N, 7.0926° W
Capital: Rabat, or Ribāṭ in Arabic
Country/Continent: Morocco is in Africa. It's bordered by the Atlantic Ocean to the west, and the Mediterranean Sea to the north. Surrounding countries are Algeria to the east and southeast, Western Sahara to the south.
Population: 37 million
National Drink: Mint tea
National Dish: Tagine and couscous
Top Export: Fertilizer, cars, consumer goods
Official Languages: Arabic and Moroccan Berber
Independence Day: November 18, 1956
Independence from: France

One of the ways a wine can be pure magic is when it starts off closed, reserved, not giving anything away on the nose or palate, and then it blossoms into something spectacular. My first impression of Marrakech was also a little bit like that. After stepping onto the tarmac, into air so hot that it rippled, my friends and I got in a cab and wound through a tangle of streets that seemed a uniform, dusty shade of terra-cotta. All I could see was the heat and that hue. We were staying in a riad, a traditional guesthouse found commonly in Morocco, and upon arrival, our host immediately greeted us with the mint tea that I would later learn is customary here; its aroma filled the air. We sipped politely in the courtyard before we were shown to our rooms. There, we were greeted by blue, green, and yellow, with black-and-white mosaic-tiled floors and a view down to a courtyard with a fountain in the middle. And it was an explosion of color, which was a huge difference from the monochrome clay palette that painted the city.

I knew then that Morocco was going to be special, like a mystery we'd have to uncover. From design to the culinary, it would be a layered adventure. And it did not disappoint.

That sense of exploration came on top of a strong surge of emotion. This girls' trip to Morocco was my first time in Africa. I had been living in Italy, determined to experience more of the world, and here I was on the Continent, with the badass Black women who were closest to me. It meant something to be on the soil where my ancestors had once stood, where most white people were the minority, for a change, and I blended in with the majority. On the streets, vendors would shout "Sister! Sister, good price for you." Nothing could take away from that—not the budget airline with uncomfortable seats that charged for bottled water, not losing my luggage in transit, not an airline strike in Italy that left me scrambling to make it to Morocco. Standing in the middle of the souks, soaking in the vibrant culture of Morocco, made the hectic journey all worth it.

When we stepped off the plane, everything looked, felt, sounded, and smelled completely different from what I was used to. I was smacked in the face by temperatures of 90-plus degrees Fahrenheit and served a side order of arid air that made it feel more like Mars, not Marrakech. The early September temperatures were what we would describe in New York City as "Africa hot." But I also felt a sense of comfort and belonging instantly. It was this mix of discovery and confidence that fueled my adventures to Marrakech. We immersed ourselves in the rituals of this Arabic nation from honoring the adhan call to prayer five times a day, to visiting hammams for a traditional cleansing. That also meant haggling in the souk for argan oil, saffron, tea sets, rugs, and leather goods to bring back as gifts, and then returning at night to eat street food at the famous stalls in the medina. What's stuck with me since, as wine has become a central part of my life, are the fragrances, spices, and smoke-kissed flavors of that trip, and a thirst to continue traveling, tasting, and exploring the world.

Looking back on Morocco through the lens of wine, I've developed a stronger appreciation for the country's terroir and culture. I think it's just as important as a traveler to look at the character of a place and how it might determine my experiences there, as it is to consider how terroir influences what it is I taste in the wine. If we define this as some alchemy of soil, climate, topography, and biodiversity, Morocco has a distinct terroir. If we layer in history and culture, we get even more complexity.

The Maghreb, or Mediterranean region of North Africa, has been home to the Berber people for a millennia. This Indigenous group remains today, despite occupations by Phoenicians, Romans, Ottomans, the Islamic Empire, and as recently as the mid-twentieth century, the French. The Spaniards have also occupied some of the country's ports, and several independent dynasties have reigned. With coasts on both the Mediterranean Sea and the Atlantic Ocean, Morocco's culture has absorbed and adapted these foreign influences seamlessly.

Moving south and east from the coasts, you'll come to the Atlas Mountains. Their highest peak stands at more than thirteen thousand feet, and these mountains provide sanctuary for Berber languages and various animal species that may have gone extinct without this shelter. In between the sea and the desert, this range has a semiarid climate; it's rich in natural resources like copper, silver, iron ore, marble, and more. Here, too, European flora and fauna come together with those more common in other parts of Africa.

And then there's the Sahara. The world's largest desert forms a neat swoop around the country's southeast. It influences people's livelihoods; tribal people are mostly reliant on raising hardy livestock and leading tours with activities such as camel trekking,

WINE PAIRING FOR THE PEOPLE

> ## Sip the Culture
>
> Although Morocco does produce wine, it's not the primary drink for the observant Muslim population. Here are some drinks you're likely to encounter:
>
> **MINT TEA.** All day, every day, you'll find sweetened mint tea. Some people choose warm drinks in hot climates because the beverage makes them sweat, ultimately cooling them off. Plus, the minty flavor can feel a little cooling.
>
> **KHUNJUL.** This is another tea, made with some of the same spices you'll find in ras el hanout.
>
> **ORANGE JUICE.** A lot of oranges grow here, so you'll find plenty of fresh-squeezed juice.
>
> **AVOCADO SMOOTHIES.** A filling drink made with avocado that's often blended with almonds, dates, or both.

sandboarding, moonlight dune hikes, or even spending the night in the desert immersed in the Berber lifestyle. As droughts become more severe and the desert even drier, many people may be forced to move into the city. Here, nights can be cold and days scorching hot—the type of diurnal swings winemakers drool over.

In the middle of all this is Marrakech, a city of about one million people, surrounded by lemon, orange, and olive groves, near the mountains and desert, set inland from the Atlantic. It's a historic center that was the national capital during some dynasties, and that has also been quite poor during others. Today, it's an important tourist hub. Some of the most misunderstood places in the world are economically poor, largely inhabited by Black people and other people of color, and yet have a strong magnetic attraction to outsiders. Maybe it's the urge of the colonizers to always look for the next place to "discover" or the next Instagram-worthy destination, but Morocco consistently remains *the* destination for culture. The ancient walled city is home to the country's largest souk, or marketplace, plus a lot of smaller ones. The result is a terroir with a little bit of everything—sights, sounds, smells, tastes waiting behind staid terra-cotta-colored walls.

On my first full day in Marrakech, before my eyelids opened, that feeling of *Where am I?* kicked in; it was becoming very familiar to me as an expat. I have taken advantage of my life abroad, traveling frequently, which usually leaves me disoriented in my new surroundings. However, that first morning in Marrakech felt different. I was awakened not by sight but by sound. It was my first encounter with adhan, the call to prayer, which is the prescribed time for prayer (or fard) in Islamic culture. Praying five times a day with your larger Muslim community is one of five pillars of Islam; since Morocco is an Islamic country, a designated role is given to the muadhin, the announcer, who recites the adhan from the minaret of the mosque. It was a powerful inner familiar feeling, yet foreign. I felt like I could see what I was hearing even with my eyes shut, as if I had been here before. I was in awe and reveled in the idea that I would be able to experience this throughout my day. Don't we all need a reminder to stop our day and check in with our spiritual self? To help us make sense of our purpose and make every day more intentional. In the same way that a glass of wine can help me embrace slower living and recenter myself at the end of a long day, the adhan did so on a spiritual level.

Like any professional wine evaluation, the ability to tap into using your senses is very important to connecting with what is in your glass. When traveling, these rules remain the same. After the sound of the adhan, sight was the next sense that was evoked and connected me to my surroundings. We secured a full-day tour through the medina of Marrakech—the walled city filled with souks, hammams, and at night, entertainment, including snake charmers, fortune-tellers, and food stalls that served delicious dishes that could rival the work of some starred chefs. I am not one for tours, but there are just some places that it is worth bringing in experts to guide you. As we weaved in and out of the Old City, with its famed architecture, we learned about its impressive, detailed arches, colorful mosaic tiles, and ornate wooden doors. In the heart of Jemaa el-Fnaa, the public square within the walled city, the air smells like ras el hanout, Morocco's ubiquitous spice blend. Ras el hanout means top of the shop, and many people and restaurants have their own custom mixes that can include some combination of cardamom, cumin, clove, cinnamon, nutmeg, mace, allspice, ginger, chile, coriander seed, peppercorn, sweet and hot paprika, fenugreek, and turmeric. Its aroma is warming, like sweet baking spice, but also savory and peppery—a study in contrasts.

When I think of a wine that evokes all of these sensations, a Syrah takes me there—a Crozes-Hermitage from the Rhône Valley in France. With this wine, you can expect both black and red berries, black peppercorn, and notes of leather and truffle. But pairing foods with all of these spices and aromas can get complicated, depending on your portion for your blend.

Morocco's Wine Regions

Wine has been produced in Morocco, off and on, since the Phoenicians occupied the area, maybe as early as 1000 BCE. There was renewed interest during French colonization, and today most wines are produced with European grapes—Carignan, Cinsault, Grenache, Alicante Bouschet, Clairette Blanche, and Muscat. Bordeaux blend varieties (Caberenet Sauvignon, Merlot, and Cabernet Franc) in addition to Chardonnay, Chenin Blanc, and Sauvignon Blanc are growing in number, but they're all pretty minor. Some wines are also produced from the indigenous blue-black-skinned red-wine grape Taferielt. Red wines make up about 75 percent of production, followed by rosé (often called vin gris, or gray wine, here), and then white.

Of the 40 million or so bottles produced annually here, between 5 and 15 percent are exported, mostly to France. The remainder is sold domestically, mostly in shops and restaurants that cater to tourists, as it's illegal to sell wine to the resident Muslim population. Wine sales may also be prohibited during Ramadan and other holidays.

The country has fourteen Appellations d'Origine Garantie (AOG) and one Appellation d'Origine Contrôlée (AOC) spread across seven regions:

Doukhala-Abda: Doukkala AOG and Sahel AOG are located in this region, which surrounds Casablanca.

Chaouia-Ouardigha: Home to Zenata AOG.

Rabat-Sale-Zemmour-Zaer: The Chellah, Zaer, and Zemmour AOGs are in this region.

Meknes-Tafilalet: Morocco's one AOC, les Coteaux de l'Atlas, is located here, along with Beni-M'Tir AOG, Guerrouane AOG, and Zerhoun AOG.

Fes-Boulmane: Beni-Sadden AOG and Sais AOC are here.

Gharb-Chrarda-Beni Hssen: Rharb is this region's only AOG.

L'Oriental: You can find Angad AOG and Berkane AOG in Morocco's only Mediterranean wine region.

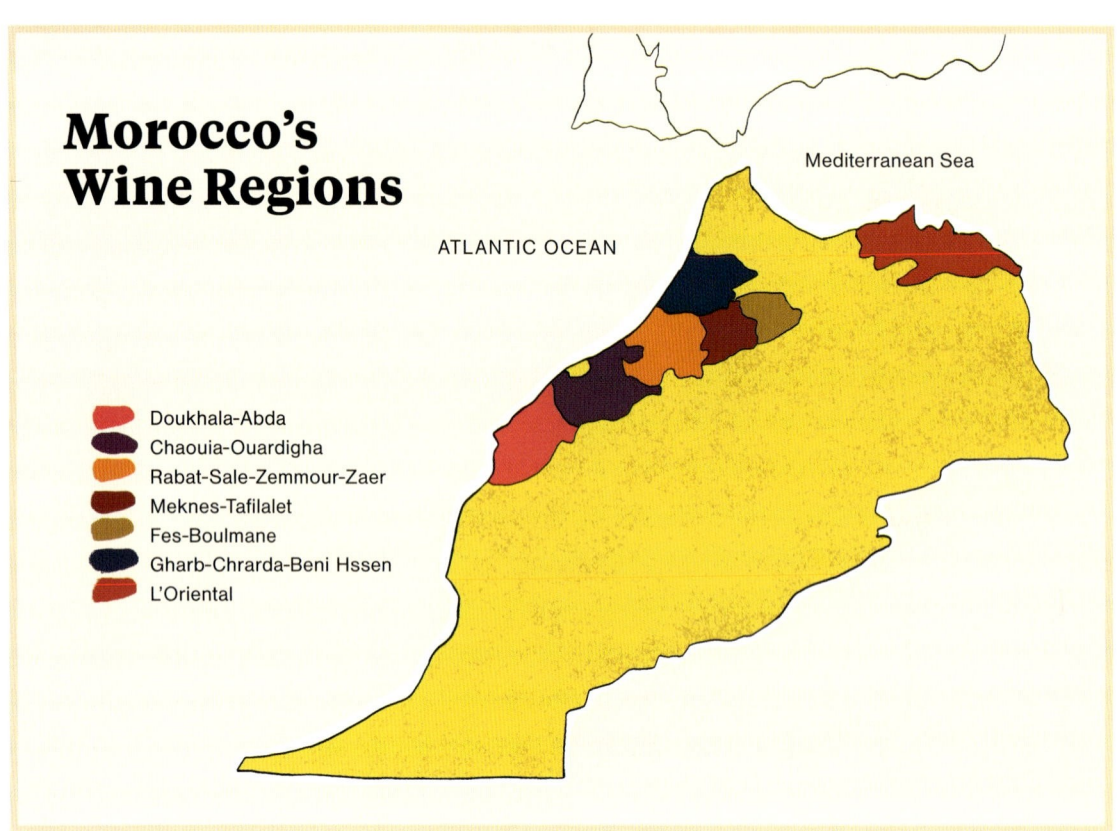

AFRICA

+ PAIRED UP

MOROCCAN SALAD AND HARIRA + NERO D'AVOLA ROSATO, SICILY, ITALY. A salad of steamed and cooked vegetables such as eggplant, beets, roasted peppers, onions, and tomatoes is often accompanied by a tomato-based soup with chickpeas and red lentils, called harira. A dark rosé made with the Nero d'Avola grape from Sicily is a crushable version of the variety that is both herbal and fruity and would pair well with the fresh tomato flavors in both the salad and soup.

BABBOUCHE + CHARDONNAY, CHABLIS, FRANCE. This snail soup is seasoned with flavors like thyme, aniseed, mint, caraway, and licorice. Chablis, a Chardonnay made in Burgundy, is known for its crisp mineral and citrus notes from Kimmeridgian soils—meaning the soil is partly made up of fossilized oyster shells. Chablis also gets some oak aging, which makes it a little richer. It's a popular pairing with escargot and a go-to for highlighting herbal flavors in slightly richer dishes, so it's basically made for babbouche.

FISH KEBABS + SAUVIGNON BLANC, MARLBOROUGH, NEW ZEALAND. At night, the stalls of Jemaa el-Fnaa turn into street-food vendors. These had numbers instead of names, and most served kebabs. To pair these night-market fish kebabs, I would lean into something fresh that has a bit of a punch to keep up with the smoky char on the fish. What comes to mind is that peppery jalapeño note that can come from New Zealand Sauvignon Blanc. The wine can be used like a condiment packed with tropical notes and the green pepper and jalapeño. It's like building a fish taco in your mouth.

MEAT KEBABS + CÔTES DU RHÔNE—RED BLEND, FRANCE. For my red wine and red meat lovers, go for the goat kebabs and choose a red wine that plays up the smoky preparation and still balances well with heartier meats. Grenache, Syrah, and Mourvèdre blend, also known as Rhône blend or GSM for short, is a great option for supporting the flavorful blend of spices with the floral notes and juicy berry flavors that come from wine being aged in stainless steel or neutral oak, both of which keep the wine approachable and fresh.

TAGINE + DRY GEWÜRTZTRAMINER, ALSACE, FRANCE. The national dish of Morocco, tagine can be described like the Old City of Marrakech: reserved and protected, but once revealed, multilayered and expressive. Tagine was one of the most memorable meals during my time in Marrakech, and when I was exploring food in the medina, I shared a chicken tagine after a hammam. Chicken pieces braised with olives, herbs, spice blend, and preserved lemon. Gewürztraminer is the perfect complement that is just as dynamic, with bold aromas and rich characteristics of lychee, passion fruit, dried mango, and floral notes of white roses and complex spices.

Senegal, Ghana, and Nigeria

Senegal

Coordinates: 14.4974° N, 14.4524° W

Capital: Dakar

Country/Continent: Senegal is in Africa. It's bordered by the Atlantic Ocean to the west, Mauritania to the north, Mali to the east, and Guinea and Guinea Bissou to the south. The Gambia is carved into a southwestern portion of Senegal.

Population: 17.3 million

National Drink: Bissap cold, spiced hibiscus tea

National Dish: Thieboudienne (broken rice stewed with fish)

Top Exports: Gold, petroleum, phosphates

Official Language: French, but Wolof is the most widely spoken language

Independence Day: June 20, 1960

Independence from: France

Even though my travels have taken me to other parts of the Continent, there's no question of the influence of West African culture on Black American experience. About a quarter of the 12.5 million enslaved Africans brought to the United States were from Nigeria, with others coming from West African kingdoms and countries like Ghana and Senegal. Everything from AAVE (African American Vernacular English) to Black food culture has direct ties to Senegal, Ghana, and Nigeria. I've experienced these cultures independently through their diaspora in New York City where more recent immigrants from these countries live, shop, and dine. My professional wine journey exposed me to West African cuisine. Upon my return to Harlem after living in Italy, I was excited to put my newfound wine knowledge to work—and the last thing I wanted was a desk job. So I took a part-time minimum-wage job working at The Winery, a boutique wine shop, which was conveniently located in the center of Harlem's Le Petit Senegal (Little Senegal), on West 116th Street, stretching from Malcolm X Boulevard (Lenox Avenue) to Eighth Avenue. It was here where I found myself exploring a new culture right in my own backyard. Eventually the aromas of nokoss, a traditional Senegalese pepper paste, filling the air, visions of butchered halal lamb being delivered, and the joy of Eid al-Fitr on the faces of men and women dressed in heavily embroidered clothes became a new norm for me and Harlem.

Though I am from Harlem, 116th Street was still unfamiliar ground from 139th Street where I was raised. Most of my family are from Uptown, basically the northern part of Harlem that was still considered undesirable then to nonnatives. The Harlem I grew up in was centered mainly around soul food—restaurants like Sylvia's were staples— and most popularly known for being the home of rappers like Cam'ron to Mase. However, 116th Street was always a different vibe, real different. During my childhood, the most iconic landmarks were Malcolm Shabazz Market and Nation of Islam Mosque No. 7 (now a Sunni Muslim mosque called Masjid Malcolm Shabazz). This was where you get to experience the intersection of African and Black American culture. The Malcolm Shabazz Market was the epitome of Afrocentric culture in Harlem, and people would come from near and far to shop for West African fabrics, art, beauty products, and jewelry from the vendors that seem to have an endless supply of vibrant, colorful kente cloth, nourishing shea butter, and intricate beaded bracelets. Restaurants such as Africa Kine played a role solidifying 116th as Little Senegal. I am certain the existing Islamic community made this area a safe space for the practicing Senegalese to call their new home. Africa Kine opened in the mid-1990s by Kine Mar and her husband, Samba Niang, in part for those tourists who would dare come north of Ninety-Sixth Street. The Senegalese community made this street their own, creating a bustling new economy to the area while bringing their homeland to Harlem.

During my time at The Winery, I was frequently asked about pairings with Senegalese food. I soon learned that most of the Senegalese restaurants like Africa Kine, which was directly across the street from the wine shop at the time, were open to BYOB, allowing guests to bring their own bottles for

---

Ghana

Coordinates: 7.9465° N, and longitude of 1.0232° W
Capital: Accra
Country/Continent: Ghana is in Africa. It's bordered by the Gulf of Guinea to the south, Côte d'Ivoire to the west, Burkina Faso to the northwest and north, and Togo to the east.
Population: 33.5 million
National Dish: Fufu
Top Exports: Gold, crude petroleum oils, and cocoa beans
Official Language: English
Independence Day: March 6, 1957
Independence from: United Kingdom

Nigeria

Coordinates: 9.0820° N, 8.6753° E
Capital: Abuja
Country/Continent: Nigeria is in Africa. It's bordered to the south by the Gulf of Guinea, Benin to the east, Niger to the north, and Chad and Cameroon to the west.
Population: 218.5 million
National Dish: Jollof rice
Top Exports: Petroleum oils and crude, petroleum gas, and fertilizer
Official Language: English
Independence Day: October 1, 1960
Independence from: United Kingdom

dine-in service. The restaurants typically did not acquire liquor licenses. I had no clue what Senegalese food entailed, but I realized I was eager to dive into this cultural gem that my wine journey was planted right in the heart of.

Years later, after I'd eaten my way through New York City's West African restaurants and was feeling confident about my pairing ability, I was motivated to focus my work on developing wine lists for underserved cuisines that I believe deserved the attention of great wine pairings. I decided to promote this myself through my wine dinner series, The Communion, which was already established as a way to make wine more accessible and was the inspiration for my own wine boutique shop. I had hit on something that was important to the culture, and it motivated me to be more intentional with my wine career. The Communion was soon adopted as part of Tastemakers Africa, a travel and commerce platform founded by Cherae Robinson connecting the African American community to Africa through authentic and modern experiences, like weeklong events for the 2018 Brooklyn AfroPunk music festival. For AfroPunk, I turned to the cuisine that I'd grown a new affinity for, Senegalese, for inspiration, and locked in with the owners of Café Rue Dix in Brooklyn to serve as my culinary partner for this experience. This dinner landed me my first major media coverage, an article in *New York* magazine's "Grub Street" segment, written by Nikita Richardson. The Communion was picking up momentum. Here is a selection of the paired courses from this experience:

The Communion
Tastemakers Africa + AfroPunk Edition
Café Rue Dix

SUMMER 2018

Force & Celeste Semillon 2017, SWARTLAND, SOUTH AFRICA
Steamed Pot of Mussels in White Wine Sauce

▼

Movia Sivi Pinot Grigio 2014, PRIMORSKA, SLOVENIA
Senegalese Spring Rolls: Spicy Vermicelli Beef and Lamb, Shrimp Rolls over Kale

▼

Château de Montmirail Gigondas Cuvée de Beauchamp 2014, RHÔNE VALLEY, FRANCE
Dibi Senegal: Grilled Lamb Chops Onion Confit, Sweet Plantains, Severed with Couscous

▼

Conterno Poderi Aldo, Nebbiolo 2013, LANGHE, ITALY
Thieboudinne: Stewed Snapper and Vegetables Served over Jollof Rice

▼

Lucchetti Spumante Rosato Special NV, MARCHE, ITALY
Caakiri: West African Pudding, Sour Cream, Couscous,
Topped with Strawberries and Bananas

AFRICA

+ PAIRED UP

SALADE NIÇOISE À LA SÉNÉGALAISE + ROSÉ, BANDOL, FRANCE. Inspired by the classic Niçoise salad from Provence, France, the Senegalese remix has a heartier and richer flavor that trades some of the traditional lighter ingredients like seared tuna, green beans, and cucumber for locally grilled fish, sweet potatoes, and black-eyed peas. Keeping the tradition alive by pairing this staple salad with a signature wine connects the other ingredients. Typical blends can include the following leading varietals: Mourvèdre, Grenache, and/or Cinsault.

YASSA POULET + FALANGHINA, LAZIO, ITALY. Marinated grilled chicken in zesty lemon, caramelized onions, and Dijon mustard with spices of black pepper, garlic, bay leaves, and occasionally chili pepper for mild heat, served with couscous, cooked until tender and served with white rice and a spicy mustard sauce. Falanghina's citrus and stone fruit flavors and bright acidity pairs well with the tangy and citrusy flavors of the dish and the mild heat.

BANKU WITH TILAPIA AND SHITO + GRÜNER VELTLINER, WEINVIERTEL, AUSTRIA. Tilapia is marinated in a blend of spices that includes, garlic, ginger, and chili. It's grilled and served with a crispy, smoky exterior, with banku, a fermented dough made from corn and cassava. Shito sauce is a spicy black pepper sauce made from dried fish, chile peppers, and ginger, giving this dish a deep, umami flavor. Austrian Grüner Veltliner complements the peppery and herbaceous flavors of the dish, and its crisp green-apple flavor balances the tanginess of the banku and the smoky notes of the grilled tilapia.

FUFU WITH LIGHT SOUP + BARBERA, PIEDMONT, ITALY. Light soup has a tomato-based broth, which is full of flavor from peppers, onions, and a blend of local spices, with protein options of chicken, goat, or fish commonly added. Fufu is a typical West African starch staple made from either pounded cassava or yam and served with light soup. Barbera is a high-acid red wine that cuts through the savory richness of the light soup without disrupting the bright red fruit flavors of cherry and plum and the black pepper finish that complement the tomatoes and peppers in the soup.

EFO RIRO + CINSAULT, RHÔNE VALLEY, FRANCE. This spinach stew is made with tomatoes, red bell peppers, onions, and sometimes Scotch bonnet peppers for heat. Palm oil adds to the rich flavor and protein choice of fried fish or beef. Cinsault is a lighter-bodied wine with bright red fruit flavors—tart cherry, red currant and raspberry—and lavender. The wine is a great match to balance the heat of the Scotch bonnet with the bright red fruit flavors of the Cinsault.

POUNDED YAM WITH EGUSI SOUP + PALM WINE. A traditional dish of Nigeria made from ground melon seeds (egusi) and cooked with greens like spinach, and tomatoes and a blend of spices with your choice of protein from beef, goat, or fish. This dish is traditionally served with pounded yam that was boiled first and serves as the starch to soak up the complex flavors. The main flavors are the rich and nutty from the egusi seeds and the earthy balance from the leafy greens, making a deep savory dish. Traditional West African palm wine is the fermented sap of palm trees. The natural alcoholic drink is a contrast pairing that brings refreshing and tangy flavors to the complex egusi soup. Expect fruity and nutty notes and a round creamy texture. A new sparkling palm wine brand, Ikenga Wines, is expected to hit the US market; be sure to support them.

(continues on next page)

CAAKIRI WEST AFRICAN PUDDING + ICE WINE VIDAL BLANC, ONTARIO, CANADA. This dessert of yogurt and couscous has a creamy texture and a milky taste with slight chewiness. Typically flavored with nutmeg, cinnamon, or vanilla, its toppings may include raisins, coconut, or lemon zest. It pairs well with the dessert ice wine—made from grapes harvested after a freeze for ultimate concentration and sweetness—from Vidal Blanc grapes, which helps balance the tanginess of the yogurt.

Judgment of Jollof

(For one version of jollof, see Chef Pierre Thiam's recipe on page 17.)

I don't know which causes a larger divide in West Africa: the FIFA World Cup match or the epic culinary debate that's more commonly known as Jollof Wars. I am glad I am able to remain neutral on this topic, as I am American born and don't see a civil ending to this war. Just kidding. But seriously, I will choose not to share my opinion and instead provide a wine pairing for each of some of the more commonly found jollof recipes.

Jollof is a rice dish flavored with tomatoes, onions, chile peppers like Scotch bonnets, and other spices. Its name originates in the Senegambian region once ruled by the Jolof Empire, spanning parts of Senegal, Gambia, and Mauritania, where rice grew. Ingredients and preparation techniques vary from country to country, region to region, and household to household. But there are some common threads, as well as some distinct differences that sparked an intense debate over which country's style is the grand cru of jollof. The controversy is a healthy rivalry between several West African countries, and now that it has made its way stateside, it gives a greater sense of pride for one's country and a shared culinary staple.

In wine, there is no greater equalizer than blind tasting. This was evident in the historic Judgment of Paris tasting event held in 1976. Several French and British wine experts as well as one American blind tasted a selection of top wines from French producers. The tasters didn't know that there were Californian wines from Napa Valley, considered up-and-coming wines from a new region, alongside the French wines. In both the red and white category the California wines received the top scores, which changed the perception of American wine and the idea that only Europe could produce world-class wines. This competition showed the power of blind tasting when judging wine or even jollof rice from different countries. I encourage you to taste each style of Jollof for quality and your preference, without origin or reputation influencing you, and to form your unbiased opinion about which is the best for you. Here are three different regional styles I have tried with a complementing wine pairing/ Hold your own Judgment of Jollof and share your favorite with others.

AFRICA

NIGERIAN JOLLOF RICE

- Nigerian jollof starts with long-grain rice that's been parboiled and washed a second time to remove some starch.
- One of the seasonings used is bay leaf, which enhances the smoky flavor. Additionally, thyme and curry powder are sometimes used.
- It's cooked over a wood fire and allowed to burn at the bottom to give it a smoky flavor.
- Vegetables are optional and can include carrots, peas, and bell peppers
- Protein options are traditional beef, chicken, goat, or fish
- Heat level is medium to high

PAIR IT WITH: Cabernet Franc from Chinon, France, which has bright red fruit flavors like cranberry and raspberry, to contrast the savory dish. However, they both share bold, smoky, and spicy characteristics that will complement each other. Cabernet Franc from Chinon typically has a hallmark earthy, smoky, and herbaceous quality; its medium tannin levels that pair well with the protein options.

GHANAIAN JOLLOF RICE

- Ghanaian jollof is made with basmati or jasmine rice. Both of these have long, slender grains with a higher starch content than the rice used for Nigerian jollof.
- The rice is not parboiled. Parboiling makes it soggy.
- Tomato stew and meat stock are used to cook the rice.
- It's seasoned with garlic, ginger, and bay leaves.
- Ghanaians use shito, an oily condiment made with hot peppers, ginger, shrimp, and onion.
- Vegetable options are typically peas, carrots, and bell peppers.
- Protein options are chicken, goat, beef or fish.
- Heat level is mild to medium.

PAIR IT WITH: Agiorgitiko from Nemea, Greece. This is a versatile grape with plum, cherry, and raspberry notes, and softer tannins to offset the dish's milder heat level without overpowering the flavor. Its good acidity pairs well with Jollof with chicken as its main proteins. You can find versions with a hint of spice that will elevate the ginger and garlic flavors in Ghanaian jollof and make these two a complementary pairing.

SENEGALESE JOLLOF RICE (THIÉBOUDIENNE)

- Thiéboudienne is often made from broken rice—a remnant from French colonizers—so the grains may be shorter than those used in other styles.
- Fish is always used to season thiéboudienne and is often served with the rice too. The dish can be cooked with fresh fish, dried fish, fermented fish, or a combination as its main protein.
- Vegetable options are carrots, cabbage, cassava, and some will include eggplant.
- Heat level is typically mild and texture is softer and wetter than other Jollof.

PAIR IT WITH: Zinfandel from Howell Mountain, California. Made from one of very few wine grapes that has red flesh, not just red skin, this is a big, bold wine. It's got ripe notes like berries and tobacco that contrast the dish's savory and umami ingredients, but it's also nice and peppery, so the contrast isn't too overpowering. This full-body and high-tannin choice can stand up to the more pronounced flavors of the oily fish and hearty vegetables.

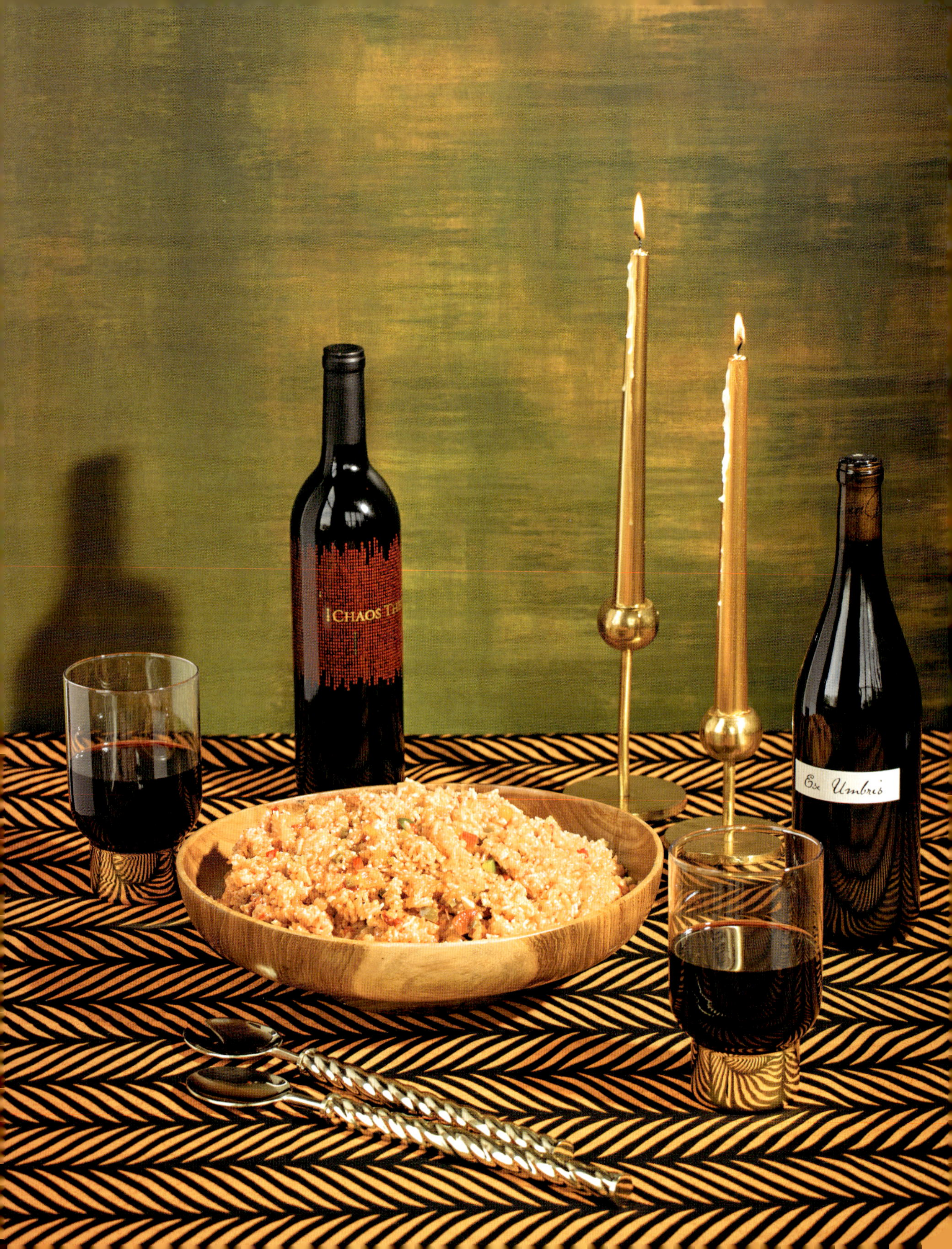
Ex Umbris

AFRICA

JOLLOF RICE + ZINFANDEL
HOWELL MOUNTAIN, CALIFORNIA

This recipe is from Pierre Thiam, who was born in Senegal and has become sort of an ambassador for West African cuisine in the United States. He founded Yolélé, a company that sells packaged foods grown by African farmers, and the New York restaurant Teranga. He's also the author of three cookbooks. In this recipe, he uses long-grain rice that isn't broken, and he flavors it with yett, which is fermented conch. He also adds a little heat with chile.

1. Rinse the rice several times until the water runs clear. Drain and set aside.
2. In a large pot, heat the oil over medium-high heat. When the oil begins to shimmer, add the onion and bell pepper. Cook, stirring with a wooden spoon, until the vegetables begin to soften, about 3 minutes. Add the tomato paste and lower the heat to its lowest setting. Continue cooking, stirring often with a wooden spoon to avoid scorching, until the tomato paste begins to darken, 5 to 7 more minutes. Add the tomatoes and their juice and stir well to combine. Add the vegetable stock, bay leaf, fermented conch (yett) or fish sauce, salt, pepper, and Scotch bonnet. Raise the heat to high and bring to a boil. Reduce the heat to low and simmer until the oil begins to rise to the surface, 10 to 15 minutes.
3. Meanwhile, in a steamer or couscoussier, add the uncooked rice, cover tightly, and steam for about 15 minutes. You'll want to stir the rice once or twice to make sure it cooks evenly. (The rice is done when it is half cooked; the outer rim of each grain is translucent but it's still crunchy to the taste.) Remove and stir to prevent clumping.
4. Transfer the rice to the tomato broth. Stir and cover with a tight-fitting lid. Reduce the heat to the lowest setting and cook until the grains are soft, about 30 minutes. Uncover and stir to release the steam and fluff the grains. Taste to see that the grains are cooked. If not, add a few drops of water, cover again, and continue cooking for a few more minutes. Transfer to a platter and serve.

Used with permission from *Senegal: Modern Senegalese Recipes from the Source to the Bowl* by Pierre Thiam and Jennifer Sit (Lake Isle Press, 2015).

SERVES 4 TO 6

2 cups jasmine rice

4 tablespoons peanut or vegetable oil

1 cup chopped yellow onion

1 cup chopped green bell pepper

2 tablespoons tomato paste

1 cup peeled and chopped tomatoes or canned diced or chopped tomatoes with juice

3 cups vegetable stock or water

1 bay leaf

1 small piece, about 2 inches, of fermented conch or yett, or a few dashes of fish sauce

2 teaspoons fine sea salt

1½ teaspoons fresh-ground black pepper

1 Scotch bonnet or habanero chile

Thin-skinned Zinfandel grapes with notes of strawberry, blackberry, tobacco leaf, and sweet baking spice that contrast with the dish's savory and umami ingredients. But it's also nice and peppery, so the contrast isn't too overpowering. This full-body and high-tannin choice can stand up to the more pronounced flavors of the oily fish and hearty vegetables.

Ethiopia and Somalia

Ethiopia

Coordinates: 9.1450° N, 40.4897° E
Capital: Addis Ababa
Country/Continent: Ethiopia is in East Africa. It's bordered by Somalia to the east, Kenya to the south, Sudan and South Sudan to the west, and Eritrea and Djibouti to the north.
Population: 120 million
Top Exports: Gold and coffee
Official Languages: Afar, Amharic, Oromo, Somali, Tigrinya
Independence Day: Freedom Day observed on May 5, 1941
Independence from: Italy's occupation ended, and Emperor Haile Selassie was reinstated

E**thiopia has always been intriguing to me.** Growing up in the Abyssinian Baptist Church in Harlem, titled with Ethiopia's historic name and cofounded by Ethiopian seamen, I felt an almost magnetic pull to the country. And on the 200th anniversary of the church, members of my church family, my godmother Kate included, embarked on a journey back to our church's roots, which connected us even more deeply to this sacred land.

I still haven't been, except for a layover on the way to Kenya. And that was enough to whet my palate, especially after a cup of Ethiopian coffee in the terminal.

It's worth acknowledging here that Ethiopia and Somalia are, like most countries, diverse places made up of different ethnic and religious groups, with different languages and cuisines. I can't speak to all of them, especially because most of my experience has been diasporic. But I do feel like I've gotten to see some of the culture, learn the history, and taste the food of Ethiopia.

When I lived in Italy for graduate school, one of my closest non-American friends, Sarah, was Ethiopian. I recall seeing her large Afro, piercing eyes, and flawless caramel skin when she was working at the local bar near my university. I knew I had to connect with her—my hair was barely surviving, and my skin was dry and hard from the chalky Roman tap water. I needed the cheat code on maintaining my crown while living

AFRICA

in Italy. But I learned more from her than just where to find a good hair braider. She also exposed me to the Ethiopian relationship to Italy. I learned that Ethiopia had defeated Italy in the Battle of Adwa, making Ethiopia the only country in Africa never to have been colonized. However, events like severe droughts, civil wars, political repression, and famine have contributed to large migration of Ethiopians as refugees to Europe, including Italy.

It's interesting to look at Italy's coffee culture through the lens of the two countries' relationship. Coffee originated in Ethiopia and Yemen, with the first domesticated coffee plants grown in Harrar, Ethiopia. In Italy, Venetian merchants started importing coffee and opening cafés in the 1500s. It became a part of Italy's cultural identity, especially when espresso was invented in Turin in the late 1800s. But coffee couldn't be grown in Italy. For a long time, Italian workers grew coffee in Brazil. The scholar Dr. Diana Garvin, who focuses on Italian, food, and women's studies, writes about how the goal of Italian-owned coffee plantations in East Africa was a motivator for the Fascist invasion. I think of this as another way in which drinks and food tie people together throughout history. It's also an example of how Europe is positioned as central in the world of food and drinks, and relies so much on African history. A centuries-long relationship that must not be forgotten started when Italy occupied the Horn of Africa and took ownership of coffee plantations in Ethiopia.

One figure emerges as part of Ethiopia's resistance against Europe: Ethiopian Emperor Haile Selassie. He reigned from 1930 to 1937, and then from 1941 to 1974. But before he was Negusa Nagast, or king of kings, he was the Ras (a title similar to duke or prince) Tafari Makonnen. During the 1930s, some Afro Jamaicans drew from Marcus Garvey's Back to Africa movement, the Bible, and Haile Selassie's crowning as emperor to form the Rastafari religion, which held Haile

Somalia

Coordinates: 5.1521° N, 46.1996° E
Capital: Mogadishu
Country/Continent: Somalia is in East Africa. It's bordered by Ethiopia to the west, Kenya to the south, the Arabian Sea to the east, and the Gulf of Aden and Djibouti to the north.
Population: 17.6 million
Top Exports: Livestock, bananas
Official Languages: Somali, Arabic
Independence Day: July 1, 1960
Independence from: Somali Independence Day celebrates the unification of states that were previously colonized by the United Kingdom and Italy

Selassie as either Jah incarnate, or a messiah. Within Ethiopia, Haile Selassie was also instrumental in fighting off the Italian Fascist army, even though he was exiled to England for most of the occupation.

A Brief History of Two Kingdoms

It's hard to know where to start discussing the history of the region where humanity likely began. But we'll jump ahead a couple of million years. Under the Axum Empire, Ethiopia became Christian around 300 CE. A Phoenician missionary named Frumentius is credited with that development. During this era, trade and relationships deepened with the Roman Empire, India, Persia, the Jewish rulers of Yemen, and beyond. Those relationships, plus growing interest from Europe, would continue through the Solomonic era, from 1270 through the 1500s. Ethiopia was a center of trade at the beginning of the 1600s, but a series of short-lived leaders, conflict between Christians and Muslims, and various other factors led to a period of isolation from Europeans. This pattern of mixing among tribes, cultures, and countries, followed by isolation, I think, is why Ethiopia feels so international but also so distinctly Ethiopian.

In 1805, England put an end to isolation, forming an alliance so that it could have a strategic military position on the Red Sea in case of conflict with the French. Other African countries were colonized at this time, but Ethiopia never was, although it was occupied by Italy.

Somalia, to its east, is believed to be the prehistoric Land of Punt, which traded myrrh and spices with ancient Egypt and Greece. Stretched out along the coast, Somalia has always had a lot of contact with other countries, especially those on the Arabian Peninsula and in Southwest Asia. That's why it was one of the first African countries to adopt Islam, with its first mosque dating to the seventh century. At times during the Solomonic era, Somalia and Ethiopia fought religious wars against each other.

In the 1500s, Somalia fought off Portuguese colonizers. Somali city-states became wealthy and powerful, largely able to fight off colonizers until the Italians came in the 1800s. Italy created a protectorate, called Italian Somaliland, in part of the country. It was bordered by British Somaliland, and following World War II, a British protectorate replaced the Italian one. In 1950, the UN put a plan into place for the country to become independent in ten years.

Like Ethiopia, Somalia has a history that has always incorporated many different cultures, from ethnic Somali, to Bantu, to Arab, and then Italian. That shows up in its cuisine and culture.

Eating Ethiopian in the United States

I've been lucky to have eaten delicious Ethiopian cuisine in Italy; Washington, DC; New York City; and Syracuse. That's where I've gotten to know the berbere spice mix of chile, paprika, fenugreek, warming spices like ginger, cinnamon, and coriander, and indigenous Ethiopian spices like ajwain and korarima. There are variations on this spice mix, and differences based on regionality and

AFRICA

Ethiopian American Population Density

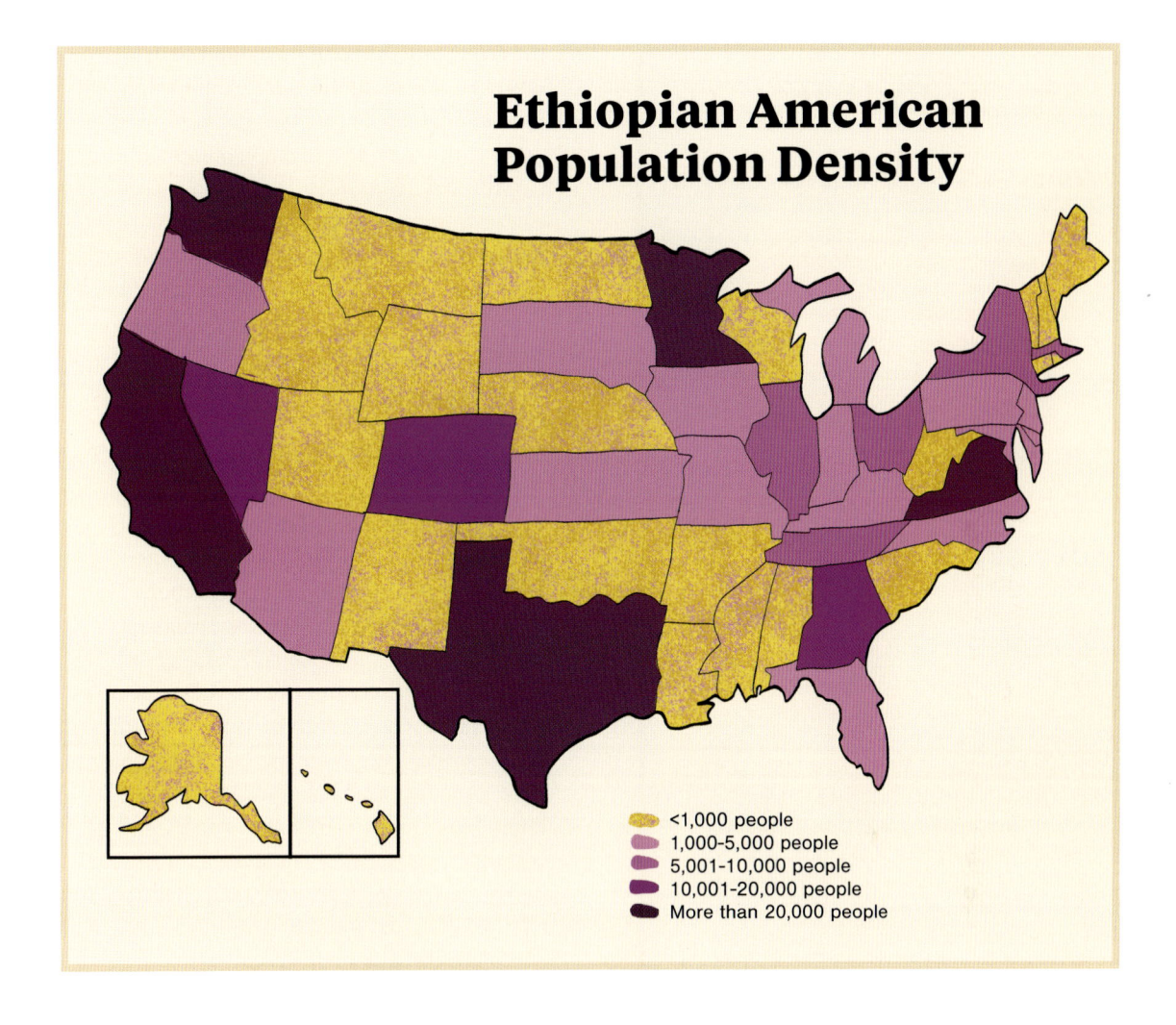

- <1,000 people
- 1,000-5,000 people
- 5,001-10,000 people
- 10,001-20,000 people
- More than 20,000 people

between individual homes. Hot and warming, this is just one complex component of meals that involve lots of ingredients served together with injera, the country's signature flatbread and eating utensil that's made from the ancient grain teff. Another popular spice mix is mitmita, made from ground bird's eye chile peppers, cloves, korarima, and salt, which is a little reminiscent of peri peri. Over its long history, Ethiopian cuisine has incorporated ingredients and cooking techniques from the Arabian Peninsula, India, and Mesoamerica, through a mixture of proximity and trading, and colonizers. One thing I love is that the style of eating—a stew or variety of stews served with injera to scoop it all up—makes it easy to try a lot at every meal, even if it makes pairing a bit of a challenge.

Washington, DC, and New York are good cities for Ethiopian food, but they're not

Sip the Culture

From its role in spreading coffee around the world to a unique honey wine, these two kingdoms have a rich drinks history that's still thriving today. Here's what to know:

COFFEE. Ethiopia is Africa's second-largest exporter of coffee, and some believe the bean was actually discovered there and then exported to Yemen by Somali merchants. It's still grown in Ethiopia and Somalia, with Ethiopian coffee being especially sought after for its light, fruity, floral flavors. Somali coffee is often spiced with ginger or cardamom.

TEA. Like Indian chai, tea in Somalia and Ethiopia is often flavored with a blend of warming spices.

T'EJ. A fermented honey wine, similar to mead, this is the national drink of Ethiopia, brewed from honey and water. What separates t'ej from mead is that it's fermented with gesho leaves, instead of yeast, and aged in clay pots. It's usually sweet, relatively low in alcohol, and the perfect way to cool your mouth between bites of hot, spicy food.

I was introduced to honey wine from the Heritage Winery by an Ethiopian family in Harlem. It was the first time I felt like I understood the "nectar of the gods" tasting description. The various styles and sweetness levels resemble a spectrum of raw honey to agave, with balanced acidity and complex flavors of white and yellow flowers to sandalwood and musk.

---

the only parts of the United States with big diaspora communities. For the best Ethiopian food on this side of the Atlantic, here are the areas with the largest Ethiopian populations.

My knowledge of Somali cuisine also comes from the diaspora, and I'll admit that I haven't had as much of it. The restaurant that introduced me to Somali food was Safari in Harlem's Little Senegal neighborhood on 116th Street, just a few doors down from my first wine job at The Winery. I was often challenged by the BYOB restaurant to help their guests decide on the best bottle for their dinners, so one day I decided to explore for myself. And that expanded to Ethiopia's neighboring country, Somalia.

There are, of course, similarities between Ethiopia and Somalia. These two countries, once kingdoms, have been interacting for thousands of years. But there are also plenty of differences. Where Ethiopian food has berbere spice, Somali has xawaash. This incredibly wine-friendly blend has warming spices like cinnamon, cloves, cardamom, cumin, and coriander, along with black pepper, turmeric, and herbs like basil, oregano, and cilantro. (Hello, Syrah and Right Bank Bordeaux!) Somalians eat anjero or canjero, also a fermented flatbread like injera, but generally made from different grains and not eaten at every meal. Instead, they serve stews with rice or pasta, as they were once occupied by Italy. In addition, people grow different types of bananas in Somalia, and they're incorporated into sweet and savory dishes.

Ethiopia is along what's called the Bean Belt, along with Brazil, Colombia, and Costa Rica, and many more places known for their coffee. Similar to the latitude 30°–50° range that's used

AFRICA

+ PAIRED UP

SAMBUSA + FRANCIACORTA EXTRA BRUT, LOMBARDY, ITALY. Sambusas can be a few things: a beef- or lamb-filled Somali dumpling, and also a lentil-filled Ethiopian dumpling, akin to Indian samosas. Whichever one you're eating, Franciacorta Extra Brut is perfect. A Brut or Extra Brut sweetness level will help balance the spicy flavors from the filling. Sparkling wines from Franciacorta are required to use the traditional method from Champagne (see page 46) as well as Chardonnay and Pinot Noir (Nero), which are also used in Champagne. Franciacorta can also include Pinot Blanc and Erbamat, a native Italian grape.

FUUL MUDAMMAS WITH PITA + TREBBIANO, TUSCANY, ITALY. This Somali fava bean and tomato stew, seasoned with xawaash spice, is nicely complemented by Trebbiano Toscano—a dry, medium-bodied white with high acidity and flavors of basil, green apples, and citrus, which will provide great texture and balance to this light bean stew.

DORO WAT + VALPOLICELLA RIPASSO DOC SUPERIORE, ITALY. This Ethiopian chicken stew is especially popular in the diaspora. It is flavored with berbere spice and also has hard-boiled eggs in it. Valpolicella Ripasso is a great style to pair with food because it's made from the grape Corvina, which has dominating red fruit flavor and tannins that can hold up to heartier dishes. The ripasso method uses grape skins from Amarone and coferments them with Valpolicella Classico to finish the maceration process, which adds complex tannins as well as dark red fruit, herbal, and savory flavors instead of sweet.

SUUGO AND BAASTA + SANGIOVESE, CHIANTI, ITALY. Somali spaghetti and meat sauce is made with cubed rather than ground beef and seasoned with xawaash spice. A Sangiovese-based wine from Chianti is known for its tomato leaf, plum, and clay notes, which complement the classic tomato sauce dish.

MALAB IYO MALAWAX + T'EJ, ETHIOPIA. Somalia's famous crepes drizzled in honey, cinnamon, and sugar go perfectly with T'ej honey wine. Look for Heritage Winery Saba T'ej. Named after the Queen of Sheba, it has honey-sweet flavor and a floral aroma. You'll get notes of fermented honey with a hint of dried apricot and high acidity.

for wine, the Bean Belt ranges from 25° north of the equator to 30° south, according to the National Coffee Association.

Along that belt, factors like climate, soil, and farming practices can affect how coffee tastes. A coffee's acidity, body, flavor, and aroma are clues to the type of coffee, the soil it was grown in, the altitude at which it was grown, temperature, latitude, crop density, genetics, and the coffee cherry's maturity when it was picked. Sound familiar? These are all factors that are important to wine.

Ethiopia is known for making coffee with blueberry and strawberry notes, for being bright and vibrant, the same way we might describe a Petite Sirah.

If *Vitis vinifera* is the species of grape most often associated with wine, coffee is a little

Catherine & Pierre Breton
2021
Ex Umbris
SHELDRA
POINT
CABERNET FRA
RESERVE
FINGER LAK
POINT WIN

more complicated. It has two major commercial species and one important emerging species. Within those, there are lots of different varieties, cultivars, and hybrids. Arabica, which originated in Ethiopia and is the main species grown there, is the most common worldwide. It's known for being a bit sweet and nutty, with some acidity and fruity notes. Robusta, the second most common variety, is grown in Vietnam, Indonesia, and other parts of Africa. It's higher in caffeine, lower in sugar, and often has nutty, chocolatey, molasses-like flavors and aromas.

Liberica coffee, named for Liberia, is gaining interest because it's more resilient to disease and can grow in warmer temperatures than Arabica. It actually became briefly popular in the late 1800s when Arabica was struggling with disease. The flavor can be vegetal, but in the right hands, it can make coffee that's sweet and smooth, with tropical fruit notes. Excelsa, once thought to be a separate species but reclassified as a variety of Liberica, is a small, round bean. Its flavor and aroma can be very intense, so it's often blended with other beans to add a little oomph. Think of it as the workhorse grape of coffee beans, the way Cinsault was traditionally used in France.

SOMALI BEEF STEW + NERELLO MASCALESE,
SICILY, ITALY

SERVES 6 TO 8

2 tablespoons canola oil

1 red onion, thinly sliced

3 garlic cloves, minced

2 tablespoons Xawaash Spice Mix (recipe below)

2 tablespoons tomato paste

2 teaspoons kosher salt, plus more as needed

2 pounds boneless beef chuck or other stew meat, cut into bite-size pieces

2 baking potatoes, cut into bite-size pieces

2 large carrots, cut into thin rounds

1 red bell pepper, stemmed, seeded, and cut into thin strips

Cooked rice, hot sauce (such as Somali Cilantro and Green Chile Pepper Sauce), cilantro leaves, lime wedges, and fresh bananas, for serving

---

XAWAASH SPICE MIX

2-inch piece of cinnamon stick

½ cup cumin seeds

½ cup coriander seeds

2 tablespoons black peppercorns

6 cardamom pods

Mix together ingredients and grind to a fine powder.

Born in Somalia, Hawa Hassan is the author of *In Bibi's Kitchen*, a James Beard Award–winning cookbook that gathered recipes of grandmothers, or bibis, all over Africa. She is also the founder of Basbaas Foods, which creates sauces and seasonings from different parts of Africa.

In this recipe, Hassan uses xawaash, a savory-sweet warming spice blend. This makes more than you'll need for the stew, so have fun playing with it in other dishes.

Nerello Mascalese, a light-bodied red wine from Sicily, has some cinnamon and leather notes that will highlight the xawaash, but it's also got great juicy red fruits to cleanse the palate. Volcanic minerality adds extra depth, so it matches the stew's complexity.

1. Warm the oil in a large Dutch oven or other heavy pot set over medium heat. Add the onion and garlic and cook, stirring occasionally, until just beginning to soften, about 3 minutes. Stir in the xawaash, tomato paste, and salt, and cook until aromatic, about 1 minute.
2. Stir in 2 cups of water and increase the heat to high. Bring to a boil, reduce the heat to low, then stir in the beef and potatoes. Partially cover the pot (leave the lid slightly ajar so steam can escape) and simmer until the beef and potatoes are just cooked through, about 45 minutes.
3. Stir in the carrots and bell pepper and cook, covered, until the beef and vegetables are all very tender, an additional 30 minutes. Season the stew to taste with salt and serve over rice with hot sauce and cilantro for topping, lime wedges for squeezing over, and bananas for eating alongside.
4. Leftovers can be stored in an airtight container in the refrigerator for up to a few days and rewarmed in a heavy pot set over low heat (stir while you heat).

Recipes used with permission from *In Bibi's Kitchen* by Hawa Hassan, with Julia Turshen (Ten Speed Press, 2020).

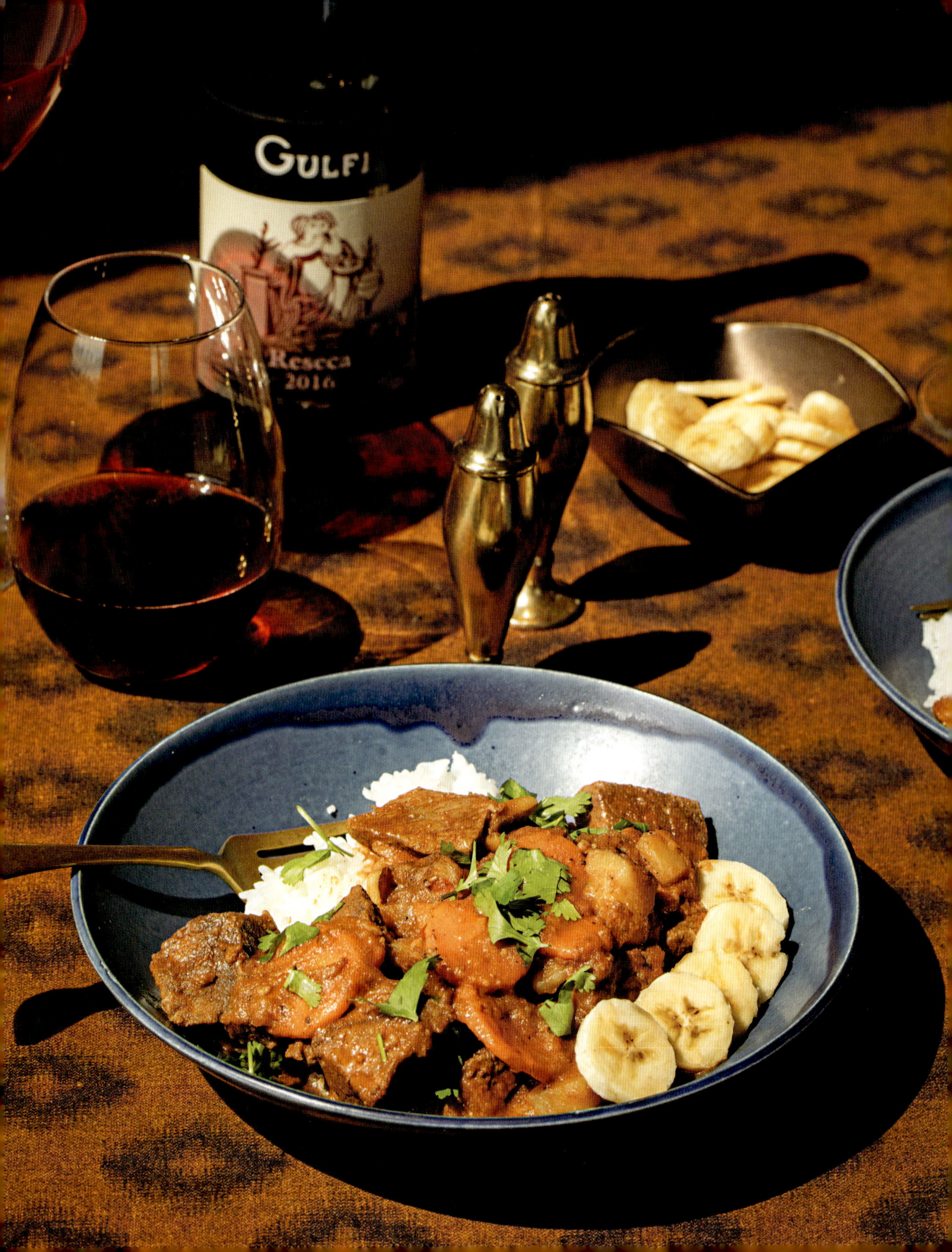
GULFI
Resecca
2016

Kenya and Tanzania

Kenya

Latitude: 0.0236° S, 37.9062° E
Capital: Nairobi
Country/Continent: This East African country straddles the equator. It's bordered by the Indian Ocean and Somalia to the east, Tanzania to the south, Uganda to the west, and South Sudan and Ethiopia to the north.
Population: 53 million
Top Exports: Tea, coffee, flowers, petroleum, titanium ore
Official Languages: English and Kiswahili
Independence Day: Jamhuri (Swahili for "republic") Day is December 12, 1964
Independence from: United Kingdom

In 2012, right after I returned from my time living in Italy, the stars aligned. As I was struggling with reverse culture shock, airline sites were glitching, and I was able to secure a few bucket-list trips with ridiculously low flight costs. If you are like me, a person who spends most of your discretionary income on travel, finding the steepest discount on the farthest destinations makes booking flights a game, or maybe even a competitive sport, especially for millennial Black travelers. A flight glitch is what helped me score round-trip tickets to Kenya for $300, but it was not my inspiration.

My friend Carolyn, who is Kenyan American, was the only member of her immediate family to be born in the United States. She was the one who discovered the inexpensive flight, called me after midnight, and encouraged me to take this trip to Kenya with her. These prices were an all-time low, and we had to act fast. I did not hesitate. This was an opportunity to see East Africa, an area of the continent Americans are not traditionally educated about. I was excited to learn from my own firsthand experience. My friend and I stayed with her relatives and saw life from a local's perspective while in Nairobi, before exploring more touristy destinations frequented by Europeans. But I also had an even more personal connection.

A few months before, I had decided to purchase DNA tests for myself and my immediate family to know more about our ancestral roots. While most American descendants of enslaved people are assumed to be West African, I had learned that my brother's, my father's, and my own DNA traced predominately to East African countries, as well as Arab nations. There was no surprise there, since the Arab world and South Asia both traded along the Swahili coast for such a long time; both cultures still have an imprint on the food of Kenya and Tanzania.

When I arrived, I was intrigued by Kenya's connection with Indian culture. East Africa is not far, geographically, from South Asia, and the two regions traded for centuries before colonization. The British, during their occupation, brought workers from India to Kenya to build railroads. Whatever cultural exchange that happened between Kenya and Tanzania and their neighbors across the Arabian Sea was solidified in a cuisine where biryani holds a place alongside ugali.

As far as wine goes, Kenya and Tanzania might be part of a new wave of emerging regions. For a long time, the common wisdom in the wine world is that *Vitis vinifera* (European wine grapes) grow well at latitudes between 30° and 50° north or south of the equator. Kenya, which straddles the equator, and Tanzania, whose southernmost point is 34° south, should be out of range. Both do produce some wine from European grapes though. In Tanzania, they were brought by missionaries in the mid-twentieth century to the Dodoma region. Kenya's wine industry is even newer, begun in 1985 in a region right on the equator. Both are tourism drivers that have grown even in the years between my visit and now. I didn't see any vineyards or get a chance to try any of their wine while visiting, but I am excited for Kenya's wine future and will be monitoring the region closely.

Maize is the principle staple food of Kenya, and it is grown on 90 percent of all Kenyan farms. As a strategy to reduce reliance on maize, which requires a fair amount of water to grow, the government embarked on a grain-diversification

---

Tanzania

Latitude: 6.3690° S, 34.8888° E

Capital: Dodoma (the largest city and de facto capital is Dar es Salaam)

Country/Continent: This East African country is bordered by the Indian Ocean to the east, Mozambique, Malawi, and Zambia to the south, Democratic Republic of the Congo, Rwanda, and Burundi to the west, and Uganda and Kenya to the north.

Population: 50 million

Top Exports: Tobacco, coffee, cotton, cashews, tea, and cloves

Official Languages: English and Kiswahili

Independence Day: December 9, 1961

Independence from: United Nations, administered by the United Kingdom

program, encouraging production and use of a flour that blends maize and wheat with sorghum, millet, cassava, and sweet potatoes. The latter, especially, have become really important crops in both countries. Small-scale farmers can plant the drought-resistant plant in often poor soils and still produce a crop for sustenance and/or a little extra income. Tanzania is the second-largest sweet potato grower in Africa, after Uganda, and here entrepreneurs are working with farming co-ops to create a range of sweet potato products. Kenya, on the other hand, is part of the Big Four plan aimed at creating food security, improving nutrition, and increasing employment opportunities in Kenya.

Tea and coffee are also important crops here. Kenya's equatorial location means tea can grow year-round. Initially planted by British settlers in 1903, tea was off limits to Kenyan farmers until 1956. Today, it's grown at high altitude in volcanic red soils without any chemicals or pesticides, and it accounts for about 2 percent of the country's agricultural gross domestic product. In Tanzania, small-share tea growers are getting a hand from a European Union–backed initiative to help improve their quality of life, and with it, the quality of the tea. Kenyan and Tanzanian coffee are both considered among the best in the world. They have the Strictly High Grown/Strictly Hard Bean designation given to coffee grown above four thousand feet, which is believed to be smoother and lighter in body. Both countries,

Sip the Culture

TEA. Under British and German colonizers, tea became an important cash crop in Kenya and Tanzania, respectively, early in the twentieth century. Today, tea growers in both countries make a wide variety of styles, but the signature black, with an amber color when it's brewed, is strong, malty, high quality, and very popular still. For breakfast, with milk and sugar accompanied by a fried dough ball, it can't be missed.

COFFEE. There's a good chance coffee initially made its way to Kenya and Tanzania from Ethiopia, thought by many to be where it originated. The Kenyan coffee industry didn't really get going until the late nineteenth century, when French missionaries started growing it strictly for export. In Tanzania, Germans mandated coffee growth and took control away from the tribes. Today, both countries produce coffee considered some of the best in the world, and there are strong efforts to make the drink as gourmet and popular domestically as it is abroad.

GIN AND TONIC. This drink isn't unique to Kenya or Tanzania, but it is a time-honored safari ritual. Once it was served because the quinine in tonic water helped cure malaria, a squeeze of lime aided in warding off scurvy, and the gin made it all palatable. It's still believed that tonic water made with real quinine from the chinchona tree can help ward off mosquitoes, plus it's a refreshing drink, so gin and tonics remain part of the safari experience.

DAWA. A cocktail of honey, sugar, lime, vodka, and ice. Its name means medicine in Kiswahili, and The Carnivore restaurant in Nairobi claims to have invented it.

AFRICA

however, export the majority of their coffee; you'll find more tea-drinking culture in both, especially Kenya.

In our two weeks in Kenya and Tanzania, I was able to experience many different terrains and terroirs, from city to beach to safari. In Nairobi, I was struck by the contrast between the big-city skyline and the rural neighborhood where my friend's family lived. We visited Mombasa, a port town where enslaved people were put on ships to cross the Indian Ocean. There was another contrast there, between the beautiful beaches with their turquoise water and the painful history that lingered in the air around us.

We also spent some time in Zanzibar, which reminded me of the flavors and colors of the Caribbean. The water was turquoise, and white-sand beaches were lined with palm trees. At night, the Stone Town culinary scene came alive. We went out at night to the cookouts in Stone Town; the seafood there and, of course, Anthony Bourdain, were basically what inspired me to hire a driver to take us to the famous, remote restaurant, The Rock. It's located on the opposite side of Zanzibar. I was excited to embark on this upscale, traditional Zanzibar culinary adventure. And it was truly one the most memorable food experiences of my life.

WINE PAIRING FOR THE PEOPLE

Africa's Popular Beer

All over Kenya, I saw the distinctive yellow label of Tusker Beer, with the beloved elephant on it. It's made within Kenya with locally sourced ingredients, which reflects the abundant agriculture of country. It is, unofficially, one of the national drinks. On later travels I learned that most African countries have a signature local beer or beloved brand. Fun fact: Nigeria, it turns out, ranks number two or three of any country in the world for Guinness consumption. Nigerians prefer Guinness Foreign Extra Stout (FES), more commonly known as Nigerian Guinness, which is known for its high alcohol content, very bitter taste, and additional hops to help the beer survive the long journey to foreign markets.

African countries have a long history of brewing local grains such as sorghum, millet, maize, and cassava for cultural practices and ceremonies. Beer is also more cost effective to produce than wine, which makes it more accessible. And of course, it is Africa, and a nice cold beer pairs well with the warm tropical climate.

Here's a look at some signature beers of different African countries.

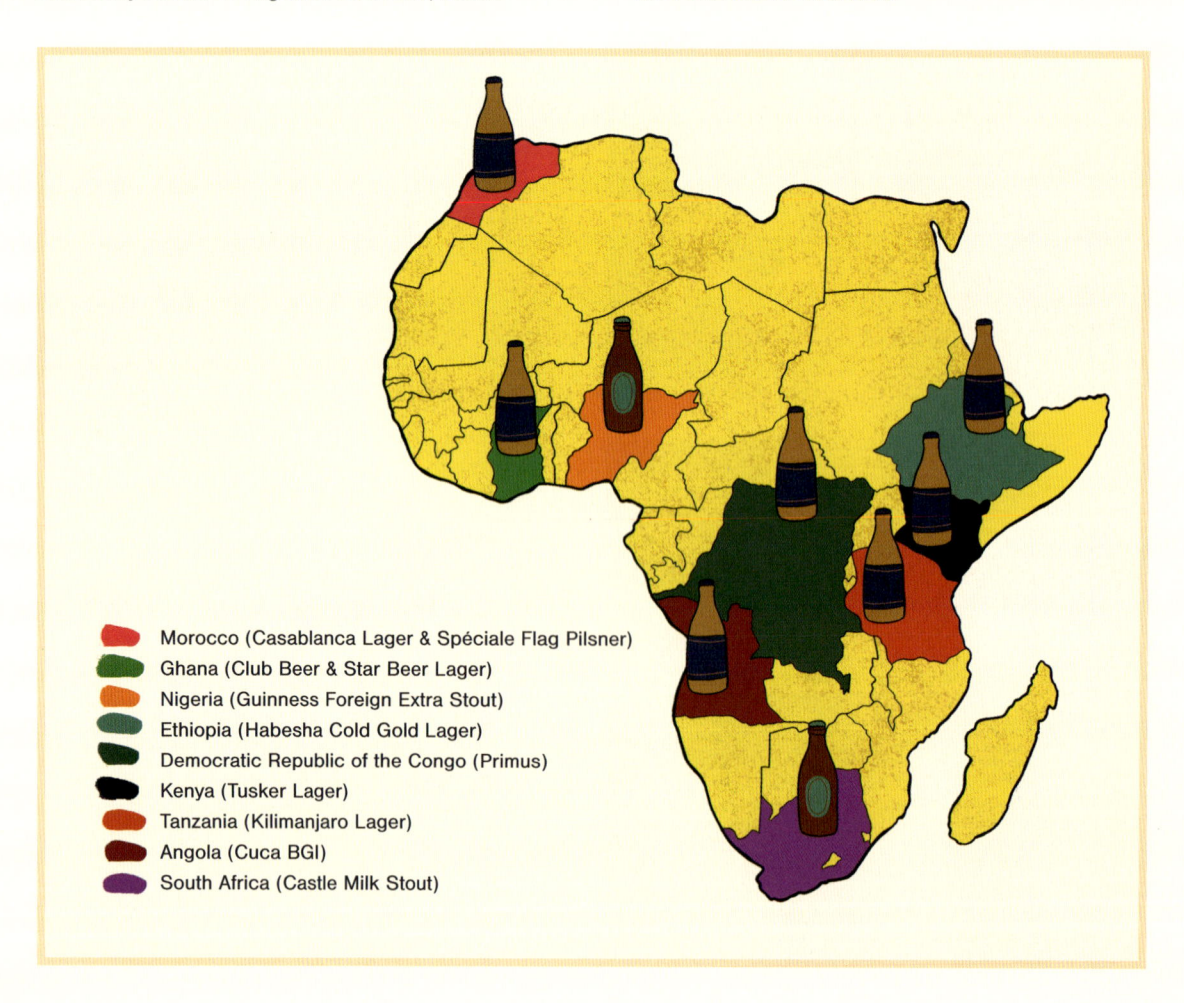

- Morocco (Casablanca Lager & Spéciale Flag Pilsner)
- Ghana (Club Beer & Star Beer Lager)
- Nigeria (Guinness Foreign Extra Stout)
- Ethiopia (Habesha Cold Gold Lager)
- Democratic Republic of the Congo (Primus)
- Kenya (Tusker Lager)
- Tanzania (Kilimanjaro Lager)
- Angola (Cuca BGI)
- South Africa (Castle Milk Stout)

AFRICA

+ PAIRED UP

CHICKEN BIRYANI + VIOGNIER, CONDRIEU, FRANCE. This Indian dish has regional variations around Tanzania. Curried meat is served with the seasoned rice, but they're not cooked together as they would be in India. Viognier, an aromatic white wine from Northern Rhône, is a full-bodied wine with peach, mango, and tangerine notes, but it's most notable for its floral notes of honeysuckle and rose.

NYAMA CHOMA + XINOMAVRO, NAOUSSA, GREECE. Meat, especially goat or chicken, is slow roasted over coals for a smoky, juicy meal that's not too far from barbecue. A red wine from Greece, Xinomavro, is known for its earthy red fruit notes of raspberry and plum and high tannins that are good for the fattiness of the grilled meats. Think of it as a blend of the perfect barbecue dipping sauce of allspice, tobacco, and red compote on the side.

EAST AFRICAN PILAU + MONASTRELL, JUMILLA, SPAIN. Rice, caramelized onions, garlic, ginger, chiles, and chicken or beef and their broth come together in this hearty, flavorful comfort food. Smoky, peppery Monastrell, which is also known as Mourvedre, is a perfectly spicy complement.

PWEZA WA NAZI + MARSANNE, SAINT-PÉRAY, FRANCE. This coconut curry has octopus as its protein, plus the usual suspects, like turmeric, chile, and lime, for flavor that will take you to Zanzibar. Marsanne is an aromatic white wine that has a creamy texture to match with the curry sauce, and its orange and beeswax notes support the contrasting sweet and savory flavors of the dish.

ZANZIBAR PIZZA + GRILLO, SICILY, ITALY. A pancake is filled with meat, vegetables, cheese, and egg then fried and served with tamarind and chili sauces. I'd pair it with a medium-body white wine that can complement the unique flavors of this dish but is also refreshing. Grillo from Sicily is packed with minerality, pink grapefruit, floral notes and a hint of rosemary.

MANDAZI + DEMI-SEC CHENIN BLANC, VOUVRAY, FRANCE. This fried doughnut is made with milk or coconut milk and flavored with cardamom. Chenin Blanc from Vouvray, in France's Loire Valley, has a waxy, mouthcoating feel, and it can be off-dry (slightly sweet), which makes it a nice option with dessert. The wine's floral aromas, sweet golden apple and persimmon, are a good accent to the mandazi's cardamom.

Angola, Mozambique, São Tomé and Príncipe, and Cape Verde

Angola

Coordinates: 11.2027° S, 17.8739° E

Capital: Luanda, also spelled Loanda, formerly São Paulo de Luanda

Country/Continent: Angola is in Africa. It's bordered by the Atlantic Ocean to the west, Namibia to the south, the Democratic Republic of the Congo (former Zaire) to the north, and Zambia to the east

Population: 35 million

National Dish: Moamba de Galinha

Top Exports: Petroleum products, diamonds, and coffee

Official Language: Portuguese

Independence Day: November 11, 1975

Independence from: Portugal

Mozambique

Coordinates: 18.6657° S, 35.5296° E

Capital: Maputo

Country/Continent: Mozambique is a coastal African country. It's bordered by the Indian Ocean to the east, and Tanzania, Malawi, Zambia, Zimbabwe, South Africa, and Eswatini to the west.

Population: 32 million

Top Exports: Coal briquettes, raw aluminum, gold, petroleum gas

Official Language: Portuguese

Independence Day: September 8, 1974

Independence from: Portugal

São Tomé and Príncipe

Coordinates: 18.6657° S, 35.5296° E

Capital: São Tomé City

Country/Continent: São Tomé is an island in the Atlantic Ocean off the coast of West Africa; the country's closest neighbors are Gabon and Equatorial Guinea.

Population: 220,000

National Drink: Palm Wine, Aquardente

National Dish: Calulu de Pieixe

Top Exports: Cocoa beans, palm oil, pepper, coconut oil

Official Language: Portuguese

Independence Day: July 12, 1975

Independence from: Portugal

AFRICA

If you've ever had peri peri chicken from the food chain Nando's, or even just bought the sauce from Trader Joe's, you have at least tasted Mozambique's global influence on today's food. I want to talk about the foods of these former Portuguese colonies—because they've worked their way into other cuisines and popular dishes worldwide without really getting their due in the media. I was able to discover the storytelling around them for myself when I moved to Portugal.

But let's back up for a minute. When I landed at the airport in Lisbon for my first visit, I wasn't sure if I was actually in Europe. Let's just say the vibe was different. I was pleasantly, delightfully in awe of the sea of brown faces smiling, waiting with signs welcoming home relatives or drivers picking up passengers. In my head, I asked, "Isn't this Portugal? Where are all of these Black people from?" During my time there, in addition to learning about the history of Port wine and lesser-known regions like Colares, I became familiar with some of the cultures and foods of Angola, Mozambique, Cape Verde, and São Tomé and Príncipe. My friends and chosen family in Portugal nourished me with the flavors of their homelands, which were former colonies, and that is how my exploration began.

I didn't know why I was so drawn to Portugal before my trip. Of course, I knew there was a lot of great wine being produced there; beyond that, I really felt a deeper soul connection. I will never forget my first time landing in Lisbon, which offered some hints of a history that has been hidden. Yes, this European city had lots of African residents. A good number of them moved here as "retornados" between 1974 and 1976, when the Portuguese government withdrew

Cape Verde

Coordinates: 16.5388° N, 23.0418° W
Capital: Praia
Country/Continent: Cape Verde is a group of Islands in the Atlantic Ocean off the coast of West Africa, specifically Senegal.
Population: 593,149
National Drink: Grogue
National Dish: Cachupa
Top Exports: Processed fish, mollusks
Official Language: Portuguese
Independence Day: July 5, 1975
Independence from: Portugal

from its countries after the Carnation Revolution on April 25, 1974. That was the day a military coup overthrew the regime of Estado Novo, which was formed as the legacy of dictator António de Oliveira Salazar, ending the rule of Portugal over its colonized nations.

African influence on Portugal dates back as far as the first Portuguese ships' arrival in São Tomé, sometime between 1469 and 1471. Portugal then trafficked enslaved people to farm sugarcane on the previously uninhabited island starting in 1493. As Portugal colonized more places and sailed between them, the cultural exchange grew.

During my time living in Portugal, I found that some Portuguese people think of their country's colonialism as a kinder, gentler version than that of other Western European nations. Portuguese settlers lived among and started families with people not just in Africa but also in other colonies like Brazil, Goa, and Macau. They worked together, too, but native Portuguese were paid more and were able to develop businesses in these countries, while Africans were restricted and enslaved in their homeland. That's part of the reason that by the middle of the twentieth century Angola, Mozambique, Cape Verde, and São Tomé sought liberation. Another reason was the Portuguese dictatorship of Salazar, which began in 1932. Salazar avoided the fascist rhetoric of his contemporaries, but he still had a brutal secret police force that would punish anyone who spoke against him, in Portugal or the colonies.

In 1961, after an uprising in Angola, the Portuguese military made a determination that it wasn't equipped to deal with guerrilla warfare. That was the beginning of the end of Portugal's colonization period in sub-Saharan Africa. In 1974, when Salazar's corporatist regime finally ended, anyone who was born in one of the colonies had full Portuguese citizenship, and people of all nationalities emigrated from southern Africa to Western Europe as citizens, not slaves. During a postcolonial dictatorship in Angola and civil war in Mozambique in the decades that followed independence, more people from those countries migrated to Lisbon, as well as a decent-size population of Mozambican people who moved to South Africa.

My first visit to Portugal in 2018 ultimately led to my decision to move to Lisbon to work in wine tourism and as a sommelier at a Michelin-starred restaurant. Being of the African diaspora and trying to find a way to succeed despite the trials of my ancestors resonated with me and connected me with the groups of African Portuguese who had moved to the country that once colonized their homelands to find better opportunities, financial stability, and safety. I learned that many people of African descent born in Portugal preferred to be recognized as simply Portuguese, and that those of native Portuguese descent born in the former colonies still consider themselves Angolan, Mozambican, or São Toméan. It's not my position to force an American definition of ethnic identities of race on them but to make room for learning. Interracial marriage is common here, and the idea of race works differently in Portugal than it does in the United States. That's not to say that racism doesn't exist or isn't an issue, but I noticed the construct is different.

While living in Lisbon, I read an article in the *New York Times* that featured Batata Doce, a Portuguese-Angolan restaurant whose name means "sweet potato." I realized that it wasn't

AFRICA

+ PAIRED UP

MOAMBA DE GALINHA + ENCRUZADO, DÃO, PORTUGAL. Angola's unofficial national dish is a chicken stew with okra, garlic, and palm paste. Encruzado is a high-acid, medium-body white wine with tasting notes of lemon, herbs, underripe stone fruit, and green melon, with white-floral aromas. This variety is produced mostly in the Dão region in the center of Portugal. It is a brisk, refreshing match to cleanse your palate while you eat this stew.

CALULU DE PIEIXE + VINHO VERDE TINTO, PORTUGAL. An Angolan and São Toméan dish of dried fish stew cooked with red palm oil, greens, garlic, bell peppers, and eggplant can be accompanied by Vinho Verde Tinto, produced using the deeply colored varietal Vinhão. When most Portuguese wine lovers think of Vinho Verde, they typically think of the white wine often with a hint of yellow-green color appearance in the glass. However, Vinho Verde, the most northern coastal region of Portugal, also produces red grapes that are often picked for an earlier or younger harvest (also known as "greener"), creating a light-bodied and low-alcohol red wine served chilled. Tasting notes are traditionally vegetal and floral forward with a hint of gravel and black cherry.

PERI PERI CHICKEN, AKA GALINHA ASADA + SKIN-CONTACT ARINTO, LISBOA, PORTUGAL. This Portuguese grape has pronounced flavors of grapefruit, beeswax, yellow flowers, and lemon zest. The grape's high acidity is tamed by skin contact and aging, which produces a more expressive and medium-bodied version of this white grape. Peri peri spice marinated on a whole roast chicken pairs well with the brightness the citrus fruit and the roundness of texture, and tannins work well with the body of this dish.

MATAPA + ALVARINHO, PORTUGAL. This Mozambican stew of cassava leaves in coconut milk is seasoned with onions and garlic. It pairs well with the grape called Alvarinho in Portugal. In the United States, it's sold more widely under the Spanish name: Albariño. Whichever name you use, this is the sweetheart grape of the Iberian Peninsula. It has a medium body that can hold up to this dish with nice saline, citrus, and savory characteristics.

CACHUPA + JAEN, DÃO, PORTUGAL. Cape Verde's national dish is a stew made with corn, cassava, and hominy (dried corn), with protein options of pork, sausage, or seafood. Jaen, a red wine from Portugal's Dão region, is actually the same varietal as Mencía from Spain. However, the Portuguese edition has smoother, softer tannins and express more black pepper and riper red fruit like raspberry, cherry, black fruit, and fresh violets. The richness of the meat and smoky notes from slow-cooked corn and beans makes for great pairing with the earthy undertones of Jaen.

just in my neighborhood of Lapa, but actually walking distance from my apartment. It is an intimate place with an eclectic décor and moody lighting, and I became fast friends with chef and owner Isabel Jacinto. There were a lot of stew- and gravy-focused dishes. In some ways, the spices reminded me of soul food, heavily seasoned vegetables and meats with starchy side dishes, exactly how my mother would prepare Sunday's dinner: low and slow. When I think about those dishes, you need a wine that could hold up to all the flavors and be able to fight the weight of the meal, finding balance.

The dishes and the story of Chef Isabel remind me of a humble grape widely grown throughout Portugal, Castelão. Its red fruit flavors from plum to strawberries, with a hint of dried meat, herbs, and mocha, make it the perfect pairing with the combination of warming spices and chiles found in Angolan dishes like moamba de galinha and even the popular dish found in many Portuguese colonies, feijoada.

São Toméan food has some similar spices and stewy dishes, but it also incorporates a lot of fish, as it is located 140 miles off the northwestern coast of Gabon. You'll find tropical produce, like breadfruit, bananas, lots of corn and cornmeal-based dishes, beans, and taro. Coffee is also grown there and used a lot as a seasoning. Because a lot of food on the islands of São Tomé and Príncipe is imported, it uses a decent amount of smoked and canned goods.

You cannot step foot in Lisbon without someone mentioning Mozambican food. As the Portuguese diet is heavily fish and seafood focused, this former colony has influenced cuisine in Portuguese coastal regions from Vinho Verde to Algarve.

I frequented Cantinho do Aziz, a Mozambican restaurant run by Khalid Aziz and his wife, Chef Jeny Sulemange, a five-minute walk from Praca da Figueira. This square is one of the most important transit crossroads between the ritzy luxury shopping street of Avenida da Liberdade to the west, the tram stop for the hilly neighborhood known for the best vistas of Lisbon, new bar scene, Graça, to the east, and the tourist destinations of Barrio Alto and Cais do Sodre. Through her cookbook, *Portugal Meets Mozambique*, her Amazon Prime show *O Meu Mundo*, and New York City pop-up dinners at the James Beard House, Jeny Sulemange has become pretty famous since I moved to Lisbon, and was rarely in town. Her menu is a perfect example of the more seafood-oriented dishes from Mozambique, compared to the heartier, stewier Angolan dishes at Batata Doce. Chef Jeny's use of crab, prawns, and of course peri peri, curry, and coconut-creamy sauces introduced me to the hallmark of Mozambican cooking and kept me coming back for more.

Though Chef Jeny prides herself on seafood, there is definitely peri peri chicken on the menu. This spicy chicken dish is named for the African bird's eye chili, also called peri peri, piripiri, or pili pili. You can find Chef Shaquay Peacock's peri peri sauce on page 39. Like all chile peppers, it's originally from the Americas, but it's been growing wild in southern Africa for centuries. The chile is blended into a sauce for chicken, and thanks to chain restaurant Nando's, this dish is taking over. It originated in Mozambique, but Nando's restaurant was cofounded in South Africa by a Portuguese man named Fernando Duarte.

And that's a point that keeps coming up: the pain of colonization still birthed beautiful food and beverage exchanges we enjoy today.

AFRICA

It wasn't just that Portuguese food influenced the cuisines of these three countries, or vice versa. Other colonies were involved, such as the Indian region of Goa. Goan curry makes its way to southern Africa, where it meets chiles brought over from Mesoamerica, and suddenly you're in Lisbon eating a dish that's calling out for an Italian or even a Georgian wine.

I don't know when or even if I'll make it to all of these countries, but I'm glad that my calling to Portugal introduced me to these cultures.

All unique cuisines share similar ingredients and DNA, and for me, they offer the comfort of finding a home away from home. Castelão and moamba de galinha is just the beginning.

Portuguese wines are vast, but they have limited representation in the global market. I selected a few to highlight with traditional dishes of Angola, Mozambique, Cape Verde, and São Tomé and Príncipe. You can be sure to enjoy these pairings whether you are in Lisbon or Luanda.

PERI PERI SAUCE

This Mozambican sauce made its way to South Africa and, through chain restaurant Nando's, the world. Peri peri chicken is a popular dish, but now that you have a recipe for the sauce, you can use it on anything.

This recipe came to us from Chef Shaquay Peacock, who has collaborated with me on several wine dinners for The Communion and also contributed as the recipe tester for select dishes in this book. Shaquay is a fellow New Yorker and has appeared on *Chopped* and *The Chew* and currently works as a private chef in the Hamptons on Long Island.

1. In a blender, combine all ingredients and puree until smooth.
2. Season with salt to taste. Use sauce in a variety of ways, as a condiment to go with seafood, poultry, vegetables, or on sandwiches.

MAKES 3 CUPS

10 red Fresno chiles, stemmed, seeded, and rough-chopped

½ red bell pepper, seeded and rough-chopped

3 garlic cloves, peeled and rough-chopped

1-inch knob ginger, peeled and chopped

1 tablespoon chopped shallot (or red onion)

1 tablespoon lemon juice (or juice from ½ lemon)

3 tablespoons chopped cilantro

¼ cup olive oil

¼ teaspoon smoked paprika

Salt, to taste

CRAB CURRY aka IKALA + BAGA ROSÉ,
BAIRRADA, PORTUGAL

SERVES 2

5 small crabs, such as mud crab, blue crab, or stone crab, cut into pieces

Neutral cooking oil, to coat pan

1 onion, chopped

2 medium ripe tomatoes, quartered

1 teaspoon tomato paste, plus more to taste

1 13½-ounce can coconut milk

Salt, to taste

Chef Jeny Sulemange became a friend when I lived in Lisbon and got to know her at her restaurant, Cantinho do Aziz. This dish was one of my favorite things to eat there. I love seafood, and the creamy coconut sauce is the perfect complement. Sulemange was born in Mozambique and lived in London and Florida before settling down and starting her family in Portugal. She and her husband, Khalid Aziz, also coauthored a cookbook, *Portugal Meets Mozambique: Cozinha Moçambicana*.

Sweet crab and coconut make this a pretty rich dish. Baga is a thick-skinned and small-bunch grape varietal that's native to the Bairrada region and mostly found in Portugal. An alternative wine selection is a Pinot Noir Rosé from Southern California. Tangy red berry notes of cranberry and raspberry in these two rosé wines will cut through the richness, but they're both delicate enough that they don't overpower the mild curry.

1. Put the crabs in a braising pan or other shallow pot with a lid, and add just enough water to cover. Bring to a boil, and cook until the crab shells are a bright orange-red color, indicating that the crabs are cooked through. It usually takes about 20 minutes, but check every 5 minutes. When they're done, drain the water and set aside the crabs.
2. Add the oil to the pan, and heat over medium. Add the onions and cook, stirring occasionally, until they start to brown. Reduce heat to medium-low, and add the tomatoes, tomato paste, coconut milk, and salt. Simmer for 2 to 3 minutes to let flavors merge. Add the crabs, and simmer for another 5 minutes so all the flavors combine.

Recipe used with permission from *Portugal Meets Mozambique: Cozinha Moçambicana* by Jeny Sulemange and Khalid Aziz (independently published, July 2020).

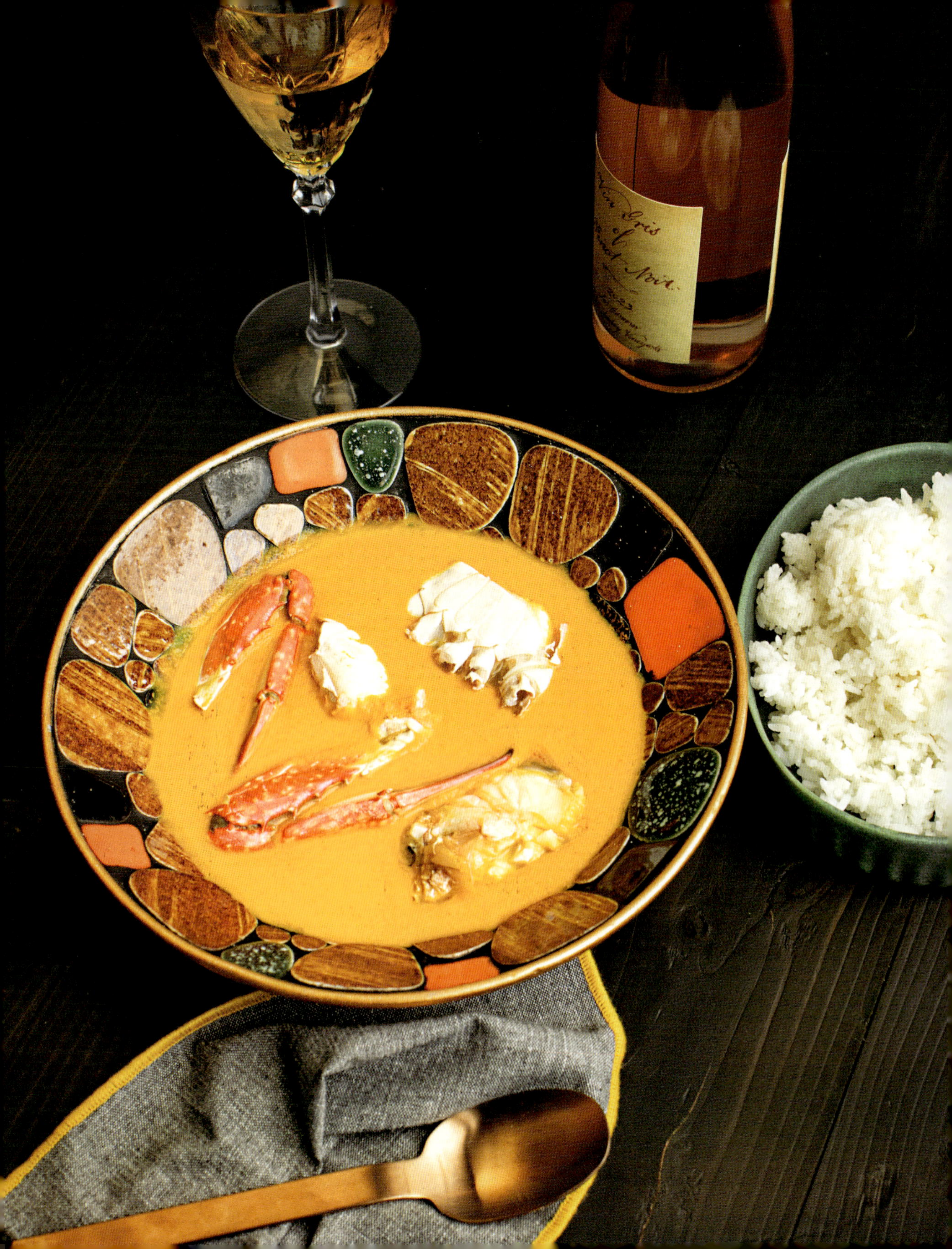

WINE PAIRING FOR THE PEOPLE

South Africa

Coordinates: 30.5595° S, 22.9375° E
Capital: Pretoria
Country/Continent: South Africa is at the southern tip of Africa. It's bordered by the Atlantic Ocean to the west, the Indian Ocean to the east, and Namibia, Botswana, Zimbabwe, and Mozambique to the north.
Population: 59.4 million
National Dish: Bobotie
Top Exports: Platinum, gold, iron ore, diamonds
Official Languages: Afrikaans, English, Ndebele, Xhosa, Zulu, Sesotho sa Leboa, Sesotho, Setswana, Swati, Tshivenda, Xitsonga
Independence Day: Freedom Day is observed on April 27, 1994, the date of the first democratic election following apartheid.
Independence from: Apartheid

I was once asked where in the world I'd want to live if money were no issue. I responded that it was distance, not money, that's stopping me from living in South Africa. This country has big, cosmopolitan cities, beautiful landscapes, a really fun and lively eating and drinking culture, and most important, some of my favorite wines in the world.

My trip here was part family vacation, part wine research. We started out in Johannesburg, or Jo'burg. Tastemakers Africa—an African experience company whose mission was to change the way people viewed the Continent—inspired me to check out the trendy Maboneng neighborhood, located downtown. It's officially named New Doorfontein on the map, but more commonly called by the Sotho word "maboneng," meaning "place of light." It's an art district with a rhythm of its own. It pulsed with Afrobeat music and wall murals. The decor in the bars and restaurants, the aesthetic around us was very chic yet traditional, paying respect with tribal decor and the use of upcycled art. While the country's violent and racist history is never far, a spirit of creativity and reinvention was present right alongside it in Maboneng.

Here I was able to indulge in a wide variety of South African wine. Some of the upscale restaurants featured more comprehensive wine lists with selections from Europe, but at the art gallery parties, hotel lobby DJ sets, rooftop parties, and at casual dining restaurants, the wine lists were predominantly domestic. Now, that might have been a matter of pricing—South African wines would be more affordable than imports, but it was exciting to see that South African wine was part of this vibrant modern culture that transcended race and class.

From Johannesburg, we went to Cape Town, affectionately called Mother City for its pivotal role in developing modern South Africa. Cape Town was a good base to start our wine journey. It felt like a beach town with city vibes, like Barcelona or Los Angeles. Although the water on South Africa's Atlantic side is too cold for swimming, it is notably great for surfing. However, it wasn't the coastline that stole the show. Everywhere I went, my eyes were drawn from the water up to the famous Table Mountain, a flat-topped mountain that overlooks the city and its harbor. (Take the cableway to the top—trust me, it is worth it.) These physical features, the closeness to nature, were a constant reminder of the terroir that affects the wines of South Africa. But just like Johannesburg, Cape Town had constant reminders of culture and history too.

My most cherished moment in South Africa was retracing the footsteps of one of my heroes, President Nelson Mandela. I made sure to carve out time in both cities to pay my respects and connect with his legacy. In Jo'burg, I visited Mandela House, at 8115 Orlando West Soweto, where I was able to witness his humble beginnings and be in the presence of his spirit. One of the most transformative museums I have ever visited was the Apartheid Museum. This multimedia museum afforded a gripping encounter, capturing the terrifying emotions and injustice during the apartheid, showing its systemic rise and its fall. You are immediately injected into a dark time that resonated with my own history as a Black person in America.

I believe these exhibitions are important to provide awareness and help ensure history never repeats itself.

And while in Cape Town, I visited Robben Island, where Nelson Mandela was imprisoned for eighteen years, just a thirty-minute ferry ride from Cape Town. Of course, I've always admired his work and leadership, but I felt a renewed connection visiting the Robben Island Museum. It is a UNESCO World Heritage site whose mission is to conserve, educate, and promote the triumph of the human spirit over extreme adversity and injustice. Here, Mandela planted a garden along the high, cracked concrete walls of the prison's courtyard, one that still thrives today. Visiting the garden and watering the plants was a full-circle moment for me, because back in Harlem, I joined a group of my neighbors to revitalize an abandoned lot behind the legendary Apollo Theater. We named it Mandela's Garden. Our mission was simple: to make our neighborhood better by fostering civic involvement and community pride, and to spread an ideal that we deserved moments of soft living, restoration, and reprieve from hard work in Harlem just as much as people in lower Manhattan. But more than anything, it was a reminder that the soil is bursting with life. It's about being rooted, not about your circumstances, and it exemplified the feeling that if plants can thrive through the concrete, so can we.

South Africa embodies the idea that terroir is culture and history. The country at the tip of the continent, with shorelines on the Atlantic and Indian Oceans, has been an attractive place to settle dating back to when the Bantu people encroached on Khoikhoi territory in the fourth century BCE.

Some parts of South Africa, such as Natal,

Wine Grapes of South Africa

South Africa grows a huge variety of grapes, many of which are used for blends or fortified wines, so we're going to focus on the largest varieties (in terms of acreage, not the size of the fruit) and the most common.

Red	White
Cabernet Sauvignon	Chardonnay
Cinsaut	Chenin Blanc
Merlot	Sauvignon Blanc
Pinotage	Semillon
Shiraz/Syrah	

still bear Portuguese names from sailors rounding the Cape of Good Hope in the late 1400s, but the country's colonial history really gets started with the Dutch in the mid-1600s, when the Dutch East India Company made the Cape of Good Hope a stop on its trade routes between Asia and Europe. This is also when its wine industry started to show promise. Dutch occupiers planted vineyards for personal use and for export. French Huguenots, seeking religious asylum, landed in South Africa at the end of that century and brought with them wine making knowledge. Wines from one particular vineyard near Cape Town, Constantia, got early international acclaim. For the most part, though, this was an era of experimentation and a lot of brandy production, which has a higher alcohol level, which can help cover up, let's call it less skillful wine making. Just as the country was starting to hit its stride with wine in the mid-1800s, in came phylloxera, an insect that feeds on the roots of European grapevines, and a protracted war between the Dutch and the British for control of the region.

Concurrently after Britain abolished slavery in all of its colonies in 1833, British rulers implemented a series of laws to continue denying pay to formerly enslaved people, and then to limit their movement, their right to vote, and their ability to own land. This gradually ramped up to apartheid, meaning apartness, a rule under which Black South Africans were subject to a totally different set of laws and had far fewer rights. By the mid-twentieth century, apartheid dictated where Black South Africans could live and work and demanded they carry special identification badges. These laws also extended to South Asian and South Asian–descended people living in South Africa. Under apartheid, and something called the dop system, rural farmworkers like those who worked in vineyards were paid partially or in full with alcohol. All of these were the sorts of injustices that the anti-apartheid movement was trying to rectify. What started in England in 1959 spread in the '60s. The United Nations passed a nonbinding resolution that condemned apartheid. In most of Europe, the Americas, Australia, and parts of Asia and Africa, people refused to buy any products that came from South Africa or from companies that did business with the apartheid government.

That extended to wine. Possibly the saving grace of South African wine was a co-op called Ko-operatiewe Wijnbouwers Vereniging van Zuid-Afrika, or KWV, which had started in 1918. KWV purchased surplus alcohol from wine growers and used it to make everything from brandy to cologne. It managed imports, exports, and the development of new grape varietals like Pinotage, a cross between Pinot

AFRICA

DECODING THE LABEL

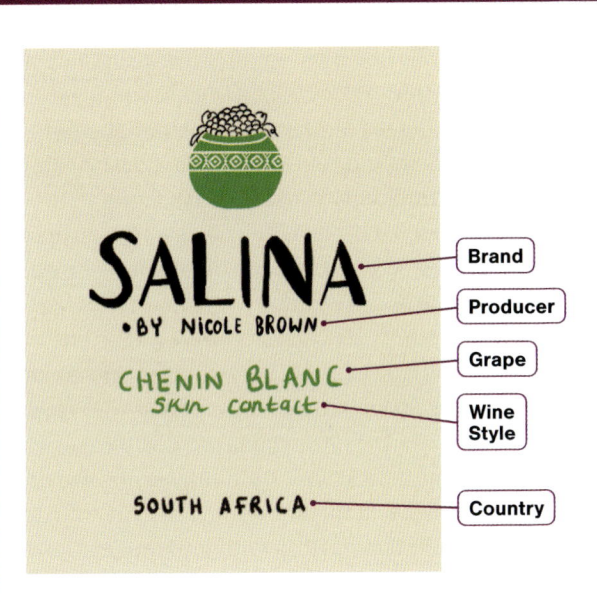

SALINA
• BY NICOLE BROWN •
CHENIN BLANC
Skin contact

SOUTH AFRICA

- Brand
- Producer
- Grape
- Wine Style
- Country

INTEGRITY & SUSTAINABILITY
Certified
WINE AND SPIRIT BOARD
www.swsa.co.za
4477
796701

The front label of a South African wine can stick to the basics, but the back label will always include this information:

Brand
Vintage
Grape
Appellation
Country
Producer's address (some will have a code that you can use to look this up)
Alcohol and bottle size
Health warning (some will use an icon instead of words)
Integrity & Sustainability label around the neck of the bottle (*above right*)

This label indicates the winemaker has gone through the following process:

- Put in an application to make certified wine with Sustainable Wines of South Africa.
- Undergone random inspections during harvest.
- Kept comprehensive records of any treatments the grapes underwent, as well as any wine made or bottled wine purchased for blending.
- Shared those records during routine inspections.
- Submitted their wine to a panel for analytical and sensory evaluation.
- Gotten a seal for their bottle labels. These seals allow anyone to trace the source of the grapes used.

WINE PAIRING FOR THE PEOPLE

South Africa Sparkles

Méthode cap classique, also known as MCC or cap classique, is a categorization for sparkling wines made using the traditional Champagne method. That means that a still wine is made and bottled, and then yeast is added to the bottle for a second fermentation, which is what creates the bubbles and adds some distinct flavors. The yeast is filtered out before the bottles are sold, so you get a clear sparkling wine. The official designation was established in 1992, but this style of wine has been made there longer.

Traditionally cap classique wines are made with Chardonnay and Pinot Noir, the same as they would be in Champagne. A growing number, though, are made from the aromatic Chenin Blanc grape for a delicious and uniquely South African take.

Noir and Cinsault. In the 1940s, it started setting minimum prices for wine, and in the 1950s, it began wine education programs. In the 1970s, KWV helped create the Wines of Origin appellation system for South Africa.

Through it all, the KWV was amassing a valuable collection of wines, art, and property that would support its privatization after apartheid ended. The organization was a stabilizing force that could buy wine from producers when the market was slow due to the boycott, and it often came up with ideas like brandy and inexpensive flavored wines to entice new buyers. We can't say what would have happened in the vineyards during apartheid without the KWV, but with it in place and regulating the market, some of the country's very old vines and vineyards were able to continue producing right up until today.

When it comes to the physical terroir of the winelands, the country has just about everything. The climate is what would be considered Mediterranean, with hot, dry summers and cool (but not cold), wet winters. Vineyards closer to the coast are often considered better because big temperature swings between day and night allow grapes to maintain their acidity while they ripen. Luckily the country has a lot of coastline. Farther inland, the climate is drier, which can mean wines that are more concentrated with ripe, fruity flavors. Mountains provide breezes for lighter-bodied wines, although some slopes get so much sun that the grapes take on a smoky, ripe characteristic, while sunny valleys lead to plush, big-bodied purple wines.

The country's soil types also vary greatly. A lot of ancient volcanic and tectonic rock formations are beneath the soil and often poke out from underground. These can give the wines a mineral characteristic. They also contribute to microclimates forming, which enhances the distinctive variety of wines available from South Africa.

South Africa's Wine Regions

The country divides its winelands into five categories. From largest to smallest, they are geographical units, regions, subregions, districts, and wards. It all gets a little confusing because not every ward is in a district or subcategory, and one ward isn't even attached to a geographical unit. Also, lots of this wine production goes into large blends or fortified

AFRICA

South Africa's Wine Regions

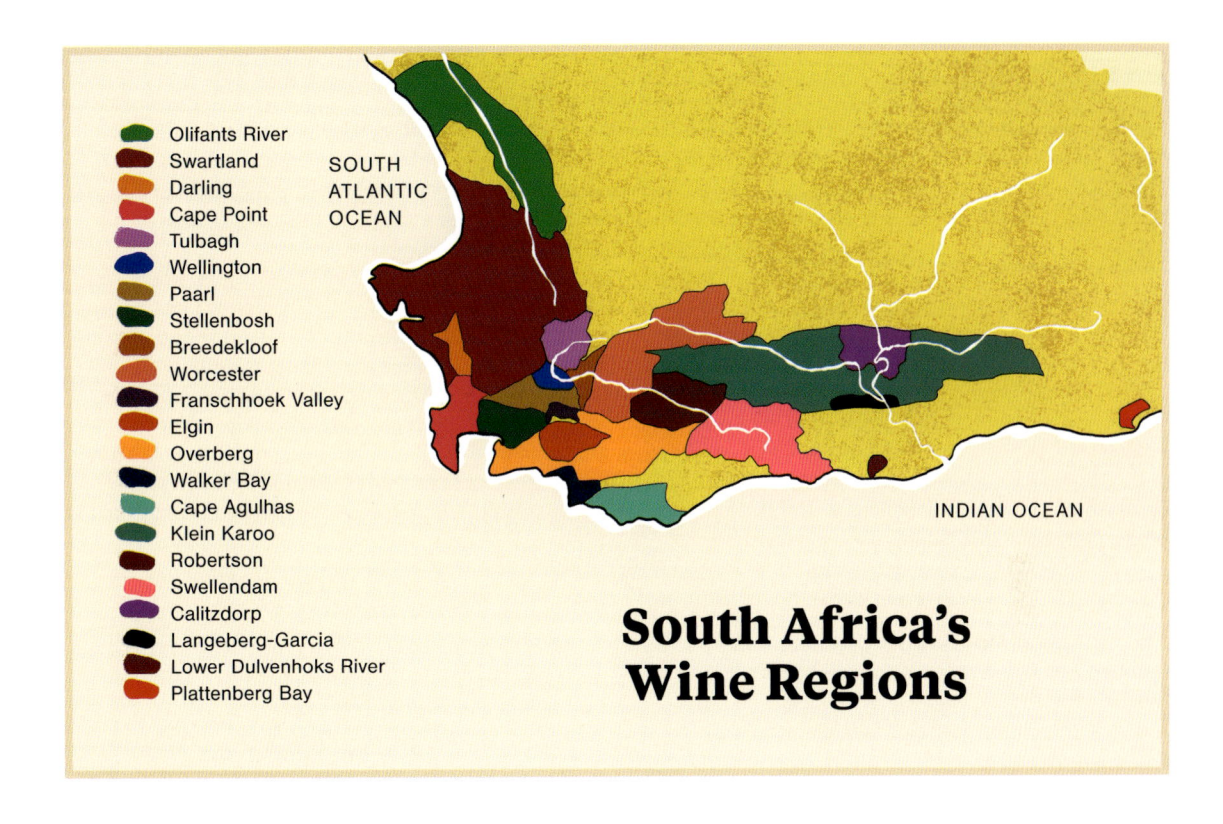

Legend:
- Olifants River
- Swartland
- Darling
- Cape Point
- Tulbagh
- Wellington
- Paarl
- Stellenbosh
- Breedekloof
- Worcester
- Franschhoek Valley
- Elgin
- Overberg
- Walker Bay
- Cape Agulhas
- Klein Karoo
- Robertson
- Swellendam
- Calitzdorp
- Langeberg-Garcia
- Lower Dulvenhoks River
- Plattenberg Bay

SOUTH ATLANTIC OCEAN

INDIAN OCEAN

wine. The most important regions for you as a drinker to know are the Wines of Origin (WO). In order for a bottle to have the label of a WO, it must be made entirely of grapes from that production area. Out of twenty-one WOs, here are the eight I'd consider most important and most available outside of South Africa:

Constantia: Once a single estate right outside of Cape Town, Constantia was established in 1685, divided up in 1715, and started producing wine in 1785. Pre-phylloxera, it was known for sweet wines made from Muscat Blanc. Today, steep slopes with cooling sea breezes and plenty of sun produce bright, complex Sauvignon Blanc and Bordeaux varieties like Cabernet Sauvignon and Merlot. A bit of sweet Muscat Blanc, known as Vin de Constance, is still produced here too.

Elgin: The country's coolest winelands are in the Cape South Coast region. The website WineAnorak.com describes it as an "elevated saucer." This valley has about three hundred meters of elevation, with mountains surrounding it on all four sides. Small hills within the valley create microclimates that are suitable for a variety of grapes (plus apple and pear orchards). Sauvignon Blanc, Chardonnay, Pinot Noir, and Syrah are particularly delicious wines grown from these shale soils.

Franschhoek: It's hard to summarize this valley that used to be part of the Paarl

Supporting Black-Owned Wine Brands

People visiting South Africa or purchasing South African wines stateside often want to buy wines from Black-owned wineries, or those made by Black winemakers. Black people are very involved in wine making in South Africa, and many wineries are investing in educational opportunities or hiring Black winemakers. I would suggest doing your research and asking about the wine-making team behind the brand, beyond the owner, to help support.

An iconic Black-owned wine brand with such beginnings is Aslina Wines, owned by Ntsiki Biyela, whom I had the pleasure of meeting once and being mistaken for at Wine Summit, a wine conference hosted in Lisbon. Biyela started Aslina Wines after earning her degree in viticulture and oenology at Stellenbosch University and working her way up to be head winemaker at Stellekaya Wines, which supported the trajectory of her growth.

There's also a question of ethnicity when we talk about culture in South Africa, in wine making and beyond. I came across several people who from my American perspective I would assume were Black from their complexion, but later learned they identified as Afrikaner, the name given to the Dutch-descended people born and raised in Africa, who speak the Afrikaans language. A lot of these descendants today have darker skin because of interracial relationships over the generations. When seeking Black-owned, be conscious of the wider ethnic identifications that are used locally.

Here is a list of Black-empowered South African wine brands to stock up on that you can find internationally and that support Black people within the industry, some of which are Black-owned wineries:

The House of Mandela: This winery was founded by Nelson Mandela's daughter, Dr. Makaziwe Mandela, who's now chairperson, and granddaughter Tukwini Mandela, who's the marketing director.

Aslina Wines: Ntsiki Biyela is the brand owner and winemaker at this label that was established in 2016. She received a scholarship to study wine making at Stellenbosch University. Upon graduating with a BSc in Agriculture (Viticulture and Oenology), she worked at Stellekaya Wines, where she claims to be the country's first Black head winemaker.

Ses'fikile Wines: Founder Nondumiso Pikashe was a schoolteacher before starting this brand.

M'hudi Boutique Family Wines: Members of the Rangaka family left other careers to start this wine and hospitality business in Stellenbosch.

Seven Sisters Vineyards: Founded by the seven Brutus sisters and run by Vivian Kleynhans (née Brutus), Seven Sisters claims to be one of only three completely Black-owned wineries in South Africa as of 2023.

Tesselaarsdal Wines: Owner Berene Sauls got her start at Hamilton Russell Vineyards before founding this brand, which is named in honor of Johannes Tesselaars, a man who donated his farmlands to servants and freed a group of enslaved people in 1810.

Black Elephant Vintners & Co.: Raymond Ndlovu is a Black man who met Kevin Swart, the company's cofounder, through their careers in finance.

PaardenKloof Estate: Co-owners Mohseen Moosa and Daphne Neethling also practice sustainable farming with native Nguni cattle and sheep.

Carmen Stevens Wines: Owner and winemaker Carmen Stevens claims to be the first Black South African to study wine making in the country, at Elsenberg College, and also to have the country's first 100 percent Black-owned winery in the country.

Highberry Farm: After working in wine in the United States and South Africa, Jabulani Ntshangase became this brand's global sales director. Vineyard manager Edward Etson is another Black person who holds a prominent role with this producer.

Kumusha Wines: World-renowned sommelier Tinashe Nyumudoka is the owner and winemaker of this brand.

appellation. It has steep hills and flat areas. The valley floor gets very little rain, while parts closer to the mountains that surround three sides get a lot. Some soils are clay, some granite, some graywacke sandstone. This diversity means that many types of grapes can find a home somewhere in Franschhoek, but producers here have chosen Semillon, Chardonnay, and Cabernet Sauvignon as signature varieties. A lot of méthode cap classique sparkling wine is made in this gorgeous area.

Swartland/Darling: Darling was once part of Swartland but got its own demarcation. One of the things that sets Darling apart is its cooling proximity to the Atlantic Ocean. Still part of the Western Cape, Swartland is north of Cape Town, so it's a bit warmer, which makes it well suited for Pinotage. Chenin Blanc and Syrah are also popular grapes in this hot, dry, shale-soiled region.

Paarl: One of the bigger regions, Paarl has been a wine making center since the French Huguenots arrived in the 1680s. It has mountains on the east and west ends, with a river running through it. This is a relatively hot region, but it does get a good amount of rain. A diversity of terrains and soils within the valley can suit a number of grapes, usually in a ripe, fruit-forward style. Think Pinotage, Cabernet Sauvignon, Syrah, Chenin Blanc, and Chardonnay.

Stellenbosch: Due to its long history of winegrowing and the Stellenbosch University, which has the country's premiere viticultural and oenological program, Stellenbosch is somewhat of a center of South African wine. The hot, dry climate is well suited to fruit-forward red wines, like Pinotage and Syrah, while areas cooled by ocean breezes also do well with Chardonnay, Chenin Blanc, and Sauvignon Blanc. Granitic soils in the 600-million-year-old mountains lend a unique and specific quality to wines grown on the district's mountainous lip.

Walker Bay: This coastal region is one of the country's coolest, subject to Antarctic breezes coming off the Atlantic. Shale and sandstone soils with a high clay content help with drainage. These factors come together to make bright, fresh, refined, mineral-driven wines using grapes like Pinot Noir, Chardonnay, and Sauvignon Blanc. With spectacular views in the shadow of Table Mountain, Walker Bay is a must-visit from Cape Town.

Bot River: North of Walker Bay and south of Stellenbosch, Bot River is a cool region with ocean breezes and sandstone soils from Table Mountain. One of its defining characteristics is fynbos, which adds a distinct herbaceous characteristic particularly to its cool-climate white wines, Chardonnay, Chenin Blanc, and Sauvignon Blanc. Chenin and Syrah are the two most planted grapes here, but you'll also find another South African signature in Pinotage.

Experience Braai

No trip to South Africa would be complete without the experience of a lekker braai, which is Afrikaans for "tasty fry." Known as tshisanyama, or "burn meat," in Zulu, this is a foodcentric social event based around barbecue, and the main star here is definitely the meat.

During my time in Cape Town, I linked with a few expats and fellow travelers to drive about thirty minutes to one of the most popular

WINE PAIRING FOR THE PEOPLE

+ PAIRED UP

BOBOTIE AND PAP + SOUTH AFRICA CAP CLASSIQUE, FRANSCHHOEK. South Africa's signature sparkling wine (see page 46) is a palate-cleansing complement to bobotie, the national dish. It's a casserole that shows a Malay influence. Ground beef flavored with warming spices is baked with a savory egg custard topping. Méthode cap classique (MCC) will also liven up your pap, a cornmeal porridge similar to grits. Typical grape varetials in the MCC blend are Chenin Blanc and Chardonnay, which bring flavors of white cherry, gingerbread, and lemon curd.

BRAAI + CABERNET SAUVIGNON, STELLENBOSCH, SOUTH AFRICA. This is the perfect South African wine for braai, because it has enough oomph behind it to stand up to the smoky, meaty spread. Cabernet Sauvignon is the country's most-planted red variety. It may be bottled on its own or used in Bordeaux-style blends with Merlot and/or Cabernet Franc. South African Cabs tend to be age-worthy, full-bodied, and spicy, with notes of green and red bell pepper, crushed black pepper, blackberry, and plum.

DURBAN CURRY + CHENIN BLANC, PAARL, SOUTH AFRICA. One of my favorite South African wines will bring a waxy, floral gentleness to balance out this very spicy chicken curry. Sometimes it's served in a hollowed-out loaf of bread, in which case the dish is called bunny chow. This high-acid, floral white grape is the most planted in South Africa and is locally known as Steen. Historically, the bulk of that production has been used for fortified wines, but still and sparkling bottlings have grown in popularity (and they're also some of my favorites).

BILTONG + PINOTAGE, STELLENBOSCH, SOUTH AFRICA. This is a savory pour to go with biltong, South Africa's answer to beef jerky, which is less sweet than what we typically find in the United States and sometimes made with venison. Pinotage is a crossing between Pinot Noir and Cinsault. Scientist Abraham Perold created the hybrid in South Africa, resulting in an interesting grape that combines fruity flavors of blackberry jam and ripe red fruit with smoke and leather. This fuller body wine is a good complement to the jerky.

BOEREWORS + SYRAH, ROBERTSON, SOUTH AFRICA. The wine's warming-spice notes and robust mouthfeel has enough body and spice to complement this rustic sausage seasoned with coriander, cloves, and nutmeg. Syrah is the country's second most-planted grape, and is grown in many regions and produced in many styles that run the gamut from ripe and fruity, to rich and chocolatey, to dry and savory.

MILK TART + VIN DE CONSTANCE, CONSTANTIA, SOUTH AFRICA. South Africa's sweet wine is a beautiful, honeyed counterpart to milk tart, a pie filled with a sweet milk custard. Vin de Constance is a historic and beloved dessert wine from Constantia region, near Cape Town, made from Muscat de Frontignan grapes. These raisined grapes exhibit flavor profiles of apricot, honey, orange blossom, spice, and high acidity. This luscious wine is a contrast to milk tart and enhance the tangy flavors.

locations beyond the tourist area of Cape Town. In a modest neighborhood far away from hotels and beachfront properties, I felt the heartbeat of Cape Town culture, music thumping from blocks away. What appeared to be a traffic jam was the entrance to this cultural experience that I couldn't wait to explore. Though it may sound like it, this was not your average cookout. We entered the party from the butcher shop, where we saw a vast selection of meat, from beef, lamb, chicken to antelope and ostrich meat, chopped into various cuts. Once you paid, you were given a ticket and escorted into a second room, which was basically where the magic happened. It was a dark rustic cave-like room filled with smoke from cooking over wood and coal. Glistening meats and savory spices from this room perfumed the entire neighborhood. I was instructed to leave my order with the braai master before heading to a third room. Last but not least was the party room, with South African wine and beers spilling over as I walked through and theDJ blasting early Amapiano music to set the vibes.

You can find parties like this (maybe not as big) throughout the townships, and they're an experience you can only have in South Africa. Don't come hungry though. There is usually a long wait, but it will be worth it.

THE WINE LIST
Africa

MOROCCO

Moroccan Salad and Harira + Nero d'Avola Rosato, SICILY, ITALY
Babbouche + Chardonnay, CHABLIS, FRANCE
Fish Kebabs + Sauvignon Blanc, MARLBOROUGH, NEW ZEALAND
Meat Kebabs + Côtes du Rhône—Red Blend, FRANCE
Tagine + Dry Gewürztraminer, ALSACE, FRANCE

▼

SENEGAL, GHANA, AND NIGERIA

Salade Niçoise à la Sénégalaise + Rosé, BANDOL, FRANCE
Yassa Poulet + Falanghina, LAZIO, ITALY
Banku with Tilapia and Shito + Grüner Veltliner, WEINVIERTEL, AUSTRIA
Fufu with Light Soup + Barbera, PIEDMONT, ITALY
Efo Riro + Cinsault, RHÔNE VALLEY, FRANCE
Pounded Yam with Egusi Soup + Palm Wine
Caakiri West African Pudding + Ice Wine Vidal Blanc, ONTARIO, CANADA
Nigerian Jollof Rice + Cabernet Franc, Chinon, LOIRE VALLEY, FRANCE
Ghanian Jollof Rice + Agiorgitiko, NEMEA, GREECE
Senegalese Jollof Rice + Zinfandel, HOWELL MOUNTAIN, CALIFORNIA

▼

ETHIOPIA AND SOMALIA

Sambusa + Franciacorta Extra Brut, LOMBARDY, ITALY
Fuul Mudammas with Pita + Trebbiano, TUSCANY, ITALY
Doro Wat + Valpolicella Ripasso DOC, SUPERIORE, ITALY
Suugo and Baasta + Sangiovese, CHIANTI, ITALY
Malab Iyo Malawax + T'ej, ETHIOPIA
Somali Beef Stew + Nerello Mascalese, SICILY, ITALY

▼

KENYA AND TANZANIA

Chicken Biryani + Viognier, CONDRIEU, FRANCE
Nyama Choma + Xinomavro, NAOUSSA, GREECE
East African Pilau + Monastrell, JUMILLA, SPAIN
Pweza wa Nazi + Marsanne, SAINT-PÉRAY, FRANCE
Zanzibar Pizza + Grillo, SICILY, ITALY
Mandazi + Demi-Sec Chenin Blanc, VOUVRAY, FRANCE

▼

ANGOLA, MOZAMBIQUE, SÃO TOMÉ AND PRÍNCIPE, AND CAPE VERDE

Moamba de Galinha + Encruzado, DÃO, PORTUGAL
Calulu de Peixe + Vinho Verde Tinto, PORTUGAL
Peri Peri Chicken + Skin-Contact Arinto, LISBOA, PORTUGAL
Matapa + Alvarinho, PORTUGAL
Cachupa + Jaen, Dão, PORTUGAL
Crab Curry + Baga Rosé, BAIRRADA, PORTUGAL

▼

SOUTH AFRICA

Bobotie and Pap + South Africa Cap Classique, FRANSCHHOEK
Braai + Cabernet Sauvignon, STELLENBOSCH, SOUTH AFRICA
Durban Curry + Chenin Blanc, PAARL, SOUTH AFRICA
Biltong + Pinotage, STELLENBOSCH, SOUTH AFRICA
Boerewors + Syrah, ROBERTSON, SOUTH AFRICA
Milk Tart + Vin de Constance, CONSTANTIA, SOUTH AFRICA

▼

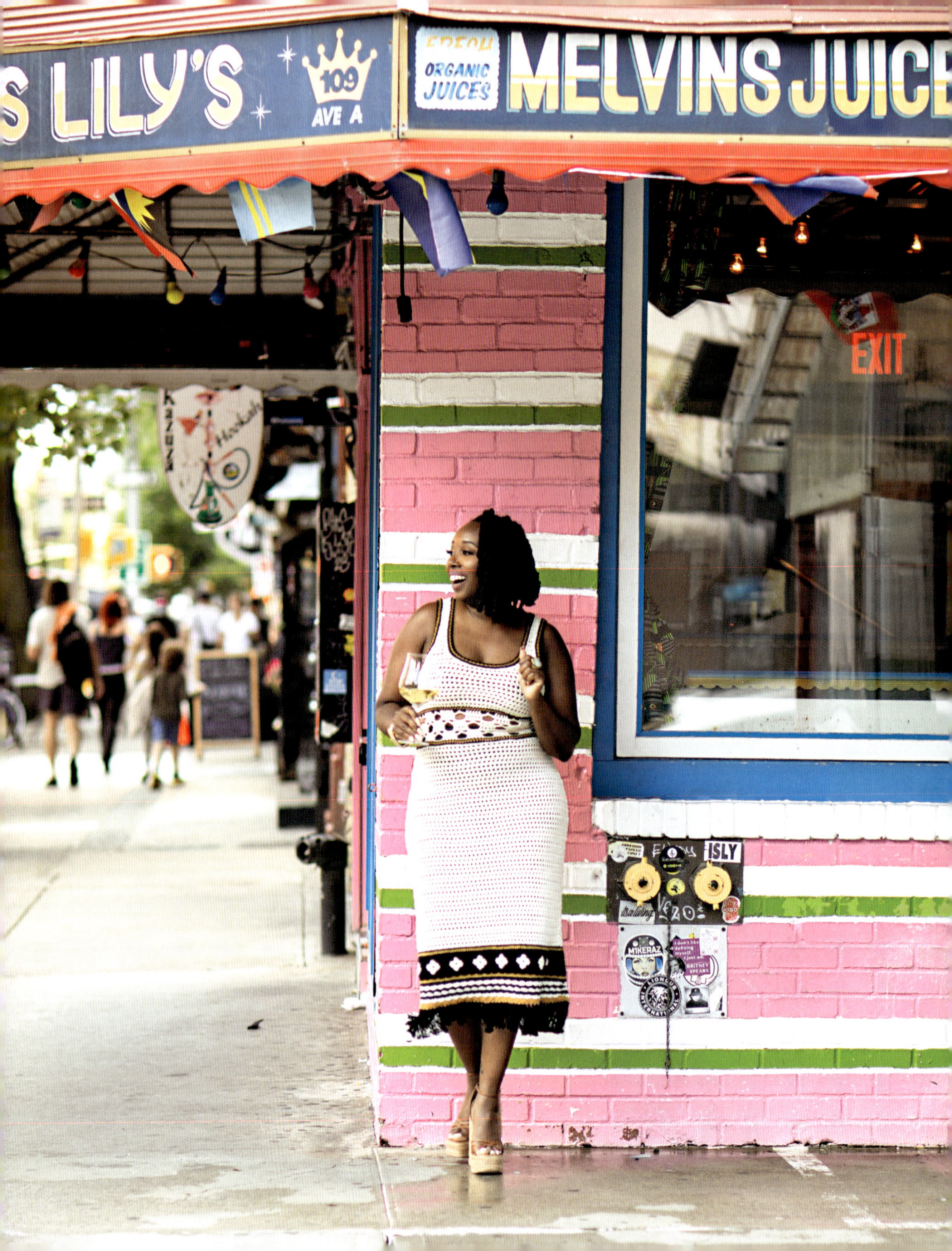
LILY'S
109
AVE A
ORGANIC JUICES
MELVINS JUICE
EXIT

The Caribbean

Puerto Rico	58
Cuba	67
Dominican Republic and Jamaica	72
Barbados	82

The Caribbean

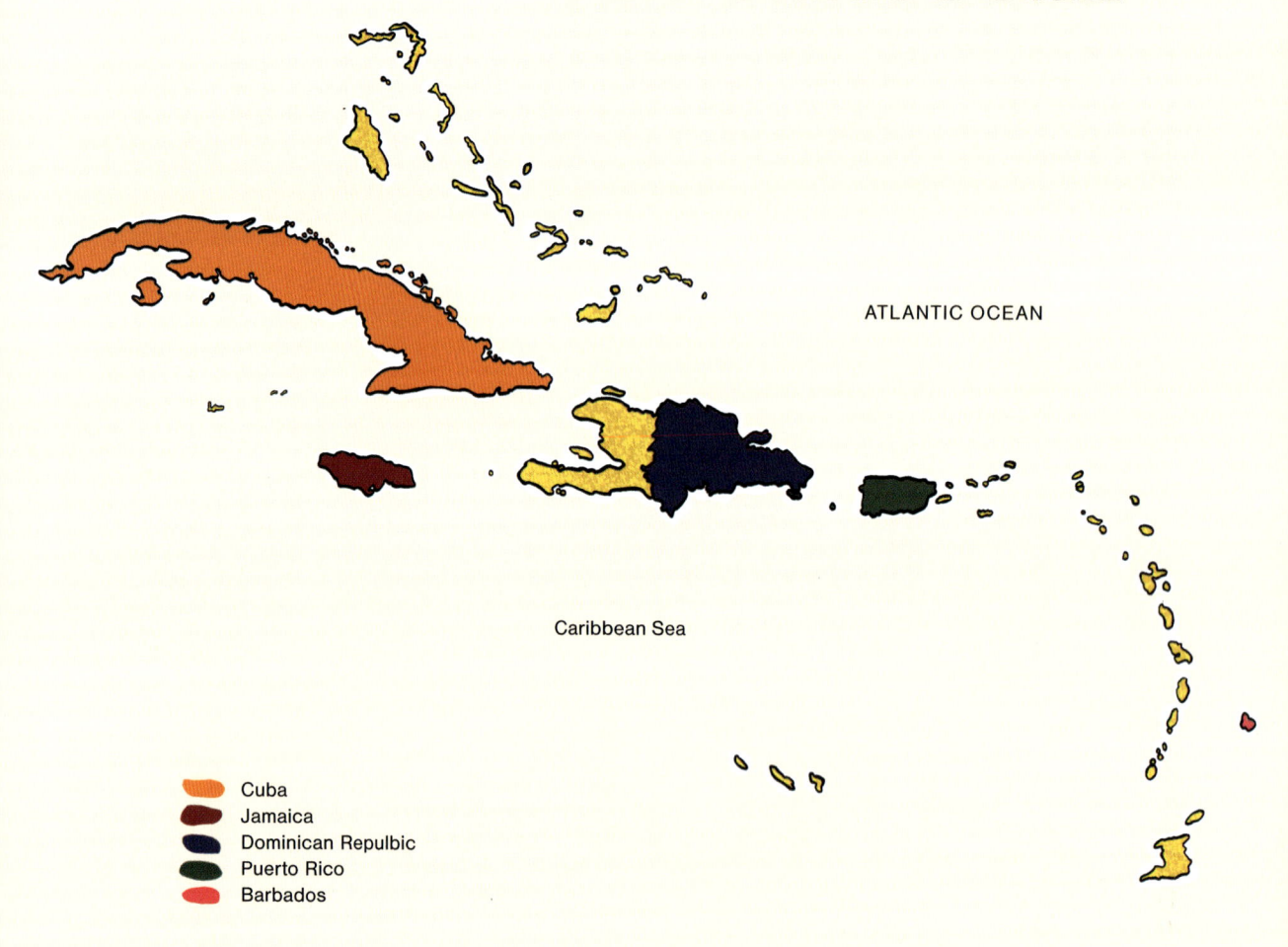

ATLANTIC OCEAN

Caribbean Sea

- Cuba
- Jamaica
- Dominican Repulbic
- Puerto Rico
- Barbados

Growing up in New York City exposes you to a variety of Caribbean cultures. In 2022, the Migration Policy Institute reported that about a quarter of the 4.4 million Caribbean immigrants in the United States live in New York, and a 2023 *Philadelphia Tribune* article states that about 20 percent of New York City's population have roots in the Caribbean. Even if I had never stepped foot on a Caribbean island, I would have had food from these islands, heard their music, and gotten to feel a bit of their lively cultures. Where you are from within the five boroughs attaches you to a specific Caribbean identity more intimately. The foods of Puerto Rico and the Dominican Republic were part of my everyday diet as a Harlem native, and I was introduced to authentic Jamican food while visiting friends who lived in Flatbush, Brooklyn.

But I have stepped foot on quite a few Caribbean islands. They're a short flight away from home, and in some cases, they became a refuge for me from bustling city life. When travel to Cuba was first allowed, you know I jumped at the chance. Same for when I was invited to a wedding in Barbados. And Puerto Rico has become a place where I feel at home, after multiple visits for relaxation and adventure.

All of this comes back around to drinks, because, of course, we're going to pair food from the Caribbean islands with wine. But also, this is the birthplace of rum, made in slightly different styles on the different islands. Like wine, it's a drink that reflects physical and cultural terroir and is deeply tied to the history of the islands, so I'm excited to share that with you.

Puerto Rico

Latitude and Longitude: 9.1900° S, 75.0152° W

Capital: San Juan

Country/Continent: The island of Puerto Rico is in the Caribbean Sea. It's east of the Dominican Republic and west of the Virgin Islands.

Population: 3.26 million

Top Exports: Pharmaceuticals, medical equipment, computers, apparel

Official Languages: Spanish and English

Independence from: Puerto Rico achieved independence from Spain in 1898. It remains a US commonwealth.

Growing up in Harlem, many of my neighbors and childhood friends were Puerto Rican. I was exposed to their culture, or at least the Nuyorican lifestyle, from an early age. Dancing salsa in their living rooms, getting full from eating too many plátanos maduros, and struggling to learn the words to Marc Anthony's "Te Conozco Bien" are some of the personal memories that slowly introduced me to the culture and manifested a bond that is very common to find Uptown. I'm talking about the chorus of the summer anthem of the early 2000s, "Oye Mi Canto" by rapper Noreaga, continuing to show pride in a connection and getting everyone in the streets of New York City singing "Boriqua! Morena!"—a kinship that has been prevalent since the beginning of hip-hop. I had relatives living in East Harlem, just north of El Barrio, also known as Spanish Harlem, which has historically been one of the largest Puerto Rican communities in New York City, as well as just over a nearby bridge, the South Bronx neighborhoods of Mott Haven, Melrose, and Hunts Point. The Puerto Rican pride was evident in wall murals and in the salsa music playing outside the bodega. Other neighborhoods with prominent Puerto Rican influence were the Lower East Side and Brooklyn's Williamsburg and Bushwick sections. As a New Yorker, this enabled me to cultivate a close connection with Puerto Rico and its people.

In 1917, the Jones–Shafroth Act granted US citizenship to Puerto Ricans, which allowed them to travel freely

THE CARIBBEAN

throughout the country, and many made New York City their home to further advance themselves, particularly after World War II and into the 1950s. There still seems to be a difference of opinion on what is the best political status for Puerto Rico—statehood, independence, or maintaining the current territorial status, which leaves them with no representation in Congress and no voting power in presidential elections.

Between the island's status and where I grew up, when I visited Puerto Rico, it felt more familiar than foreign, like a cultural extension of New York City. I have been traveling to Puerto Rico since I was a teenager. My family are avid cruisers—in a single-parent household, cruises were the best way to explore on a budget, with some cruises leaving right from the Hudson River on the westside of Manhattan. Puerto Rico was often the port city for our departures around the Caribbean, and we took advantage of the days before and after the cruise to get to know San Juan.

Today, my typical San Juan itinerary is focused on healing and recharging. A boutique hotel, the Dreamcatcher, has become my haven. I spend my time exploring the different neighborhoods and becoming reacclimated with what is new since my last trip. I love waking up to the sounds of the beach in Ocean Park. My hotel embodies the simple beauty of Puerto Rican island vibes and hospitality, comfort, and wellness. I have been staying here since one of the original owners, Sylvia De Marco, managed the property. Her inspiration was to turn her own home into a communal space to host travelers, and she succeeded, helping us feel at home in Puerto Rico. The hotelier has since grown her portfolio and continues to incorporate community and wellness as part of her new properties, La

> **DRINK NOW: San Juan**
>
> One thing is certain: wherever there is a modern, hip food scene, there is a wine movement close by fermenting. The wine list of Vianda made it evident that there was more to the wine scene for me to explore in Puerto Rico. Here are a few bars, retailers, and restaurants that are focused on great quality and low-intervention wine selections worth checking out while in San Juan:
> - El Vino Crudo
> - Bar La Penúltima
> - Café Caleta
> - CRU Wine Shop
> - Pío Pío Restaurant & Wine Bar

Botanica Hotel in San Juan and Finca Victoria in Vieques. To me, Sylvia's work defines the aesthetic of modern Puerto Rican design and lifestyle.

In the afternoon I hit the urban heartbeat of San Juan and explored the art galleries and culinary scene of Santurce. When in Santurce, be sure to café-hop—modern cafés are great spaces to retreat from the sun and meet locals. Puerto Rican coffee production may have decreased since its prime in the nineteenth and early twentieth centuries, but Puerto Ricans' love for the drink is still thriving. Be sure to sample the local coffee producers like Café Lareño, Hacienda San Pedro, and Sandra Farms.

No trip to San Juan would be complete, of course, without meandering the streets of Old San Juan until sunset. I find myself wandering the cobblestone streets, taking in the beauty of the colonial architecture, letting the energy of Calle de San Sebastián lead me to salsa dancing at the now-closed Nuyorican Café or a nightcap at one of my favorite bars, La Factoría. La Factoría was ranked number eighteen in North America's 50 Best Bars ranking in 2024 and has

Sip the Culture

Puerto Rico is not new to the beverage scene. Its rich rum history has been making the island a leading spot for top bar experiences and talent. Enslaved Africans were brought to the island to produce sugarcane, which was introduced to the island by Spanish colonizers. Rum, a byproduct of distilled sugarcane, has been made there since the 1500s, so it's had a little bit of time to birth some great rum cocktails. We know that most recipes, for food or drinks, don't have a single inventor or point of origin, but here's a look at some of the drinks that are part of the island's drink lore and culture. Make sure you enjoy these cocktails with Puerto Rico's own Ron del Barrilito or Don Q rum. If you find yourself on the island, let the professionals handle it at La Factoría, which repeatedly makes the World's 50 Best Bars list for North America, for innovative cocktails as well as the classics.

PIÑA COLADA. The official story is that Ramón "Monchito" Marrero, a bartender at the Caribe Hilton Hotel in San Juan, invented this combination of pineapple, coconut, and rum in 1954. In 1978, it became the island's official drink. Still, other bars and bartenders on the island have claimed the drink, and a 1950 *New York Times* article mentioned the drink in Cuba. Regardless of its exact origins, though, this is the official cocktail of Puerto Rico.

MOJITO. The mojito is from Cuba. There's no denying that. But the mix of mint, lime, simple syrup, rum, and club soda is everywhere in Puerto Rico, and it's very much part of my experience there. In a story for Whetstone, Israel Meléndez Ayala wrote that maybe it's just come to be seen as another tropical cocktail. Or maybe during the US blockade of Cuba, when some rum producers moved operations to Puerto Rico so that they could sell their product to the United States, the cocktail came too.

COQUITO. Coconut milk, rum, and baking spices like cinnamon and nutmeg come together in this sweet, creamy drink often made around the holidays. Some recipes use evaporated and/or sweetened condensed milk. Some may use eggs. No one is sure of the drink's exact origin story, but it's undoubtedly Puerto Rican and a staple for the Christmas season.

---

consistently been on the list. Each room has a different experience from a wine bar to a dance floor for salsa beginners and experts.

During the pandemic, I realized that I did not want to travel far, but like most of us, I was still in need of a new environment beyond my apartment. In search of reprieve, I found myself in San Juan to celebrate my birthday and just simply life. It was an easy destination to get to after a year of lockdown. I immediately recognized that since my last visit, in 2017, the same year as Hurricane Maria, there was a renaissance in the food and beverage scene that was beyond the traditional culinary landmarks. Rising chefs were returning to the island to open their establishments after years of working in kitchens in the States and Europe. I enjoyed my birthday dinner at Vianda, an intimate farm-to-table restaurant focused on native ingredients, founded by the husband-and-wife duo Amelia Dill and Francis Guzmán, after they spent years working at popular restaurants like Range in San Francisco, and Blue Hill and the Modern in New York City.

Vianda is just one example of the modern fine-dining experience that highlight Puerto Rican heritage.

Road Tripping

Exploring Puerto Rico beyond San Juan was a bucket-list trip for years after I became well acquainted with the city. I was ready to explore beyond the city limits and recruited my fellow Alpha Kappa Alpha sorority sister Kali, who had moved from Queens to Fajardo, in eastern Puerto Rico. She was just as eager as I was to embark on this adventure. One July Fourth week, we packed up a rental car and started on a three-hundred-mile journey around and through the main island.

Traveling along the rim of the island was the best way to absorb the diverse topography of Puerto Rico. In addition to its superior uninhabited beach coastal plains, we were able to take in everything from vast mountainous interiors to rainforest. In the interior of the island, between the Central Mountains, are the fertile valleys where the farmland and agriculture industry dominate, and top crops such as bananas, coffee, yams, and citrus are grown. At the mountain foothills are a system of rivers and streams on the east and west end of the island, where sugarcane, coconuts, and a wide range of fruits are produced.

We checked into the different cities in each region, soaking in the sun and the taste of the western, southern, and interior culture. Loaded with everything from the serenading sounds of Marc Anthony to the hip-thrusting vibes of Daddy Yankee on our playlist, we were ready for our visits to Aguadilla, Rincon, a pit stop in Guanica, Ponce, and then through Caguas on Highway 52 (PR-52) back to San Juan. The Taíno, Spanish, African, and Caribbean influences were the visible thread that connected each city, especially through its food. Whether enjoying a cookout on Crash Boat Beach or enjoying street food along the highway, Taíno cooking techniques like barbecuing and roasting were our daily meat options, accompanied with yuca. Spanish colonizers brought with them some of the staple ingredients that now contribute to the unique style of seasonings that are key elements of Puerto Rican cuisine. Sofrito is a great example of this fusion, a mixture of finely chopped onions, garlic, peppers, culantro, tomatoes, and cilantro that is a base of many Puerto Rican traditional recipes, like the national dish, arroz con gandules.

Enslaved Africans were brought to Puerto Rico just like they were to other Caribbean islands. In the 1500s, members of the Yoruba tribe settled in what's now Loíza, just east of San Juan on the island's north shore. Loíza has its own styles of music, plena and bomba. It has its own art, vejigante masks worn during Carnaval. And it has its own food. The area is famous for its frituras, or fritters, and for El Burén de Lula, where Lula, a woman in her eighties, uses a traditional clay burén to cook foods that would have been eaten before anyone from Spain got here. It's an easy day trip, and after taking in some beach time at Playa Piñones, you can find me at the kiosks enjoying everything from alcapurrias de jueyes and pinchos to fresh oysters. Some Spanish and Taíno culture has crept into Loíza, but it still has its own distinct West African culture that keeps me coming back for more.

WINE PAIRING FOR THE PEOPLE

MARRERO FAMILY COQUITO

SERVES 12

1 cup raw sugar

¼ cup crushed cinnamon bark or 10 cinnamon sticks

½ vanilla bean or 1 teaspoon vanilla extract

2 ripe coconuts

1¼ cup white rum

1¼ cup aged rum

One 12-ounce can sweetened condensed milk

One 12-ounce can evaporated milk

1 tablespoon fresh-grated nutmeg, for garnish

Every family, household, and even person has their own recipe for coquito, a spiced coconut-milk drink fortified with rum and served around the holidays. Lynnette Marrero is an educator, advocate, and consultant in the bartending world. She's cofounder of Speed Rack, a cocktail competition for women and femmes, with Ivy Mix (page 111) and has herself racked up all sorts of awards. She's sharing her coquito recipe with us, filled with holiday cheer.

It uses fresh coconut milk and it isn't thickened with egg yolk. But if you have to have your yolks, you can add them after step 6.

1. Heat the oven to 350°F.
2. In a medium saucepan, bring 1 cup water and the sugar to a boil to make a simple syrup. Add the cinnamon and vanilla to the water. Let it boil for 2 minutes, then sit for 1 hour, and strain.
3. Once the oven is hot, place the coconuts on a baking sheet and bake them until you see cracks start to appear, 10 to 15 minutes. Remove them from the oven and, when they're cool enough to handle, wrap one in a towel, and tap it with the side of a heavy knife or with a hammer until it breaks into pieces. Repeat with the second coconut. Separate the meat from the shell and remove brown skin. Wash, drain, and grate the meat.
4. In a blender, pour ½ cup white rum, ½ cup aged rum, and add about ⅓ of the grated coconut meat. Blend thoroughly at high speed until it looks pureed. Strain and squeeze through muslin cloth.
5. Pour the strained liquid back into the blender, add ⅓ coconut meat, blend, and strain.
6. Pour the strained liquid back into the blender again, add balance of grated coconut meat, blend, strain, and add 2 cups of the liquid back into the blender.
7. Add condensed and evaporated milk, and mix well.
8. With the blender still running, slowly add the simple syrup you made in step 2, the cinnamon, and the vanilla.
9. In a large bowl, mix the liquid thoroughly with the remaining ¾ cup white rum and ¾ cup aged rum
10. Bottle and store in the refrigerator. Before serving, shake the bottle well, pour into punch cups, and sprinkle with ground nutmeg.

THE CARIBBEAN

The Mofongo Chronicles

I decided to make mofongo my treat whenever I visited Puerto Rico, as everyone should. It's not the island's official dish, but it might as well be. Green plantains are fried and then mashed with chicharron and garlic. There are variations of chicken and seafood, so I made it my mission to taste as many as possible when traveling around Puerto Rico. I allow myself to overindulge since I rarely eat mofongo in New York and have given myself permission in the name of "research" to order it whenever I find a new variation on the menu. I've tried different styles found in each region of the island during my road trip, fine-dining restaurants, and the traditional spots. Here's my wine-pairing guide to mofongo:

Wine + Mofongo = WINEFONGO

MOFONGO	WINE
Mofongo de Camarones (mofongo stuffed with jumbo shrimp and a creole butter lemon sauce)	**Chardonnay, Pfalz, Germany** (citrus, green apples, and slight minerality; typically, no oak or neutral oak allows for the freshness and high acidity to shine)
Mofongo de Chicharron (mofongo stuffed with fried pork skins or, for people who don't eat pork, fried chicken)	**Gran Reserva Cava Brut, Penedès, Spain** (baked green and yellow apple, toasted almond, brioche, and spice notes; traditional sparkling wine from Spain with high acid and creamy mousse)
Mofongo de Carne Guisada (mofongo stuffed with beef stew)	**Tannat, Madiran, France** (blackberry and plum and high structured tannins; does well with age and notes of tobacco leaf, cedar, and pepper)
Chuletas Rellenas de Mofongo (pork chops with mofongo stuffing)	**Crianza Rioja, Rioja Oriental, Spain** (ripe red cherry, dried fig, and, from the oak aging, characteristics of vanilla and spice)

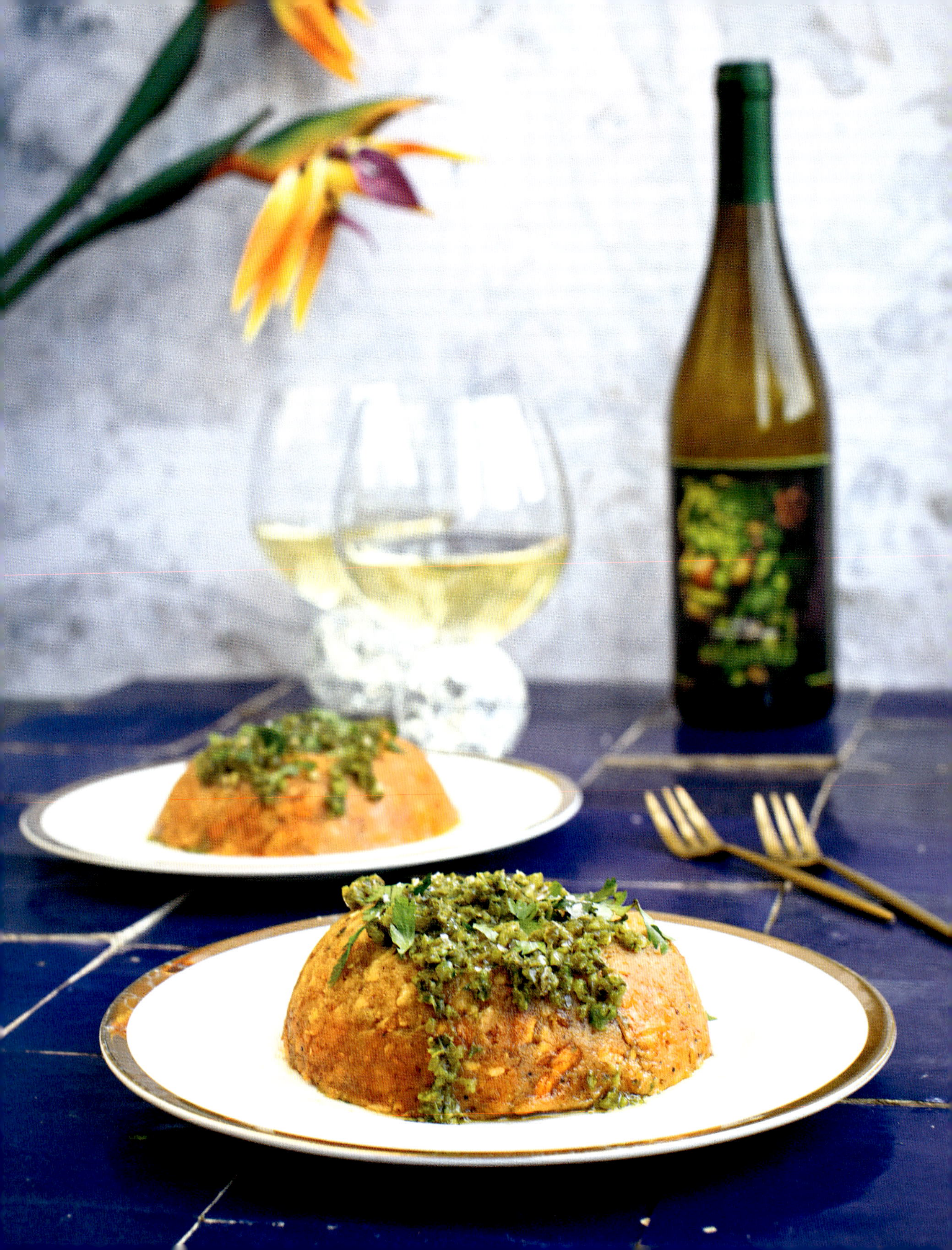

THE CARIBBEAN

VEGAN MOFONGO + RIOJA BLANCO,
RIOJA ALVESO, SPAIN

This recipe came from Alicia Kennedy, a food writer who lives in San Juan and grew up on Long Island. She's of mixed Puerto Rican descent and writes about how living on the island has given her a new appreciation for the seasonality and availability of certain ingredients and dishes—among other things. She's the author of *No Meat Required*.

Rioja Blanco white wine blends only make up about 10 percent of what's produced in Spain's Rioja region. The dominant, indigenous grape is Viura (aka Macabeo), which is required by Rioja DOC to make up at least 51 percent of the blend. Other grapes can include indigenous Malvasía de Rioja, Garnacha Blanca, Tempranillo Blanco, Maturana Blanca, and Turruntés de Rioja, as well as Chardonnay, Sauvignon Blanc, and Verdejo. Viura's primary notes of honeydew, lime, and lemon curd balanced with tarragon and hazelnut complement the flavors of this vegan mofongo, which accentuates the flavor-packed plantains. Either a fresh, joven style or aged Reserva, with its complex flavors of caramelized honey, preserved lime, and roasted pineapple, will pair well. Look for Lopez de Heredia Rioja Vina Tondonia Reserva Blanco, Viña Ilusion Blanco, and El Mozo Wines "Herrigoia" Blanco.

1. Remove the plantain skins by cutting through the skin vertically, then peeling back the thick skin. Cut each into about 1-inch thick pieces. Soak the pieces in a bowl of water with 2 teaspoons salt, for 2 hours and up to overnight.
2. When ready to make mofongo, start by smashing the garlic, miso, and smoked paprika together in a pílon or mortar and pestle. Alternatively, grate the garlic cloves into a large mixing bowl, then mash in the miso and paprika to make a paste. Set aside.
3. Heat frying oil to 325°F. Drain the plantains and pat dry. Fry in batches until golden brown: Don't rush them, as if they brown too much on the outside, they won't cook within.
4. Remove the plantains from the oil when ready directly into the pílon or mixing bowl and mash as they're ready, allowing any residual hot oil to come in with them. Drizzle in olive oil to ease

SERVES 4 TO 6

3 medium green plantains (870 grams or 1 pound, 15 ounces after skins are removed)

5 cloves garlic

1 tablespoon miso (red or white)

1 teaspoon smoked paprika

Oil for frying

Olive oil, flaky sea salt, and sofrito, for serving

Pique (chile-infused vinegar) and cilantro, optional, for garnish

---

SOFRITO

MAKES ABOUT 1 CUP OF SOFRITO

¼ cup recao (aka culantro)

¼ cup cilantro, with stems

¼ yellow or white onion, rough-chopped

5 ají dulce (sweet peppers), rough-chopped

1 cubanelle or green bell pepper, rough-chopped

1 clove garlic

1 teaspoon salt

¼ cup olive oil

Blend together until smooth. Adjust salt or olive oil to taste as needed.

(recipe continues on next page)

the mashing and allow the mofongo to come together. It will be ready when it is smooth, nearly uniform in texture. Taste for salt and fat; add more salt or olive oil if needed.

5. To serve, you can drizzle the sofrito under or on top of the mofongo. To form the servings of mofongo, spoon mixture into a ramekin, mashing to pack it tight, and then turn it out onto the plate. Drizzle with more olive oil and pique, if desired, and sprinkle with flaky salt. Garnish with cilantro leaves.

+ PAIRED UP

PINCHOS + SYRAH, SAN LUIS OBISPO, CALIFORNIA. These skewers are usually served hot off the grill with barbecue sauce, and all I want to drink with them is a red that can be served with a chill. Syrah from the San Luis Obispo coast in Northern California is that, plus it will complement the herbs and seasoning of the chicken or pork. Syrah from cool climate regions provide higher acidity, red fruit flavor, and a blend of crushed tricolor peppercorn.

ALCAPURRIAS DE JUEYES + CARIÑENA ROSADO, CATALONIA, SPAIN. Deep-fried savory pastry stuffed with local land crab was my ultimate snack on the beach, and there was nothing I wanted more than a nice chilled rosé to complete the moment, even though my Medalla Light got the job done. Balancing the flavors from the banana leaf wrapping to the stewed crab meat called for a much richer-style rosé that can hold up to the flavors but also provide freshness. Spanish Rosado made from Carignana grapes has notes of ripe red berries and red currant, with baking spices and minerality.

PERNIL + ST. LAURENT, BURGENLAND, AUSTRIA. Pernil is how you know it's Christmas. This bone-in pork shoulder that usually takes at least twenty-four hours of marinating with sazón, garlic, and herbs is the crown jewel of the season. Holiday dinners always call for wines that are compatible with the various flavors and dishes, which makes the fruit-forward St. Laurent an easy alternative to your cousin's Pinot Noir. Lesser-known St. Laurent has traditional bright red cherry, raspberry flavor with black pepper, forest floor, and sweet baking spices.

FLAN DE QUESO + MOSCATEL DE SETÚBAL, SETÚBAL, PORTUGAL. The caramelized sugar and cheese in this cheesecake-like custard melts with the raw honey, white floral notes of Muscat of Alexandria and is enhanced with the finish of navel orange and peach skins.

THE CARIBBEAN

Cuba

I traveled to Cuba during the Obama administration. When you travel internationally from the United States, it always matters who the current president is and the political relationship between your home country and the one you are visiting. US politics is global politics, our voting decisions affect us and other countries, and traveling internationally is the best way to understand the international perspective.

The tension between the United States and Cuba dates back to the end of the Cold War, when the United States placed an embargo on Cuba for Fidel Castro's relationship with the former Soviet Union during the Cuban Revolution of 1959. As a result of the trade blockade, US citizens were banned from traveling to Cuba for five decades.

Ten years before I wrote this book, the Obama Administration changed this policy in an effort to reestablish diplomatic relations and strengthen efforts to control drug trafficking, illegal migration, and counterterrorism. After a Cuban embassy reopened in the United States and a US embassy reopened in Cuba in 2015, travel restrictions were eased, and in 2016 commercial flights from the United States were allowed to fly directly to Cuba, and I was on one of them.

Congress ultimately made the decision that kept the embargo in place, however it allowed for expanded categories of authorized travel to the country. I took advantage of President Obama's approach that connecting the United

---

Latitude and Longitude: 21.5218° N, 77.7812° W

Capital: Havana

Country/Continent: The island of Cuba is in the Caribbean Sea and sits between Florida and the Bahamas to the north, Turks and Caicos and Haiti to the east, Jamaica and Cayman Islands to the south, and Cancun, Mexico, to the west.

Population: 11.3 million

National Dish: Ropa Vieja

National Drink: Cuba Libre

Top Exports: Nickel, cane sugar, cigars, metal ores

Official Language: Spanish

Independence Day: October 10, 1868, and May 20, 1902

Independence from: Spain in 1868 and the United States in 1902

States with Cuba was better than isolation. Coincidentally, my friend Dash Harris, who owned a travel company, Afro Latino Travel, which conducted tours in Panama, was expanding her travel business to Cuba. I connected with Dash to create an educational heritage tour for me that would fulfill one of the twelve approved categories of travel, and booked a flight on Jet Blue with a few friends for the cultural experience of a lifetime.

During our time in Cuba, we had to tick off the tourist checklist driving around Old Havana in a 1950 Ford convertible and visiting El Capitolio, Plaza de la Revolucion, and the neighborhood of El Cerro. Like Rome, Havana's architecture and our ride felt like we were in a time capsule that gives the city an open-air-museum feeling of the Spanish colonial era. History feels alive here, as do the decades of neglect. The colorful colonial-era buildings in many areas looked like ancient ruins—missing windows, roofs, and sometimes even the building facade. The midcentury cars, thanks to the embargo, that cruised the streets made it feel like we took a time machine not a plane to get here. Our deep dive into Afro-Cuban history started as soon as we stepped into Museo Casa de Africa, a cultural center with an exhibition of art, and we were able to experience a tambores guitar demonstration and participate in a rumba dance workshop. Our visit to Asociación Cultural Yoruba de Cuba was an immersive overview of the Santería religion, and we learned about the major orishas (Yoruban deities/saints). We were even invited to a private Santería ceremony, and I will always cherish witnessing the transcendent experience of its parishioners.

Havana may feel isolated from the world with its nostalgic architecture, fashion, and rich history, but at night we were able to experience the ingenuity of the culture. The tourist-filled neighborhoods had plenty of fine-dining restaurants, however they were state run and typically focused on traditional Cuban cuisine, thanks to the island's agricultural abundance from the land and the Caribbean Sea. However, my most memorable food experience was visiting the different paladares. Paladares are family-owned restaurants that typically operate in a section of the family home that was converted into dining area for guests. Paladares provide an intimate dining experience that lets you get to know locals and are an opportunity for each family to showcase their family recipes and creativity.

THE CARIBBEAN

+ PAIRED UP

ROPA VIEJA + RIOJA RESERVA, RIOJA ALTA, SPAIN. This shredded beef stew, the name of which means "old clothes," pairs well with Rioja Reserva. Tomato and herb notes always make this wine a good accompaniment to stew. A Reserva, which has been aged somewhat, will have mellow tannins to match the beef's soft texture.

VACA FRITA + MERLOT, COLUMBIA VALLEY, WASHINGTON. This is another beef dish. In this one, shredded beef is seasoned with lime and garlic and fried until crispy. Columbia Valley Merlot from Washington State is soft and silky to smooth the meat's edges.

MEDIANOCHE + MENCÍA, BIERZO, SPAIN. The precursor to the Cubano sandwich is made with bread that's soft and sweet, thanks to the use of eggs. It can be compared to challah or brioche. Many believe the Cubano was originally from Florida. Roasted pork, ham, Swiss cheese, mustard, and bread-and-butter pickles come together on a soft roll. Bierzo Mencía, a light-bodied red wine from Spain, has enough acidity to match the pickles and mustard, and just enough body to stand up to the meat and cheese.

LECHON ASADO + SAVATIANO, ANCHIALOS, GREECE. Cuba's roast pork dish is marinated in and served with a garlicky, citrusy mojo sauce. The Greek white grape Savatiano is known for pairing well with marinated meats like this. The notes of resin, honeydew, lemon, and green apple that are packed into this medium-plus-body wine will lift the flavors of the sauce.

AJIACO CUBANO + GODELLO, VALDEORRAS, SPAIN. This stew can be a different thing, depending on who you ask on what day of the week. It can have pork, beef, chicken, corn, and root vegetables like yucca, malanga, calabaza, plantains, and boniatos, along with seasonings like cumin, garlic, lime, and peppers. Pair it with full-bodied, citrus-forward, briny Godello from Spain, which will act like an extra seasoning.

PICADILLO + SUPER TUSCAN, TUSCANY, ITALY. A hash of ground beef, tomatoes, onions, olives, capers, and sometimes raisins (they're controversial), picadillo is served over rice. Pair it with a Super Tuscan. These red wines take their name from an era when winemakers in the Tuscany region of Italy started working with nonindigenous grapes like Merlot and Cabernet Sauvignon, so they couldn't get official appellation status. Instead, they made their own name and blend. Today, you will find a large amount of Sangiovese supported by those other grapes to create a full-bodied red with flavors of plum, cherry, cassis, sweet baking spices, and a cedar finish.

More Than Just a Cigar

Cigars are a lifestyle in Cuba from several smoke shops and outdoor lounges to the iconic Cigar Ladies. You can find Cigar Ladies taking pictures, for a price of course, with tourists in Plaza de la Catedral dressed in headwraps, colorful dresses, and with some of the rarest and boldest cigars carefully balanced on their lips. I was fortunate during my visit to Cuba that I was able to tour the iconic Real Fábrica de Tabaco Partagás (The Royal Partagás Cigar Factory) in Havana. Partagás was a cigar factory museum, the home of the famous Habanos cigars and one of the oldest cigar factories.

Arriving at Partagás was a similar experience to driving down St. Helena Highway in Napa Valley during harvest with fresh fruit aromas and hard work filling the air; but this musky yet sweet smell of tobacco gave a pleasantly warming and familiar feeling. At that moment I felt an unexpected connection to wine. Watching the workers at different stations, separating the tobacco leaves, stuffing and rolling, weighing and cutting the ends, counting and inserting into the cigar boxes, and finally stamping the boxes with the factory code and date was all done by hand. Cigars like wine are a true labor of love.

It is common to find tasting notes of cigars or cigar box or even tobacco leaf in wine imparted from oak barrel aging. Oak aging is a winemaker's preference, and it has become synonymous with many Old World wine styles, like wine from Bordeaux, France, and Rioja, Spain, and in the New World, like wine from Napa Valley, California. Typical flavors you can expect to find in your wine beyond cigars are vanilla, clove, caramel, smoke, and even coconut. A winemaker may choose to use oak to help slowly expose the wine to oxygen, resulting in a wine with smoother texture and less astringent tannins. It is also a more favorable environment for malolactic fermentation, which gives wine a creamier texture.

The three more commonly used oak are French oak, American oak, and Eastern European. Like cigars and wine, oak also has terroir, imparting flavors from its natural environment that can be attributed to the soil, climate, and time. However, guaiacol is the primary organic compound of the oak barrel that is exposed to the wine after the barrel has been toasted. Having this intimate, up-close connection with the smell of tobacco and cigar box gave me a tangible memory to draw from when tasting wine aged in oak barrels, and I am grateful for this experience.

When pairing wines and cigars, I search for complementary pairings to body, profile, and sweetness levels. Here are a few examples of high-quality cigars listed by various styles and the type of wines to enjoy with them:

THE CARIBBEAN

FULL BODY WINE + FULL BODY CIGARS

Wine Pairing: Search for full body, higher alcohol, pronounced aromas, intense profiles

Examples of wine to consider: Syrah, Malbec, Zinfandel, Gran Reserva Rioja, Brunello di Montalcino

EPC (Ernesto Perez-Carrillo) Pledge
Cigar Notes: Robust wood notes, balanced by a hint of sweetness and baking spice with a smooth coffee finish

Oliva Serie V 135th Anniversary Edicion Limitada
Cigar Notes: Dark chocolate, espresso, black pepper, caramel, malt, cedar, and black raisins

MEDIUM BODY WINE + MEDIUM BODY CIGARS

Wine Pairing: Search for medium body, medium alcohol, and medium intensity aromas with an oak aging profile.

Examples of wine to consider: Pinot Noir, California Chardonnay, Barolo, Vintage Champagne

Tatuaje Black, Nicaragua
Cigar Notes: Oak, dark cocoa, nuts, spice, and hints of dark fruit

Alec & Bradley Kintsugi, Honduras
Cigar Notes: Earthy, wood, chocolate, nuts, and pepper

Plasencia Alma Fuerte Colorado Claro, Nicaragua
Cigar Notes: Toasted bread, cream, cedar, leather, and espresso beans, with a floral finish

LIGHT INTENSITY WINE + MELLOW CIGARS

Wine Pairing: Search for wines with what we call medium-minus body and medium-minus alcohol, meaning a little lighter than medium and a little fuller than light, plus creamy texture, fruit forward flavors, and floral notes.

Examples of wines to consider: Chardonnay, Viognier, Trebbiano, Marsanne, Beaujolais

Foundation Highclere Castle
Cigar Notes: Creamy, baking spices, nuts, and cedar

Macanudo Gold Label
Cigar Notes: Smooth, almonds, lemon sweetness, and buttercream

Perdomo Double Aged 12-Year Vintage
Cigar Notes: Cream mixed with caramel and cedar and a buttery finish

Dominican Republic and Jamaica

Dominican Republic

Coordinates: 18.7357° N, 70.1627° W
Capital: Santo Domingo
Country/Continent: This Caribbean nation occupies the eastern portion of the island it shares with Haiti. Puerto Rico lies to the east, and Turks and Caicos to the north.
Population: 11.12 million
National Drink: Mamajuana
Top Exports: Ferronickel, cigars, plastics, electrical equipment, bananas
Official Language: Spanish
Independence Day: February 27, 1844
Independence from: Haiti

My experiences with these two countries have been predominantly in New York City, and somewhat in Florida. Even though both are pretty easy to travel to, with plenty of inexpensive flights on budget airlines, I just haven't made it, yet. Sometimes the easiest travels are the ones that get put off the longest. And I know which neighborhoods will immerse me in these cultures at home when I am in the mood. I can see, hear, smell, and taste the Dominican Republic in Harlem and Washington Heights. And when craving Jamaican, the hour-long subway ride on the 3 train from Harlem to Brooklyn does the trick.

Immigration from the Dominican Republic to the United States, and specifically to New York City, really took off during the 1970s, and it kept going. The country was ruled by a violent dictator, Rafael Trujillo, from 1930 until he was assassinated in 1961. It seems like with a lot of dictators, countries are eventually safer and more peaceful once they're out of power, but in the immediate aftermath, there's political and economic instability. That's the story with the Dominican Republic; people left to find better lives here. The Migration Policy Institute says that in 1960, there were around twelve thousand Dominican people in the United States. There were more than ten times that number by 1980. As of

THE CARIBBEAN

2016, there were more than six hundred thousand people of Dominican descent living in the New York City metro area, according to the Migration Policy Institute. So for most of my life, if I wanted to hear bachata or eat mangú (mashed green plantains), I didn't have to go far.

Even though I've been geographically close to the cuisine and culture, it still took exploring with a native from the Heights to really get to know it. During my freshman year at Syracuse University, I met my friend Chayri, one of the few Black engineers who was Afro Dominican and grew up not far from me in Washington Heights, just north of Harlem in Manhattan. Often I was able to hitch a ride with her and her father from the Heights to Syracuse. Along that four-hour drive, I was able to learn more about her culture and get some of the food from her care packages that her father cooked up for her return to campus. Lucky for me, that also meant visiting hole-in-the-wall Dominican restaurants not far from the George Washington Bridge, making sure I have the mojo sauce with my roasted chicken and tostones, and learning how to really appreciate the flavors of Dominican culture and the differences between Dominican and Puerto Rican cuisine. I learned quickly that there wasn't mofongo at her house but instead mangú, and that the sofritos from each island are not the same. The same way the right pairing of food and wine can make or break a meal, intentionally pairing the right food with the right sauce can make a meal sing, similar to the "what grows together goes together" theory.

New York City's Jamaican population is centered in Brooklyn. It's a little less clear cut what drove Jamaican immigration, but there was an increase in the twentieth century. In the same way that I can walk through Washington Heights and along Broadway in Harlem and feel fully immersed in Dominican culture, I can walk through parts of Flatbush and Crown Heights and feel like I'm in Jamaica—smell the jerk chicken smoking over pimento wood, and

> **Jamaica**
>
> **Coordinates:** 18.1096° N, 77.2975° W
> **Capital:** Kingston
> **Country/Continent:** Jamaica is an island in the Caribbean Sea and has Cuba to the north and Haiti to the east.
> **Population:** 2.8 million
> **National Dish:** Ackee and saltfish
> **Top Exports:** Aluminum oxide, bauxite, sugar, rum, coffee, yams
> **Official Language:** English
> **Independence Day:** August 6, 1962
> **Independence from:** United Kingdom

WINE PAIRING FOR THE PEOPLE

hear reggae and dancehall blasting the speakers from cars to restaurants.

I didn't start exploring these neighborhoods and their foods until after college—Brooklyn is a trek from Harlem—so when I did, I got to learn how wine-friendly Jamaican food is. Like wine, it can combine smoky and wood flavors with warming spice, savory characteristics, and green herbs.

+ PAIRED UP

MANGÚ CON LOS TRES GOLPES + PINOT GRIS, WILLAMETTE VALLEY, OREGON. Pinot Gris and Pinot Grigio are the same grape. When the French name, gris, is used, it usually refers to a juicier, more full-bodied wine with apple and pear or tropical-fruit notes, while grigios are lighter, leaner, and more citrus forward. Oregon Pinot Gris often splits the difference, though, with juicy tropical notes but a lighter body with zingy acidity. That balance of bold flavors and acidity is the perfect match for this dish. Mangú, or boiled and mashed green plantains, are creamy and starchy, so the wine's acidity can stand up to the golpes—fried salami, fried cheese, and a fried egg. This is a traditional breakfast meal, but people eat it any time of day.

LA BANDERA DOMINICANA + NEGROAMARO, PUGLIA, ITALY. A traditional lunch, this meal is meant to represent the Dominican flag, with beans standing in for the color red, rice for the white, and meat (beef, pork, or chicken) for the blue. It's typically served with some sort of salad and platanos too. Negroamaro, from the Puglia region of Southern Italy, is known for its dried herb notes, which make it the perfect rustic match for this hearty meal.

SANCOCHO + ASSYRTIKO, SANTORINI, GREECE. This stew bursts with flavor no matter the chosen protein. Traditionally made with beef, plus a variety of starchy ingredients like potatoes, yuca, and plantains, the melody of seasonings and heavy garlic steals the show. Pairing it with a high-acid wine, like Assyrtiko, made with a Greek white wine grape, will help as a palate cleanser. No one does garlic like the Greeks, and Assyrtiko is no stranger to garlic pairing. Common notes are lime, passionfruit, and flint for this light- to medium-body white wine.

ARROZ CON POLLO + CANNONAU, SARDINIA, ITALY. Also called locrio de pollo in the Dominican Republic, this one-pot meal is pure comfort. Slow roasted chicken and rice are cooked together with onions, garlic, tomato, and pepper. The dish can include vegetables like carrots and squash, and some people add green olives. The whole mix is generously seasoned with spices like oregano and cumin for an earthy flavor, and lime juice. Cannonau is a red wine from Sardinia—an island wine with an island dish—that also has a comfort-food vibe, thanks to its smooth texture and tannins. Its peppery notes will liven up the dish.

MONDONGO + RIOJA TEMPRANILLO ROSADO, RIOJA, SPAIN. This tripe stew uses a tomato base and is flavored with onions, garlic, peppers, celery, cilantro, and lime. Some people may add crushed red pepper to spice it up. A rosado (or rosé) made from the Tempranillo grape in Spain's Rioja region brings in bright red apples and red berry flavors of raspberry and strawberry to contrast this earthy, flavorful stew. It has enough acidity to match the tomato base and enough body, thanks to skin contact, to stand up to the food's meatiness.

THE CARIBBEAN

MORO DE GUANDULES + GARGANEGA, SOAVE, ITALY. Rice and pigeon peas are cooked with coconut milk and seasoned with the usual garlic, onions, peppers, and tomato, plus oregano and often olives, capers, or both. White wine made from the Garganega grape in Italy's Soave region adds the perfect refreshing lift. It's high in acidity, with delicate notes of peaches and melon, and a white blossom aroma that will accent the dish's coconut flavors.

BIZCOCHO DOMINICANO (AKA DOMINICAN CAKE) + MOSCATO D'ASTI, PIEDMONT, ITALY. Both airy and moist, this cake practically melts when you bite into it. Its traditional meringue frosting, called suspira, is just as light and melty. Moscato Bianco, a fizzy wine from Piedmont that's made with low alcohol in a slightly sweet style, is a good match. Orange blossom and honeysuckle are the leading floral notes of this aromatic wine with ripe fruit flavors of pear, orange, and Meyer lemon.

VEGGIE PATTIES WITH COCO BREAD + AVESSO, VINHO VERDE, PORTUGAL. The vegetarian answer to beef patties are made of potatoes, peas, and cabbage seasoned with curry powder, thyme, and sometimes pepper sauce wrapped in pastry crust and served on coco bread, a slightly sweet bun. It finds a match in a high-acid white wine with bitter green almond, white grapefruit, and peach flavors.

JERK CHICKEN + ALICANTE BOUSCHET, ALENTEJO, PORTUGAL. The chicken's smoky heat can be tamed but not overpowered by Alicante Bouschet, a very big, very red wine from Portugal with dark berry and tobacco notes.

STEW CHICKEN + GARNACHA, PRIORAT, SPAIN. This mild, soothing stew is made with chicken in a brown gravy stew. A rustic expression of Garnacha from the Priorat, Spain, exhibits a unique character of this common varietal. Priorat is known for its old vines, which date back fifty to a hundred years and give the local Garnacha a complex character of deep black fruit flavors of cherry and plum, and savory notes of herbs and spices, with a signature licorice finish.

OXTAIL STEW + SHIRAZ, MCLAREN VALE, AUSTRALIA. The food is rich from caramelized sugar and a little spicy with Scotch bonnet peppers. So is Shiraz from South Australia, which has blueberry and chocolate notes that are a great balance with this dish.

CURRY GOAT + TORRONTÉS, SALTA, ARGENTINA. This stew is deliciously spicy and gamy, thanks to Scotch bonnet peppers and bone-in goat meat. It will go well with a contrast of flavors from the aromatic, medium-body, high-acid white wine Torrontés, known for its notes of rose petal, geranium, and citrus.

ACKEE AND SALTFISH + GRECHETTO, UMBRIA, ITALY. Jamaica's national dish—a mix of salty dried fish cooked with ackee, a fruit in the lychee family that has a savory flavor and scrambled-egg-like consistency—finds a good partner in Grechetto. This Central Italian wine has historically been used to add structure to white wine blends. On its own, it's got medium body and delicate herbal notes.

FISH ESCOVITCH + LOUREIRO, VINHO VERDE, PORTUGAL. This pan-fried mild fish topped with pickled vegetables is not that far from a lot of Portuguese dishes that marry mild fish and tangy vinegar sauces. That's why a Portuguese wine, like Loureiro, is a good bet here. Known as the Riesling of Portugal for its high acid and petrol notes, Loureiro also has sage, peppermint, and green apple flavors.

GRILLED JERK LOBSTER TAILS + ALVARINHO,
MONÇÃO E MELGAÇO, PORTUGAL

SERVES 4

4 lobster tails, halved
3 tablespoons vegetable oil
Kosher salt
¼ cup store-bought jerk sauce, such as Nyam

Brittney "Stikxz" Williams is a New York City chef of Jamaican descent. She's done pop-ups around the city and has been on Food Network's *Taste of Jamaica*, *Chopped*, *The Kwanzaa Menu*, and *Ciao House*. This recipe mixes the classic flavors of jerk, traditionally smoked with pimento wood, and puts a seafood spin on it.

Marinated lobster in a spicy jerk seasoning is a contrast to the fresh and smoky flavors that I would highlight in this dish. The pronounced flavors of jerk from Scotch bonnet peppers, allspice, thyme, and garlic are a welcoming combination for the Alvarinho from the Vinho Verde region. Alvarinho has natural high acidity and charismatic fruit notes. This varietal is fruit forward—you can find everything from green apple to pineapple and even a hint of lemon oil. Other fruit-forward wines like Gewurztraminer work here, too. The acidity helps cut the rich buttery texture of the lobster, as the citrus notes help balance the heat from the jerk.

> **DRINK NOW:** Vinho Verde Alvarinho Producers
> - Luis Seabra Granito Cru Alvarinho, Vinho Verde, Portugal
> - Mendes Muros de Melgaço, Monção e Melgaço, Portugal
> - Quinta de Santiago Vinho Verde, Monção e Melgaço, Portugal

1. Light the grill and let it get hot, or heat a grill pan on the stove over medium-high heat.
2. On a sheet pan, lay your lobster tail shell side down. Take a pastry brush and lightly coat the meat with a touch of vegetable oil. Sprinkle salt lightly on each tail. Liberally brush each piece of lobster tail with your choice of jerk sauce.
3. Lay your lobster tail pieces meat side down on the grill for 3 to 4 minutes. Flip and finish cooking for another 3 to 4 minutes or until preferred doneness. Set aside.

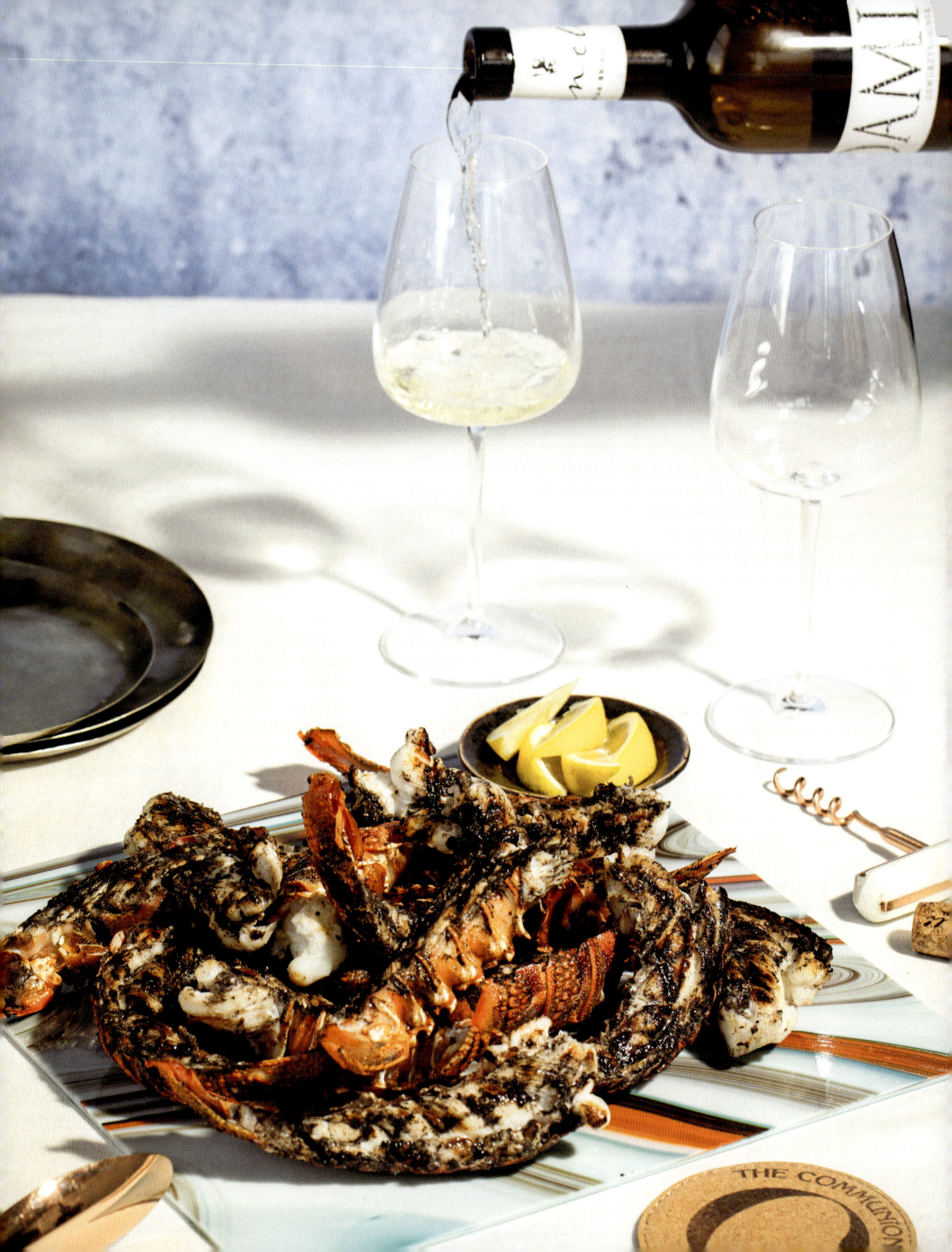
THE COMMUNION

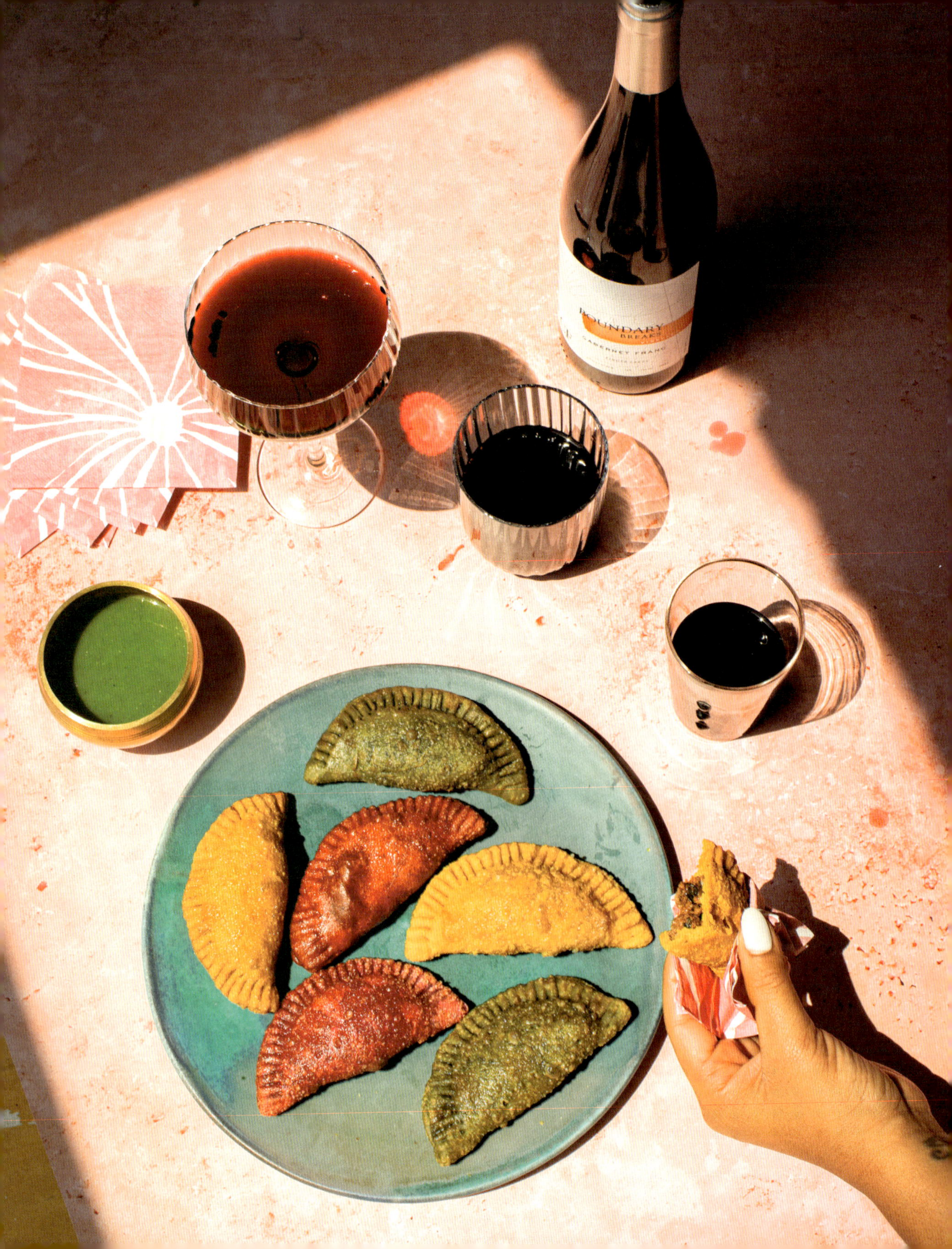
BOUNDARY
BREAKS
CABERNET FRANC

THE CARIBBEAN

RAINBOW PASTELITOS (EMPANADAS) + PETITE SIRAH, NAPA VALLEY, CALIFORNIA

Paola Velez is a Bronx-born chef and activist who focuses her talents on Afro-Dominican food. In the spring of 2020, she held a donut pop-up called Doña Dona to benefit undocumented workers in Washington, DC, where she lives. In the uprisings that followed the brutal police killing of George Floyd, her pop-up evolved into an organization called Bakers Against Racism, which she cofounded to help connect bakers from all backgrounds who want to make the world better. Her first cookbook, *Bodega Bakes*, draws on her Dominican and New York City heritage.

Pastelitos, called empanadas in many Spanish-speaking cultures, are baked dumplings. They can be filled with sweet or savory ingredients, and depending on what country you're talking about, you might find them wrapped in pastry, a corn-based wrapper, or a bubbly-crisp wheat dough. These pastelitos are the latter, with a colorful twist on a classic.

Ground beef-stuffed pastry packs bold rich flavors into this buttery casing, the perfect snack for a rare French varietal, Petite Sirah, which is mostly found in California today. If you can't find it, Cabernet Franc works here, too. Deep colored with rich black fruit flavors of black plum, blackberry, and blueberry, dark chocolate, and black tea, Petite Sirah does not not overwhelm the dish but enhance the flavors of the seasoned meat filling.

DRINK NOW: Napa Valley Petite Sirah Producers
- Turley Wine Cellars Petite Syrah Hayne Vineyard, Napa Valley, California
- Barra of Mendocino Petite Sirah, Mendocino, California
- Stags' Leap Winery Petite Sirah, Napa Valley, California

1. Whisk together the flour, baking powder, and salt in a large mixing bowl until well combined.
2. Make a well in the middle of the flour mixture. Add ¾ cup room-temperature water and 3 tablespoons vegetable oil to the well in the mixing bowl.

MAKES 9

Dough
- 2 cups all-purpose flour, plus more for work surface
- 1 teaspoon baking powder
- 1 teaspoon kosher salt
- 3 tablespoons vegetable oil, plus more for frying
- 1 tablespoon dragonfruit powder
- 1 tablespoon turmeric powder
- 1 tablespoon spinach powder

Filling
- ½ red onion, small diced
- 1 tablespoon minced garlic
- ½ pound ground beef
- ½ teaspoon dried oregano powder
- 1½ to 2 teaspoons adobo powder
- 2 tablespoons tomato paste
- 2 to 4 teaspoons chopped fresh cilantro
- 2 teaspoons oil to cook filling
- Salt and pepper, to taste

(recipe continues on next page)

3. Using your hands, mix the ingredients together until the dough is tacky but not sticky. If dough is dry, add water in 1-teaspoon increments until dough comes together.
4. Use a scale to divide the dough into three equal portions. Mix dragonfruit powder into one, turmeric into one, and dehydrated spinach into one.
5. Form each portion of dough into a ball, and place each ball in its own bowl. Cover with a dish towel and let rest at room temperature for 30 minutes to 1 hour. Meanwhile, let's cook the filling!
6. In a large skillet, heat up the oil and add the onion and garlic. Sauté until aromatic; remove from the pan and set to the side.
7. Add the ground beef, oregano, and adobo, and sauté until the ground beef is golden and delicious. Add the onion and garlic mixture, tomato paste, and cilantro, and stir vigorously to coat the beef with the tomato paste. Taste and season if needed with salt and pepper.
8. Lightly flour the countertop. Divide each dough ball into three 2-ounce balls.
9. Using a rolling pin, roll out each ball into a 4-inch disk.
10. Spoon 1 tablespoon beef mixture onto half of each disk, making sure not to overfill.
11. Dab finger or pastry brush in small bowl of water, tap off excess moisture, and run it around the outside edge of the empanada dough on the half containing filling. Fold dough edge over to form half-circle; crimp with a fork to seal. Place on a lightly floured rimmed baking sheet, and repeat the process with the remaining dough. If the empanadas are too soft to pick up from the tray, chill 10 minutes before frying.
12. Pour oil to a depth of 2 inches in a large Dutch oven; heat over medium to 350°F.
13. Working in 4 or 5 batches, fry empanadas until golden, 90 seconds to 2 minutes per side. Place them on a paper towel–lined plate or baking sheet.
14. Serve immediately, or cool completely and refrigerate in an airtight container for up to 5 days.

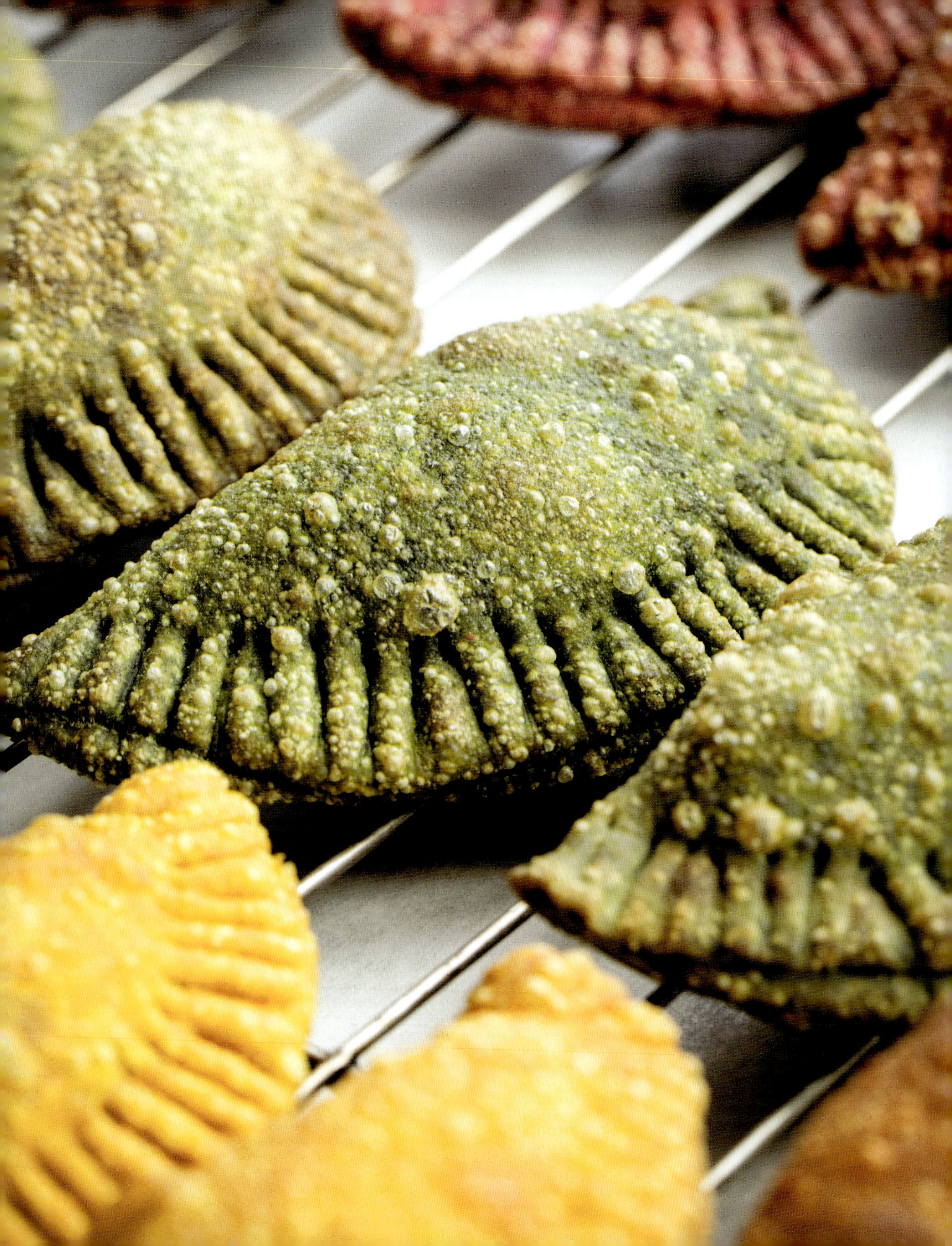

Barbados

Coordinates: 13.1939° N, 59.5432° W
Capital: Bridgetown
Country/Continent: Barbados is an island in the Caribbean Sea. It is east of the Virgin Islands.
Population: 281,000
National Dish: Cou-cou and flying fish
National Drink: Mauby
Top Exports: Petroleum oils, beverages, pharmaceuticals
Official Language: English
Independence Day: November 30, 1966
Independence from: United Kingdom

Before my first trip to Barbados, for my Alpha Kappa Alpha sorority sister Tamish's wedding, I admit that I didn't really know much about the country beyond that it was a British colony and the birthplace of Rihanna. I'd already been to the nearby islands of Puerto Rico and Cuba, so I had some idea what it might look like, but when it came to cuisine, I was eager to explore.

As I was flying in, I saw that Barbados is very lush. My plane left New York around midnight, so we arrived right before sunrise. The whole island looked like a big patch of green. I was very much in awe—it felt like we were landing in the Amazon, because that's how dense the trees were. My initial impression made me anxious to explore the island—not just to see it but to smell and taste what Barbados had to offer. I got a sense that the food might also be just as lush as its topography, with lots of tropical fruits that were unfamiliar to me.

For the wedding, we stayed at an all-inclusive resort. I didn't have to leave, but I needed to venture out of the walled area to get familiar with the local culture. To have an authentic Bajan experience, I had to go out and explore on my own. I made plans to meet with rum distiller and advocate Maggie Campbell, but rum wasn't the only thing I wanted to dig in to.

THE CARIBBEAN

Sip the Culture

Barbados is somewhat of a rum capital and is said be the birthplace of rum. Its cocktail culture reflects that. But its drinks culture moves away from rum, too.

RUM PUNCH. Brazil has its caipirinhas, Morocco has its mint tea, and Barbados has its rum punch. It's almost like a daiquiri, made with dark rum, lime juice, and sweetener. Simple, delicious, ubiquitous.

CORN 'N' OIL. This cocktail uses rum made with blackstrap molasses, called black rum or blackstrap rum, plus falernum (a liqueur with flavors of lime, ginger, and almond), lime juice, and bitters. Its name comes from the appearance of black rum layered with yellowish liquid.

BANKS BEER. This is a lager, and it's the official beer of Barbados. The brewery was founded in 1961 by a Guyanese entrepreneur. It's crisp, easy to drink, and can be found all over the island.

MAUBY. Made from the bark of the mauby tree boiled with warming spices like cinnamon, nutmeg, and allspice, plus orange peel. It's bitter, sweet, and mostly made in people's homes. It can be sipped on its own or added to cocktails and is the official drink of Barbados.

I learned how important fishing was to Barbados's history and economy. Fishing was one of the main sources of income for families in Barbados, supporting the demand for fish exports in the 1960s during the time of transition from British rule to becoming an independent nation. No visit to Barbados would be complete without spending time at Bridgetown's Oistins Fish Market. Everyone goes there. You will find locals and tourists enjoying the food and sounds of the market past midnight on the weekend. Filled with different stalls with a wide range of options, it is like the seafood version of the Grand Bazaar in Turkey or the Souk Semmarine in Marrakech, and there is a wide range of flavors and a variety of sea creatures, including of course fish. This is the scene for energetic nightlife, from live calypso bands to DJ booths woven into the maze of food stalls. The pier is easily accessible from the market, and that's where fishers bring their catch from the day, so it can be served grilled, fried, or even sautéed fresh. There is a wide variety of fish and seafood options here. The stall I ate at offered flying fish, blue marlin, tuna, king fish, dolphin (mahi-mahi), shrimp, and lobster. Seafood is one of the defining features of the food in Barbados.

At the fish market and at my hotel, the British influence on the country was apparent. People were proper and spoke the Queen's English. This hospitality had a formal feel that could, at times, come across as stark and reserved. It was a contrast to the the lush greenery, the welcoming fisherman at the market, and to the warming rum that flowed through the island. And so that's Barbados to me: a beautiful, verdant, rum-soaked tropical island with a posh veneer.

WINE PAIRING FOR THE PEOPLE

- Bahamas (Ricardo Rum)
- Barbados (R.L. Seale, Mount Gay)
- Brazil (Seleta, Avuá)
- Colombia (Dictador)
- Costa Rica (Ron Centenario)
- Cuba (Havana Club)
- Dominican Republic (Brugal, Atalantico)
- Guatemala (Zacapa)
- Guyana (El Dorado)
- Haiti (Rhum Barbancourt)
- Jamaica (Wray + Nephew, Appleton)
- Martinique (Rhum Clément, Rhum J.M)
- Nicaragua (Flor de Caña)
- Panama (Ron Abuelo)
- Puerto Rico (Bacardi, Don Q)
- Trinidad and Tobago (Angostura)
- Venezuela (Diplomatico)

Rums of the Caribbean

Caribbean Sea

And a Bottle of Rum

Before visiting Barbados, I knew rum was made on the island, but I didn't know that the spirit is thought to have originated here. According to the island's tourism bureau, the British colonized Barbados in the 1600s to grow tobacco or cotton, but were unsuccessful. The Dutch were growing sugarcane in Brazil and introduced the idea to Barbados. At that time, there was already an unrefined sugarcane spirit called "kill devil." Over the course of the 1600s, that became commercial rum distillation as we know it today.

I made time to connect with Maggie Campbell, the newly appointed estate rum manager for Mount Gay, the country's most iconic distillery, which was founded in

THE CARIBBEAN

1703. She had just arrived to Barbados from Massachusetts, where she was the president and head distiller for Privateer Rum. I wanted to taste the island with her, which led to an informative deep dive about the terroir of rum.

I learned about the ocean influence, the position of the barrels where rum ages in relation to the sea breeze, and how that can affect the liquor's taste and much more.

At present, there aren't designated appellations or protections for rums the way there are for wine or other spirits, like Scotch and Kentucky bourbon. There are people working toward achieving that, but in the meantime, it's important for us in the drinks business to say when we can that Barbados is the birthplace of rum (see map on page 84). These kinds of regulations aren't just for marketing purposes. They offer some protection and status for independent farmers and distillers, usually Black in the case of Barbados, from corporations that can buy whatever cane or cane plantations are cheapest and label their rums as being from the country where they're bottled, removing the identity of the place of origin of the sugarcane.

I got a glimpse of this in action when I visited Foursquare Rum Distillery in Barbados. Dario, my guide, was native to Barbados and was very informative about the history of rum making and very passionate about its future. His family runs the bar that doubles as a gift shop for the distillery and has the event space upstairs. His family has worked for the distillery for generations, so even though he isn't an owner, he was able to start his tour-and-tasting business on Foursquare's property and seemed thankful for their partnership.

DECODING THE LABEL

Young Pirate Black Label Superior Barbados Rum

- Country
- Brand
- Quality Designator
- Alcohol Level — 40% alc.vol / 80 proof
- Volume — 750 mL
- Distillery Location — Blended and Bottled by R.L. Seale and Company Limited, Four Square, St. Phillp, Babados

Spotlight on the Crop Over Festival

Over the years, it's always been fun to see Rihanna return home and participate in "playing mas" for the Crop Over Festival, dancing to calypso on a masquerade band's float with pride, adorned in an elaborate costume of vivid, colorful feathers and sparkling jewels. After visiting the island and becoming more acquainted with Barbados and its history with sugarcane, I have a new appreciation for Crop Over and can't wait to play mas one day myself. A harvest festival—literally, the crops are over—this celebration dates back to the late 1700s, when sugarcane growing was really starting to take off there. Similarly in wine, there are parties held within wine villages to celebrate the end of grape harvest, like November's Hospices de Beaune wine auction held in the region of Beaune in Burgundy, France, in the region of Beaune.

Crop Over is six weeks long and ends in August. There are craft fairs, street-food festivals, live music, and all kinds of celebratory events, leading up to Grand Kadooment. That's where you will find Rihanna on a float. Kadooment is a Bajan word for a party or celebration. Grand Kadooment is a big parade with people in bright, feathered costumes dancing on trucks and in the street. Others are jumping and dancing along the sidewalk.

To have all of this dedicated to sugarcane is a reminder of the important role rum plays in Bajan identity.

With Dario, I was able to taste the Real McCoy rum, produced by Foursquare. Obviously, a real McCoy has to try the Real McCoy. This is a fourth-generation family-owned business. During Prohibition in the United States, Bill McCoy would sail his rum up the Eastern Seaboard and sell it offshore. While I'm used to the smell of barrel rooms, the aroma here was a lot sweeter. The molasses filled the air, and I got to learn more about how the sugarcane became the rum in tasting glasses in front of me. It really drove home for me how much the history and geography of this spirit needs to be protected and respected.

Other countries around the Caribbean also have their own history and culture around rum. They produce different styles, which can usually be loosely sorted into white rum, dark rum, and sometimes categories like rhum agricole or other sugarcane spirits like cachaça. Here's a look at which styles are most closely linked with which countries, and which are exported most to the United States, meaning they're accessible for you all to find and try.

THE CARIBBEAN

+ PAIRED UP

FLYING FISH AND COU COU + VERMENTINO, SARDINIA, ITALY. Barbados's national dish is made up of fish with a cornmeal pudding, served with a spicy gravy. This pairing is an example of a maritime wine pairing well with seafood. This white wine has a lot of saline and mineral notes that are palate cleansing with fish. When it's grown on the Italian island of Sardinia, it also takes on herbal notes that complement the gravy.

BAJAN PEPPERPOT + VALPOLICELLA SUPERIORE, VALPOLICELLA, ITALY. Tough cuts of meat are braised with garlic, warming spices, herbs like basil and thyme, and Scotch bonnet peppers in this spicy, hearty stew. Red wines from this Northern Italian region can range from light and fruity to deep and rich. The Superiore classification falls on the lighter end of the spectrum. It also has cinnamon, clove, and dried thyme notes similar to the pepperpot, making it a perfect pairing.

JUG JUG + RKATSITELI, KAKHETI, GEORGIA. According to Barbados's tourism authority, jug jug may have been brought to the country by Scottish people in the 1600s, inspired by haggis. Meat is ground up with pigeon peas and corn flour to create a dish that's somewhere between porridge and sausage. It's served on Christmas Day. Rkatsiteli, a white wine from the republic of Georgia, brings in brightening green-apple notes.

PUDDING AND SOUSE + PICPOUL DE PINET, LANGUEDOC, FRANCE. Different parts of the Caribbean have their own versions of souse, but this is a dish of cold, vinegar-pickled meat, usually pork. In Barbados, it's served with sweet potato, which is the "pudding" element. With really tart dishes like this, it's important to choose a wine with good acidity. Otherwise, the wine can feel flabby and bland next to the food. Picpoul de Pinet, a white wine from Southern France, brings the acidity along with white flowers, rocks, lime, and salinity.

BEEF WITH POTATO ROTI + DOLCETTO, PIEDMONT, ITALY. Roti is also eaten around the Caribbean. This flaky flatbread is an example of the South Asian influence on the islands' food. This one is stuffed with curried beef and potatoes that have a bit of heat. Dolcetto, a red wine from Northern Italy, has plump blackberry and plum notes that will lessen the heat and provide juicy refreshment with this starchy dish, leading into a nice cocoa and violet finish.

CONKIES + SÉMILLON, BORDEAUX, FRANCE. Cornmeal, coconut milk, raisins, and pumpkin are steamed in a banana leaf to make this pudding. Sémillon, especially one with a bit of sweetness to it, will add juicy apple and pear notes that bring a cozy fall feeling to anything with raisin and pumpkin flavors.

BAJAN RUM CAKE + TAWNY PORT, DOURO VALLEY, PORTUGAL. Also called black cake, this rum-soaked cake is flavored with dried fruit and warming spices like cinnamon and allspice. Tawny Port is one of Portugal's fortified wines. It's made by blending different vintages that have been barrel aged. It has similar notes of dried fruit and baking spice, plus a nutty note that enhances the dish.

THE WINE LIST

The Caribbean

PUERTO RICO

Mofongo de Camarones + Chardonnay, PFALZ, GERMANY

Mofongo de Chicharron + Gran Reserva Cava Brut, PENEDÈS, SPAIN

Mofongo de Carne Guisada + Tannat, MADIRAN, FRANCE

Chuletas Rellenas de Mofongo + Crianza Rioja, RIOJA ORIENTAL, SPAIN

Vegan Mofongo + Rioja Blanco, RIOJA ALVESA, SPAIN

Pinchos + Syrah, SAN LUIS OBISPO, CALIFORNIA

Alcapurrias de Jueyes + Cariñena Rosado, CATALONIA, SPAIN

Pernil + St. Laurent, BURGENLAND, AUSTRIA

Flan de Queso + Moscatel de Setúbal, SETÚBAL, PORTUGAL

▼

CUBA

Ropa Vieja + Rioja Reserva, RIOJA ALTA, SPAIN

Vaca Frita + Merlot, COLUMBIA VALLEY, WASHINGTON

Medianoche + Mencía, BIERZO, SPAIN

Lechon Asado + Savatiano, ANCHIALOS, GREECE

Ajiaco Cubano + Godello, VALDEORRAS, SPAIN

Picadillo + Super Tuscan, TUSCANY, ITALY

▼

DOMINICAN REPUBLIC AND JAMAICA

Mangú con los Tres Golpes + Pinot Gris, WILLAMETTE VALLEY, OREGON
La Bandera Dominicana + Negroamaro, PUGLIA, ITALY
Sancocho + Assyrtiko, SANTORINI, GREECE
Arroz con Pollo + Cannonau, SARDINIA, ITALY
Mondongo + Rioja Tempranillo Rosado, RIOJA, SPAIN
Moro de Guandules + Garganega, SOAVE, ITALY
Bizcocho Dominicano + Moscato d'Asti, PIEDMONT, ITALY
Veggie Patties with Coco Bread + Avesso, VINHO VERDE, PORTUGAL
Jerk Chicken + Alicante Bouschet, ALENTEJO, PORTUGAL
Stew Chicken + Garnacha, PRIORAT, SPAIN
Oxtail Stew + Shiraz, MCLAREN VALE, AUSTRALIA
Curry Goat + Torrontés, SALTA, ARGENTINA
Ackee and Saltfish + Grechetto, UMBRIA, ITALY
Fish Escovitch + Loureiro, VINHO VERDE, PORTUGAL
Grilled Jerk Lobster Tails + Alvarinho, MONÇÃO E MELGAÇO, PORTUGAL
Rainbow Pastelitos + Petite Sirah, NAPA VALLEY, CALIFORNIA

▼

BARBADOS

Flying fish and Cou Cou + Vermentino, SARDINIA, ITALY
Bajan Pepperpot + Valpolicella Superiore, VALPOLICELLA, ITALY
Jug Jug + Rkatsiteli, KAKHETI, GEORGIA
Pudding and Souse + Picpoul de Pinet, LANGUEDOC, FRANCE
Beef with Potato Roti + Dolcetto, PIEDMONT, ITALY
Conkies + Sémillon, BORDEAUX, FRANCE
Bajan Rum Cake + Tawny Port, DOURO VALLEY, PORTUGAL

▼

221
LEYENDA
CÓCTELES

Latin America

Mexico	94
Chile	104
Argentina	118
Brazil	125

Latin America

- Mexico
- Brazil
- Chile
- Argentina

Latin America is one of the most exciting parts of the world for wine. The historic, high-altitude wines of Chile and Argentina have been making waves internationally for a while—almost every wine lover has enjoyed an Argentine Malbec at some point. And for me, Chile holds a special place in my heart and my career because I spent a three-month solo trip there exploring its wines early in my wine journey. But lately I've been loving the wines coming out of Mexico and Brazil. Both countries obviously have a history of wine from Spanish and Portuguese colonizers, the same way Chile and Argentina do, but they're a little newer to the wine market in the United States, reviving their production and industry.

In these countries, history is such a huge part of wine making. When we talk about cultural terroir, it's the legacy of Indigenous people descended from some of the oldest civilizations in the world, and the ways that they interacted with enslaved Africans.
The story of colonization, of the European influence and later the influence of the United States, comes up a lot in the history and wine of Mexico and South America, and there's so much awareness that is needed to highlight the resilience and ingenuity each country is contributing to the future of the wine industry. There's also so much to celebrate when we sit down to a meal from any of these countries and pair them with wine.

WINE PAIRING FOR THE PEOPLE

Mexico

Coordinates: 23.6345° N, 102.5528° W
Capital: Mexico City
Country/Continent: Mexico is part of North America. It's south of the United States and north of Guatemala and Belize. Its east coast is on the Gulf of Mexico, and the Gulf of California and Pacific Ocean lie off its west coast.
Population: 127.5 million
National Drink: Paloma
National Dish: Mole poblano
Top Export: Machinery and transport equipment, steel, electrical equipment
Official Languages: None. Spanish is most widely spoken, and the government recognizes sixty-eight Indigenous languages.
Independence Day: September 27, 1821
Independence from: Spain

My first experience with authentic Mexican culture was a trip to Mexico City. New York City has a large Mexican community, but for a lot of people who grew up here, we tend to indulge more in the fast food and inexpensive margarita options over authentic cuisine. It was an easy, and dare I say decent, option for me as a young adult to elevate from Taco Bell to Blockheads. Both were a starting point to at least build a vocabulary around some of the culinary staples of Mexican cuisine, such as guacamole, quesadillas, and burritos (and, yes, I know that the style of burritos common here is very different from anything served in Mexico). These establishments made Mexican food feel recognizable even if it was Americanized. However, after my first trip to Mexico City, I learned that they had left out the soul of the people, the diversity of the cuisine, and the beauty of culture.

After living in Italy, I returned to the United States with a new vision of the world, and I couldn't wait to explore further. While on a group trip to Turkey (more on this trip on page 212), I made friends with a Mexican woman named Gaby. After learning about my love for travel, she spent most of our time in Turkey advocating for me to visit her in Mexico City. Gaby shared how large a city it was, which appealed to me as a New Yorker. She broke down the unique vibes of each neighborhood, from the floating markets and mariachi bands of the Xochimilco district to spending a day in the footsteps of

LATIN AMERICA

Sip the Culture: Agave Spirits

Making wine more accessible and equitable for Black and brown people has become my mission. I have spent a decade developing my wine knowledge, getting a grasp on the various regions, and understanding the wine market to stake a claim in this industry. I realized, after all this time, that the Black and brown wine community can learn a lot from what has already been done in the spirits industry.

Many spirits originated in areas of the world that are inhabited by Black and brown people who have the history to claim ownership but struggle with getting consumers to drink more intentionally and purchase from the descendants of the original producers. After years of chasing vineyards, I embarked on a journey to Tequila, Mexico, to understand the terroir of this beloved agave spirit directly from its people. Like a lot of wines, Tequila has protected Denomination of Origin (DO) status in Mexico that lays out rules for how and where it can be produced.

This trip also provided an opportunity to learn about other spirits made from agave, a large succulent plant indigenous to Mexico:

MEZCAL: Known for its smoky flavor, mezcal is made by roasting the piña, or heart, of the agave plant before fermentation and distillation. It can be made using many different types of agave, and the majority of production is in Oaxaca. In Mexico, it's traditional to drink it straight, but it's become popular in cocktails in the United States.

TEQUILA: Its DO status means that tequila has to be made from blue agave in one of five states: Jalisco, Michoacán, Guanajuato, Nayarit, and Tamaulipas. The spirit comes in a few styles: blanco (unaged, clear, and mild), reposado (aged up to one year, with a light golden color and nutty notes as well as honey-like agave flavors), and añejo (aged in oak barrels for one to three years, with an amber color; usually for sipping as opposed to cocktails). Some less common styles are extra añejo (aged for more than three years), cristallino (añejo or extra añejo that's filtered so that it's clear), and joven (blanco with a bit of reposado or añejo mixed in to give it a little color).

PECHUGA: Mezcal or raicilla that's been distilled with a chicken or turkey breast in addition to spices and fruits was usually made for special occasions, historically. Its origin story is unclear, but you can think of it as an agave spirit with a little bit of extra heart.

SOTOL: I'm cheating a little bit, because sotol is made from a close relative of agave, a succulent called dasylirion. Originating in the deserts of Chihuahua, it has DO status and must be produced in Chihuahua, Durango, or Coahuila. It also comes in reposado and añejo styles as well as an unaged plata style.

COMITECO: Sharing a name with the type of agave it's made from, comiteco originated in the southern Mexican state of Chiapas. Unlike the other spirits we've discussed here so far, it's made from the agave sap. The process of collecting the sap makes this a more labor-intensive spirit to produce.

BACANORA: Technically a type of mezcal, bacanora comes from the northern state of Sonora. It has DO status that dictates it has to be made with a specific type of agave called angustifolia, pacifica, or yaquiana. But with a long history, bacanora's been made with all sorts of agave types historically.

RAICILLA: With DO status, raicilla must be made in Jalisco. It's similar to mezcal and tequila in that it uses the piña of the agave plant. It uses a more rustic still, in an open-air distillery, drawing comparisons to moonshine. Even though the piña is roasted, raicilla can have a fresh, green, herbaceous flavor to it.

WINE PAIRING FOR THE PEOPLE

DRINK NOW: Agave Spirit Producers

Here are some agave-spirit producers of tequila to explore:

- Fortaleza
- La Gritona
- Arette
- Chacolo
- La Venenosa

DRINK NOW: Mexican Wine Producers

- Bichi
- Fractura Rosa
- Vinos Pijoan Arbol De Fuego
- Cava Garambullo
- Octagono
- Pouya Wines
- Tres Parlas

artist Frida Kahlo to enjoying the craft cocktail and food scene of Roma. Sold.

Six months later, I was on a flight to Mexico City, commonly known as DF, Distrito Federal, by the locals. It was a trip that changed my entire perspective of Mexican culture and its people. I stayed with Gaby in the upscale neighborhood of Polanco, five miles from the historic city center. Polanco is a tree-lined, affluent neighborhood most famous for its museums, like Museo Soumaya and Museo Jumex. High-end hops on Avenida Presidente Masaryk are often compared to those on Rodeo Drive, And mixed-use high-rise buildings with fine-dining restaurants, such as the Michelin-starred Pujol, makes Polanco the swanky borough.

She was right. I fell in love with the complex city life, accessible transportation, vivid art scene, and creative bar and restaurant culture. I visited Mexico City three years in a row after Gaby and I met in 2012. It has become one of my favorite travel destinations. She invited me into her home, and I will forever be grateful for her and her sister's hospitality. With so much media attention on crime in the country, I was surprised yet happy to learn that American Express Travel reported that in 2023 American tourists were going beyond the all-inclusive beach vacations and choosing Mexico City as one of their top destinations.

Mexico's Wine Regions

As early as the 1500s, European colonizers saw that grapevines and olive trees would thrive in Mexico's dry, sunny interior. Spaniards brought over the Listan Prieto grape, but then wine growing started to take off, and Mexico competed with European wine and olive oil industries, so in 1600, wine making was banned except for church purposes.

But it was too late. Vineyards had already taken root in a sparsely populated northern region of the country. Bodegas del Marques de Aguayo and Casa Madero were founded in 1593 and 1597, respectively, and are still operational today. Mexico's wine growing also helped shape wine making in California and Texas, thanks to the efforts of the nonprofit organization Hispanics in Wine and programs like the Latinx Wine Summit, two organizations that are diligently working to amplify the Hispanic and Latinx roots in the wine industry, create community, and share resources for upward mobility by connecting vineyard stewards to winery executives.

After Mexico got its independence from Spain, wine making ebbed and flowed. In the 1980s, quality and production both started to pick up, and now Mexico is producing great wines and developing its enotourism industry. Here are the major regions to know:

LATIN AMERICA

Baja California: The leading wine-producing state accounts for more than half of all wine from Mexico and produces a variety of wine styles. It has mineral-rich soil from the Sierras de Baja California mountains, and sandy, infertile soil of decomposed granite near the dry riverbeds contribute to the minerality found in this region's wine. An arid valley west of the mountains and a Mediterranean climate cooled by Pacific breezes make for good growing conditions. Baja California is home to the Guadalupe Valley, which has its own Ruta del Vino (wine route) with more than a hundred wineries to explore. Known for its full-bodied reds, this region grows an abundance of Cabernet Sauvignon, Merlot, Tempranillo, Zinfandel, and Nebbiolo.

Wine Grapes of Mexico

Red

Cabernet Sauvignon
Tempranillo
Mexican Nebbiolo (which was brought to Mexico after World War II and may or may not be the same grape as the Nebbiolo grown in Italy)
Syrah
Merlot
Cabernet Franc
Malbec
Pinot Noir
Mourvèdre
Grenache
Petite Sirah

White

Sauvignon Blanc
Chardonnay
Viognier
Chenin Blanc

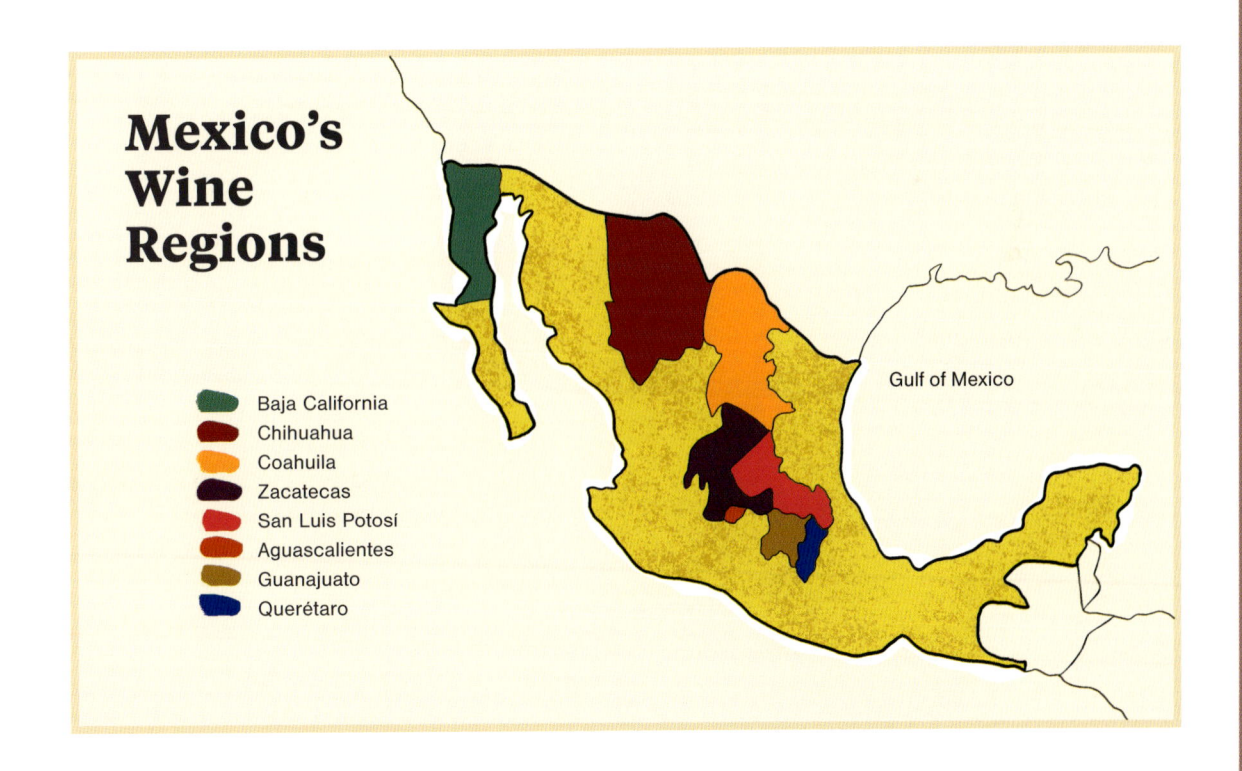

Mexico's Wine Regions

- Baja California
- Chihuahua
- Coahuila
- Zacatecas
- San Luis Potosí
- Aguascalientes
- Guanajuato
- Querétaro

Gulf of Mexico

Coahuila: This is where Casa Madero has been making wine for more than four hundred years. It's a region of snowy mountain peaks, with some vineyards at almost seven thousand feet. Its elevation and diurnal swings are attracting a new generation of winemakers from Spain. Here you will find a strong focus on sweet dessert and fortified wines.

Querétaro: Just a few hours from Mexico City, Querétaro pushes the boundaries of how far south good wine can be made. It's wetter than the country's northern regions too, but high altitude tempers the heat to produce wines with good acidity. Sparkling wines are making a statement in this region using the traditional method and the Champagne varietals of Pinot Noir and Chardonnay.

Zacatecas: This is another Mexican wine region that some might consider extreme. It has no major river and little rainfall. But it's cool, dry, and has some of the country's highest-altitude vineyards. The high altitude offers a great environment for white-wine making and innovative sparkling wine.

Aguascalientes: Named for its hot springs, this is a moderate and productive region. It also has many high-altitude vineyards, where it gets a decent amount of rainfall and occasional hail. Red varieties like Nebbiolo and Malbec are popular here.

San Luis Potosí: A desert region, this area has very hot summers and cold winters, sometimes in the twenties. Sparkling wine does well here.

Chihuahua: A big state with diverse terrains, Chihuahua has attracted a lot of interest and is still finding its wine identity. In the past, brandy and table grapes have been its strong suits, but some winemakers are having success growing Bordeaux varieties at high altitudes.

Guanajuato: Maybe Mexico's fastest-growing wine region, Guanajuato has high altitude and good seasonal and diurnal temperature swings. Those conditions make it easier to produce wines that are light-bodied, low in alcohol, and refreshing. That's probably why it's become Mexico's center of natural wine.

LATIN AMERICA

Taco Tour

During my time wandering the streets of the Centro Historico near Palacio Nacional, I was able to feel the true spirit of Mexico. The bustling city of mixed cultures has proud heritage that still plays a role not only in the culinary scene but also in the architecture, music, and fashion.

With 22 million people and almost double the size of New York City, it's no wonder tacos are famous here. They make a filling on-the-go meal that you can enjoy anywhere at any time. At their simplest, tacos can be defined as a tortilla made from corn or wheat, wrapped around something. Usually they are filled with a protein and vegetables, and dressed with a sauce. Taco fillings have no boundaries. They include stews, chicken, beef, or fish, and there is even a type of taco referred to as "nothing tacos" (tacos de la nada). These tacos are rolled up tortillas with just salt, which shows you how simple and accessible tacos are.

One of Mexico City's signature tacos, as we know them today, are said to be inspired by Lebanese immigrants' kebabs. This hallmark taco style is known as shepherd's taco (taco al pastor) or taco oriental, and it is filled with thin slices of marinated pork, carved off meat that's sometimes marinated with pineapple to tenderize it then cooked on a vertical spit that spins in front of an open fire. The meat is added to a hot tortilla with chopped onions, cilantro, salsa, and pineapple chunks from the whole fruit roasting on top of the spit.

One of my favorite memories of Mexico City is doing a taco crawl with Gaby and her friend to check out old and new stands that are elevating and expanding the taco experience, whether at a restaurant, stall on a city block, or at a food market. Mexico City is a melting pot, where all the thirty-two states of Mexico come together, no two taco spots are the same. Here is a list of just a few popular taco styles that I have encountered on menus during my trip, with complementing wine pairings.

Regional Tacos and Pairings

Al Pastor (Mexico City) + **Primitivo,** PUGLIA, ITALY

Carne Asada (Sonora) + **Malbec,** CAHORS, FRANCE

Birria (Guadajalara) + **Syrah,** ELQUI VALLEY, CHILE

De Canasta/al Vapor (Mexico City) + **Grenache,** BAROSSA VALLEY, AUSTRALIA

Pescado (Baja) + **Verdejo,** RUEDA, SPAIN

+ PAIRED UP

CHILAQUILES + CHENIN BLANC PÉT-NAT, VALLE DE GUADALUPE, MEXICO. Brunch and bubbles go together like bacon and eggs. This dish of fried tortilla chips sauteed in a red sauce and topped with fried eggs is satisfying without being heavy. Pét-nat—short for pétillant naturel, which means naturally sparkling—made from Chenin Blanc has the grape's signature funky-yet-bright white grapefruit and yeasty notes, and light acidity on the palate. Chenin Blanc is growing more relevant in Mexico's Valle de Guadalupe, but you can also find pét-nat made with it from producers in California and the Loire Valley.

TAMALES + VERMENTINO, SARDINIA, ITALY. These dumplings made with masa harina are a hearty and filling street snack. Fresh cornmeal gives them a fragrant quality that finds a refreshing, bodacious match in Vermentino. For a little extra body and creaminess, seek out the Italian version from the island of Sardinia, which will have bright acidity, medium to full body with mineral flavors, green apples, and floral notes of jasmine and acacia.

QUESADILLAS + CHARDONNAY, MARGARET RIVER, AUSTRALIA. This classic, comforting dish comes in different variations depending on where in Mexico you are. Sometimes they're fried, and other times they're baked. Sometimes the cheese is the main event, and other times the tortillas are the star. Regardless, they're a delicious combination of starch and melted cheese that only needs a little something to really sing. Margaret River Chardonnay combines minerality, tangy notes of lemon and peach, and a bit of texture from a little bit of oak age. Its flavors act like a squirt of lime and a pinch of salt on the quesadilla, and it has just enough body to match the melted cheese.

ELOTE + CAVA ROSÉ, PENEDÈS, SPAIN. One of the best street foods there is, elote is grilled corn topped with mayo, cheese, lime, and chile. It's a flavor bomb that combines tangy, hot, sweet, and creamy flavors. All it needs by its side are bubbles with enough texture and body to cleanse the palate. A rosé Cava—Spain's signature sparkling wine that's made the same way as Champagne—has crisp acidity and a bit of fruitiness that will play beautifully off the chile.

MOLE POBLANO + NERO D'AVOLA, VALLE DE GUADALUPE, MEXICO. There are many moles in Mexico, because mole is a word for sauce. This one, from Pueblo, is one of the most famous for its use of chocolate. It's spicy and savory, made with chiles, sesame seeds, and warming spices like cinnamon. The unsweetened chocolate in it adds a deep, earthy flavor. Mole poblano can be served over a variety of proteins. Nero d'Avola is a red wine from Sicily, but be on the look out for the version from Mexico. This wine pairs well with any of the mole versions. It has a good amount of body and tobacco, pepper, and black plum notes that work in harmony with the mole.

POLLO EN BARBACOA + BOBAL, REQUENA-UTIEL, SPAIN. Mexico's take on barbecue chicken is smoky, spicy, and rich with warming spices. Bobal, a red wine from Spain, has a plush, velvety texture that won't overwhelm the chicken. Its fruity notes will highlight the chiles' fruity flavors, and it's got plenty of acidity to keep you refreshed between bites.

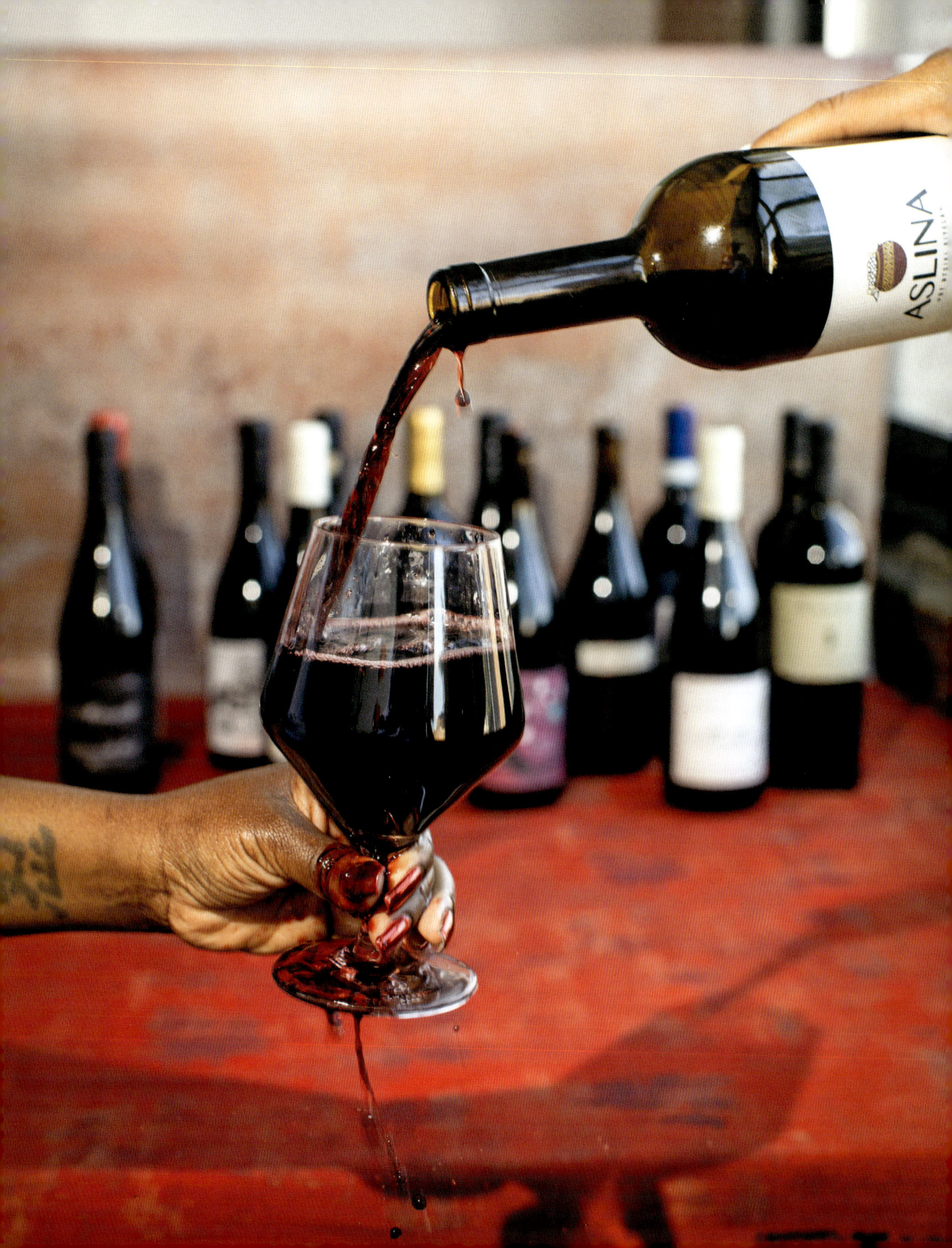
ASLINA

VERACRUZ-STYLE SNAPPER + ROSÉ,
BAJA CALIFORNIA, MEXICO

SERVES 4

- 3 tablespoons extra-virgin olive oil
- 4 red snapper fillets (6 ounces each)
- Salt and fresh-ground black pepper
- ¾ cup chopped onion
- 4 garlic cloves, minced
- 1½ cups canned crushed tomatoes with juice
- 1 Anaheim chile, stem and seeds removed, cut into strips
- 1 bay leaf
- 1 teaspoon crumbled dried oregano
- ½ cup halved pitted green olives
- ¼ cup capers, drained

Marcela Valladolid calls herself a "curator of beautiful things from Mexico" in her Instagram bio, and this recipe from her first cookbook is one of those things. Valladolid grew up in Southern California and studied cooking in Tijuana and France, so she understands the mixing of European technique and flavors from elsewhere. In addition to writing six cookbooks, she's hosted or competed on several Food Network shows.

This dish hails from Veracruz, on the coast of the Gulf of Mexico in the south of the country. As a seaside region, it enjoys a lot of fish. This one is braised in a chunky tomato sauce with capers and olives, for the perfect amount of brine and tang.

Rosé from Mexico's Baja California has bright red fruit—think strawberry and watermelon—as well as tropical notes midpalate, plus a spicy finish.

1. Heat the oven to 350°F.
2. Heat 1 tablespoon of the oil in a medium sauté pan over medium-high heat. Season the snapper fillets with salt and pepper. Add the fish to the sauté pan and cook until opaque and just cooked through, about 2 minutes per side. Transfer the fish to a glass baking dish that fits the fillets snugly.
3. In the same sauté pan, heat the remaining 2 tablespoons of oil over medium-high heat. Add the onion and garlic, and cook until the onion is translucent, about 5 minutes. Add the tomatoes, Anaheim chile, bay leaf, and oregano. Reduce the heat to medium, cover the pan, and simmer until the chile is soft, about 6 minutes. Uncover the pan, add the olives and capers, and let simmer for 4 minutes to merge the flavors. Season to taste with salt and pepper.
4. Pour the sauce over the fish in the baking dish. Bake for 5 minutes.
5. Serve the fillets topped with the sauce.

Used with permission from *Fresh Mexico: 100 Simple Recipes for True Mexican Flavor* by Marcela Valladolid (Clarkson Potter, 2009).

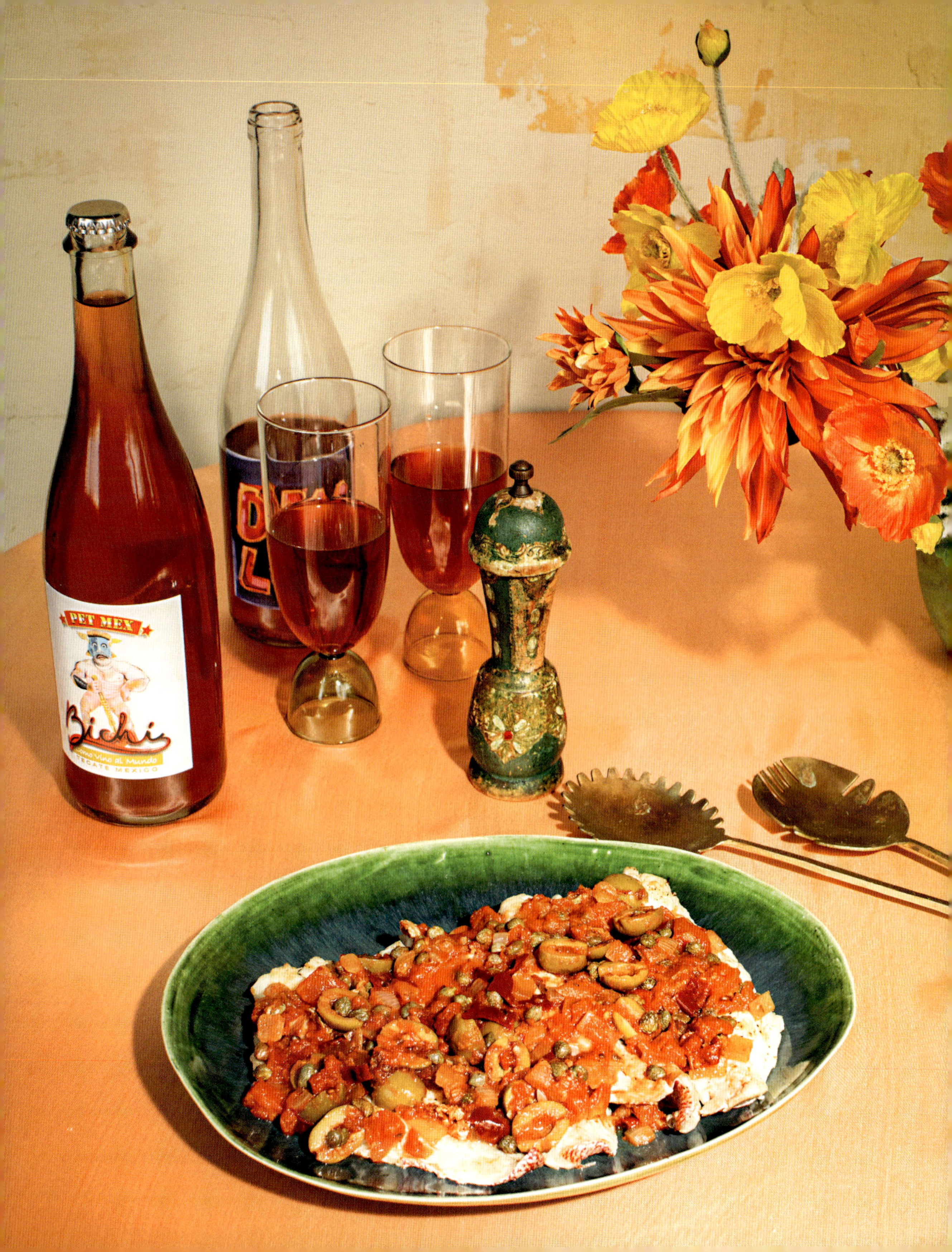
PET MEX
Bichi

WINE PAIRING FOR THE PEOPLE

Chile

Coordinates: 35.6751° S, 71.5430° W
Capital: Santiago
Country/Continent: Chile runs along the west coast of South America. It's bordered on the south by the Pacific Ocean and, at its southeasternmost point, the Atlantic Ocean. Peru lies to the north, Bolivia to the northwest, and to the west, in the world's third-longest border, Argentina.
Population: 19.5 million
National Drink: Pisco Sour
Top Exports: Copper ore, refined copper, raw copper, fish fillets
Official Language: Spanish
Independence Day: September 18, 1810
Independence from: Spain

My time in Chile marks a pivotal professional moment in my wine journey. I realized I was willing to risk my successful career in civil engineering—working on construction sites to renovate luxury retailers, museums, and universities in New York City—for wine. To do that, I made up my mind that I would set boundaries around my corporate job, which took full advantage of my time since I was unmarried and had no children. Like most of my peers, I had made my career my life in my midtwenties to early thirties, eager to climb the corporate ladder to the corner office. However, that left little to no room for exploring hobbies or enjoying life.

At that time, I was working part-time at The Winery on the weekends and eager to continue to learn about wine so that I could one day transition fully into the industry. I envisioned a future life in which I could travel around the world learning, teaching, and building community around wine. I had the power to manifest that new life but would need to put myself in the driver's seat to go after this goal. I talked to a colleague about taking time off, and realized I was asking for a sabbatical. But let's be real, this was corporate America, not a university. There was no sabbatical benefit for employees at my company. I knew that I was devoted to my engineering career and was a highly valued employee to my team, so I had to remove fear and stand on faith, which led me to ask the vice president of my department for two and half months off.

To be honest, I had no plans for where I was going or what I was going to do when I asked for the time off. I just knew I needed dedicated time to be surrounded by wine and to focus on learning, exploring, and connecting. When it was time to make a decision, I was torn between South Africa and somewhere in South America, and I was driven by a feeling of wanting to be somewhere unfamiliar. I had already visited South Africa, and English is widely spoken there. I knew I could easily meet people from Argentina and taste Argentine wines in New York, so that left me with one choice. Chile became the frontrunner because I knew the least about the country or the wine, and I knew it would set me apart in the industry because it was a lesser-known region that was still emerging in the global market at the time. I bought a ticket and left the day after Thanksgiving.

I wasn't 100 percent sure I'd have a job to come back to. HR did not approve my sabbatical. But my boss recognized my workload was beginning to slow down for the holiday season and the hard work and dedication I had put in all year, so he agreed to not share my whereabouts as long as I checked my email. I thought that if I was going to be away for that long, I should go the distance. I went from willing to take an unpaid break for three months to working remotely from Chile (prepandemic). Not everyone is willing to put their job on the line like I did, and I'm not saying anyone should. This is my "do not try this at home" disclaimer. But for me, taking an unsanctioned leave of absence and going to Chile solidified my commitment to a career in wine and travel. That's the intuition and commitment that allowed me to transition to wine with confidence and to obtain the success I have achieved thus far.

I flew to Santiago from New Orleans, and I'd be lying if I said it was an amazing wine adventure from the moment I landed. I arrived in the Southern Hemisphere during the peak of summer, which was also around the Christmas holiday season. It didn't hit me until I was on a full flight with other Chileans flying home from the United States that I wouldn't be celebrating with any family. I'll admit at that moment that I questioned whether I was doing the right thing. I didn't even speak Spanish; whatever I had picked up in Spanish Harlem and Washington Heights, I quickly learned, did not work when communicating with locals speaking Chilean Spanish. I had just shown up with only the contacts of the Chilean producers I had been introduced to from working at the wine shop, hoping to be able to work with one of them during my time there, before harvest season. I wasn't in Chile for vacation, but I also didn't know, at first, exactly what I *was* there to do and how to go about establishing my uncharted focus on Chilean wine. But I had taken this leap, this risk, so now I had no choice but to push through the anxiety and dive into this immersive experience that ended up becoming the blueprint for how I traveled to other wine regions in the future.

I think I stared for at least an hour out the window of a luxury apartment in the home of my Airbnb host's parents in the Providencia neighborhood of Santiago de Chile. Their 360-degree views were a mix of sprawling cityscape and the Andes, one of the largest mountain ranges in the world. I am from New

York City—skyscrapers don't usually faze me, but this metropolis mixed with mountains so vividly in reach felt like something in a movie. Santiago de Chile is located in a valley, hemmed in by the Andes on one side and the Chilean Coastal Range on the other, so there are literally mountains surrounding the city. It was a drastically different view from New York City or anywhere I have ever visited. But as I got acclimated over time—from what could have been altitude sickness—it was also a reminder of why I was here, to explore and connect to a culture that felt foreign from my own.

Chile's geography plays a major role in its diverse landscape and its food and beverage culture. It is the longest and thinnest country in the world, stretching 2,670 miles north to south, which is just shy of the width of the United States from New York to California, 2,892 miles. Chile has lots of variation and microclimates, but if I had to name the two notable factors that define the Chilean wine terroir, they are the mountain and ocean influences.

The Central Valley subregion of Maipo Valley became my first point of exploration of Chilean terroir. I was able to take the Metro Line 4 from my Airbnb apartment to my first winery visit, which was just one hour south of the bustling city center of Santiago. The Chilean wine culture didn't feel highbrow because it was more accessible to everyone— quality wine at every price point and you can find it everywhere from the supermarket to the neighborhood bars, and of course in upscale restaurants. I was able to pay an equivalent to one US dollar for public transportation and arrive in front of an award-winning winery. As I entered the gates of Viña Cousiño-Macul, with the Andes to my right, I stood in awe of the vineyards directly in front of me, with the sprawling urban environment directly behind them. This experience gave me a new perspective on the important roles of urban wineries, and how mass transportation plays a role in wine accessibility, which makes life easier for workers and also makes wine more a part of the lifestyle.

I experienced a different side of the country when I visited Viña del Mar, just north of the coastal city of Valparaíso. Anywhere in the world where vineyards are near the sea, the wine is usually fresher and brighter thanks to the cooling breezes off the water. Ocean breezes provide cool temperatures to the vineyard during the hot season, stable moisture to the vines during dry periods, and reduce disease pressure. A lot of Chilean vineyards get these benefits from the Humboldt Current, named after the geographer Alexander von Humboldt, who conducted extensive research on South America's climate, geography, and ecosystems. Off the coast of Chile and Peru, this current brings colder water from deeper in the ocean close to the surface. This cold surface meets with hot air and creates fog. This is the same idea as the Humboldt fog in the San Francisco Bay Area. The fog protects wine grapes from harsh summer sun, which helps maintain the grapes' freshness.

Cha's Wine Traveler Tip: If you don't know where to begin wine exploring, find the best wine bar, boutique wine shop, and/or wine-focused restaurant in town. Employees at these establishments will undoubtedly have traveled to regions and wineries themselves and can give you the best advice on which winery will have the best experience.

LATIN AMERICA

And then there are the mountains. I got my sample of the Andes when I went for a horseback ride while visiting the southern region Valdivia. I was already so far out of my comfort zone that I felt, Why not do something else different? The guided ride was inexpensive, so I thought it would be a short trail ride. I was wrong. The group I went with was continuing to the other side of the Andes to Argentina. I hadn't brought my passport, so my journey ended at the Chilean border, but I still got a little preview of the huaso life. (Huasos are

107

Sip the Culture

Drinks in Chile tell the story of its Indigenous people, colonizers, and the waves of immigrants who followed.

BEER. The influx of German immigrants to southern Chile in the second half of the nineteenth century means there's a big beer scene in the south. Pilsners and other pale lagers have historically been the style popular here, but craft IPAs have also come along more recently.

CHICHA. This word describes precolonial fermented drinks from the Andes and Amazon regions, so there are lots of different styles. People associate it with a corn-based drink, but in Chile, most chicha is made with apples.

MATE. This is a highly caffeinated tea popular in Argentina and Chile. Black, green, and white teas are all made from the *Camellia sinensis* plant, but mate is made from a totally different plant called *Ilex paraguensis*. The traditional way to drink it is to combine shredded leaves with hot, but not boiling, water in a gourd, and then to sip through a straw that filters out the leaves.

PISCO. Chilean pisco is made like a traditional brandy: grapes are made into wine, and then the wine is distilled into a higher-alcohol spirit. The country's regulations allow pisco to be distilled more than once and aged, if the producer wants to. Pisco is made mostly from the Muscat grape in Chile.

TERREMOTO. This is a cocktail of pipeño table wine, pineapple ice cream, and grenadine or Fernet. There are variations. Some people may add rum or pisco. Its name means earthquake, because it will leave your legs shaking.

Chile's version of gauchos: cowboys.) We brought lunch with us, so we could eat and drink wine in the mountains, completely unplugged. It was simple and slow, definitely a once-in-a-lifetime experience.

The Andes form Chile's eastern border with Argentina, the Central Mountains are in the middle, and the Coastal Mountains provide lots of ocean-facing slopes. These mountains are high and windy, with slopes that help drainage—all things wine grapes love, so you will find plenty of vineyards here. The Atacama region in the north of Chile is arid and where you will find the Atacama Desert, which is one of the driest in the world. Central Chile is more of a valley and this is where most of the vineyards and major cities are found. In southern Chile you can find lush forests, lakes, and snowcapped volcanoes. Lastly, Patagonia and Chilean Antarctica in the southernmost region are home to picturesque landscapes of glaciers and national park Torres del Paine. Chile's diverse topography and weather make it one of the most interesting countries in the world for wine making.

Many wine-growing regions in Chile are quite dry, to the point that they're becoming unusable. A 2022 Reuters article says that wine-growing land decreased by 4 percent over the five years ending in 2020. The southern part of the country gets more rain, but it's also colder, so not everything can grow there. Chilean winemakers have reinvented themselves before, and they face a steep battle doing so again in the face of climate change.

Earthquakes are another fact of Chile's geography. The line between the South American and Nazca Plates runs along Chile's coastline. According to *Physics Today*, the two plates move toward each other by about eight centimeters per year. One of the ways that affects wine specifically is that for a long time it wasn't practical or feasible to build railroads through the mountains to connect Chile to other countries for trade. There was a long-standing wine culture to produce cheap table wines for domestic consumption. That's more about cultural terroir, but it is interesting to think that Chile, where wine growers didn't have to worry about phylloxera mites, has a much bigger threat to its wine market.

With Peru in the north and Antarctica in the south, the best way to begin understanding Chile is by dividing it into three parts, North, Central, and South. I spent most of my time learning about Chilean wine exploring producers located in the Central Valley wine region, with Santiago de Chile as my home base.

Santiago is home to seven million people, or Santiaguinos, as the locals are called. They are known for being industrious. And this cosmopolitan city I can tell you from experience, has one hell of a nightlife. It should be on the list for travelers who are looking to explore a new urban landscape. In the Barrio Lastarria neighborhood, I was introduced to the Bocanáriz wine bar by a friend of a friend. Jenny is a native Chilean living in Harlem, who was in Santiago visiting her family for Christmas and became my local expert. Bocanáriz became my go-to wine bar during my stay. I spent weeks dissecting their proud Chilean bottle list with more than three hundred wines available, which is considered a very extensive wine selection to serve by the glass (also known as a BTG list), and also a wine-by-the-taste menu that allows for a flight of multiple Chilean wines. Bocanáriz literally translates to "mouth nose," and it became my palate's gateway to exploring all of Chile's wine regions. After just a few visits and feeling like a regular, the sommelier invited me down to the cava, the wine cellar, to geek out over some of their favorite producers and rare bottles, like Vik by Viña Vik and Seña by Viña Errázuriz. I returned for a couple of winemaker nights, for deep-dive tastings held in their private dining room with a photography exhibit, highlighting black-and-white portraits of Chilean winemakers.

As I settled in, I got to explore the markets, which were abundant and overflowing with fresh summer produce. If you love to travel for food, I always recommend going to the market in whatever country you are visiting. Those in Chile were some of the most beautiful markets I've ever visited. I felt like even the fruits and vegetables were a reminder of the impeccable agriculture and the hopeful future for premium wines from Chile. With almost 2,700 miles facing the Pacific Ocean, Chile embraces seafood. At the market, I had my favorite version of a fisherman's stew. It was a brothy mix of seafood with a sort of curry base to it. Even though people recommended Peruvian food, Chile has its own cuisine and influences. Mapuche cooking, and ingredients like potatoes, corn, and beans, remains after Spanish colonizers brought over ingredients like pork and wheat. This merging of Spanish and Indigenous foodways is common throughout Central and South America and the Spanish-speaking Caribbean. In Chile, an influx of German immigrants in the late nineteenth and early twentieth centuries added their pork preparations and baked goods to the mix, while Italian immigrants brought pasta and prosciutto.

Wine also came to Chile from Europe, even though the Indigenous people were drinking something fermented from fruits and vegetables, now called chicha, long before the first Spanish colonizers arrived (more on chicha at page 108). The country's first wine grape harvest is attributed to conquistador Francisco de Aguirre in 1551. There's not much record of what those first wines were, but the red-wine grape País was common. In the mid-1800s, French varieties like Cabernet Sauvignon and Merlot were introduced.

Chile was untouched by the phylloxera that decimated so much of the European wine economy in the late nineteenth century. Even some of Argentina's vines were affected, but not Chile's. So that brings up a question: If Chilean vineyards are filled with wonderful old vines and centuries of wine-making culture, why is it only in the last thirty years or so that it's been exported and celebrated internationally? And the answer to that, I learned, is politics. Chile's socialist leader Salvador Allende campaigned on a revolution with the "flavor of empanadas and wine," and while food and wine were plentiful under his rule, quality and export were not the priorities in wine making.

When dictator Augusto Pinochet came into power in 1973, he brought brutal violence and a drive to open Chile up for trade. By the 1980s, Chilean wines were becoming popular in the United States for delivering quality on par with Bordeaux at a fraction of the price. And Spanish and French winemakers began relocating to the country to explore Chilean terroir further.

The End of the Allende Era

Before my trip to Chile, when I thought of a socialist political regime, I often confused them with the strong-armed communist leaders and breadlines—leaders who reject capitalism and typically are not beloved. However, when talking to Chileans about former President Salvador Allende, I learned a different perspective. Allende was elected democratically and was progressing the country gradually toward socialism by nationalizing major industries and expanding access to food and education. He was president from 1970 until his tragic death in 1973. His tenure left many Chileans with mixed feelings about the future of the country. Some people reflected on a life that was good and hopeful during his term. The working class celebrated the efforts of nationalizing the private large companies and creating land reforms. Under the Agrarian Reform Law, his administration broke up large wine estates and redistributed their land to vineyard workers. This led to a state-run cooperative that dramatically affected the quality of wine. Exports were only allowed to other socialist countries and traditionally markets such as the United States decreased tremendously due to political and economic uncertainty.

In 1973, the CIA (the United States's Central Intelligence Agency) backed a coup d'état murdering Allende and putting the Chilean commander in chief Augusto Pinochet in power. Pinochet was all about opening the market, opening the country to foreign trade—basically advocating for capitalism and what's come to be known as neoliberalism. But he was

(text continues on page 112)

LATIN AMERICA

BUENA ONDA

Ivy Mix cofounded Speed Rack, a drinks competition, with Lynnette Marrero (page 62). She's also the owner and head bartender at Leyenda, a Brooklyn bar and restaurant that celebrates the spirits of Latin America. This one does just that, combining pisco made from the Torontel grape, a name for certain Criollo grapes in Chile and Peru, with yerba mate, an Argentine tea that's also popular in Chile, into a variation of a pisco sour, one of Chile's national drinks.

1. Combine all the ingredients except for the garnish in a cocktail shaker. Shake and strain shake into a coupe glass.
2. Garnish with bitters hearts

MAKES 1 COCKTAIL

2 ounces yerba mate–infused Torontel pisco (recipe below)
½ ounce lemon juice
½ ounce lime juice
¾ ounce simple syrup
½ ounce egg white
3 dashes Bitterman's Hopped Grapefruit Bitters
Angostura Bitters, for garnish

YERBA MATE-INFUSED PISCO

4 teaspoons yerba mate
1 750-ml bottle Torontel pisco

Combine yerba mate and pisco, and let steep for around seven hours. Strain out the yerba mate with a fine-mesh strainer.

also a brutal dictator. An official report said that he was responsible for three thousand deaths.

Pinochet stayed in office until 1990, and his policy of encouraging international trade was a huge change from Allende for the wine industry. A turning point was in 1985, when famous wine critic Robert Parker praised a Chilean Cabernet for being as complex as anything from Bordeaux, at a much lower price. While Allende's goals led to a downturn in the quality of wine in Chile, they helped support the working-class people. I would be remiss not to mention that Pinochet's efforts are a darker, uglier side of Chile's history and are not the right way to unify and grow the wine industry or to show support for the country.

Chile's Wine Regions

The country's department of agriculture established wine regions in the mid-1990s. While not every winegrower was happy about the designations, they are easy for consumers to understand. There are six regions, each with subregions defined by valleys. Because the country is so long and narrow, they run north to south, one after the other.

Atacama: This dry, desert region to the north has two subregions, Copaípo Valley and Huasco Valley. A lot of vineyards are planted closer to the ocean, where the air is a little more humid. Even though this region gets plenty of sun and is closer to the equator, cool-weather grapes like Chardonnay, Sauvignon Blanc, and Pinot Noir are commonly planted.

Coquimbo: Each subregion here has its own distinct characteristics. The Elqui Valley has vineyards up to 6,500 feet in altitude, some

Chile's Wine Regions

- Atacama
- Coquimbo
- Aconcagua
- Central Valley
- Sur
- Austral

of Chile's highest. The altitude helps cool temperatures a little, but because it's so dry and sunny here, grapes are still likely to get very ripe and produce high-alcohol wines, which is probably why this area has traditionally grown grapes for pisco. Now, Syrah is becoming

LATIN AMERICA

a signature. The Limarí Valley, Coquimbo's central region, benefits from the cooling Camanchaca fog, which makes it well suited to Sauvignon Blanc, Chardonnay, Pinot Noir, and Syrah. The cool Choapa Valley grows Cabernet Sauvignon and Syrah, with vineyards owned by large producer De Martino, which is in the Central Valley.

Aconcagua: Wine regions that are considered among the country's best are in this region that was mostly livestock farms until the 1980s. Valleys run west to east, carrying through Pacific breezes and moisture. Fog created by the Humboldt Current has a cooling effect, so grapes ripen slowly and maintain great acidity. This is another area good for cool-climate grapes Chardonnay, Sauvignon Blanc, and Pinot Noir.

Central Valley: The country's largest wine region is made up of really diverse subregions. The Maipo Valley is both one of the oldest and, because it's so close to Santiago, most tourist friendly. Some of the country's biggest wineries, like Concha Y Toro, Santa Rita, and Undurraga are here. Cabernet Sauvignon is its star, followed by Merlot and Carménère. South of Maipo is the Rapel Valley, which is home to the subregions of Cachapoal Valley and Colchagua Valley. Cachapoal is fertile and produces Cabernets and Syrahs with great concentration. The ones from higher altitudes can also be very elegant. Colchagua, like Maipo, is one of the country's historic wine regions, with a steam-powered wine train for touring. But this is also a forward-looking region where winemakers are producing skin-contact wines, rosés, sparkling wines, and grapes like Mourvedre and Carignan. Travel south to Curicó Valley, and you'll find affordable

Wine Grapes of Chile

Red

Alicante Bouschet
Cabernet Franc
Cabernet Sauvignon
Carignan
Carménère
Merlot
País
Syrah

White

Chardonnay
Sauvignon Blanc
Semillon
Torontel

wines in different styles. This region did grow wine under Spanish colonization, which was revived in the late 1970s by Spanish winemaker Miguel Torres. Finally, the southernmost part of the Central Valley is Maule Valley, which gets more rain than a lot of the country's other areas. It produces bulk red and white wines, but there's some movement to preserve historic vineyards and make more expressive wines with finesse.

Sur: The country's southernmost wine-making region until pretty recently, the Sur has two major valleys: Itata and Bío Bío. The Itata Valley is a historic region with lots of old vines, and *New York Times* wine writer Eric Asimov called its Cinsault "among the most interesting Chilean wines" in an August 2019 column. The Bío Bío Valley gets good rainfall, and its cool temperatures can be a benefit in good years, giving grapes a long, slow growing season but also a challenge.

Austral: One of the southernmost wine-growing areas in South America, this is a new

113

+ PAIRED UP

MACHAS A LA PARMESANA + TORONTEL, ITATA VALLEY, CHILE. Light-bodied and dry Torontel will add some delicate floral notes and a light lift of acidity to really make machas a la parmesana shine. It can be used for pisco or to produce dry, aromatic white wines. Machas a la parmesana, an appetizer, is made with a saltwater clam native to Chile and Peru and shows the Italian influence on cuisine. It's made by shucking the clam from the shell and then adding it back and baking it with wine, butter, and cheese such as parmigiano.

PLATEADA + MALBEC, MAULE VALLEY, CHILE. The wine can be your braising liquid and your pairing for this wine-braised beef dish. Plateada is also the name of the cut of beef, and it's one that US butchers don't cut, but it's similar to a boneless short rib or brisket. Both the wine and the meat will have a silky, tender feel in your mouth, and the wine will bring plenty of pepper to enhance the meat. Not a whole lot of Malbec is grown in Chile, but what's there can be very good. It tends to be lighter in body than Argentine Malbec, with a silky texture and plenty of black fruit and black pepper notes. Some of the best Malbecs come from Maule, and Colchagua is also producing good options.

CHARQUICÁN + CHARDONNAY, ACONCAGUA, CHILE. Chile's cooler coastal regions are great for this grape. Often, it's given a lot of oak, for a buttery chard like you might find from California, with lively apple and pineapple notes. Chardonnay in the Casablanca region typically gets some body from oak aging, but it maintains good acidity and bright citrus flavors, just the thing to serve with one of Chile's precolonial dishes. Charquicán is a stew that takes its name from the charqui, or jerky, that used to be used to season it. This is a seasonal vegetable stew—squash and potato in winter, corn and beans in summer—that's served topped with an egg. Today it's typically made with fresh meat or seaweed for a vegetarian version.

PAILA MARINA + SAUVIGNON BLANC, CASABLANCA, CHILE. These Sauvignon Blancs, such as Caldillo de Congrio, benefit from the Humboldt Current, which keeps the wines fresh and high in acidity, plus granitic soils that add a hint of minerality. This is another example of a wine growing near the sea pairing well with food from the sea, in this case paila marina, or Chilean seafood stew. Made with a mix of fresh fish and shellfish and seasoned simply with garlic, onion, and sweet red pepper, this stew tastes fresh and homey at the same time when paired with the bright wine. Light-bodied Chilean Sauvignon Blanc features a lot of the grape's best qualities: It's super aromatic, with lots of tropical fruit, peach, and grapefruit notes, but it's also got a lot of herbaceous and grassy characteristics that keep it from being a fruit bomb.

JALEA + SPARKLING CHARDONNAY, CASABLANCA, CHILE. These sparkling chards have a little oak influence and a lot more bubbles, which works well with a seafood dish from Peru: jalea. This is a platter of mixed fried seafood with yuca, fried plantain chips, and a red onion and tomato salad. The sparkling wine is a refreshing, palate-cleansing partner.

COMPLETE HOT DOG + PAÍS, ITATA VALLEY, CHILE. Technically Listan Prieto and also known as the Mission or Criollo grape, this black-skinned grape produces juicy, crunchy, light-bodied and easy-drinking wines with cherry, strawberry and herbal notes. This native grape shines alongside a dish that's easy to enjoy but deceptively complex. Meet the complete, Chile's hot dog topped with ingredients like avocado, tomatoes, sauerkraut, and mayonnaise.

LATIN AMERICA

> **LOMO SALTADO + CABERNET SAUVIGNON, MAIPO VALLEY, CHILE.** Chile's most-grown grape is also the one that put the country on the map for international wine collectors. A lot of Chilean Cabernet is refined and savory, while some are richer, with more plush black fruits, closer to a Left Bank Bordeaux style. The wine's rich, dark fruit flavors stand up well to Peru's stir-fried beef, lomo saltado. Some red cherry notes in the wine provide brightness to keep the meat and French fries from feeling heavy. This dish is an example of Peru's chifa cuisine, which blends in the influence of Chinese workers who immigrated to the country in the late nineteenth and early twentieth century.
>
> **AJI DE GALLINA + SEMILLON, COLCHAGUA VALLEY, CHILE.** Once accounting for almost a third of Chile's wine grapes and made into cheap table wine, this Bordeaux variety was largely replaced by Sauvignon Blanc in the second half of the twentieth century. It's creeping back though, now creating beautiful fine wines with notes of straw, dried herbs, and honey. This grape maintains its bright acidity even when it gets a bit of oak for structure and body. Its dried herb characteristics really enhance Peru's signature comfort food, aji de gallina. This creamy stewed chicken dish seasoned with aji pepper gets just the right amount of brightness from the wine.
>
> **CHILEAN CEVICHE + SAUVIGNON BLANC, LIMARÍ VALLEY, CHILE.** In Chile, ceviche tends to be made with lemon, instead of the lime or orange that are more common in Peru, which Limarí Valley Sauvignon Blanc has plenty of.

wine region. Its first vineyards were planted in 2000. With plenty of rain and volcanic soils, it has great potential, even though only about seventy-five acres are planted so far.

The Carménère Affair

If Argentina has Malbec, Chile has Carménère. This is a grape variety from Bordeaux, and it's related to Cabernet Sauvignon. Imported to Chile in the mid-nineteenth century, it quickly blended in with Merlot.

For years, Carménère was thought to have died out with phylloxera. Research by Jean-Michel Boursiquot, a French ampelographer (a scientist who studies grapevines), and confirmed by further DNA testing at the University of California–Davis by Dr. Carole Meredith in the mid-1990s, revealed that large quantities of it were being grown and vinified as Merlot in Chile. The same was happening in parts of Italy and France.

Since then, Chile made the grape its own and has become the world's largest Carménère producer. Growers made adjustments, like less irrigation and an earlier harvest, to make the most of the medium-size, thick-skinned, deep-purple grape. Today, Chilean Carménère is bright and fruit forward with a peppery streak.

One of the best ways to experience these grapes is by pairing them. Here are some of my favorite matches with Chilean and Peruvian dishes.

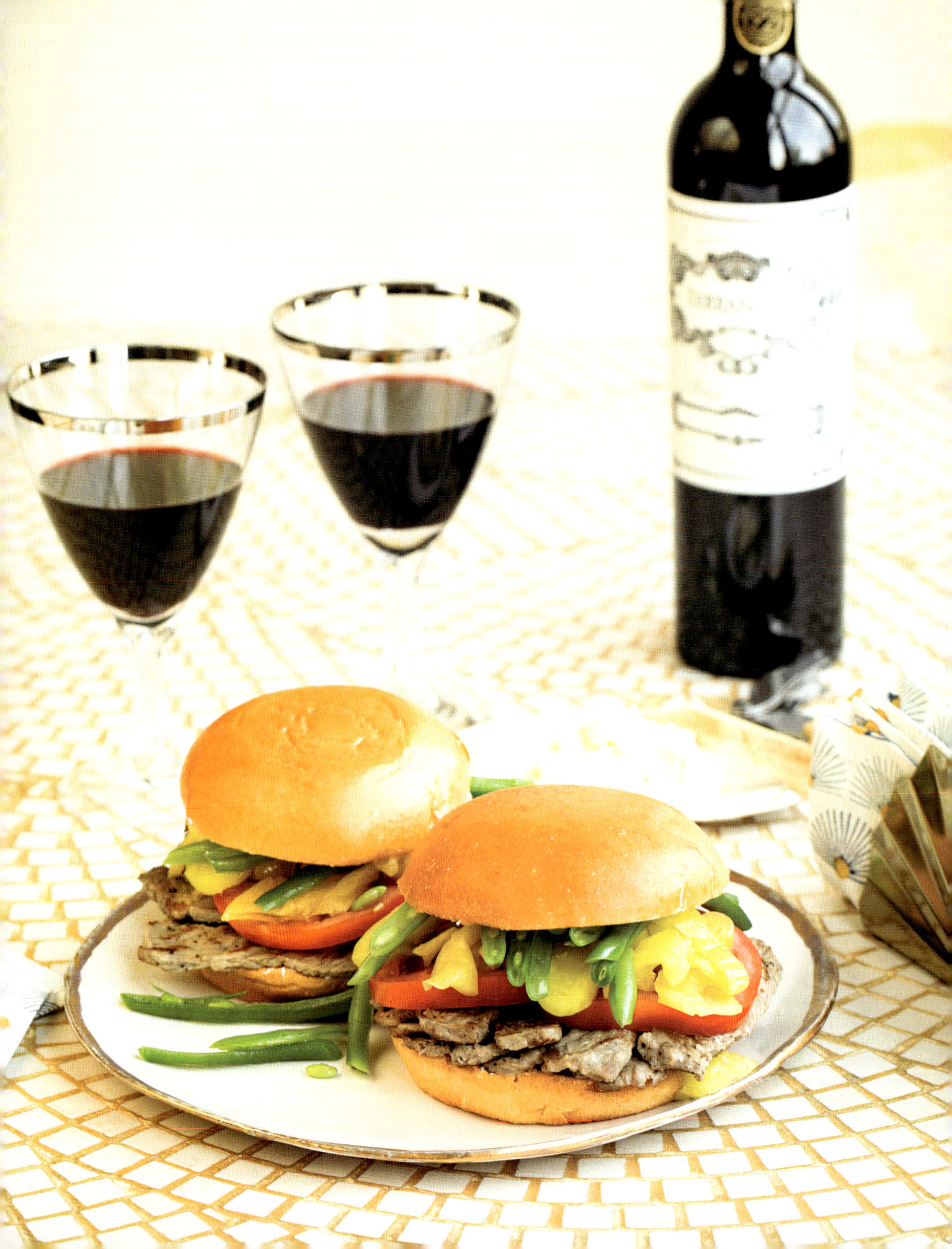

LATIN AMERICA

CHILEAN CHACARERO SANDWICH + CARMÉNÈRE, CACHAPOAL VALLEY, CHILE

Philly has the cheesesteak, Vietnam has the bánh mì, and Chile has the chacarero as its iconic sandwich. This recipe comes from Pilar Hernandez, who was born and raised in Chile, where she studied medicine. Then she moved to the United States and had to navigate foreign groceries in a foreign language to recreate the dishes that would taste like home. She started a blog about the process, and that grew into a cookbook.

I had to pair the national wine with the national sandwich. The wine's peppery notes are always welcome with beef, and its bright, playful nature sets the right tone for a good sandwich.

1. Wash the green beans, cut the ends, and cut them lengthwise with a knife. Place them in a bowl and add a splash of water and sprinkle of salt. Cook in the microwave for 6 minutes, taste, and cook until tender but still crisp. In my microwave, they take 8 minutes. Or cook in a pot in salted boiling water, 3 to 5 minutes.
2. Drain the green beans and cover with ice water to preserve the bright green color once cool. Drain and pat dry with paper towels and dress with salt and oil.
3. Cut the steak into thin slices. Add salt and pepper to the meat.
4. In a medium skillet over high heat, heat 1 teaspoon oil and cook the steak 1 minute per side.
5. Season the tomato slices with salt.
6. Cut and smear the bread with butter and mayonnaise, if using. Place the meat, then tomatoes and peppers if using, and finally the green beans.
7. Serve immediately.

Used with permission from *The Chilean Kitchen* by Pilar Hernandez and Eileen Smith (Skyhorse, October 2020).

SERVES 2

1 cup green beans
1 pound New York strip or rib-eye steak
Kosher salt and black pepper
2 slices tomato
2 brioche rolls
1 tablespoon butter
Mayonnaise, optional
Sweet banana pepper, optional

WINE PAIRING FOR THE PEOPLE

Argentina

Coordinates: 38.4161° S, 63.6167° W

Capital: Buenos Aires

Country/Continent: Argentina is in South America, bordered by Chile to the west, the Atlantic Ocean to the east, Bolivia and Paraguay to the north, Uruguay to the northeast, and Drake Passage to the south

Population: 45.8 million

National Drink: Mate tea and wine

National Dish: Asado

Top Exports: Corn, soybean meal and oil, wheat

Official Language: Spanish

Independence Day: July 9, 1816

Independence from: Spain

F**inally! I made it to Buenos Aires after spending** close to twenty hours traveling, for a trip that was supposed to take less than one hour from Santiago de Chile. During my short stint living in Chile, I violated rule number one of international travel: *research*. Before you go, research the country you are visiting, its political relations with your home country, travel requirements, and restrictions. Chile did not require a visa for me to enter as a US citizen, so I didn't think twice when purchasing my flight to Argentina.

At the time of this writing, the US passport is ranked the eighth strongest in the world, allowing for visa-free access to 184 of the 227 countries. Most Americans assume you can fly to most countries freely, and you would be wrong. But on this trip, I realized that traveling around South America wouldn't be like my time in Western Europe. Different countries, different historical and political relationships with the United States, different rules. Today Americans can visit Argentina for ninety days without a visa, but in 2014, that was not the case, and I learned the hard way. I had to miss my original flight and the next two until my visa was completed at the Chilean airport. When I finally did land, it was well after midnight, which I soon learned meant the night had just begun in Buenos Aires.

Weeks before my trip to Chile, I connected with a friend, Rich, a fellow Harlem native and my fraternity brother of

Alpha Phi Alpha. He was completing his MBA program with a semester abroad in Argentina. Before he returned to Harlem for the holidays, I thought it was the perfect time to visit Mendoza, Argentina's premier wine region, and spend time exploring Buenos Aires with Rich as my guide.

Once I arrived, I messaged Rich from the airport to let him know that I had landed, and I hoped for the best in trying to find my way to his apartment. I realized that, without cell-phone service, I could not get in contact with Rich once I left the airport.

I went straight to his apartment building in the Palermo neighborhood of Buenos Aires, and as I pulled up to the dimly lit area anxiety kicked in. *I am a Black woman, sitting outside of an apartment building with luggage in the middle of the night in one of the largest cities in the world. I don't speak the local language, and I don't have phone service. This can go wrong real fast.*

After a long wait and a few prayers, I gained access to the lobby from a neighbor, and eventually Rich arrived, out of breath and sweaty, like he had just finished a CrossFit workout, but full of smiles. He rushed me upstairs to his apartment, exclaiming that I needed to change clothes quickly and we needed to get back to his roommates, fellow classmates whom he had left in the club. I was a bit confused why we were returning to the club when it was already two a.m., assuming things should be closing. Little did I know we had until six a.m. to party in Buenos Aires. We arrived at the entrance of the Makena Cantina nightclub, and when the crowd parted like the Red Sea, giving Rich familiar head nods and letting us walk right past everyone on line, I realized my evening had just begun. Rich later shared his love for his semester abroad in Buenos Aires and even said, "I can breathe here"—a complicated response to the fear he lives with as Black man in New York City relating to Eric Garner's last words, "I can't breathe," as he was killed by a New York City police officer.

The rest of the week, I was able to get a glimpse of Rich and his roommates' (also Black men from the United States) perspectives of living in Argentina, while back at home, the assassinations of Black men were repeated in headlines across the media this year alone: Eric Garner in July, Michael Brown in August, and Tamir Rice in November, all due to police brutality. In Argentina, they were able to experience joy, to breathe, and they wanted to celebrate life to the max, enjoying a sense of freedom here. But I also witnessed that when we were not distracted by flowing cocktails, loud music, and strobe lights, they were not detached from the pain of what was happening stateside.

Argentina has a history of being a safe haven

Wine Grapes of Argentina

Red

Bonarda
Cabernet Franc
Cabernet Sauvignon
Criolla Grande
Malbec
Pinot Noir
Syrah

White

Cereza
Chardonnay
Semillon
Torrontés
Torrontés Riojano

for foreigners. Though colonized by the Spanish, it took in a large number of Italian immigrants in the late nineteenth and early twentieth century, who have left a big impact on its culture. Notoriously, Southern parts of Argentina became home to Nazis fleeing prosecution after World War II, but many Eastern European Jewish refugees also came to Argentina for refuge.

However, the country was less hospitable to the enslaved African people who were brought there. A 2021 Associated Press story by Christiana Sciaudone states that about a third of Argentina was of African descent in the early nineteenth century. In 2010, the census recorded only 150,000 Black people in the country. Sciaudone reports that the number is probably closer to two million. As I have learned in other travels, Black can mean something different depending on where you are. There are different theories as to why the Black population dwindled so much. Some say most of the Black people were recruited into the army and killed in battle, a conscious effort to have a whiter country. Others say the government just flooded the country with white Europeans to create, over generations, a majority of people with lighter skin and more European features, to overshadow both Black and Indigenous people.

Now, according to Sciaudone, a growing number of activists have been working to reclaim Black and Indigenous space and heritage, including the Black influence on Argentina's national dance, the tango. I'm excited to visit again, to see what that looks like.

Despite some leaders' efforts to make Argentina a European country, the food shows all its cultural influences, which makes it exciting to pair. The country's wine regions are big and diverse, meaning I didn't get to see it all, but I did treat myself to a bike tour in Mendoza. Mendoza is about a two-hour flight from Buenos Aires. Once you're there, it's common to visit the wineries by bicycle. On the opposite page is a map of the bike route and stops from Maipú, a subregion of Mendoza.

Argentina's Wine Regions

Argentina is divided into three large areas—the North, Cuyo, and Patagonia and the Atlantic. Within these are Geographic Indications or GIs. Some of them are smaller subregions within the regions listed below—the country has more than one hundred GIs.

North

Salta: A really high-altitude region with vineyards 5,000–10,000 feet above sea level, Salta, and specifically the Cafayate Valley, is exciting for well-structured Cabernet Sauvignon and Tannat wines that thrive in the high-altitude vineyards. Torrontés is a great white wine from the area. Jujuy, a newer subregion of Salta, is one of the highest regions in the world. Its lower areas are still more than 5,000 feet above sea level. The Moya vineyard, at 10,922 feet up, is considered the highest in the world. Very little rain falls here, and the red wines produced are dark, inky, and well structured.

Tucumán: This high-altitude region is home to part of the Calchaquí Valley (the valley spans into Salta too), which is the largest-producing wine region in the country, and also home to one of its oldest vineyards, planted to Torrontés. This valley is perfectly built for wine

LATIN AMERICA

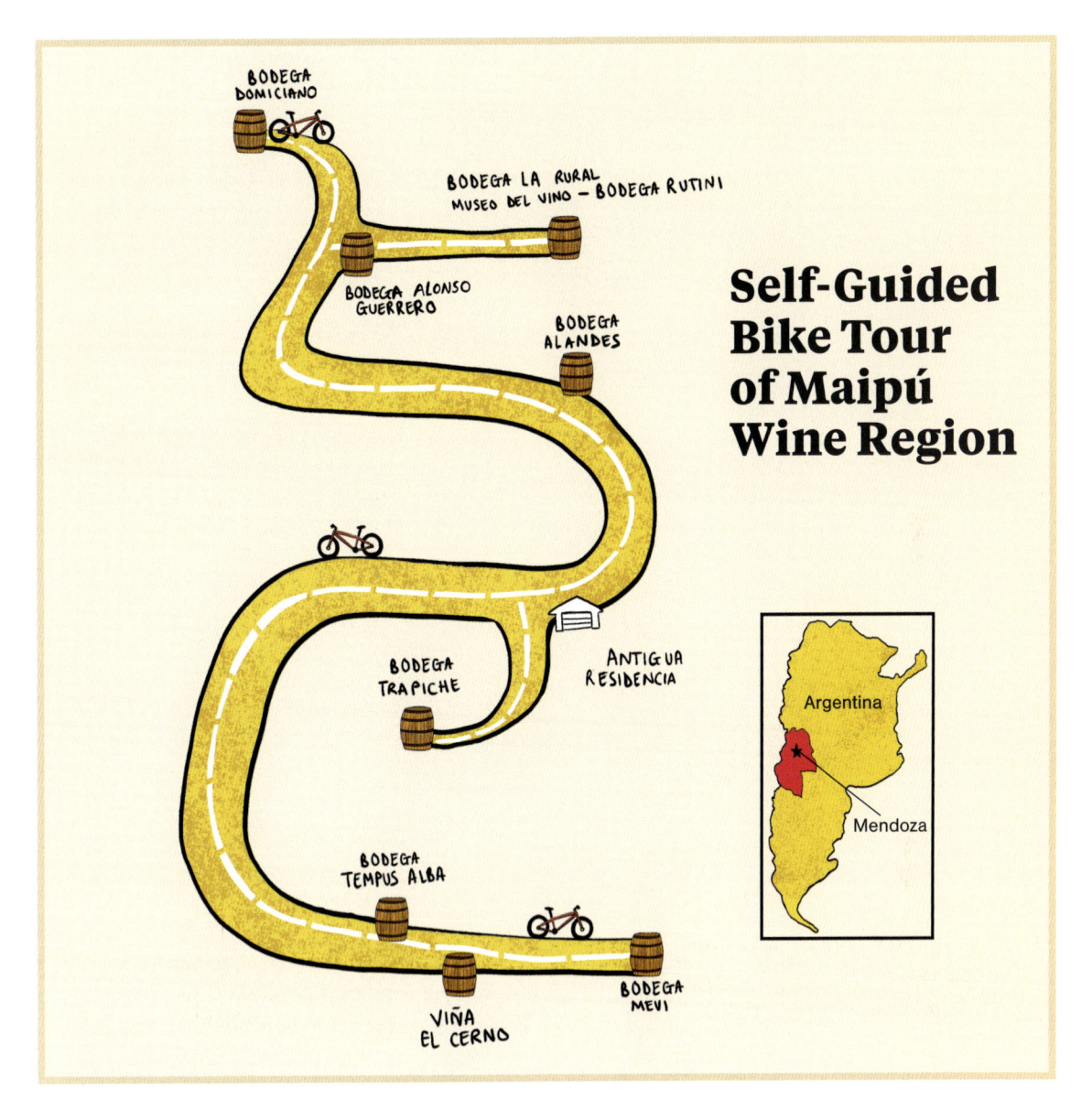

Self-Guided Bike Tour of Maipú Wine Region

Stops shown along the route:
- BODEGA DOMICIANO
- BODEGA LA RURAL – MUSEO DEL VINO – BODEGA RUTINI
- BODEGA ALONSO GUERRERO
- BODEGA ALANDES
- BODEGA TRAPICHE
- ANTIGUA RESIDENCIA
- BODEGA TEMPUS ALBA
- VIÑA EL CERNO
- BODEGA MEVI

Inset map: Argentina, with Mendoza marked.

growing, with lots of sunshine, good drainage, and big diurnal swings.

Catamarca: Because of its mountains, this region of mountain valleys that run north-south stayed pretty isolated while other parts of the country were being planted in the colonial era. At the southern end of the North district, Catamarca is also lower in altitude, ranging from about 2,000 to 4,500 feet above sea level (still considered very high altitude for the rest of the world). Wine growing started

+ PAIRED UP

EMPANADAS + BONARDA, CALCHAQUÍ VALLEY, ARGENTINA. A bright, fruity, carbonically macerated bottle of this wine, made from a grape that originated in the French Alps, is a fun, easy-drinking accompaniment to savory empanadas. Serve the wine chilled.

ASADO + MALBEC, SAN JUAN, ARGENTINA. The wine brings serious concentration to mixed grilled meats served with chimichurri, a condiment made with parsley, garlic, and chile peppers. The Malbec's dark fruit and coffee notes will stand up to this rich, smoky, spicy spread, while its silky texture won't fight with the chimichurri the way a more tannic wine might.

CHORIPÁN CHORIZO SANDWICH + CRIOLLA GRANDE, MENDOZA, ARGENTINA. This is another example of a pairing of light, fruit-forward wine—this one made from a native red grape—that brings just enough sophistication and complexity to match a flavorful street food.

PROVOLETA + TORRONTÉS, SALTA, ARGENTINA. Argentina's signature white wine has beautiful floral notes that will add elegance to Italian-inspired provoleta. This dish of grilled, melted provolone, served with bread seasoned with oregano and chili flakes, also benefits from the wine's bright acidity.

FUGAZZA + CHARDONNAY, MENDOZA, ARGENTINA. This thick flatbread with onions and sometimes other toppings is reminiscent of Italian focaccia. Oak-aged Chardonnays are rounder and fuller in body, making them a good option with complex notes of toast, butter, and hazelnut—the perfect complement to this easy dish.

ALFAJORES + CREAM SHERRY, JEREZ, SPAIN. Argentina's beloved sandwich cookie bound together by dulce de leche also brings me back to Europe. Pair with a cream sherry, which is made when a dry sherry is blended with a sweet sherry, and then they're aged together, creating a semisweet wine. It will have hallmark nutty notes like the dulce de leche, but still maintain good acidity.

---

here in the 1930s. A lot of the production is Torrontés and Cereza that are used in bulk wine, but Syrah and Bonarda grown here are starting to generate some interest for higher-end wine.

Cuyo

La Rioja: Bordering Catamarca, this region of parallel valleys has its own unique terroir. It's relatively warm but still dry, which helps the grapes ripen without some of the risks, like mildew, that come from a more rainy area. The slopes and valley floors create lots of different microclimates. La Rioja has its own Torrontés Riojano grape that makes up the majority of vineyards, but Malbec and Cabernet Sauvignon are also important to the region.

San Juan: This is considered Argentina's second most important and largest producing region; 16 percent of the country's vineyard acreage is here. Like La Rioja, it's made up of a series of warm, sunny valleys and primarily

LATIN AMERICA

Argentina's Wine Regions

Legend:
- Salta
- Tucamàn
- Catamarca
- La Rioja
- San Juan
- Mendoza
- Patagonia and the Atlantic

Mendoza: Probably the country's best-known region accounts for around 60 percent of the country's wine production and 75 percent of its vineyard acres. Some areas are mountainous, which creates a lot of different microclimates. Wine regions at high elevations are cooler, windier, and better draining, so they make lighter-bodied, higher-acidity wine. Historic vineyards on the valley floor produce wines that are plusher and more ripe.

Patagonia and the Atlantic

Argentina's southernmost region has extreme weather and high altitude in some areas, while others are warmer, grassier, and even tempered by the Atlantic Ocean. The subregion of **La Pampa**, for example, serves as a transition between the Andes in the west and the Atlantic to the east. It's still about a thousand feet above sea level, and mostly grasslands (*pampas* translates loosely to prairie). It's relatively warm and planted mostly to red varieties. Malbec is prominent here.

The climate in another subregion, **Neuquén**, doesn't sound quite as nice: drought, hot days, cold nights, constant wind. But all of that comes together to grow good wine grapes. This region doesn't have the same history as some of the others; it started getting attention in the 1990s, when a local man named Julio Viola came up with an irrigation system that used snowmelt, making it easier to grow in the dry climate. Now it produces a variety of grapes.

One of the country's lowest-altitude subregions, **Río Negro** slopes toward the Atlantic coast, along the Colorado and Negro rivers. Cold winters and strong winds help grapes here ripen slowly, which makes wines

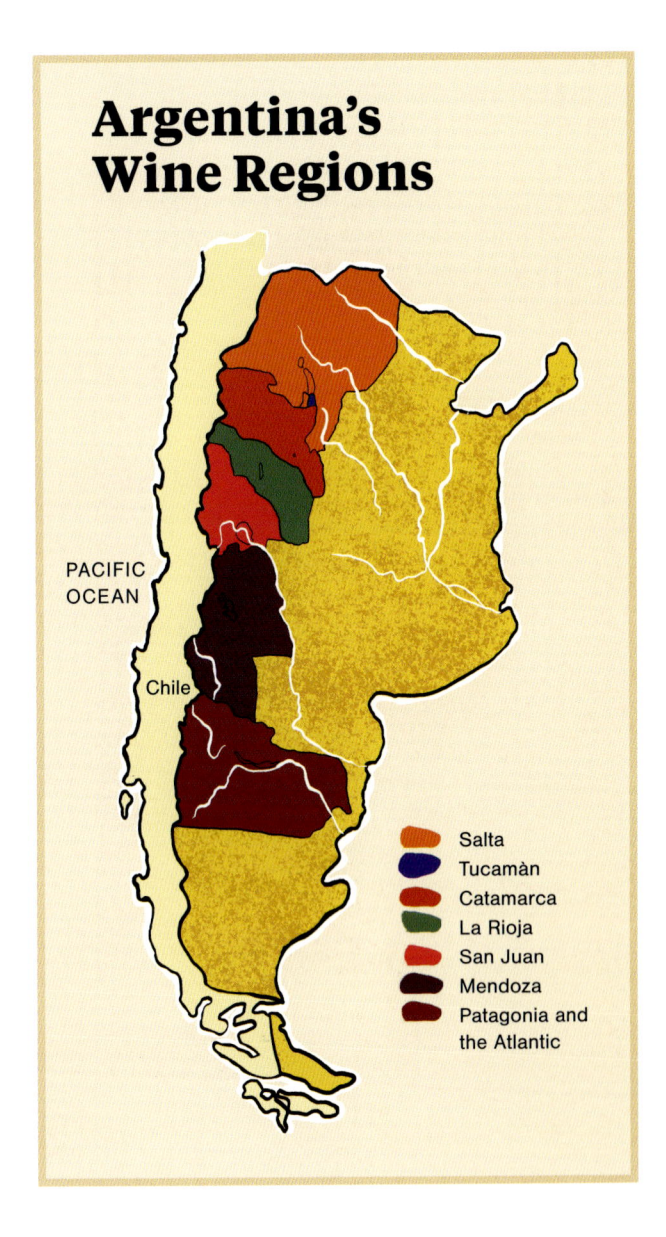

clay and sandy soils. Wines produced here tend to have a fruit-forward characteristic. Malbec, Cabernet Sauvignon, Bonarda, and Torrontés are all important here, but Syrah is really one of the signature grapes.

with complexity. White wines here, mostly Sauvignon Blanc and Semillon, can take on mineral characteristics too.

The subregion of **Chubut** is home to the southernmost vineyard in the world. And you've got to remember that in the Southern Hemisphere, south equals cold. With strong winds and frosts, this can be considered a cold-climate wine region, which means Pinot Noir, Chardonnay, Sauvignon Blanc, and even Gewürztraminer produce bright, fresh wines with some fruitiness.

The country's newest subregion, **Buenos Aires**, started producing wine in the early 2000s. The terroir here is lower mountains and plains. It's warm and humid, but ocean breezes give the grapes a fresh character. This region is good for sparkling wines, plus cooler-climate grapes like Chardonnay, Sauvignon Blanc, and Pinot Noir.

LATIN AMERICA

Brazil

My first trip to Brazil was also my first time traveling with a group of strangers. Back when I was still living in Italy, my obsession with traveling had led me to a Facebook group of like-minded people who used whatever disposable income they had to see the world. My friends in New York City considered traveling to be hopping on a flight to Cancun for a weekend to party, but can you blame them? It took a several-month queue for an interview for a ten-year visa and a fee, at the time of my trip, for just a one-week vacation to Brazil. In the Facebook tribe, I gained access to a group of young Black and brown Americans living in Sweden, South Korea, and Italy, like me, who welcomed the challenges of travel, collecting passport stamps like marathon medals. Nomadness Travel Tribe, founded by Evita Robinson in 2011, connected members in the United States and abroad who were ready to travel to destinations beyond what is typically marketed to us and was looking for others outside our personal circle to share experiences, travel tips, destination inspiration, and most important, community for our next adventure. After returning home from living aboard in Italy in 2012, a Nomadness Trip to Brazil was posted, and I jumped at the chance to meet more members IRL and explore South America for the first time. We were a group of ten women flying in from different cities around the United States straight into Rio de Janeiro at the tail end of Carnival.

Coordinates: 14.2350° S, 51.9253° W
Capital: Brasília
Country/Continent: Brazil is on the east coast of South America, with the Caribbean Sea to the north and the Atlantic Ocean to the east. It's bordered by Uruguay to the south; Argentina, Paraguay, Bolivia, and Peru to the west; and Colombia and Venezuela to the northeast.
Population: 215.3 million
National Drink: Caipirinha
National Dish: Feijoada
Top Export: Iron ore, crude petroleum, soybeans
Official Languages: Portuguese
Independence Day: September 7, 1822
Independence from: Portugal

WINE PAIRING FOR THE PEOPLE

> ## Sip the Culture
> ### Cachaça and Caipirinhas
> During my first trip to Rio de Janeiro, I might as well have had an IV drip of caipirinhas. It's a simple drink—crushed ice, limes, sugar, and cachaça—that's everywhere, refreshing, and delicious, and it offers relief from the heat.
>
> Drinking all those caipirinhas led me to want to learn more about cachaça. It's made from sugarcane, like rum. The difference between the two is that rum is made from molasses, which is sugarcane juice that's been cooked, so that it thickens and caramelizes, taking on a more intense flavor that sometimes has a little edge of bitterness to it. Cachaça is made from fresh sugarcane juice that can have a little bit of a green, herbaceous character. The end result is a more terroir-focused flavor profile.
>
> Those differences carry over to the finished spirit. Unaged cachaça will be a little greener and sometimes a bit funky. Aged bottles will get more mellow and round, and they'll take on barrel characteristics like baking spice and toast, just like rum does.

Globally Carnival is known for its extravagant costumes, parades, and dance parties; however samba is the heartbeat of Rio Carnival, and escolars de samba (samba schools) are able to showcase their years' worth of training in this highly competitive showcase. This festival sees millions of visitors over this weeklong cultural extravaganza. I arrived just in time for the real party, celebrating with the winning samba school, Viradouroto, and the locals. This trip to Brazil was one of my favorite travel experiences, because of the bonds I formed with these women on the journey with me, spending time in the favelas jamming to the bass of Brazilian Funk, learning how to samba in heels in Ipanema, and sipping Caprinhas on Copacabana Beach with Bossa Nova in the background. I fell in love with Brazilian culture and immediately knew I would return.

Before I arrived, I had a mixture of impressions of the country thanks to the propaganda. First of all, I knew it was huge. The length of the country is about the same as the distance from New York City to Seattle. I also knew from my MBA studies that it was a BRIC country, projected to be one of the world's dominant suppliers of raw materials by 2020. I knew what I saw portrayed in the movie *City of God*. I was also aware that the 2014 World Cup would be hosted there, but that no matter where the World Cup was, soccer was a big deal here. I *thought*, based on the miles and miles of beaches, that it would be easy for me to find seafood to eat. I got that last part a little wrong, but I loved Brazil anyway and returned a few more times to explore more of this massive country.

Brazil is a large country with intense regional differences in culture, cuisine, and climate. Bustling cities, culturally rich coastal

The five-day festival coincides with the pre-Lent season ending on Ash Wednesday, generally around February or March, and was introduced by Portuguese colonizers in the nineteenth century. Samba was birthed from dances and music created by freed enslaved Africans who blended their traditions with Indigenous and European styles. It's believed that it was invented in today's Afro-Brazilian neighborhoods of Praça Onze and Cidade Nova.

areas, and naturally abundant rainforest are just a few of the vastly divergent lifestyles and terroir throughout the country. It's considered to have the highest population of people of African descent of any non-African country in the world.

On my next trip to Brazil, I was inspired to explore the Afro-Brazilian cultural heartland in the port city of Salvador in the northeast region of Bahia. The rhythm of the drum is the pulse that matches the eclectic smiles of its people, the vibrant colors, and the spiritual energy of the city. Though Salvador has a dark history as one of the hubs for the transatlantic slave trade, the joy I received when I arrived is a sign of the strength and resilience of the diasporic spirit. Officially a UNESCO City of Music, the drum is in the DNA of the African heritage of Salvador and is the legacy of African-Brazilian culture and the birthplace of music genres such as axé, bossa nova, samba, and tropicalism. The unique music is the soundtrack to the beach lifestyle, but its seafood-focused cuisine is the perfect pairing and a contrast to Brazil's beef production, which contributes to rodízio culture. Rodizo-style dining waiters bring meats on skewers to your table rotating different cuts throughout this all-you-can-eat experience at a traditional Brazilian steakhouse.

In a two-hour flight south, I went from the sunny festive beach vibes of Salvador to the bustling city living of São Paulo. It was a stark contrast, especially from the one marketed about Brazil, to fly into the gray skies filled with skyscrapers. As a New Yorker, I was familiar with this environment and welcomed the opportunity to explore this grand metropolis. Known as the Gotham City of South America, São Paulo holds

> **DRINK NOW: Cachaça Producers**
> - Avua Amburana
> - Yaguara Cachaça
> - Novo Fogo

the title of the largest populated city of the Americas, with 12.8 million in comparison to New York City, with 8.5 million documented inhabitants. I jumped right into exploring the street-art culture, making my visit to Beco do Batman (Batman Alley) in the Vila Madelena neighborhood one of my first stops. Batman Alley is an urban art gallery that originated in the 1980s with an image of Batman, and now has inspired a maze of colorful images that covers walls and surrounding streets created by different artists and in various styles. I continued my art appreciation by paying a visit to the Museum of Art of São Paulo in the heart of the city, where I saw pieces from Europe's Renaissance period in a permanent exhibit.

São Paulo checks the boxes for a great city, from museums to grand parks, but no city would be complete without an appetizing dining scene. One of my most memorable restaurant experiences was dinner at Figueira Rubaiyat. Located in the swanky Jardins district, this outdoor-indoor fine dining experience under a 150-year-old tree in the middle of the bustling city was an escape to the Amazon. The Iglesias family are considered pioneers in the farm-to-table movement in São Paulo, bringing their cattle, poultry, and produce to supply their restaurants as far back as 1957. Today they continue to work with farmers who supply quality products from land and sea. For a more local experience, I found myself in Mercado de Municipal adventuring through rare fruits that are special to the

Wine Grapes of Brazil

Red
Cabernet Sauvignon
Merlot
Pinot Noir

White
Chardonnay
Moscato Branco
Glera

Amazon—pitaya (dragonfruit), cupuaçu, maracuja do mato (green passion fruit), abiu, and seriguela, to name a few. Like any large city, São Paulo has attracted foreigners from near and far and is now famously known for being the largest Japanese settlement outside of Japan. If you plan a trip to Brazil do not forget to explore the neighborhood of Liberdade to dig further into Japanese-Brazilian culture (see page 193) and visit the Saturday Japanese market for a fusion of flavors, just like its vibrant city.

Brazil's Wine Regions

The Portuguese first arrived in Brazil with vines in the 1500s. However, it is said that the grape growing was unsuccessful due to a tropical storm off the coast of São Paulo. Later in the 1600s, the Jesuits brought Spanish vines and made sacramental wine in the Rio Grande do Sul region, which produces the majority of Brazilian wine today. In the 1700s, Azorean settlers brought with them vines from the Azores islands and Madeira as well as the knowledge of growing grapes in hot weather. Their production was minor; however, it did bring American hybrid varietals and Azorean native grapes, like Isabella, which has contributed to the long legacy of American vines and use of *Vitis labrusca* in Brazil. It is currently estimated that 80 percent of the vines are from American hybrids and native grapes. However, the Portuguese banned the production of wine in the 1780s, putting a halt to what could have been a fruitful future for Brazil's wine industry.

Wine making as we know it in Brazil today was established in the late nineteenth century. Once Brazil gained its independence from Portugal in 1822, there was an influx of Germans, French, and, most notably for wine development, Italians. In the 1870s, the Serra Gaúcha region, which was home to one of the largest Italian immigrant populations in Brazil, was incentivized to help develop southern Brazil, which is currently where the country's most premium wines are being produced. In 1973, Champagne producer Moët & Chandon saw great potential for sparkling wine in the high-altitude, subtropical southern areas of the country, so it started Chandon Brasil. It wasn't until the 1990s, though, that the Brazilian wine industry really began focusing on fine wine and exports, establishing Denominations of Origin (DOs). Here's a look at some of the country's more productive wine regions.

Vale do São Francisco: Brazil's northernmost and closest-to-the-equator wine region focuses mostly on reds Cabernet Sauvignon, Merlot, and Syrah. Because of its warm climate, growers can get multiple harvests in a year.

Serra Gaúcha: This mountainous region in the south is home to Chandon Brasil. This area gets a decent amount of rainfall, so winemakers are experimenting with hybrid grapes in the sparkling region.

LATIN AMERICA

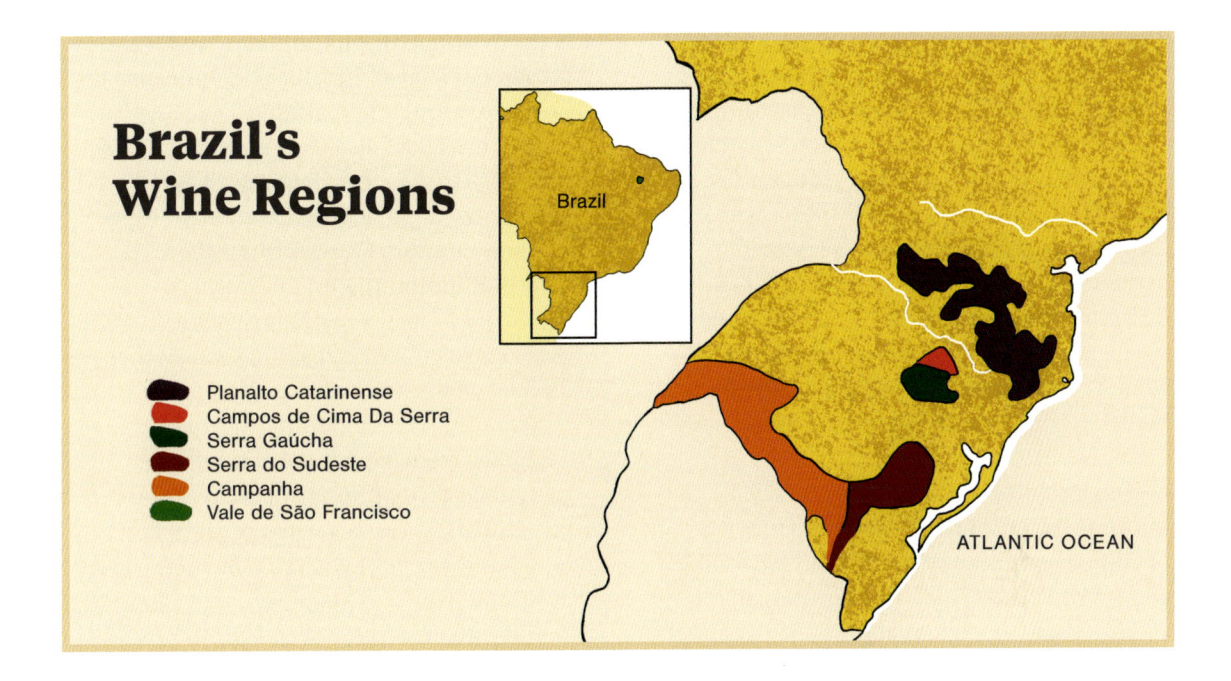

Brazil's Wine Regions

- Planalto Catarinense
- Campos de Cima Da Serra
- Serra Gaúcha
- Serra do Sudeste
- Campanha
- Vale de São Francisco

Planalto Catarinense: South of Serra Gaúcha, and drier, this region grows Pinot Noir and Sauvignon Blanc with finesse.

Campanha: On the border with Uruguay, this dry, hilly region is known for soft and fruity red wines with complexity.

Serra do Sudeste: The country's smallest and southernmost wine region borders Uruguay. Grapes here are sent to other regions to be made into wine. They include whites and reds.

Campos do Cima da Serra: This tiny, high-elevation region has been planting grapes typically used in Portugal's Vinho Verde.

The New Capital of Bubbly

As Brazil's wine-making scene keeps growing, one style is emerging as its signature: sparkling wine. I sell Brazilian sparkling wine in my store, The Communion Wine & Spirits, and they can range from crisp and refreshing in the south, where it's colder, to fruity and luscious in the north. Here is a breakdown of the most common ways to produce sparkling wine. The traditional method, established in Champagne, France, also known as the méthode champenoise, is used by many of Brazil's sparkling wine producers following the same intricate process. They produce fine bubbles that can compete with many sparkling wines in the market today for a fraction of the average price.

Traditional method/méthode champenoise: After wine is made, additional yeast and sugar (usually in the form of grape must) are added to the bottle, which gets a temporary crown cap, for a secondary fermentation that traps carbon dioxide bubbles in the bottle. These bottles are aged, and in that period of contact with the yeast, wines can take on a bready, brioche sort of a flavor.

After aging, the bottles go through a process called riddling. A special rack holds bottles at a 35-degree angle, and they're rotated or shaken periodically to move the yeast, now called lees, into the neck of the bottle. Finally, the yeast is removed, and the bottle is closed with a mushroom-shaped cork that can withstand the pressure of the carbon dioxide.

This method is also used in Spain for Cava, in South Africa for méthode cap classique, and in other regions of France for Cremant wines.

Tank method/Martinotti method/Charmat method: With this method, secondary fermentation happens in a pressurized tank. The sparkling wine is then drained off the lees and into the bottle.

Sparkling wines made this way have a brighter, fresher quality than a lot of traditional-method wines, because the tank gives them less contact with the yeast. Prosecco is probably the most popular tank-method wine as well as many Lambruscos.

Pét-nat/pétillant naturel/méthode ancestrale: This method is older than the traditional method. Fermentation is stopped while the wine still has active yeast and sugar that hasn't been fermented. It's transferred to bottles, which are capped with a crown cap, like a beer bottle, and then fermentation resumes. The carbon dioxide from fermentation becomes trapped in the bottle, forming bubbles.

Pét-nat tends to have less pressure in the bottle, so it's a softer bubble than the foamy mousse a traditional-method wine can have. This method is not limited to region, but it is often associated with natural wines.

DECODING THE LABEL

[Champagne label diagram with the following labels pointing to parts of an André Glouet Champagne label:]

- Quality Designation (Grande Réserve)
- "Champagne"
- Producer
- Wine Style (Brut)
- Subregion (Bouzy, France)
- Alcohol Content (12% Vol.)
- Volume (750ml)

Obviously, the French region of Champagne is seen as the historical home of sparkling wine, and its method for making them has come to be known in some regions as "traditional method." Only sparkling wines made in Champagne, using this method, can be labeled as Champagne (except for Korbel California Champagne, which was founded before the laws were in place around Champagne labeling and fought to keep its name). Champagne is one of the earliest wine regions to have international protection, which dates back to Treaty of Madrid in 1891 and the Treaty of Versailles in 1919. Though the Appellation d'Origine Contrôlée (AOC) was not put in place until the 1900s, it was important to protect the reputation and heritage of Champagne to uniquely identify this style of sparkling quality as other regions and countries started making traditional-method sparkling wines. When selecting Champagne here are some key identifiers you want to find on the label to help you make a selection of fine bubbles:

- **Produit de France** (with associated legal code) may seem obvious, but this and the actual use of the word "Champagne" are key identifiers you have the real thing.
- **AOC/AOP designation** (Appellation Champagne Contrôlée)
- **Méthode traditionnelle** is the required method but may not be listed
- **Grand Cru/Premier Cru** (optional) gives you an idea of the status level
- **Village or vineyard name**—knowing the designated areas and identifying them on the label can give you intel on the terroir and on which grape varietals are going to be more dominant.

+ PAIRED UP

For most dishes from anywhere in the world, there's a sparkling wine that will go well too. Brazil's no exception, but its cuisine is as varied as its terrain, made up of all the cultures within the country and influences from other countries that were colonized by Portugal. Here's a look at some classics and how to pair them.

FEIJOADA + ISABELLA, AZORES, PORTUGAL. Brazil's beloved pork and black bean stew has made its way around the Portuguese-speaking world. It can be made with offal and sometimes vegetables like tomato and cabbage, but the beans are the star. Try it with Isabella, preferably Isabella a Proibida, made in the Azores. The Isabella grape is a hybrid of *Vitis vinifera* and *Vitis Labrusca*, which makes red wines high in acidity, a perfect counterpart to a rich, earthy dish like this.

CHURRASCO + TANNAT, CANELONES, URUGUAY. Brazil's version of a variety of grilled meats and salads needs a big, smoky, chewy wine to match it note for note. Look next door for Uruguayan Tannat. Soft tannins work well with different cuts of meat, as do black fruit flavors such as blackberry, black cherry, and black plums.

MOQUECA + VERDEJO, RUEDA, SPAIN. Brazil's seafood and coconut stew—one of my favorite types of dish, no matter where I am in the world—has plenty of garlic, lime, and cilantro. The Spanish grape Verdejo brings more lime notes, but it's got a savory edge with fennel and grapefruit pith, to cut through the rich coconut broth.

BOLINHO DE BACALHAU + BRAZILIAN SPARKLING WINE. This cod fritter is quintessential Brazilian food. Fried food and bubbles are always good together, so it only makes sense to pair it with a dry Brazilian sparkling wine. Look for a blend of Chardonnay and Pinot Noir, like Cave Geisse Amadeu Brut.

ACARAJÉ + PINOT NOIR ROSÉ, PATAGONIA, ARGENTINA. A direct link to Nigerian akara, these black-eyed-pea fritters stuffed with shrimp and spicy paste are a popular street food. This bright, fresh rosé has the acidity you need to cleanse your palate when you're eating something fried. Its red fruit and berry notes will cool the dish's spice.

PÃO DE QUEIJO + CHARDONNAY, SANTA RITA HILLS, CALIFORNIA. A cheese bread that has gained popularity in the United States in recent years in part because it's gluten free, but it's also light, airy, and delicious. Pair it with an oaked Sta. Hills Chardonnay from California, like Pizzato Gran Reserva Legno Chardonnay or Californian-style Donnachadh Estate Chardonnay, and enjoy cheesy-buttery goodness.

LATIN AMERICA

VIERA COM VATAPÁ + ALBARIÑO,
RÍAS BAIXAS, SPAIN

Emme Ribeiro Collins has done it all. She's run her family's restaurant, done catering, worked as a private chef, held pop-ups, and even been the district chef for Seattle's public schools. She was born in Brazil but grew up in Seattle, where she's always worked to honor her Afro-Brazilian roots through food. You can see that in this dish's peanut and red palm oil sauce, vatapá, which also happens to be the name of a stew that's often made with shrimp. In this case, though, it's made with viera, which are scallops, adding a creamy luxuriousness.

Pair this dish with Albariño from Rías Baixas, Spain, or for a little extra body and creaminess, seek out the Portuguese version from the region of Monção e Melgaço. Both are known for mouthwatering acidity and a saline finish, with notes of green almond, lime, honeysuckle, and beeswax.

SERVES 8

2 tablespoons red palm oil

1 teaspoon minced ginger

1 teaspoon minced garlic

1 tablespoon finely chopped dried shrimp

8 super colossal (U10) scallops

Kosher salt and black pepper

Banana leaves cut into 8-inch squares

2 cups vatapá (recipe follows)

1. In a small sauté pan, heat palm oil over medium high heat. Add ginger, garlic and dried shrimp, and cook while stirring until fragrant, 1 to 2 minutes. Remove from heat and let cool.
2. Season scallops with salt and pepper in a shallow dish. Add dried shrimp mixture and mix until well incorporated.
3. Lay the banana leaves out and place ¼ cup of the vatapá in the center of each leaf. Top it off with a scallop.
4. Fold the sides of the leaves over the scallop and then tuck under the top and bottom to make a packet.
5. Place the banana leaf packets into a steamer basket.
6. In a medium saucepan over high heat, add 2 cups water; when it boils, reduce the heat to a simmer, place the steamer basket into the pan, and cover. Cook for 3 to 5 minutes, until scallops are cooked through.

(recipe continues on next page)

VATAPÁ–RED PALM OIL PEANUT SAUCE

½ onion, chopped
1¼ cup shelled, dry-roasted, salted peanuts
2-inch piece of ginger, peeled and chopped
One 13.5-ounce can unsweetened coconut milk
3 tablespoons palm oil

1. Place onion, peanuts, ginger and coconut milk in a blender and blend until mixture is pureed and smooth.
2. Place palm oil in a medium sauce pot and cook over medium heat for about 30 seconds. Add the pureed blend and let simmer, stirring occasionally until sauce thickens, about 5 to 10 minutes.
3. Strain sauce through fine-mesh strainer. Keep warm until ready to serve.

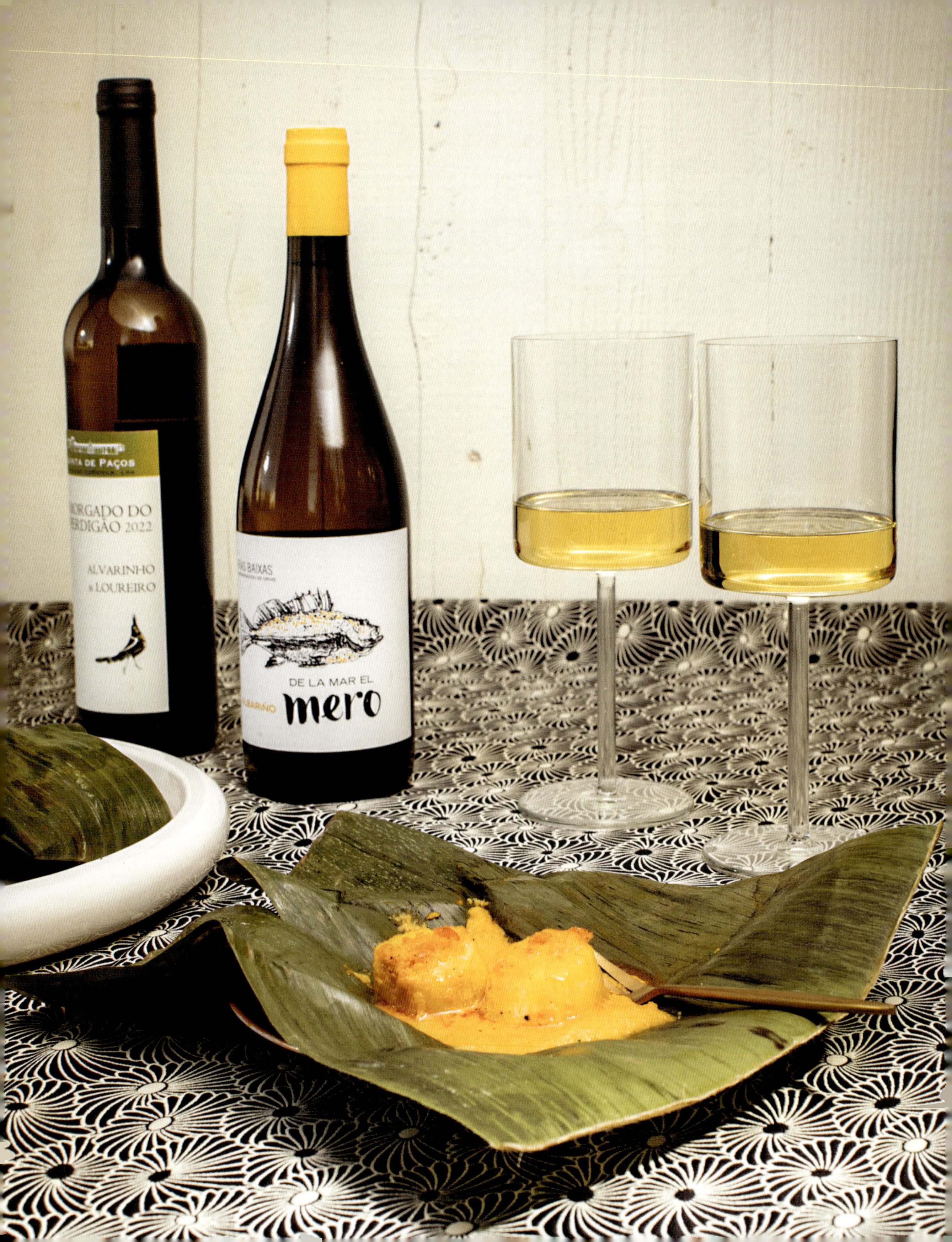
2022
ALVARINHO
& LOUREIRO
DE LA MAR EL
mero

THE WINE LIST
Latin America

MEXICO

Tacos al Pastor + Primitivo, PUGLIA, ITALY
Carne Asada Tacos + Malbec, CAHORS, FRANCE
Birria Tacos + Syrah, ELQUI VALLEY, CHILE
De Canasta/al Vapor Tacos + Grenache, BAROSSA VALLEY, AUSTRALIA
Pescado Tacos + Verdejo, RUEDA, SPAIN
Chilaquiles + Chenin Blanc Pét-Nat, VALLE DE GUADALUPE, MEXICO
Tamales + Vermentino, SARDINIA, ITALY
Quesadillas + Chardonnay, MARGARET RIVER, AUSTRALIA
Elote + Cava Rosé, PENEDÈS, SPAIN
Mole Poblano + Nero d'Avola, VALLE DE GUADALUPE, MEXICO
Pollo en Barbacoa + Bobal, REQUENA-UTIEL, SPAIN
Veracruz-Style Snapper + Rosé, BAJA CALIFORNIA, MEXICO

▼

CHILE

Machas a la Parmesana + Torontel, ITATA VALLEY, CHILE
Plateada + Malbec, MAULE VALLEY, CHILE
Charquicán + Chardonnay, ACONCAGUA, CHILE
Paila Marina + Sauvignon Blanc, CASABLANCA, CHILE
Jalea + Sparkling Chardonnay, CASABLANCA, CHILE
Complete Hot Dog + País, ITATA VALLEY, CHILE
Lomo Saltado + Cabernet Sauvignon, MAIPO VALLEY, CHILE
Aji de Gallina + Semillon, COLCHAGUA VALLEY, CHILE
Chilean Ceviche + Sauvignon Blanc, LIMARÍ VALLEY, CHILE
Chilean Chacarero Sandwich + Carménère, CACHAPOAL VALLEY, CHILE

▼

ARGENTINA

Empanadas + Bonarda, CALCHAQUÍ VALLEY, ARGENTINA
Asado + Malbec, SAN JUAN, ARGENTINA
Choripán Chorizo Sandwich + Criolla Grande, MENDOZA, ARGENTINA
Provoleta + Torrontés, SALTA, ARGENTINA
Fugazza + Chardonnay, MENDOZA, ARGENTINA
Alfajores + Cream Sherry, JEREZ, SPAIN

▼

BRAZIL

Feijoada + Isabella, AZORES, PORTUGAL
Churrasco + Tannat, CANELONES, URUGUAY
Moqueca + Verdejo, RUEDA, SPAIN
Bolinho de Bacalhau + Brazilian Sparkling Wine
Acarajé + Pinot Noir Rosé, PATAGONIA, ARGENTINA
Pão de Queijo + Chardonnay, SANTA RITA HILLS, CALIFORNIA
Viera com Vatapá + Albariño, RÍAS BAIXAS, SPAIN

▼

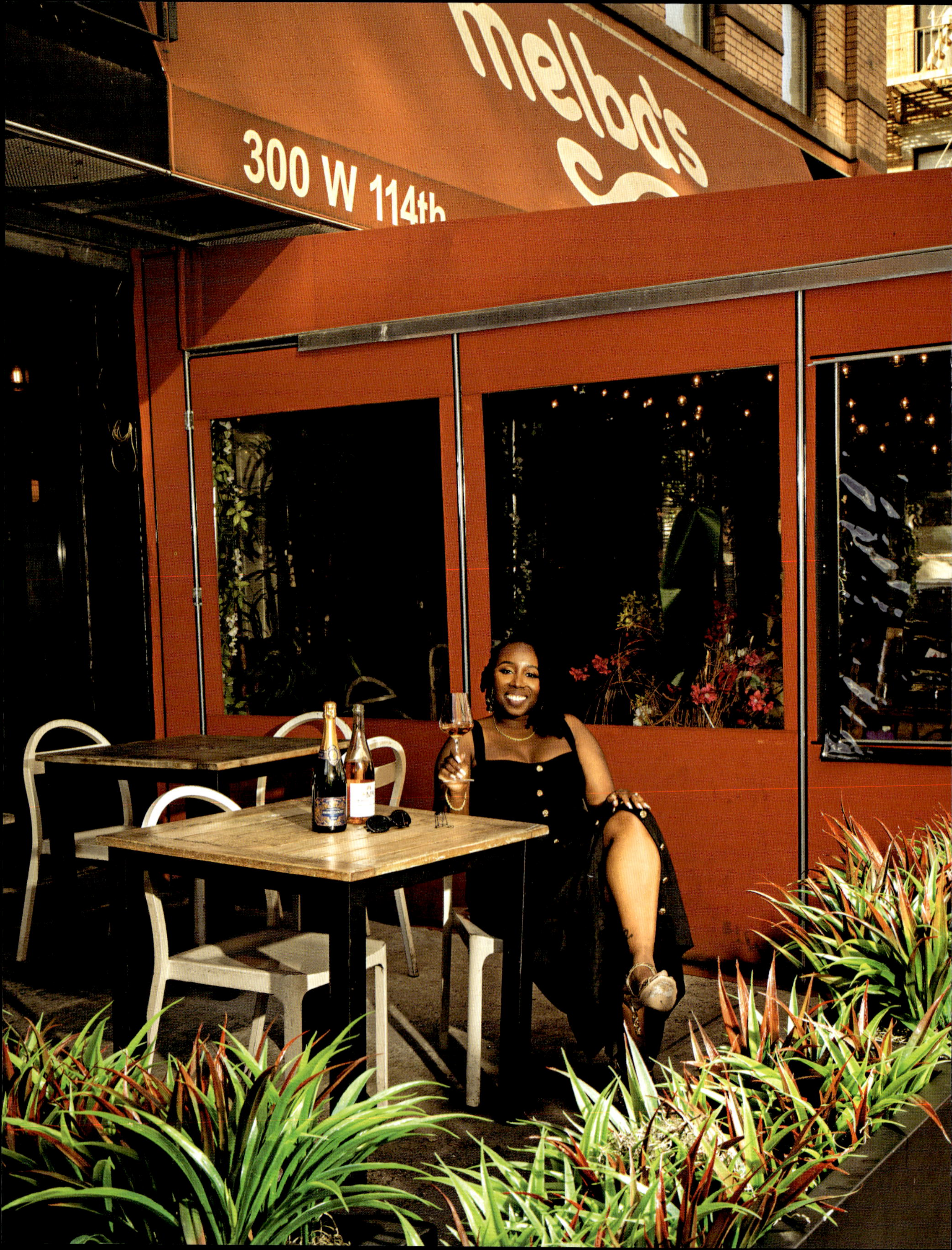
melba's
300 W 114th

United States of America

Soul Food	142
Lowcountry	153
Barbecue	159
Creole	169

United States of America

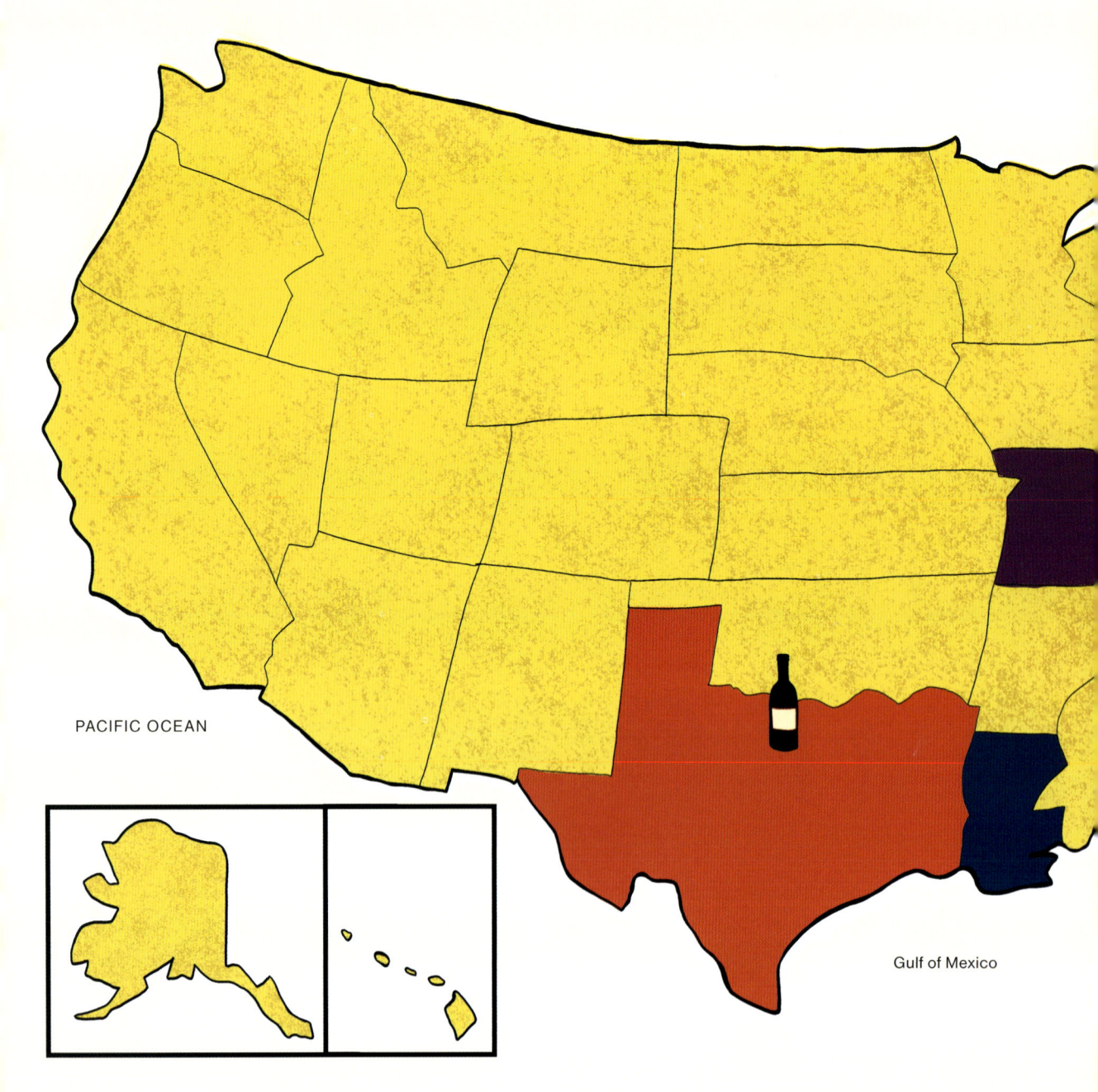

PACIFIC OCEAN

Gulf of Mexico

ATLANTIC OCEAN

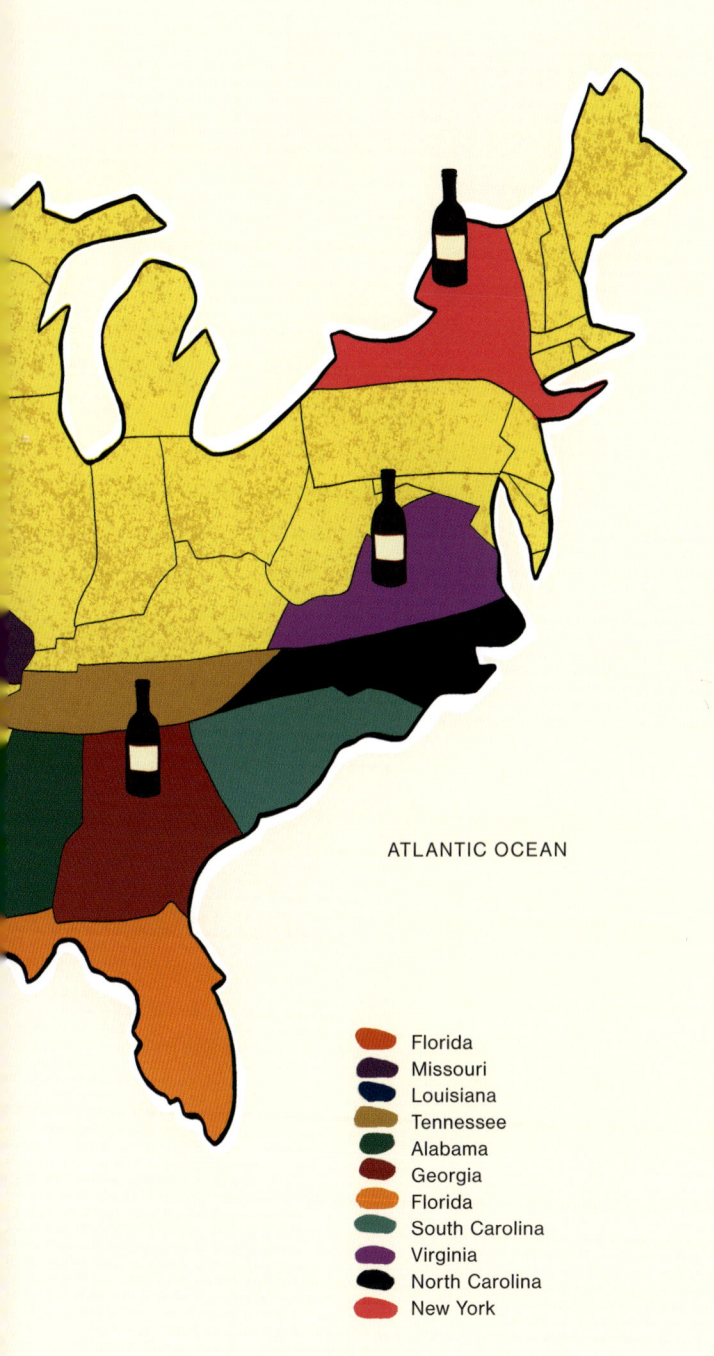

- Florida
- Missouri
- Louisiana
- Tennessee
- Alabama
- Georgia
- Florida
- South Carolina
- Virginia
- North Carolina
- New York

This chapter is a little bit different from the others, because it's not organized by country. The United States has some of the best African diasporic food in the world, in my opinion. These foodways originated in Southern states like the Carolinas, Georgia, Florida, Louisiana, and Alabama, and they spread and developed new dimensions in Tennessee and Texas. I thought this would be a good opportunity to dive into some of the differences among various types of Black American cuisines.

"Soul food" gets thrown around a lot as an all-encompassing term, and sometimes it's used as a synonym for Southern food, but I believe soul food as something that's more specific and bigger than Southern food. That's because the cuisines we're going to get into in this section have a lot in common with each other. One other thing they have in common is that these dishes may have been deemed unworthy of wine pairings because they are viewed as simple or even peasant food, or traditionally wine may not havebeen the beverage enjoyed with these dishes as much as the more accessible beer. There's nothing wrong with that, but I hope this chapter helps you to consider other options to give these flavorful, historic cuisines the pairing they deserve.

WINE PAIRING FOR THE PEOPLE

Soul Food

As I've said, "soul food" has become a catch-all term for all food that's Southern or Black, but it means something a little bit more specific. Adrian Miller, aka the Soul Food Scholar, defines it as the food of landlocked areas of the Deep South, in Alabama, Mississippi, and Georgia, that was transported north during the Great Migration. He calls soul food a subcategory of Southern food—the most flavorful and celebratory dishes.

Other people besides myself and Miller have broader definitions that include elements of Creole and Lowcountry food, and even barbecue. Most people agree: Soul food was born in what Miller calls the Black Belt or Cotton Belt of inland Alabama, Mississippi, and Georgia. It was created by enslaved people from West Africa combining ingredients and techniques they brought with them and dishes and ingredients they were using in the Southern American kitchens of the people who enslaved them. You can also see the influence of Indigenous people in the use of cornmeal, for dishes like cornbread. There's an element of using what was available, like ham hocks to flavor pots of greens, or less desirable cuts of meat, like chicken wings to make fried chicken, pigs' feet, and intestines to make chitterlings.

The name "soul food" came into wide use in the 1960s. In 1962, poet Amiri Baraka published an essay called "Soul Food," in response to an article that claimed that Black people don't have a cuisine of their own. That same year, Sylvia's

Restaurant opened in Harlem. Sylvia Woods became known as "the Queen of Soul Food." The name itself was probably born out of the Black Power movement happening at the time, led by groups like the Black Panthers. The word "soul" was shorthand for Black nationalism. Soul music by artists like James Brown and Nina Simone told stories of Black culture and pride. People were calling each other soul brother and soul sister. And so it made sense that their cuisine that tells the story of Black people would also be called soul food, which was another expression of their artistry.

So what actually is soul food? What are the dishes that make up this cuisine? It's the savory okra that came from West Africa and the bitter collard greens that Black people learned to transform to smoky and earthy for the white people who were already growing them. It's the first crunch when you bite into perfectly crisped fried chicken and fried catfish. It's knowing the perfect baking temperature for sweet potatoes that were reminiscent of African yams to make candied yams. And knowing how to preserve the bits of pork—cuts that were "low on the hog"—needed to season it all. It's sweet delicacies like pound cake, sweet potato pie, and red velvet cake that made use of ingenuity and the ingredients that enslaved people could get their hands on. The reasoning behind the name is that this is food made with love, heart, and soul. It's a cuisine that used scraps and what could be grown in small kitchen gardens that was so iconic and delicious that it became a staple of American cooking.

My parents are New Yorkers whose families were part of the Great Migration. My maternal grandmother, Lorraine, was from Lawrenceville, Virginia, and my paternal grandmother, Fannie, from Jacksonville, Florida, and born in Savannah, Georgia. Along with their hope for a better life, their recipes came with them to Harlem, New York City.

To earn some extra cash, my maternal great-grandmother, Nannie, was famous in her apartment complex on 144th Street for selling hot plates on Saturday night and inspired my mother's Sunday dinners when I was growing up. Nannie's signature menu included red rice, fried chicken, collard greens, and potato salad. For a quicker meal, some neighbors opted for the fried leg and thigh chicken sandwich. My paternal great-grandmother, Lucille, was a domestic worker for a wealthy family on Long Island. My father gives her credit for teaching him how to cook, and our family's famous peach cobbler recipe derives from her.

Rarely did we dine out for soul food, as it was considered just typical Sunday dinner in my house. When I was growing up, my mother worked three jobs to keep us afloat, and she found it hard to keep up with Sunday dinner, so eventually we started ordering from neighborhood churches to make sure we still received our Southern classics and comfort food. With my mother serving on the Prayer Night Usher Board for Abyssinian Baptist Church and my aunt Pat on the Meet & Greet committee famous for her mini sweet potatoes, which she sold at the church, my brother, Chu, and I were in the perfect position to access the kitchen team. Salivating during the sermons as children kept us alert enough in church to be first in line for our go-to order of chicken livers with sauteed onions, grits, salmon cakes, and cheesy scrambled eggs after service. And for dinner, "smothered turkey wings, collard greens, and candied yams" was my regular order from the church closer to our apartment on Eighth Avenue, the United House of Prayer.

No Pork on My Fork

Harlem became a reflection of Malcolm X's influence. Malcolm X referred to some soul food dishes as "slave food," and the African American community reclaimed our freedom through our diets. When enslaved, Black people were forced to eat scrap foods, such as chitterlings, but we now have the choice to reject pork and choose healthier diets. Because of these beliefs, many African Americans born in the Northern states have completely removed pork from their diet or, as in my case, have never eaten it at all. My father was introduced to the Nation of Islam and the teachings of the Honorable Elijah Muhammad while incarcerated. Before I was born, he committed to a new life of intellectual awakening, which introduced him to the Muslim dietary standards called halal. Permissible foods include most seafood, uncontaminated plant-based foods, and meat and poultry from animals slaughtered according to specific guidelines called zabihah. This diet prohibits pork and its byproducts, alcohol, animals that died naturally, and blood. Though my father did not convert to Islam, my maternal uncle Sherman and paternal aunt Linda eventually did. It is now a cultural diet tenet I find as a connection among African Americans who are descendants of the Great Migration, regardless of our religion.

The search for alternative and healthier options birthed the bean pie into the Black Muslim community to substitute for the commonly high-in-sugar, sweet desserts. Beans were considered to be blessed according to Muhammad and were used as the filling to provide protein, fiber, vitamins, and minerals, making bean pies a more nutritious dessert. My mother leaves the baking to Muhammad Mosque No. 7, the local mosque in our neighborhood, to get her favorite dessert and support their fundraising efforts for community initiatives.

Harlem born and bred, my parents were raised in a post–Harlem Renaissance era but still reaped the benefits of this thriving period for African American culture. I can only imagine them as a young couple hustling through the night scene of Harlem, enjoying live music at 22 West Lounge and artisanal cocktails at Perks Bar, not before eating at one of Harlemites' favorite soul food spots, Copeland's, for mac and cheese, smothered chicken, fried catfish, and collard greens.

One Harlem restaurant that made a lasting impact on soul food was Wells Restaurant, also known as Wells Supper Club. Opened in 1938 and closed in the 1980s, it was one of my parents' favorite soul food restaurants, known for serving the late-night dining crowd after enjoying or working the popular jazz clubs. Everyone from Billie Holiday to Nat King Cole frequently dined there, arriving late at night or early in the morning for Copeland's signature dish, fried chicken and waffles. The restaurant popularized this unusual dinner and breakfast combo. Wells became the after-party social spot servicing hungry musicians until two in the morning and birthing a new soul food staple. Today Melba's Restaurant is continuing the Harlem legacy of soul food and a lively social scene, and we are honored to include her legendary fried chicken and waffles recipe (page 147).

UNITED STATES OF AMERICA

✚ PAIRED UP

When we're talking about soul food, it's usually a meal for a gathering with several main and side dishes, so I've paired wine to pour with typical menus for specific occasions, rather than for singular dishes.

BREAKFAST/BRUNCH
Salmon croquettes
Corn fritters
Chicken & waffles
Pancakes
Grits
Bacon

Sparkling wine is a great option, as many of the main dishes here are breaded, and I took into consideration a complementary pairing between the bread notes. Champagne and sparkling wines using the Champagne method undergo a second fermentation and a process called yeast autolysis, which contributes the flavor of biscuit, brioche, and toasty notes. Mimosas and Bellinis are popular options, however a better pairing would be something bright and playful. An extra-dry Prosecco from Valdobbiadene, made from the Glera grape, using the Charmat method (page 130) will add brunch-friendly notes of melon and grapefruit, plus some nutty pistachio notes and white blossom aromas.

There are good still wine options, but those usually take a back seat to sparkling wine and unlimited mimosas. Aromatic white wines that have pronounced ripe fruity and sweet floral notes—such as Pinot Bianco from the Alto Adige region of Italy, Moscato d'Asti, and off-dry Gewürztraminer from Alsace, France—offer a range of sweetness levels for you to explore.

THE COOKOUT
Corn on the cob
Potato salad
Macaroni salad
Beef skewers
Deviled eggs
Grilled chicken wings
Fish and chips
Fruit salad

Cookouts are a celebration of summer, especially during notable holidays such as Memorial Day, Juneteenth, and Labor Day. Though the menu may be similar in many households, the seasonings and marinades set each cookout apart. Regardless of if someone adds raisins to the potato salad or not, these are the wines I would suggest that you bring to the cookout:

Lambrusco di Sorbara, from the Emilia-Romagna region of Italy, is a refreshing red sparkling wine. A blend of eight grapes, it comes in various sweetness levels. Lambrusco has become my secret weapon, because it pairs with everything from burgers to ribs straight off the grill on a sunny day. Red and blue berries and floral notes are complemented by the vibrant acidity, which make it the perfect match for the variety of dishes you will enjoy at the cookout.

If you can, get your hands on one, wine made from Concord, an American native grape that's part of the *Vitis labrusca* species, is making a huge comeback in New York's Finger Lakes

(continues on next page)

region. Look for bottles from some low-intervention wine producers such as Wild Arc Farm. Often described as grapey, it is very reminiscent of grape-soda flavor with notes of tart black cherry, violets, and spice.

A refreshing white wine option to consider is dry Welschriesling from either Austria or Germany, and if you can find this same variety from Croatia, where it's known as Graševina, you will note its bright acidity and typically light body with notes of lime, pear, and elderflower.

SUNDAY/HOLIDAY DINNER

Smothered chicken
Turkey wings
Pineapple ham
Macaroni and cheese
Braised collard greens
Candied yams
Black-eyed peas

Sunday family dinner, when I was growing up, meant a selection of protein, starch, and vegetables. On holidays at my grandmother Fannie's house, it was the Super Bowl of Sunday dinners. All the dishes were displayed at once for a feast of flavors. I like a red wine to stand up to all these rich foods. Depending on how much you're eating and how much of what you're eating is meat, you may want a light- to medium-bodied wine, like Burgundian Pinot Noir or Zweigelt. For something in the medium- to full-bodied range, try Touriga Nacional or Châteauneuf-du-Pape.

DESSERTS

SWEET POTATO PIE + VIN SANTO DEL CHIANTI CLASSICO, TUSCANY, ITALY. Sweet potato is cooked, mashed up, and mixed into a custard with baking spices like cinnamon and nutmeg. Some say this is what pumpkin pie wishes it could be. Vin Santo del Chianti Classico, a sweet wine made from grapes that are left on the vine until they wither, also has some of those baking-spice notes, plus bright acidity to cut the pie's sweetness.

7UP BUNDT CAKE + ASTI SPUMANTE, PIEDMONT, ITALY. Moist lemon-lime cake should be just the right amount of sweetness, and so is the sparkling version of Moscato d'Asti, Asti Spumante. The wine- and soda-based cake will add fresh acidity, and its floral notes will add complexity to the cake's sweet tang.

BEAN PIE + LATE-BOTTLED VINTAGE PORT, DOURO VALLEY, PORTUGAL. Bean pie is what it sounds like. Beans (usually canned navy beans) are mashed up and made into a sweet custard that may also have baking spices and vanilla. Even though the beans, on their own, don't have a whole lot of flavor, they give the custard a rich texture and slightly earthy note. Portugal's fortified wine only gets vintage designation in certain years. A late-bottled vintage is aged longer, which gives it smooth toffee notes.

UNITED STATES OF AMERICA

MELBA'S SIGNATURE CHICKEN AND EGGNOG WAFFLES + VINTAGE CHAMPAGNE BLANC DE NOIRS, BOUZY, FRANCE

Representing the new generation of classic Harlem soul food restaurants, Chef Melba Wilson opened Melba's in 2005. That was after she worked at other New York City institutions like Sylvia's and Windows on the World. Melba's is all about comfort, but she puts a little glitz on it, like the homemade eggnog in her waffles and the strawberry butter.

Pair this dish with a vintage Champagne. Sparkling wine is always a good choice with fried chicken. Its bubbles and acidity cleanse the palate while you're eating. To add a hint of fruit flavor, seek out a blanc de noirs, made from Pinot Noir, or a rosé, which gets added body from skin contact. Vintage Champagne uses all grapes from a single year's harvest, instead of a blend, and requires a minimum of three years aging. This additional time spent on its lees (see page 130 for more about how sparkling wine is made) gives this wine complex flavors of brioche and baked fruit, which pair perfectly with the eggnog flavor in the waffles and berry topping.

1. In a large bowl, combine the flour, baking powder, cinnamon, and nutmeg. In another bowl, whisk together the eggnog, egg yolks, and melted butter. Stir the wet ingredients into the dry ingredients just until combined, with no lumps, being careful not to overmix.
2. In a clean bowl, whisk the egg whites until almost stiff, and fold them into the batter. The batter should be a pourable consistency at this point. If it's too stiff to pour evenly into the waffle iron, fold in milk to thin it out. (This will depend on the consistency of your eggnog.)
3. Heat a waffle iron and spray it with nonstick cooking spray. Ladle ¼ cup of the batter into the middle of the hot iron and close the lid. Cook for 3 to 4 minutes, until cooked through and golden brown. Repeat with the remaining batter, respraying the waffle iron before each addition.
4. Serve with the strawberry butter, if desired.

SERVES 4

Eggnog Waffles

2 cups all-purpose flour, sifted

2 teaspoons baking powder

Pinch of ground cinnamon

Pinch of ground nutmeg

1½ to 2 cups eggnog, homemade (recipe follows) or store bought

2 large eggs, separated

4 tablespoons unsalted butter, melted

Whole milk, as needed

Nonstick cooking spray, for the waffle iron

Strawberry butter (recipe follows), optional

(recipe continues on page 149)

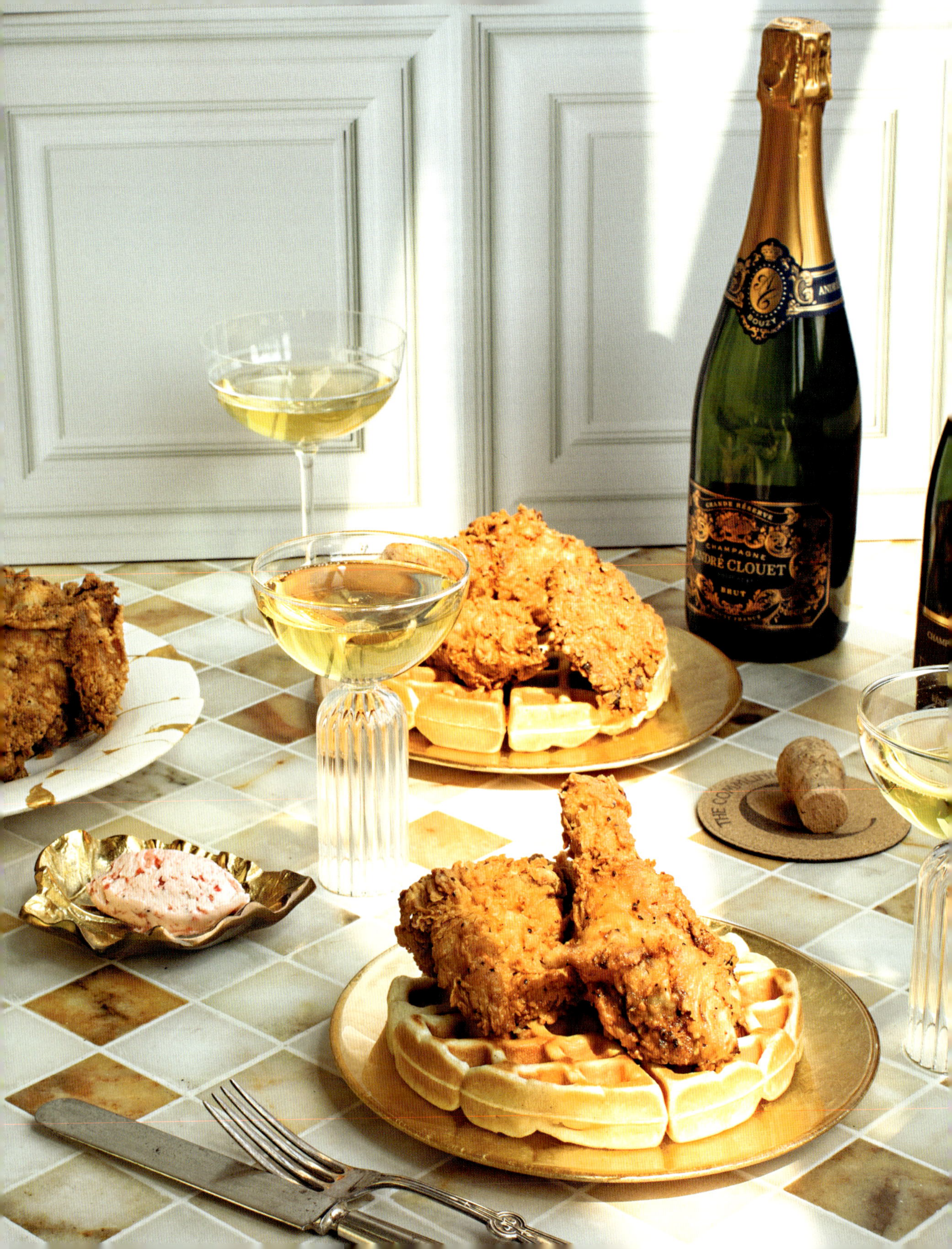
BOUZY
GRANDE RÉSERVE
CHAMPAGNE
ANDRÉ CLOUET
BRUT

EGGNOG

1½ cups whole milk
½ cup heavy cream
1 tablespoon pure vanilla extract
½ teaspoon ground cinnamon
Pinch of ground nutmeg
4 large eggs, separated, plus 2 yolks
¾ cup sugar
2 ounces rum, bourbon, or alcohol of your choice (optional)

1. Combine the milk and cream in a small pot over medium-low heat and bring to a slow boil. Whisk in the vanilla, cinnamon, and nutmeg.
2. Place the 6 egg yolks in a large heat-proof mixing bowl. Slow ladle half the milk and cream mixture into the yolks, whisking vigorously. Pour the mixture back into the pot with the rest of the milk and cream, raise the heat to high, and continue whisking until the mixture thickens to the consistency of a loose pudding.
3. Transfer the mixture back to the bowl, cover with plastic wrap, and refrigerate to chill.
4. While the yolk mixture is chilling, place the 4 egg whites in the bowl of an electric mixer. Using a whisk attachment, mix on high until they begin to thicken. Continue beating as you gradually add the sugar; the whites will continue to stiffen. Remove the yolk mixture from the fridge, hand whisk into the beaten whites, and stir in the rum or bourbon, if you like.

STRAWBERRY BUTTER

1 cup unsalted butter, slightly softened
4 ounces strawberries, hulled and sliced (about ½ cup)
A few drops of grenadine syrup
Salt, to taste

1. Put the butter in a food processor fitted with a metal blade and blend until smooth.
2. Add the strawberries and grenadine and pulse until there are just a few small pieces of berry visible.
3. Season to taste with salt.
4. Serve at once with your waffles or refrigerate until needed, up to 5 days.

(recipe continues on next page)

FRIED CHICKEN

One 3-pound chicken, cut into 8 pieces
2 teaspoons kosher salt; more to taste
1 teaspoon fresh-ground black pepper
1 teaspoon sweet Spanish paprika
1 teaspoon poultry seasoning
1 teaspoon garlic powder
1 tablespoon brown mustard
2 cups buttermilk
Peanut or vegetable oil, for frying
3 cups all-purpose flour
2 teaspoons Goya Sazonador seasoning

1. Put the chicken pieces in a bowl. Sprinkle with the salt, pepper, paprika, poultry seasoning, and garlic powder. Add the mustard and, using your hands (clean, of course), rub all the seasonings into the meat. Pour in the buttermilk, cover with plastic wrap, and marinate in the refrigerator for at least 2 hours.
2. When ready to cook, pour 3 inches of oil into a deep, heavy-bottomed skillet (preferably cast iron) and heat to 325°F over medium heat.
3. While the oil is heating, combine the flour and Sazonador seasoning in a large brown paper bag. Add a few pieces of chicken at a time to the seasoned flour and shake the bag like you really mean it.
4. Fry the chicken in batches until it is beautifully brown and crispy on one side, about 15 minutes. Then turn and cook on the other side until the chicken registers 160°F on an instant-read meat thermometer, about another 15 minutes.
5. As the pieces are done, transfer them to paper towels to drain. Season to taste with salt.
6. Serve with waffles and strawberry butter, if you like.

UNITED STATES OF AMERICA

ROASTED PINEAPPLE CORNMEAL CAKE + SAUTERNES, BORDEAUX, FRANCE

Chef Adrienne Cheatham has worked with Chefs Eric Ripert and Marcus Samuelsson, some of New York's best, and she channeled that experience into *Sunday's Best*, her first cookbook. She's competed on *Top Chef*, where she says that judges encouraged her to stop overthinking things and do what she does best. That combines soul food influences from her Chicago upbringing and current home in Harlem with her own spin, like this dessert cake that adds a bit of tropical flavor through pineapple and a rummy caramel that forms in the pan.

Bordeaux's signature dessert wine is sweet, made from Sémillon, Sauvignon Blanc, and Muscadelle. It has beautiful apricot and coconut notes that will really highlight the cake's caramelized pineapple.

SERVES 12 TO 16

- 6 cups fresh pineapple chunks (from 1 large, ripe pineapple)
- ¼ cup dark rum
- 1½ cups all-purpose flour
- ½ cup fine yellow cornmeal
- ¾ cup granulated sugar
- 1 tablespoon baking powder
- ½ teaspoon kosher salt
- Zest of ½ orange
- ½ cup coconut oil, melted
- 1 cup whole milk, coconut milk, or nondairy creamer
- 2 large eggs
- 1 teaspoon pure vanilla extract
- ½ cup (1 stick) unsalted butter
- ½ cup packed dark brown sugar

1. Heat the oven to 425°F.
2. Spread the pineapple in a single layer on a baking sheet. Roast until the edges begin to turn dark brown, 10 to 15 minutes. Stir the pineapple and continue roasting until the juices in the pan have started to brown. Remove the baking sheet from the oven and pour the rum around, stirring to loosen the caramelized juices. Let cool. Reduce the oven temperature to 350°F.
3. In a large bowl, combine the flour, cornmeal, granulated sugar, baking powder, salt, and orange zest. In a separate medium bowl, whisk together the coconut oil, milk, eggs, and vanilla. Stirring with a wooden spoon, gradually pour the liquid mixture into the dry ingredients and continue stirring until the batter is smooth.
4. Scrape the roasted pineapple and all the liquid into a food processor, and pulse until the pineapple is fine-chopped.
5. Line a baking sheet with parchment or aluminum foil.
6. Heat a 10-inch cast-iron skillet over medium heat, and add the butter and brown sugar. Cook, stirring occasionally, until the sugar is bubbling and slightly darkened, about 5 minutes. Remove the pan from the heat, and let it cool for a couple of minutes.

(recipe continues on next page)

7. Carefully spoon the pineapple over the butter-sugar mixture, and use a spatula to spread it into an even layer almost to the edges of the pan. Pour the cake batter over the pineapple, and spread it into an even layer. Place the skillet on the prepared baking sheet, and transfer it to the oven.
8. Bake until a cake tester or toothpick inserted into the center comes out clean, about 45 minutes. Place the skillet on a rack or cool gas burner grate, and let it cool for 10 minutes.
9. Once the skillet is cool enough to handle, place a large serving plate upside down over the skillet, and flip the skillet, turning the cake onto the plate. Spoon any pineapple remaining in the pan over the cake. Let it cool for a few more minutes, and then serve warm.

Used with permission from *Sunday Best: Cooking Up the Weekend Spirit Every Day* by Adrienne Cheatham with Sarah Zorn (Clarkson Potter, April 2022).

UNITED STATES OF AMERICA

Lowcountry

Some people will argue that the Lowcountry is only South Carolina, in the region sandwiched between the Savannah River and the Atlantic Ocean. However, geographically speaking, the region stretches from just north of Charleston, South Carolina, passing through Savannah, Georgia, down to Jacksonville, Florida. This area is dense with history and culture that make it a unique region in the South. Rice cultivation was the leading factor in wealth generation in the Lowcountry due to its ideal growing conditions and accessibility to trading in the port cities of Charleston and Savannah. Slave traders specifically looked for West African people with expertise in growing rice and trafficked them to South Carolina and Georgia for production. Many of those people migrated to the Sea Islands, Edisto, James, and Johns Island, where they have protected their foodways, dialects, and Geechee and Gullah traditions. Their legacy has spread along the Atlantic to North Carolina and northern Florida.

My paternal grandmother, Fannie, was born in Savannah, lived in Jacksonville, Florida, and migrated to Harlem in the late 1940s, making my father her first child of five at the time to be born in New York. Later, she would birth three more children there, for a total of eight. When I was growing up there were not many stories shared about my family's lifestyle in the Lowcountry, however, through my work in wine, I was able to establish my connection. One of the most memorable

Where to Drink in Charleston

Wine

Graft Wine Shop
Bar Rollins
The Tippling House
Wine & Company
Three Sirens (North Charleston)

Cocktails

The Gin Joint
Last Saint
Citrus Club
Little Palm
Bourbon N' Bubbles

experiences was when I passed the Certified Sommelier exam for the Court of Master of Sommeliers in Charleston and celebrated with an impromptu road trip after the exam to Hilton Head and Savannah with my mother. More recently I established a deeper admiration for the region when I took on the role of head of beverage for the Charleston Wine + Food Festival, which gave me the opportunity to become involved with that city's dynamic food and beverage scene. I learned a lot about Lowcountry culinary history while working with the community. Monthly visits over two years included meeting with locals and natives who opened their hearts over a glass of wine or two. I got to work with some of the leading chefs, sommeliers, brewers, and mixologists not just in the South but in the country. I was able to feel the magic of the people and of Charleston's iconic culinary scene.

The Lowcountry cuisine is serious about its seafood and Carolina Gold rice. Staples such as okra and tomatoes are also important here. It's fresh food, more likely to be grilled than fried, and it takes advantage of the farming knowledge from the West African ancestors. Of course, it has its ties to soul food, Creole cooking, and even barbecue, but it carries the "merroir" of salt air, taking in the influence of the sea.

The Lowcountry means "low" in terms of altitude, but its name refers to the fact that it's below the fall line, where elevated hard rock ground meets a soft, sandy coastal plain. A good portion of the Lowcountry is salt marsh or winding river, making it just as easy to get oysters, crab, and shrimp as it is to grow fruits and vegetables. This sort of aquatic ecosystem is fragile in an era when hurricanes and flooding are more extreme and less predictable than they used to be. And waterfront real estate is valuable. It's a struggle to preserve this land, but the people whose families have lived here for generations are committed to it. For them, it's not just land but their culture and their heritage.

UNITED STATES OF AMERICA

+ PAIRED UP

SHRIMP AND GRITS + ROSÉ, PROVENCE, FRANCE. Shrimp is served in a gravy flavored with bell peppers, hot peppers, garlic, and onions. Some recipes use tomato paste, while others don't. Some also add bacon, sausage, or even heavy cream. This is all served over creamy grits. Shrimp and grits can be breakfast, brunch, lunch, or dinner. A dry rosé from Provence is just as versatile. In addition to its palate-refreshing acidity, it will add a dried-herb note that really enhances the meal.

BRUNSWICK STEW + SANGIOVESE, ADELAIDE HILLS, AUSTRALIA. A tomato-based stew made with beans and game meat, Brunswick stew is smoky and hearty. A red with good acidity is a good call. Sangiovese, an Italian grape, has those qualities plus an herbaceousness that always goes well with tomato-based dishes. Bottles from Southern Australia can also take on a meaty, gamy flavor that's perfect here.

SHE-CRAB SOUP + ARNEIS, PIEDMONT, ITALY. This dish, a creamy crab bisque, historically would have been made with crab carrying roe, but now catch regulations discourage that. Some cooks will still add roe, as well as sherry and shallots. With its creamy texture and delicate flavors, it does best with something aromatic and a little bit mouthcoating, like Italian Arneis, a medium-body, aromatic wine with peach, yellow apple, honeysuckle, and nutmeg notes.

FROGMORE STEW + CINSAULT ROSÉ, RHÔNE VALLEY, FRANCE. Also known as a Lowcountry Boil, this is a summery dish of fresh corn, new potatoes, shrimp (heads and shells on!), and smoked sausage. It is best enjoyed outside with a glass of rosé. Cinsault, a grape grown mostly in parts of Southern France, makes rosé that's brisk and refreshing but also delicate and a little bit saline. A simple dish that's all about fresh ingredients deserves a wine that will act like the gentlest squeeze of lime and pinch of salt.

SAVANNAH RICE + FRAPPATO, SICILY, ITALY. This stewy, tomato-based rice dish may have a connection to West African jollof (see page 14) and is sometimes called red rice. Pair it with Frappato, a juicy, spicy, light-bodied red wine from Sicily.

OKRA PILAU + FRIULANO, FRIULI, ITALY. Another rice dish, this one's made with okra, obviously, and usually bacon, peppers, and onions. Pair it with Friulano from Friuli, Italy, which is a light-bodied, herbaceous white wine that has plenty of acidity to refresh your palate while you're eating the rice.

PEACH COBBLER + VERDELHO MADEIRA, MADEIRA, PORTUGAL. Fresh, ripe peaches baked with sweet biscuit dough are a good excuse to tap into the region's history with Madeira. I like a Verdelho Madeira that's sweet but dryer than some other Madeiras and has caramel and citrus notes that are delicious with peaches.

The Madeira Connection

The Lowcountry is not known as a wine-making region, except for wines made from muscadine, *Vitis rotundifolia*, grapes, which are big, sweet purple grapes indigenous to the southeast of the United States. However, I would agree with writer Jonathan Miles, in his 2013 article for *Garden & Gun* magazine, that Madeira wine is the original drink of the South. And Southern food experts Matt and Ted Lee wrote for *Punch* that Charleston was America's Madeira-consumption capital. From the 1700s until shortly before the Civil War, this fortified wine was central to high society in Charleston and throughout the South, and you can find traces of Madeira's history at the Bar & Patio at Husk in Charleston and at the Davenport House Museum in Savannah.

Madeira is a fortified wine made on an island of the same name off the Atlantic coast of Morocco. The Portuguese colonized the island, and during the Age of Exploration, their ships would stop there for fuel and other resources as part of the transatlantic slave trade. They planted Portuguese wine grapes—Sercial, Verdelho, Bual, and Malvasia, also known as Malmsey, and Tinta Negramoll. Madeira wines can be dry or sweet, vintage or nonvintage. They used brandy to fortify the wine made with these grapes, to stabilize it for travel on ships. One of the unique characteristics of Madeira was that the demand and therefore value of the wine increased as it completed long voyages. Madeira enthusiasts appreciated the enhanced flavor profiles the wine was exposed

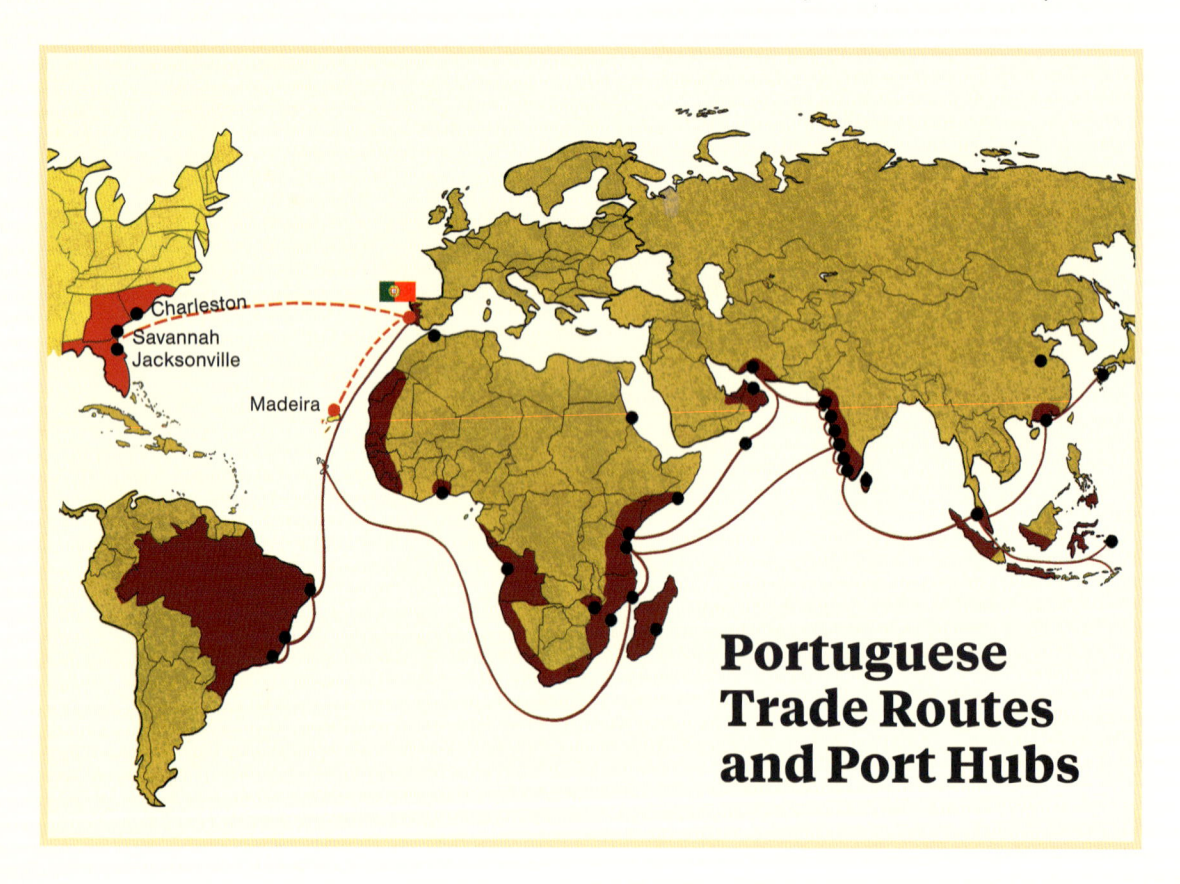

Portuguese Trade Routes and Port Hubs

to on the ships and were willing to pay more for Madeira that had endured long voyages. These Madeiras, called Vinho da Roda (meaning "rolled wine," for the motion of the sea), were intentionally sent out in barrels for extended journeys along other trade routes to develop more complex aromas and tasting notes, which at the time was the preference and considered high quality. Here is an illustration of a few typical routes that shows the extent to which sellers were willing to go to produce these well-traveled wines.

It's been called the eternal wine, because it can be cellared for easily over a hundred years. While living in Lisbon, I was fortunate to taste a rare bottle from the 1800s at my local wine bar. Its longevity is because of how it's made. The island of Madeira is hot, and so the wine is exposed to heat several times throughout its production. Historically, it was then exposed to more heat and rough conditions as it crossed the Atlantic. As the wine was heated and oxidized, it changed to an amber or dark-brown color. This process became known as "maderization," and it made the wine basically impervious to heat and very resilient. It also gave Madeira what we call oxidative flavors, or delicious notes of walnuts, vanilla, burnt caramel, and stewed fruits. But it still maintains bright, refreshing acidity and citrus notes, making a chilled glass the perfect sip in a hot city like Charleston.

In the 1850s, an outbreak of mildew slowed Madeira production, then came Civil War blockades that kept ships out of Charleston, phylloxera in Madeira vineyards, and Prohibition, so the city lost its connection with Madeira, but it's an interesting part of Lowcountry's history.

DECODING THE LABEL

BROADLEAF — Producer
MADEIRA — Wine Style
RESERVE — Quality Designator
5 YEARS OLD — Time Aged in Barrels

WINE PAIRING FOR THE PEOPLE

CRAB RICE + GARGANEGA, SOAVE, ITALY

SERVES 4

1 cup long-grain white rice, uncooked

Small pinch of salt

2–3 strips thick-cut bacon, diced

1 stalk celery, diced

½ bell pepper, any color, diced

1 small onion, diced

1 pound crabmeat, cooked (lump preferred, but any will do)

Garlic powder, onion powder, salt, and black pepper to taste

Amethyst Ganaway is a rising legend of Lowcountry food. She was born and raised in Charleston, where I met her through my work with the festival, and she's a scholar of Geechee Gullah history and food. You might find her out in her waders catching her own crab, but she was generous enough to suggest others can use store-bought crabmeat.

Garganega, a white wine from Northern Italy, has lots of pretty flower aromas, but it's best known for its peach, honeydew, and tangerine fruit notes and its marjoram and nutty finish, which is really good with rice and will show off the rich crab flavor.

1. Rinse the dry rice under cool water 3 to 4 times and drain. Put the rinsed rice into a small pot, cover with 2 cups of water, add a pinch of salt, and bring to a boil. Turn the heat to low, cover the pot, and let the rice cook undisturbed for 20 minutes. Remove from heat, crack the lid of the pot so that the rice can stop cooking, and set aside.
2. In a small skillet, fry the bacon pieces over medium-low heat until all the fat is rendered and bacon is crispy, about 3 to 5 minutes. Carefully remove the bacon pieces and set them aside. Reserve the rendered fat in the pan.
3. Over medium heat, add the celery, bell pepper, and onion to the pan with the bacon fat, and sauté until vegetables have softened and onions are translucent, about 5 minutes. Then add the crabmeat and cook for an additional 5 to 10 minutes, until the crab has begun to crisp.
4. Add the cooked rice, bacon, and seasonings to the pan with the vegetables. Incorporate all ingredients until evenly mixed, turn to low, and let cook for an additional 5 to 10 minutes. Serve hot and enjoy!

UNITED STATES OF AMERICA

Barbecue

It was truly a culinary blessing to be born in a city as gastronomically diverse as its people. However, there are some cuisines you can't just eat—you have to experience them to get the true sense of their flavors. Barbecue is more than a sauce. It is a technique, a lifestyle, a culture with its own terroir.

In 2012 and 2013, the *Village Voice* and *Esquire* called New York a barbecue capital. I am sure these articles raised more than a few eyebrows. New York has a lot of great barbecue restaurants, but a capital? Wouldn't that mean that New York has its own style? In Syracuse, where I opened The Communion Wine & Spirits shop while teaching wine as an adjunct professor, I had my fair share of one of New York State's favorite barbecue, Dinosaur Bar-B-Que. Even its owners say that they were inspired by the pit cooking styles of the South, so that is where we will explore to understand this dynamic cuisine.

In my frequent visits to South Carolina, as the head of beverage for the Charleston Wine + Food Festival (CHSWF) I took advantage of the opportunity to understand barbecue culture and its nuances. What I cherished about my role was how it challenged me to create experiences that inspire a forward approach to the traditional food and beverage scene. I recognized the importance of barbecue to the local culture, and I was excited to lean in and learn from my colleague, Jenna Kepley, the festival's program manager. During my

WINE PAIRING FOR THE PEOPLE

tenure, Jenna would lead the direction of the food experiences, and I would curate the beverage experiences and pairings.

Though she is now officially a local fixture in the bustling culinary scene in Charleston, she is originally from Lexington, North Carolina, which is considered by some to be the barbecue capital of the world, and once I learned this fact, I began to affectionately call her the Barbecue Baddie or the Queen of R&B (Rubs & Barbecue). The nicknames didn't stick, but her passion for barbecue culture was undeniable. Researching Lexington helped give this New Yorker some context to Barbecue 101. Lexington-style barbecue is known for the use of pork shoulders slow cooked over coals.

The type of protein, wood species, meat preparation, sauces, and the technique of

The Barbecue Belt

The United States is big, but its barbecue belt is a bit more concentrated around the Southern states. They are mostly in warm-climate regions, which is more suitable for all-year outdoor cooking and helps with the long hours of low heat needed for good barbecue. Barbecue capital cities tend to be located in proximity to agriculture states with more access to farmland for pork and beef. The legacy and craftsmanship of barbecue technique has now been passed down, making these areas the premier locations for barbecue in the United States. Here are the top cities known for their barbecue and their unique styles.

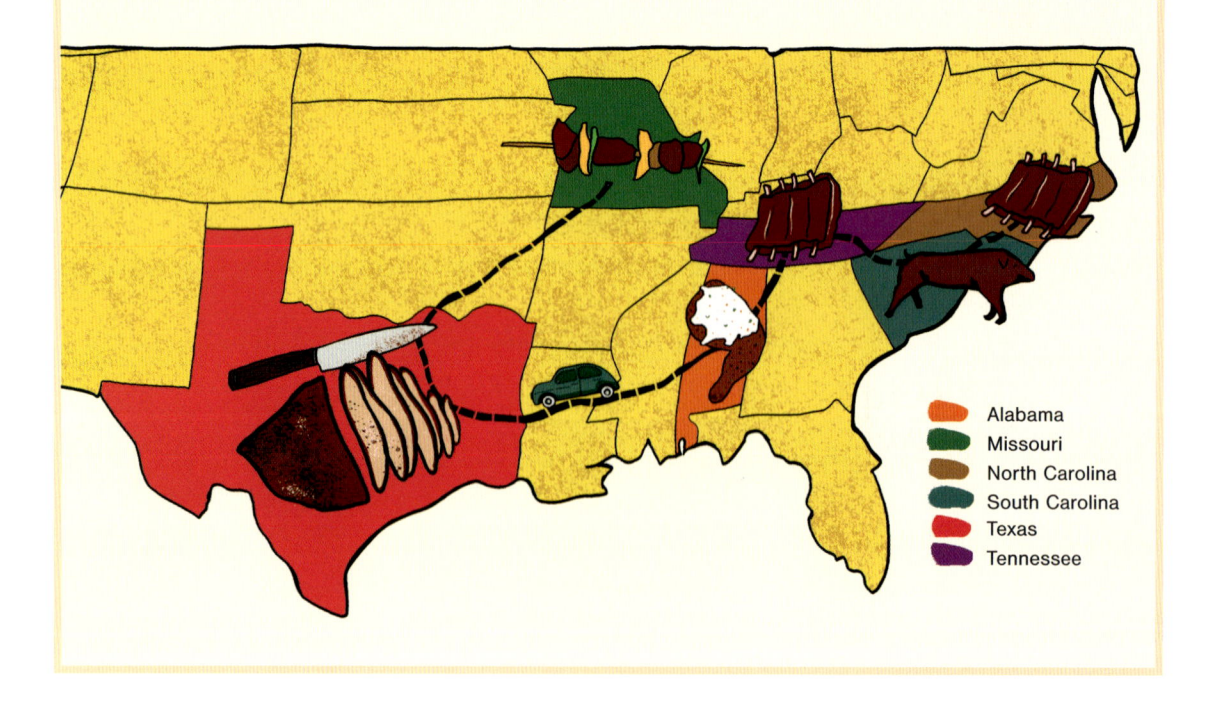

- Alabama
- Missouri
- North Carolina
- South Carolina
- Texas
- Tennessee

160

UNITED STATES OF AMERICA

+ PAIRED UP

EASTERN CAROLINA WHOLE-HOG BARBECUE + ALICANTE BOUSCHET, ALENTEJO, PORTUGAL. Also called just Carolina barbecue, this style is known for its vinegar sauce with chili flakes. It's usually pork—whole hog or ribs—and it's often smoked over pecan wood, which imparts a bit of sweetness and baking spice. Pair it with Alicante Bouschet, which is a bold and full-bodied red wine that's still juicy enough to work with the vinegar sauce.

SOUTH CAROLINA BARBECUE PULLED PORK + AGLIANICO ROSATO, CAMPANIA, ITALY. Yes, it's a thing that's separate from eastern Carolina, but it's still usually pork. It's smoked over oak or more assertive hickory, and the signature sauce is mustard-based and tangy. Pair it with Aglianico Rosato (rosé), which will match the acid level and complement the flavor profile of bright red fruit flavors of strawberry and tangy cranberry balances the mustard bite.

KANSAS CITY BARBECUE BEEF RIBS + AGIORGITIKO, NEMEA, GREECE. This is all about the sauce, which is tomato based and thick, flavored with molasses and brown sugar. The average bottle of store-bought barbecue sauce is based on this style from Kansas City, Missouri. The meat can be beef, pork, or chicken. It's not too particular about the wood either, but it must be smoked low and slow. Agiorgitiko will bring a savory, herbaceous note to keep the sauce from becoming cloying.

MEMPHIS-STYLE BARBECUE PORK RIBS + BONARDA, CALCHAQUÍ VALLEY, ARGENTINA. This Tennessee style is usually pork ribs or pulled pork that's been smoked over hickory. It's defined by a complex spice rub that includes salt, pepper, cayenne, paprika, brown sugar, celery seed, onion powder, garlic powder, and more. Pair dry-rubbed meats with Mencía, a Spanish grape with complex fruit and floral flavors that can keep up with the spice rub. Its "wet style" is also mopped with a sauce that's similar to Kansas City style but thinner and tangier. Pair it with Bonarda, an Argentine red wine that has a bit more twang to it.

ALABAMA BARBECUE CHICKEN + PETIT VERDOT, NAPA VALLEY, CALIFORNIA. A thickened, spiced, tangy, mayo-based white sauce is the hallmark of this style. Chicken is popular as the meat, but it can be anything, smoked over any type of wood. Petit Verdot, a red grape from Bordeaux that used to be used mostly for blends, is a bold red with dried herbal notes that will pair nicely with the white sauce.

TEXAS-STYLE BARBECUE BRISKET + TEMPRANILLO, TEXAS HILL COUNTRY, TEXAS. Brisket rubbed with salt and pepper and smoked over oak, which creates a mild aroma, is a signature, but you can also find smoked sausages in Texas. Pair it with Texas notable Tempranillo with black plum and black and blue berries with notes of cedar and cigar box that will complement the weight of the wine and balance with the spice flavor.

DRINK NOW: Texas Wine Producers
- Cheramie Wine
- McPherson Cellars
- William Chris Vineyards
- Messina Hof

cooking gives clues to identifying a regional style, which you can learn about in this chapter's Paired Up section. Charleston and eastern North Carolina are known for whole-hog barbecue. Through CHSWF, I was able to witness and appreciate this style of cooking and be introduced to BJ Dennis, a chef who has dedicated his life's work to sharing the unique Gullah Geechee culture, which sets Charleston's barbecue apart from the rest of South Carolina. BJ's marinades and rubs highlight West African spice blends, local coastal ingredients, and traditions that make his barbecue distinct.

In addition to working with him, I also got to know notable pitmaster Rodney Scott—an inductee into the Barbecue Hall of Fame and only the second pitmaster to win a James Beard Award. His slow-roast whole hog has now become a tradition for the festival's grand finale event.

Creating wine and food pairings for CSHWF live series for thousand of participants, such as Side Hustle in 2022 and the World of Cue in 2022, was exhilarating. Celebrating the culture with intention and spotlighting everything from the important roles of side dishes (like rice, coleslaw, and collard greens) to the expansive culture of barbecue (whether it's the Carolinas, Texas, and Tennessee) was a way for us to highlight the global barbecue connection to Jamaica, Puerto Rico, Argentina, and beyond.

Barbecue can mean different things depending on where you go in the country, and a lot of people feel strongly that their barbecue is the correct barbecue. The origins of barbecue are just as controversial. For a long time, the accepted theory was that Taíno people in the Caribbean practiced open-fire cooking, called barbacoa, and Spanish explorers brought the technique to what's now the United States. But in his book *From Barbycu to Barbecue: The Untold History of an American Tradition*, author Joseph R. Haynes said that the barbacoa was the rack used by Taíno people to cook or dry foods over a fire (and to hide valuable items). Haynes wrote that the pit cooking over coals that evolved into the US definition of barbecue came from collaboration among enslaved Africans, Indigenous people, and English colonizers, probably in Virginia.

Like soul food, barbecue is born out of collaboration and was mostly done by Black cooks. That's not the only crossover either. A lot of the side dishes that are served with barbecue fall under the heading of soul food. When you go to a barbecue restaurant, you might order collard greens or macaroni and cheese on the side, and both types of cooking originate in the South. It would be nice if we could categorize things neatly all the time—this is soul food, that's barbecue—but history is messy, just like ribs.

Back to barbecue's regional styles. These came about mostly because different parts of the country raise different livestock and have different types of wood available for smoking meat. In some places, regional barbecue styles grew to include specific sauces or spice mixes, but at its heart, barbecue is meat and smoke, and so regional styles mostly come down to what kind of meat and smoke were the most

UNITED STATES OF AMERICA

available before supermarkets and shopping online.

One thing they all have in common is big, smoky, meaty flavor. Even if you're eating barbecued chicken, it's going to be smoky and meaty. Typically, if people are drinking alcohol with barbecue, they're going to reach for beer, because there's a real fear that the rich, meaty intensity would clobber a wine, taking out all its intensity. But if you think about some of the different barbecue sauces out there, they're tangy, full-bodied, and maybe a bit smoky or fruity. Wine can bring all of that to the table too.

Big State Calls for Bold Wine

I cannot talk about barbecue and wine without mentioning Texas's fast-growing wine regions. Currently with eight AVAs (American Viticultural Area), Texas High Plains and Texas Hill Country are two of the largest and more established. Texas is growing rapidly and is currently the fifth largest wine-producing state after New York. Texas is a large state with diverse terroir from limestone-rich soils of the Hill Country to cool temperatures and high altitude in the High Plains. Top varietals to try are Tempranillo, Tannat, and Sangiovese for red wine. As for white wine, seek out Viognier, Roussanne, and Albariño.

Wine in the USA

American wines are plentiful, varied, and delicious. All fifty states make wine. California is the biggest; Oregon and Washington also fall into that heavy-hitter category. But the states highlighted on the US map (see pages 140–41) are the up-and-comers in the market that I'm most excited about: Virginia, Texas, and, well, of course I'm partial to New York wines.

DECODING THE LABEL

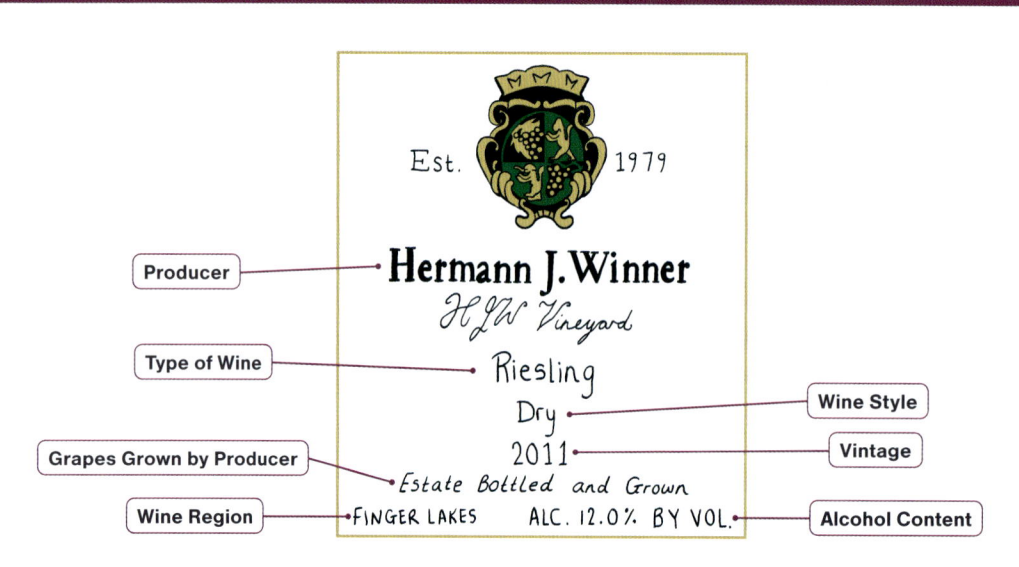

Label annotations:
- Producer: Hermann J. Winner
- Grapes Grown by Producer: HJW Vineyard
- Type of Wine: Riesling
- Wine Style: Dry
- Vintage: 2011
- Estate Bottled and Grown
- Wine Region: Finger Lakes
- Alcohol Content: ALC. 12.0% BY VOL.
- Est. 1979

In the United States, wine labels are regulated by the Alcohol and Tobacco Tax and Trade Bureau (commonly known as TTB). They are less strict than the European Commission, but both regulate the required label information for appellation of origin, which grapes are in the wine, and alcohol content. The TTB concentrates on monitoring health warnings and marketing terms, whereas in Europe the protected designation of origin (PDO) is more focused on preserving quality levels and geographic identity. The United States's equivalent is an American Viticultural Area (AVA), which is a federally regulated and identified geographical area that is defined by a particular feature, such as type of soil, weather patterns, altitude, or climate. The AVAs are regulated by the TTB and, if included on the label, the wine must adhere to requirements about including a certain percentage of grapes grown within the AVA as well as where the wine production is completed. Labels are required to provide certain information to help guide your purchases. Currently there are not requirements to share ingredients, but many people are advocating for that to change for more consumer transparency. For now, here's an example of what to expect when deciphering an American wine label:

- **Producer**
- **Type of wine**
- **Where it's from** (state or American Viticultural Area; "American Wine" means the grapes can be from anywhere in the country)
- **Alcohol by volume**
- **Volume of liquid in bottle**

UNITED STATES OF AMERICA

RODNEY SCOTT'S SPARERIBS + CABERNET SAUVIGNON, MAIPO VALLEY, CHILE

Rodney Scott is a James Beard Award–winning whole-hog pitmaster legend. He learned how to smoke whole hogs as a child, at his family's variety store and barbecue spot in South Carolina and then went on to open his own restaurant in Charleston. This recipe is one of the Carolina styles, but not the mustard-based sauce that's sometimes associated with South Carolina barbecue. His spareribs, he says, aren't as tender as baby back ribs. They're not supposed to fall off the bone. But they will still be tender, smoky, and delicious.

Pair these ribs with Chilean Cabernet Sauvignon, known for black fruit flavors like black plum and black currant, green bell peppers, black pepper, and thyme. This wine is a complement to the smoky, savory, and spicy flavors of this dish and a great match between fat and tannins.

SERVES 6 TO 12

3 slabs pork spareribs, membranes removed

1½ tablespoons rib rub (recipe follows)

2 to 3 cups Rodney's Sauce (recipe follows)

1. Heat the grill to between 200° and 250°F.
2. Season each slab with the rib rub. Make sure you get under the flap, the little piece of meat that dangles on the bone side of the ribs.
3. Place the seasoned ribs on the grill grate bone side down, with the fatty end toward the middle of the grill. The middle of the grill tends to be hotter, so that will ensure that the thicker part of the rib gets cooked properly. Close the grill and cook: You are looking for caramelization on the ribs before you flip them. That should take about 1½ hours. Open the grill and look for caramelization on the bone.
4. If it's ready, mop sauce onto one side, flip the ribs, and mop sauce onto the other side. Close the grill. Bring the grill back up to a temperature between 200° and 250° F. Cook the ribs until the second side gets that same caramelized look. To check doneness, we pick up a slab of ribs with a pair of tongs and check how much give there is. When you pick the slab up, it should sag or flop easily. If a slight tear develops in the meat between the bones, that's another sign of doneness.

(recipe continues on page 167)

165

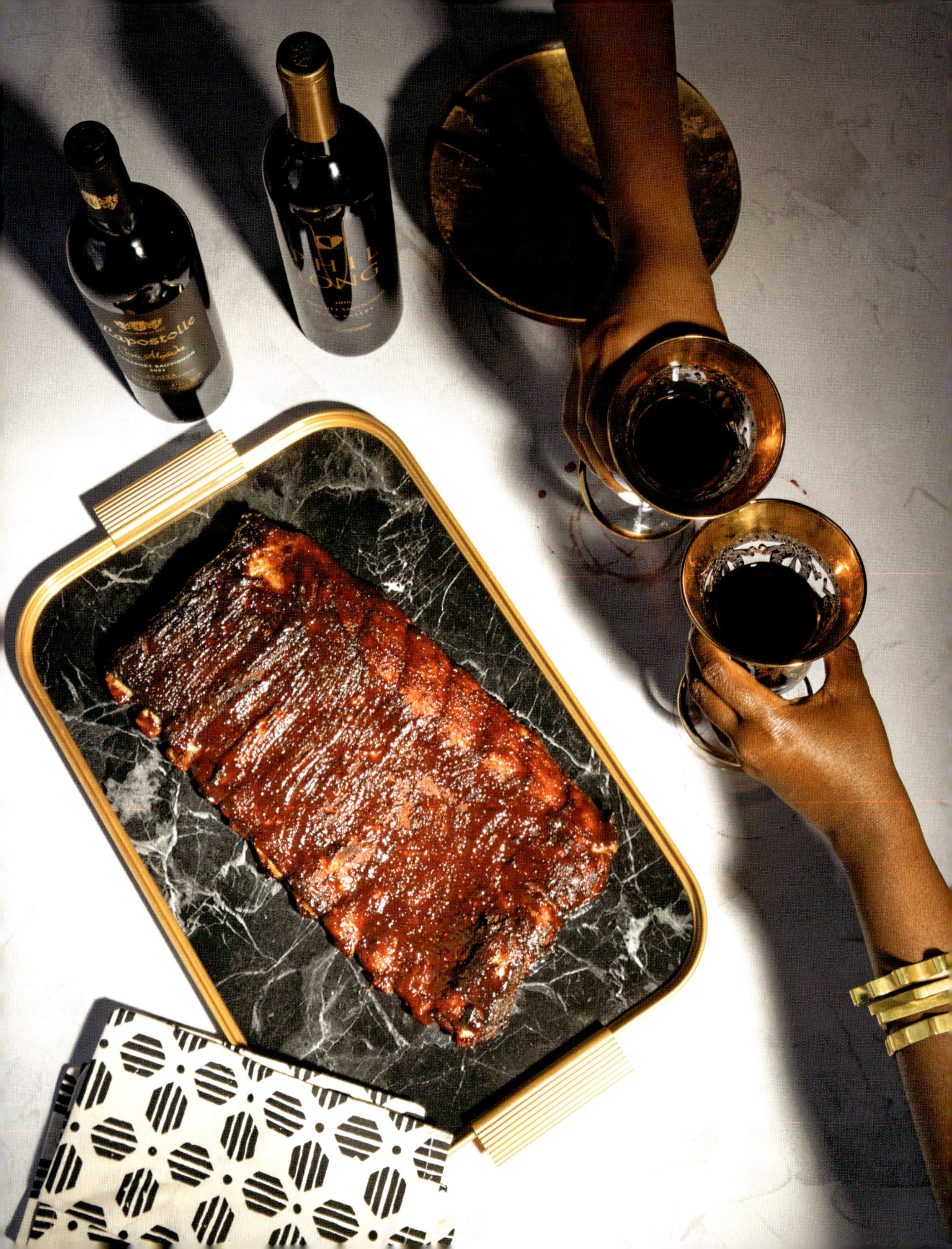

UNITED STATES OF AMERICA

RODNEY'S RIB RUB

MAKES 2 CUPS

½ cup Diamond Crystal kosher salt
¼ cup monosodium glutamate
¼ cup freshly ground black pepper
¼ cup paprika
¼ cup chili powder
¼ cup packed light brown sugar
2 tablespoons garlic powder
2 tablespoons onion powder
1 teaspoon cayenne pepper

Mix all the ingredients and place them in an airtight container. Cover and store in a cool dry place until ready to use.

RODNEY'S SAUCE

MAKES 1 GALLON

1 gallon distilled white vinegar
1 lemon, thinly sliced
½ cup ground black pepper
⅓ cup cayenne pepper
1¼ tablespoon red pepper flakes
2 cups sugar

1. In a small stockpot, warm the vinegar over medium-high heat. After about 5 minutes, when the vinegar reaches 150°F on an instant-read thermometer, just before it starts to simmer, add the lemon slices and continue to cook until the lemon peels begin to soften and wilt, about 10 minutes more.
2. Whisk in the black pepper, cayenne, pepper flakes, and sugar. Continue to cook over medium-high heat until the sugar is completely dissolved and the sauce reaches 190°F, about 10 minutes. Remove from the heat and allow to completely cool before using. Once the lemon is removed, the sauce can be refrigerated in an airtight container for up to 8 weeks.

Used with permission from *Rodney Scott's World of BBQ* by Rodney Scott and Lolis Eric Elie (Clarkson Potter, 2021).

WINE PAIRING FOR THE PEOPLE

BARBEQUED SPATCHCOCKED CHICKEN + CABERNET FRANC, SENECA LAKE, NEW YORK

SERVES 4

1 cup unsweetened grapefruit juice

½ cup packed brown sugar

¼ cup apple cider vinegar

¼ cup kosher salt

¼ cup fresh-ground black pepper

1 tablespoon cayenne pepper

1 whole chicken

¼ cup Bavarian mustard

True Made Foods Ed's "Mother of All" Rub

True Made Foods Ed's Kansas City BBQ Sauce, for serving

Father-son team Ed and Ryan Mitchell are experts of and ambassadors for North Carolina barbecue. Eastern Carolina whole-hog pit smoking is one of their calling cards, but they do a good whole chicken too. But they don't just share good barbecue—they also share the history of barbecue as part of Black history and the Black legacy in American food.

For those who are new to spatchcocking, it means that a whole chicken gets cut in a way that flattens it out. Some people say this helps it cook more evenly, but I think the big payout is more crispy, smoky, seasoned skin and juicy, tender meat.

Pair it with a Cabernet Franc from New York's Finger Lakes, a medium-bodied yet vibrant, red fruit-forward wine. It has rustic strawberry, red currant, and black cherry on the mid palate with notes of green herbs including bell pepper, tomato leaf, and sage, with vibrant acidity that cuts through the crispy skins. Finger Lakes Cabernet Franc tends to be fuller-bodied than the Loire Valley style, with more fruit-forward flavor.

1. In a bowl or tub large enough to hold a whole chicken, mix 2 cups water, grapefruit juice, brown sugar, vinegar, salt, black pepper, and cayenne, and stir until the sugar and salt have dissolved. Add the whole chicken and submerge it in the brine. Refrigerate for 8 hours.

2. Heat the oven to 400°F. Remove the chicken from the brine and pat dry (discard the brine). Using kitchen shears, split the chicken spatchcock-style, cutting down the ribs. The wings should be sticking up toward you and the breast should be down. Slather with the mustard to coat on both sides, then cover the whole chicken evenly with dry rub. Place breast side down in a baking pan and cover with aluminum foil.

3. Roast the chicken on the bottom rack of the oven for about 1 hour, removing the foil from the pan after 30 minutes. Serve with barbecue sauce.

Used with permission from *Ed Mitchell's Barbeque* by Ed and Ryan Mitchell with Zella Palmer (Ecco, June 2023).

UNITED STATES OF AMERICA

Creole

In 1995, one of the largest celebrations of Black culture commenced in New Orleans. The first Essence Music Festival was designed as a one-time event to honor the twenty-fifth anniversary of *Essence* magazine. *Essence* highlights Black women, celebrates the Black experience, and underlines the important issues facing the Black community. The celebration was such a success that it became an annual music festival, now known as the Essence Festival of Culture that focuses on popular genres like R&B, hip-hop, and soul, and over the years it has expanded to include reggae, Afrobeat, and, of course, jazz. From New York, Essence Fest seemed to me like the most important Black experience to attend in one of the most important cities for Black culture in the United States.

Essence Fest was my introduction to New Orleans and its distinct culture. Held annually around the Fourth of July weekend, it provides a different type of expression of independence to African Americans celebrating Black Excellence in business, music, and gastronomy. After making my initial pilgrimage to New Orleans I opted to experience more of the city and not attend as many of the official events for my second Essence Fest. This led me on an adventure that gave me the same feeling when traveling internationally—curiosity to explore deeply a new culture of food, drinks, and music.

While dancing in the street under the Fourth of July fireworks another spark was ignited. I met a group of New

WINE PAIRING FOR THE PEOPLE

Sip the Culture

Home of the Museum of the American Cocktail and Tales of the Cocktail, a massive trade event for people in the drinks industry, New Orleans has become the authority on cocktail culture. Some people have even called it the birthplace of cocktails, but the word "cock-tail" was used in a Hudson, New York, newspaper in 1806, decades before Antoine Peychaud allegedly invented the cocktail in New Orleans. Today, you can still get signature Big Easy cocktails in the bars where they were invented.

It is true that Peychaud, an apothecary owner, invented Peychaud's Bitters for medicinal purposes. He discovered that they tasted good mixed with cognac, sugar, and water. That combination became the Sazerac, one of many New Orleans signature cocktails. Today, the Sazerac is made with rye whiskey or bourbon whiskey and served in a glass that's been washed with absinthe or Herbsaint, another New Orleans creation. Here are some other cocktails invented in New Orleans.

VIEUX CARRÉ. Invented at the Carousel Bar in 1938, the Vieux Carré is made with brandy, rye, sweet vermouth, French herbal liqueur Bénédictine, Angostura Bitters, and Peychaud's Bitters.

HURRICANE. The story with the Hurricane is that it was invented to use up excess rum. Pat O'Brien is said to have invented this drink in the 1940s at Pat O'Brien's Bar. Made with light and dark rum; lime, orange, and passion fruit juices; and grenadine, Hurricanes go down easy.

GRASSHOPPER. The story goes that Philibert Guichet, who bought the restaurant Tujague's from the Tujague family in 1910, invented this sweet, green drink for a New York cocktail competition. Because of Prohibition, none of this would have been publicized, so it's hard to know exactly what year it was invented, but probably 1919 or the 1920s. It's equal parts crème de menthe, crème de cacao, and cream, and it's still served at Tujague's today.

Orleans natives and my love affair with the city and its people began. I was transformed from being an annual festivalgoer to making monthly trips to spend time with my then boyfriend, Benjamin. He became my Crescent City connect, fully immersing me in his culture and everyday living in NOLA beyond the tourist traps, an experience that I welcomed. He lived in the Harvey Gretna area but his parents were originally from Uptown. I transitioned from Bourbon Street to Frenchman Street in search of the best live brass-brand experience. And I eventually traded in my Hand Grenades, the signature green cocktails consumed by tourists, for a Sazerac, which is considered the official cocktail of New Orleans. One of my guilty pleasures when in the city was to find a late-night oyster bar and, after a long day, clear a dozen or more oysters either raw or in the famous charbroiled style alongside a gin cocktail.

I soon learned the importance of festivals beyond Essence Fest to the history and experience of New Orleans, and of course the city's main cultural event, Mardi Gras. This pre-Lent experience was introduced to the United States by French colonizers near New Orleans. Today the city has the largest celebration in the country and has taken on a new expression of Black culture. The French Carnival tradition of masquerade balls is still upheld and hosted by social clubs called krewes, as well as elaborate masks and costumes by parade participants and attendees. Mardi Gras is an expression of New Orleans's cultural diversity, of French, Spanish, African, and Caribbean influences, which are also reflected in the city's rich culinary scene of Creole food.

Creating Creole

The word "Creole" is used throughout the Caribbean to refer to people who are of mixed African and European descent. In Louisiana, it's expanded to refer to culture and cuisine too. That mixing of people from different backgrounds over hundreds of years is one of the reasons that New Orleans feels so different.

An explorer named Robert Cavelier de la Salle claimed what's now New Orleans in the name of the French crown in 1682, disregarding the Chitimacha, Atakapa, Caddo, Choctaw, Houma, Natchez, and Tunica people who already lived there. About a hundred years later, the colony was given to Spain as part of a larger treaty deal, and then in 1800, France acquired it back. Louisiana didn't become part of the United States until 1803, in the Louisiana Purchase.

France and Spain were guilty of the same brutal treatment of enslaved Africans and Indigenous people as their English counterparts in the rest of what's now the United States. We're not going to call them better colonizers, but they did infuse a different culture, language, and architecture, which all make New Orleans feel as much like a part of the Caribbean as part of the United States.

French and Spanish colonizers also brought Catholicism, which was very important in making New Orleans culture different from the parts of the country originally colonized by the Protestant British.

In more recent years, New Orleans can be credited with everything from being the birthplace of jazz—Ferdinand "Jelly Roll" Morton and Louis Armstrong are both from the city—to the place where a young Ruby Bridges integrated the school. The city's energy is alive. Even in places where the buildings were destroyed by Hurricane Katrina, people's spirits remain lifted.

New Orleans in New York

I quickly learned the daily diet in New Orleans is very different than in New York. I enjoyed the festival season, but it was the time spent immersed in the cooking at Benjamin's parents' home that I soon realized my heat tolerance or lack thereof and New Negro diet of no pork didn't translate here. With a lot of Creole food, the things that set it apart from soul food are not just what people eat but when and how. Red beans and rice are a Monday night tradition, for one. Mondays were traditionally known as laundry day. This was before washers and dryers, so women made a dinner that they could leave simmering all day on the stove while they did the laundry. In some homes, they'd have a leftover ham bone from Sunday dinner that they could use to season the dish. In New Orleans, seafood dishes are not even safe from meat. If you're getting a seafood boil, or when I was in town for crawfish season, it was common to find turkey neck in the bag for seasoning. A dish that soon became one of my favorites, so much so that Benjamin's father would cook it for me, was barbecued shrimp—but it did not originally begin as such.

WINE PAIRING FOR THE PEOPLE

+ PAIRED UP

CRAWFISH ÉTOUFFÉE + DOLCETTO, PIEDMONT, ITALY. Crawfish gets simmered in broth thickened with roux. A Dolcetto from Italy's Piedmont region is a perfectly peppery pairing with blackberry, cocoa, and plum notes.

BARBECUED SHRIMP + LAMBRUSCO DI SORBARA ROSÉ, EXTRA DRY, EMILIA-ROMAGNA, ITALY. This one confused me the first time I ate it. It is *not* shrimp that's cooked on a barbecue. It's head-on, shell-on shrimp braised in butter and Worcestershire sauce. Pair it with a tangy Lambrusco Rosé full of fresh red-berry fruit flavors. Look for a slightly sweet version of Extra Dry, which is typically 12–17 grams of residual sugar for sparkling wines.

CHARBROILED OYSTERS + PROSECCO RIVE DI SAN PIETRO DI BARBOZZA BRUT, VALDOBBIADENE, ITALY. This is a briny and sweet way to take advantage of a favorite New Orleans seafood. Pair them with a Prosecco Rive di San Pietro di Barbozza Brut, which is a Prosecco of the highest quality that will bring a bright acidity and saline character that are unique to this region.

JAMBALAYA + CABERNET FRANC, CHINON, FRANCE. This one-pot rice dish is made with sausage, ham, shrimp, and Creole cooking's "holy trinity" of onions, celery, and bell peppers. Pair it with Cabernet Franc from the Chinon region of France's Loire Valley. This wine has a great balance of minerality, which is a nice, austere counterpoint to richer dishes, and fruitiness to match the jambalaya's fun spirit.

SHRIMP PO'BOY + CRÉMANT DE BOURGOGNE BRUT ROSÉ, BURGUNDY, FRANCE. New Orleans' iconic sandwich piles fried shrimp (or oysters) on a light, crusty roll with remoulade sauce on it. Remember: bubbles always go well with fried food. In this case, I'd reach for Crémant de Bourgogne Brut Rosé—a sparkling rosé from Burgundy that has delicate, juicy raspberry notes.

BEIGNETS + DEMI-SEC CHAMPAGNE, ÉPERNAY, FRANCE. A good beignet might make you reject donuts. Try this deep-fried square of dough topped with powdered sugar with a demi-sec Champagne to match its sweetness and cut through the powdered sugar.

The first time he served it, I was expecting charred grilled shrimp that were marinated in sweet and savory barbecue sauce. Instead, I was served head-on shrimp in the shell that hadn't seen a grill but were braised in white wine, butter, and Worcestershire sauce and seasoned with a copious amount of red pepper flakes, paprika, and cayenne pepper, along with herbs. You can understand how my Yankee palate did not originally comprehend this dish with "barbecue" in its name, but I grew to love it as much as I did the culture. Eventually, I learned how to adapt to the spice. I will never forget when Benjamin's mother sent a care package to us in New York to help adjust his palate after relocating. I soon incorporated these seasonings into our pantry to bring a taste of New Orleans to New York: Tony Chachere's, Slap Ya Mama, Louisiana Brand Hot Sauce, Louisiana Brand New Orleans–Style Fish Fry Seafood Breading Mix, Zatarain's Creole Seasoning, and Utz's Zapp Kettle Potato Voodoo Flavor Chips.

UNITED STATES OF AMERICA

THE PARISH

Tiffanie Barriere, aka the Drinking Coach, has done it all in the cocktail world: she's done panels and demonstrations at food and drinks festivals like the Charleston Wine + Food Festival, contributed recipes to books and magazines, judged competitions, and appeared on Netflix shows *Drink Masters* and *High on the Hog*. She weaves history into her work, and especially the ways in which Black women have contributed to drinks culture. She says that moonshine is often sipped neat, but it can be incorporated into a punch like this one, which she says might be shared at a crawfish boil or reunion. There's no better person to share a moonshine punch with us.

SERVES 12 TO 16

4 lemons
4 lemons, juiced
1½ cups white sugar
1 750-ml bottle of moonshine
½ pint dark rum
½ pint cognac
2½ cups pineapple juice
2 bottles sparkling water
Pineapple rings, for garnish

1. In a punch bowl, slice 4 lemons into wheels.
2. In the punch bowl, combine the lemon juice and sugar and whisk into a sand-type mixture. Add moonshine, rum, cognac, and pineapple juice, and whisk until sugar is dissolved.
3. Add a large dense block of ice to the punch bowl.
4. Top with sparkling water and pineapple rings.

WINE PAIRING FOR THE PEOPLE

CHICKEN AND SAUSAGE GUMBO + CARIGNAN, LANGUEDOC-ROUSSILLON, FRANCE

SERVES 8 TO 12

- 8 boneless skin-on chicken thighs
- 2 teaspoons kosher salt; more to taste
- ½ cup unsalted butter
- ½ cup all-purpose flour
- 3 cups ¼-inch-diced yellow onion
- 1½ cups ¼-inch-diced green and red bell pepper
- ⅓ cup ¼-inch-diced celery
- 3 cloves garlic, minced
- 1½ pounds andouille sausage, cooked, sliced
- 2 fresh bay leaves
- 2 teaspoons dried thyme
- 2 teaspoons cayenne pepper
- 1 teaspoon black pepper; more to taste
- 1 to 2 teaspoons crab boil seasoning

"Gumbo is a very particular thing," is what Chef Dominick Lee said when we asked him for a recipe. He was born in New Orleans and displaced by Hurricane Katrina. He went to culinary school in Houston, and in early 2024, he opened a Creole restaurant there. So he gets to be particular about gumbo. In between finishing culinary school and opening his latest venture, he studied some of the roots of Creole cooking in Europe, opened a New York City restaurant that served Louisiana alligator, and worked with me at the Charleston Wine + Food Festival. There are plenty of gumbo variations that still fall under the umbrella of being true and authentic to Creole food, and I'm excited to share this one with you.

I like to pair this with Carignan because it's fresh and berry forward to balance out the meat, but it has some earthy, forest-floor notes that match the roux's nutty flavors.

1. In a large pot, cover chicken with water and add a teaspoon of the salt. Bring the water to a boil, and then reduce to a simmer until the chicken is fully cooked, about 20 to 25 minutes.
2. Strain water and reserve.
3. Remove cooked chicken from pot, allow to cool, then shred into small pieces. Cover and set aside.
4. In a large pot, combine butter and flour. Cook over medium heat, frequently stirring with a whisk to make a dark brown roux, about 15 minutes. In the last 5 minutes make sure to continuously stir so the roux does not burn.
5. Add onion, bell peppers, celery, and garlic. Sauté until vegetables are tender, about 8 to 10 minutes.
6. Add andouille sausage. Cook for 10 minutes, stirring occasionally.
7. Add bay leaf, thyme, cayenne, pepper, and remaining 1 teaspoon of salt.
8. Stir in the reserved liquid from step 2, one cup at a time until the stew reaches your desired consistency. If you use all of the liquid and want to thin it more, you may add more liquid, such as hot water or chicken broth.

UNITED STATES OF AMERICA

9. Simmer over medium-low heat for approximately 35 minutes with pot loosely covered, stirring occasionally.
10. Add cooked shredded chicken and simmer for an additional 15 minutes.
11. Turn off heat and slowly stir in the crab boil seasoning. Taste and season with more salt and pepper as desired.

THE WINE LIST
United States of America

SOUL FOOD

Breakfast/Brunch

Extra Dry Prosecco, VALDOBBIADENE, ITALY; Pinot Bianco, ALTO ADIGE, ITALY; Off-Dry Gewürztraminer, ALSACE, FRANCE; Moscato d'Asti, PIEDMONT, ITALY

The Cookout

Lambrusco di Sorbara, EMILIA-ROMAGNA, ITALY; Concord Grape Wine, FINGER LAKES, NEW YORK; Welschriesling, NIEDERÖSTERREICH, AUSTRIA

Sunday/Holiday Dinner

Pinot Noir, MUSIGNY, FRANCE; Zweigelt, BURGENLAND, AUSTRIA; Touriga Nacional, DOURO VALLEY, PORTUGAL; Châteauneuf-du-Pape, SOUTHERN RHÔNE, FRANCE

Melba's Signature Chicken and Eggnog Waffles
Vintage Champagne Blanc de Noirs, BOUZY, FRANCE

Desserts

Sweet Potato Pie + Vin Santo del Chianti Classico, TUSCANY, ITALY
7UP Bundt Cake + Asti Spumante, PIEDMONT, ITALY
Bean Pie + Late-Bottled Vintage Port, DOURO VALLEY, PORTUGAL
Roasted Pineapple Cornmeal Cake + Sauternes, BORDEAUX, FRANCE

▼

LOWCOUNTRY

Shrimp and Grits + Rosé, PROVENCE, FRANCE
Brunswick Stew + Sangiovese, ADELAIDE HILLS, AUSTRALIA
She-Crab Soup + Arneis, PIEDMONT, ITALY
Frogmore Stew + Cinsault Rosé, RHÔNE VALLEY, FRANCE
Savannah Rice + Frappato, SICILY, ITALY
Okra Pilau + Friulano, FRIULI, ITALY
Peach Cobbler + Verdelho Madeira, MADEIRA, PORTUGAL
Crab Rice + Garganega, SOAVE, ITALY

▼

BARBECUE

Eastern Carolina Whole-Hog Barbecue + Alicante Bouschet, ALENTEJO, PORTUGAL
South Carolina Barbecue Pulled Pork + Aglianico Rosato, CAMPANIA, ITALY
Kansas City Barbecue Beef Ribs + Agiorgitiko, NEMEA, GREECE
Memphis-Style Barbecue Pork Ribs + Bonarda, CALCHAQUÍ VALLEY, ARGENTINA
Alabama Barbecue Chicken + Petit Verdot, NAPA VALLEY, CALIFORNIA
Texas-Style Barbecue Brisket + Tempranillo, TEXAS HILL COUNTRY, TEXAS
Rodney Scott's Spareribs + Cabernet Sauvignon, MAIPO VALLEY, CHILE
Barbequed Spatchcocked Chicken + Cabernet Franc, SENECA LAKE, NEW YORK

▼

CREOLE

Crawfish Étouffée + Dolcetto, PIEDMONT, ITALY
Barbecued Shrimp + Lambrusco di Sorbara Rosé, Extra Dry, EMILIA-ROMAGNA, ITALY
Charbroiled Oysters + Prosecco Rive di San Pietro di Barbozza Brut, VALDOBBIADENE, ITALY
Jambalaya + Cabernet Franc, CHINON, FRANCE
Shrimp Po'Boy + Crémant de Bourgogne Brut Rosé, BURGUNDY, FRANCE
Beignets + Demi-Sec Champagne, ÉPERNAY, FRANCE
Chicken and Sausage Gumbo + Carignan, LANGUEDOC-ROUSSILLON, FRANCE

▼

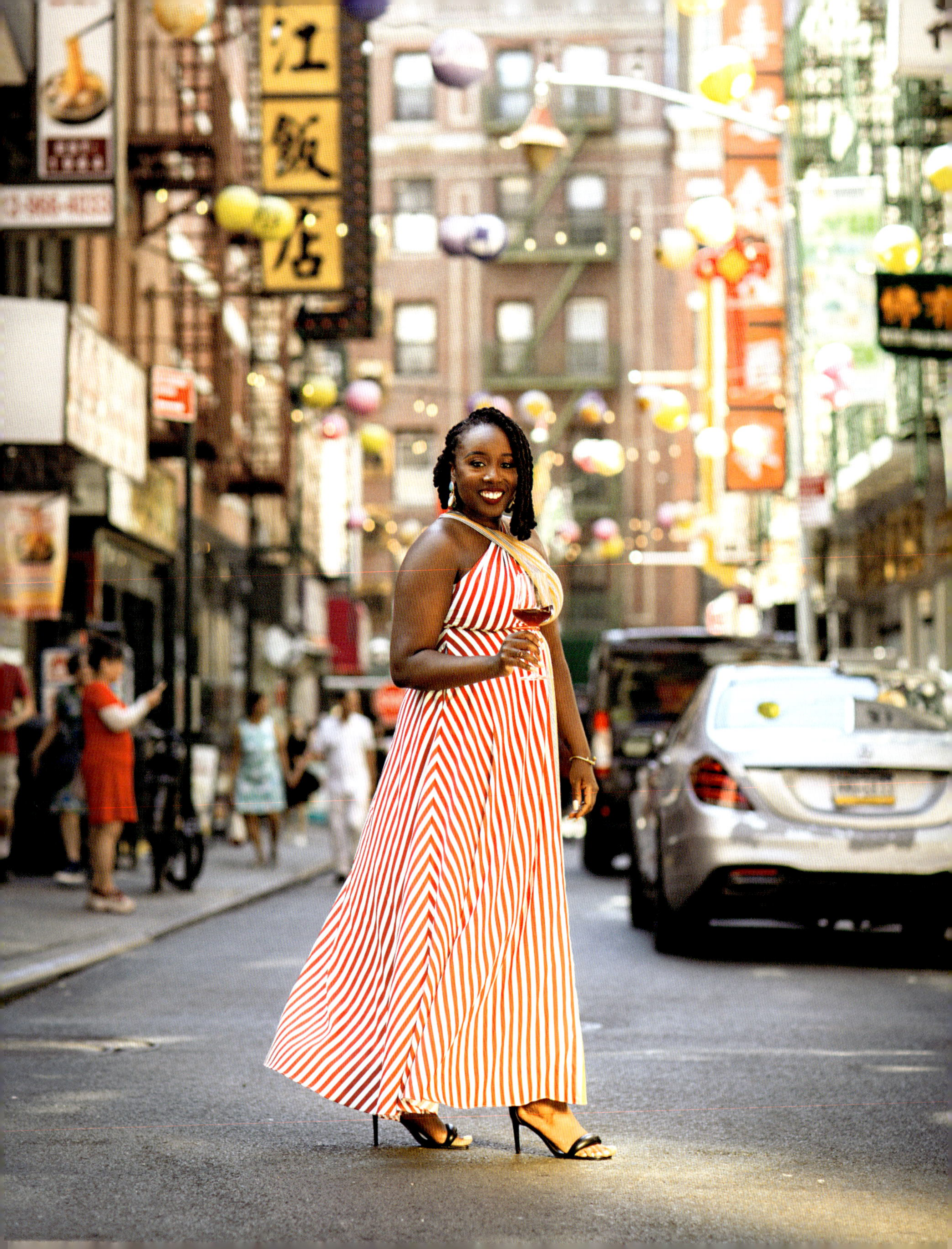
江飯店

Asia

China	182
Japan	192
South Korea	199
Southeast Asia	204
Turkey	212
Georgia	218
United Arab Emirates	227
India	230

Asia

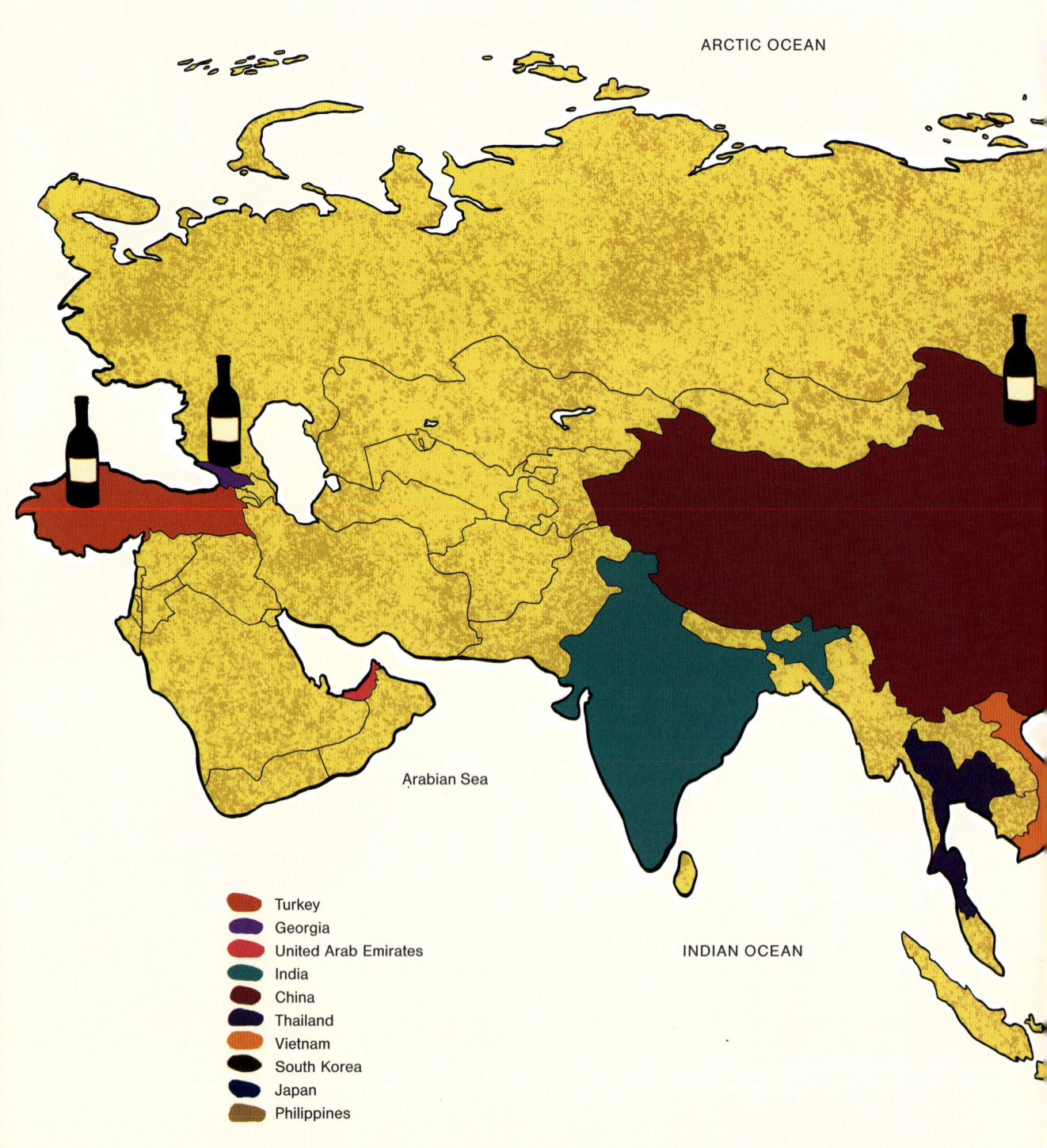

ARCTIC OCEAN

Arabian Sea

INDIAN OCEAN

- Turkey
- Georgia
- United Arab Emirates
- India
- China
- Thailand
- Vietnam
- South Korea
- Japan
- Philippines

I started this book in Africa because that's where life itself began. We're ending with Asia because that's where wine began. These are my alpha and omega—my culture and ancestors, and my career and passion.

I'll admit that Asia is not necessarily the continent that comes to mind when you think of the African diaspora. But Asian cuisines, like Chinese food, have their place in Black communities, and I wanted the opportunity to shed some light on wine pairing for a few of them. Plus, some parts of Asia, like Georgia and Turkey, are essential to the history and development of wine, and others, like India and Turkey, have had an impact on the development of African and African American food via the spice trade dating back hundreds of years before the transatlantic slave trade.

This section will cover everything from the ancient wine-making traditions of Georgia and Turkey to the connection between Chinese takeout and urban neighborhoods across the United States. Some Asian countries also have growing wine-making cultures that we'll dive into. Plus I've got you covered on how to pair your sushi, your pad thai, and more.

China

Chinese food is as much a part of growing up in New York City as taking the subway. I'm talking specifically about the American Chinese takeout spots that open early and stay open late, selling Cantonese-inspired dishes like General Tso's and chicken wing combos. It's hard to get a solid count on how many of these restaurants are open in New York City, but it looks like more than two thousand. By comparison, there are around two hundred McDonald's at the time of this writing. But it's more than just a New York thing, and it's more than just sheer numbers. In New York and other big cities, Chinese restaurants are popular in urban Black neighborhoods. There's a connection.

Kurt Evans is a Black chef and activist who opened Black Dragon Takeout, an American Chinese takeout restaurant in Philadelphia that he hopes to turn into a chain. In an April 2023 interview, he told *Philadelphia Magazine* this:

"There are three types of Chinese restaurants [in America]. You've got the sit-down places in Chinatown, where they bring you a menu and all that. You have Chinese buffets in the suburbs, where you get all-you-can-eat type food. Then you have the hood Chinese store—desolate neighborhoods, high security, they buzz you in, a lot of them have bulletproof glass."

The proliferation of Chinese restaurants in the United States dates back to the 1849 California Gold Rush. Chinese immigrants went there to find their fortune. In 1862, as the Civil War was being fought, work started on the transcontinental railway. Chinese workers were recruited for this labor. Eventually, people came from China specifically to work on the railroad. An April 2022 *Smithsonian Magazine* article by Matt Stirn estimates that twelve thousand Chinese people did the blasting and laid tracks out west. An April 2023 History Channel article by Lesley Kennedy puts the number at fifteen thousand and twenty thousand.

When the Civil War ended and suddenly more people needed jobs, some people turned their hostility toward the Chinese laborers for "taking" those railway jobs. That led to the Chinese Exclusion Act being passed in 1882. But starting in 1915, Chinese people classified as merchants could be granted visas. Restaurateurs counted as merchants. Suddenly there was an incentive for people to open restaurants, especially small ones with low start-up costs.

In a 2018 *Philadelphia Inquirer* article, Roseann Liu writes that during the Reconstruction era, Chinese merchants opened grocery stores in the Mississippi Delta. These stores sold goods at a cheaper price than the plantation commissaries available to formerly enslaved people working as sharecroppers, and they let Black customers in during the Jim Crow days. During the Great Migration and the redlining that created Black neighborhoods in US cities, this pattern stayed: Chinese merchants would open small grocery or convenience stores and restaurants in Black neighborhoods, and they were able to offer lower prices than other businesses a majority of the time.

Because Chinese cuisine in China is extremely regional and varied, and these business owners had to adapt to what their customers liked, even American Chinese food became regional. Someone who knows New Orleans yakamein, a beef noodle soup, would be surprised by Baltimore's yat gaw mein or yakamein, which is thick udon noodles in a brown gravy. Both might be upset that they can't find it in New York. Just like you, I can't find the big, bubbly-skinned New York–style egg roll in San Francisco, where egg rolls are smaller and lighter in color, closer to what I call a spring roll. So even though it doesn't have gourmet status, depending on who you ask, I still think of Chinese takeout from the hood Chinese spot as a cuisine, with all the care and attention that it deserves, including wine pairing.

I grew up with a Chinese food experience that showed me that level of care. My father was introduced to Hop Kee by his uncle JJ in the late 1970s. It became his gateway to Chinatown. The Cantonese food and the hospitality must have made a lasting impression on my father, as Hop Kee has been adopted as our "family's restaurant."

Hop Kee opened in 1968 on the corner of Mott and Mosco streets, and it's one of the oldest restaurants in Chinatown. I have been eating at Hop Kee my entire life. My mother shared that she had cravings for its food during both her pregnancies with me and then my brother, and my father would drive from Harlem to Chinatown at three a.m. to satisfy them. Throughout the years we have been dining at this no-frills, very simply decorated restaurant to celebrate everything from birthdays to graduations, and we've been fortunate to develop a bond with the waiters, cooks, and the owner.

I will never forget in 2001, weeks after the

WINE PAIRING FOR THE PEOPLE

DECODING THE LABEL

Label 1 annotations:
- Producer
- Vintage

Label 2 annotations:
- Producer
- Vintage
- Type of Wine
- Ingredients
- Date Bottled
- Winery Location
- Volume, Alcohol Content, Sugar Content
- Health Warning

Label 2 text:
Ao Wine
2017
Cabernet Sauvignon
Red Wine
Contains: grapes, tartaric acid, sulfites
Made 23/04/04 by
Ao Wine Importers and Distributors
27 Cabernet Street
Bottle City
750 ml | 14% alc | 5 grams/liter sugar
WARNING: WINE HAS HEALTH EFFECTS

Chinese wine labels will always have the following info on the back label:

- **Name/brand of product**
- **Product type** (i.e., Grape Wine, "red," "white," "sparkling," "semi-sparkling," "fortified," "sweetened fortified," etc.)
- **Ingredients list** (exempt for products made of one ingredient)
- **Volume** in ml or liters (usually 750 ml)
- **Alcohol content** (%)
- **Production date** (yy/mm/dd)
- **Producer/Distributor/Importer** name and address
- **Sugar content** (g/L)
- **Health Warning statements**

attack on the World Trade Center, which is walking distance to Chinatown, when my father called the family with a declaration: "We've got to go to Hop Kee!" We learned from the news about the decline of business due to the lack of tourists in New York City, and about government employees who had worked in the neighboring courts and federal buildings, who were traumatized and did not want to return to the area. My father understood the power of the dollar, and he made sure each of us played a role in ensuring the security of the small businesses in Chinatown.

My father was loyal to his love for Hop Kee,

and on the last birthday before his transition, I was able to share some favorites with him and our family in the hospital. On my birthday, just one week after his funeral, I went down to Hop Kee. Everything looked the same as it had my entire life, but it felt different. As soon as I put in my order the manager and waiter recognized me.

"You are Tony's daughter, right? How is he doing? We heard he is not well," the waiter said. I took a deep breath and shared the news of his passing. They offered their condolences, and I began crying and tried to finish what I could of my large family-size order. Then the waiter returned and offered me dessert. (Wait, they have dessert?) They cut a slice of the famous fluffy cheese sponge cake, which was clearly an off menu item, and they sat down and enjoyed it with me.

I am going to be honest: I have never read the menu at Hop Kee—I have been ordering from memory for years. Here are few of my family's favorite dishes for you to try: Cantonese crab, pan-fried flounder, snails in black bean sauce, in-shell barbecue shrimp, snow peas with oyster sauce, shrimp lo mein, string beans in garlic sauce, fried lobster, and for my mother, the roasted Peking duck. My father always made us tableside iced tea with the piping hot black tea they served, but he would order a bottle of Tsingtao Beer for himself. The light lager was his official pairing, as he was big on drinking like the locals everywhere he ate.

Back in 2019, I officially invited friends to join me at Hop Kee for my birthday, and we easily finished about a case of Champagne with our food. Since then, I have never arrived without wine. It turns out, my father and I were ahead of the trend. Recently, sommeliers have gotten media attention expressing their love for Chinese BYOB spots, either for the sport of finding the perfect pairing between wine and food, or just sharing wine with friends. The support seems to be welcomed by the establishments, as it highlights these old-school restaurants that may lack the attention that newer spots get. Beyond my beloved Hop Kee, other sommeliers' favorites are Peking Duck House and Spicy Village in Manhattan.

China's Wine Regions

Not a whole lot of Chinese wine makes it to the United States as of this writing. The label you're most likely to find is Ao Yun, which is owned by Louis Vuitton Moët Hennessy. But the London Wine Competition notes that China is the sixth-largest wine-producing country by volume and that there's evidence of wine making there all the way back to 2600 BCE.

In more recent years, China has seen interest and investment from winemakers in Champagne and Bordeaux, plus a huge amount of growth in domestically owned wineries. As its wine production continues to grow, its regions will change too. For now, here are the major regions:

Shandong: On China's east coast, between Beijing and Shanghai, Shandong produces about 40 percent of the country's wine. It has a cool maritime climate, with some higher-altitude regions further inland. It has investors and grapes from Bordeaux—Cabernet Sauvignon, Cabernet Franc, and Carménère—as well as Syrah, Chardonnay, and Riesling.

Hebei: Just north of Shandong, Hebei has warm springs and summers, but cold winters.

Its coastal subregion, Changli, is called China's Bordeaux, and gets some humidity from the Bohai Sea. Another subregion, Shacheng, is drier and sunny. Hebei is known mostly for Bordeaux grape varieties. A third subregion, Tianjin, was where Chinese and foreign winemakers first worked together in the late 1970s and '80s—the Sino-French Tianjin Dynasty Wine Company. It produces mostly sweet wines with Black Muscat.

Xinjiang: This region is in northwest China, bordering Kyrgyzstan and Mongolia. Among the Tianshan Mountains, a lot of the high-altitude desert vineyards here are prone to extreme weather and dramatic diurnal swings. Mostly sweet wine is produced here, and it's the country's second-largest grape-growing region, but mostly for table grapes. It's also one of the oldest—Greek settlers started making wine here in the fourth century BCE.

Ningxia: A mountainous region in northern China, Ningxia is dry with a lot of sunshine. It's best known for Bordeaux grape varieties. Bordeaux blends from here have even beat wines from Bordeaux in international competitions. That's why it's gotten subsidies from the government and investment from major winemakers.

Shanxi: This relatively small region east of Hebei has some prestige attached to it. Mostly a plateau surrounded by mountains, it's got four

China's Wine Regions

- Xinjiang
- Ningxia
- Yunnan
- Shanxi
- Hebei
- Shandong

PACIFIC OCEAN

ASIA

seasons, dry winds, big diurnal swings, and low humidity, which combine for pretty ideal wine-growing conditions. That's why it's attracted some high-profile winemakers. Its most popular varieties are Chenin Blanc, Merlot, Cabernet Franc, and Cabernet Sauvignon.

Yunnan: In southern China, Yunnan borders Myanmar, Laos, Vietnam, and Tibet. It's pretty far south for wine growing, but its Himalayan altitude helps keep it cool. It's humid and sunny, with a long growing season. It's attracted investment from Louis Vuitton Moët Hennessy.

Pairing with China's Regional Flavor Profiles

Chinese food is usually divided into eight regional styles. Are there variations within these styles? Yes, and there are entire regional and ethnic cuisines that aren't included in these eight. For example, there's Uyghur food. The Uyghur are a persecuted Turkic minority group whose food reflects their ancestry. Hong Kong has its own cuisine, and Taiwan (an independent country that China considers part of China) has its own cuisine. And then these cooking styles are different in diaspora too. But we'll start here to get an overview of the cuisine and what wine to pair with their most popular dish.

Sichuan is known for its signature mouth-tingling peppercorns. The cuisine also uses a lot of pickled and fermented ingredients, as well as garlic and ginger. It's strong and spicy.

Try: Kung Pao Chicken (宫保鸡丁, Gōng bǎo jī dīng), stir fried with chile peppers and peanuts, with off-dry Alsace Gewürztraminer. Depending on your heat tolerance, you can go with a dry or off-dry style—the off-dry will do more to offset the dish's heat. The common lychee, pink grapefruit, and ginger notes balance well with the Sichuan peppercorns, Hoisin sauce, and peanuts.

Hunan is another cuisine with a spicy flavor profile, but Hunan food uses mostly dried chiles, instead of numbing Sichuan peppercorns. Many dishes have smoky flavors, plus shallots, garlic, and fermented and pickled ingredients for umami.

Try: Chairman Mao's Red-Braised Pork (毛氏红烧肉, Máo shì hóng shāo ròu), a rich dish of pork belly braised in a spicy sauce flavored with star anise and ginger—with Gamay from the Willamette Valley. This light-bodied red wine from Oregon has refreshing acidity, plus dark fruit and tobacco notes that provide a nice boost to the dish's warming spices.

Jiangsu is a coastal southeastern province, sometimes called the land of fish and rice, even though one of its signature dishes is salted duck, and another is braised meatballs. But yes, there is a lot of fish. The food here is known for being light, salty, and letting the flavor of the ingredients shine through.

Try: Sweet-and-Sour Mandarin Fish (松鼠桂鱼, Sōngshǔ guì yú), a whole fish that's been cut so that small pieces stick out while staying attached to the bone, then fried and served with a sweet-and-sour sauce. I'd pair it with Auxerrois Blanc from Alsace, because something crisp and mineral-driven will pair well.

Zhejiang is also a pretty mild, fresh, and light cuisine. It also uses a lot of fish, but usually lake fish, plus poultry and fresh vegetables.

Common seasonings are vinegar, shallots, garlic, and ginger. Shaoxing cooking wine is from here, and it's known for being slightly sweet up front, with a dry, tart, slightly astringent finish.

Try: Beggar's Chicken (叫化鸡, Jiàohuà jī). A whole chicken, plus herbs and aromatics, are steamed together wrapped in lotus leaves and clay. The whole thing comes out tender and steeped with delicate flavors. A Bordeaux Blanc is a white wine blend that has the waxy characteristic of Semillon, so it won't be overwhelmed by this flavorful dish, and the lemon-and-herbs quality of Sauvignon Blanc will enhance the flavors.

Fujian is another coastal region where spicy seafood soups and stews are common. Even a lot of seasonings, like fish sauce and shrimp paste, come from the sea. There's also a lot of woodland ingredients like mushrooms and bamboo shoots, and warming spices like cinnamon and star anise. This region has a lot of international influences on its food.

Try: Buddha Jumps Over the Wall (佛跳墙, Fó tiào qiáng). This is an incredibly layered and complex soup, made with a lot of big, bold ingredients from seafood to eggs to red meat. It's tempting to reach for a hearty red wine, but that would clobber some of the food's more delicate aspects. Slovenian skin-contact Pinot Grigio is an orange wine that is packed with notes of dried fruit and tea. The skin contact gives this wine some viscosity to help it stand up to the stew.

Shandong, one of China's oldest cuisines, is known for being fried but not greasy. Soups and braises also play a large role, and a lot of dishes use seafood. Some of the more common flavors are ginger, garlic, and scallion, but there are some sweet-and-sour dishes here too.

Try: Braised Intestines in Brown Sauce (九转大肠, Jiǔ zhuǎn dà cháng), which is fried pieces of intestine in a brown gravy, will go well with Xinomavro. With rich food, a little bit of funk from this Greek wine will add richness to match the dish's.

Anhui is China's mountain cuisine. It uses herbs, mushrooms, and bamboo shoots, as well as smaller game meat like frogs and turtles. It's heavy on stews, soups, and braises.

Try: Wang's Smelly Tofu (王小臭豆腐, Wáng xiǎo chòu dòu fu), aka stinky tofu, originated in Anhui. This spicy fermented tofu goes well with a lighter-bodied red wine. Spätburgunder, the German word for Pinot Noir, will match this food in herbaceous and earthy characteristics.

Cantonese is the style of cooking closest to American Chinese food. It's less spicy than Sichuan or Hunan cuisine. Garlic is a major flavor, plus ginger and five-spice powder. Cantonese food also uses a lot of sauces like plum sauce, black bean sauce, and sweet and sour.

Try: Peking Duck. The iconic dish of a whole, slow-roasted duck goes beautifully with Viognier. A wine with high acidity will cleanse your palate from these rich, mild dishes, but you still want something aromatic to accent the anise notes of five spice and the fruity, floral notes of some sauces.

ASIA

+ PAIRED UP

GENERAL TSO'S CHICKEN + ROSADO, NAVARRA, SPAIN. Crispy chicken pieces tossed in sweet-and-spicy sauce call for a wine with a bit of texture that can stand up to all the dish's flavor. Bright strawberry-pink rosado made from a blend of Tempranillo and Garnacha is a great option for this dish. Intensely flavored red fruit, like strawberry, raspberries, and cherries, and refreshing acidity are great at providing balance for this powerful dish.

ORANGE CHICKEN + FIANO, CAMPANIA, ITALY. This is another dish that starts with crispy chicken pieces and adds a sweet-and-spicy sauce (What can I say? It's a formula for success). This one, though, is flavored with orange, as you may have guessed from the name. Fiano, a white wine from Southern Italy, has a sort of waxy quality that works well with a sticky, syrupy sauce like this one. It also has notes of orange peel that match well with the chicken.

SWEET-AND-SOUR CHICKEN + DE CHAUNAC PÉT-NAT, FINGER LAKES, NEW YORK. Chicken fingers in a light, airy batter and a sauce that is, like the name says, sweet and sour, are great with a sparkling wine that can cleanse the palate. De Chaunac is a French American hybrid wine grape used to make red wine. In the Finger Lakes, you can find light-bodied sparkling options with black cherry and violet notes.

FRIED CHICKEN WINGS + GRENACHE BLANC, RHÔNE VALLEY, FRANCE. This Spanish white wine is rich and refreshing at the same time. It has enough body to stand up to deliciously greasy, salty, crispy wings, but bright, tangy notes of citrus zest, Asian pear, and green plum add freshness.

BEEF AND BROCCOLI + TROLLINGER, WÜRTTEMBERG, GERMANY. A classic, soothing dish of beef and broccoli stir-fried with a garlicky, gingery brown sauce deserves a little fun. Trollinger, a red wine grape from Germany brings that. It's light in body and high in acidity to liven up the brown sauce. Fruity notes of pomegranate, raspberry, and red cherry will really accentuate the dish's ginger flavors.

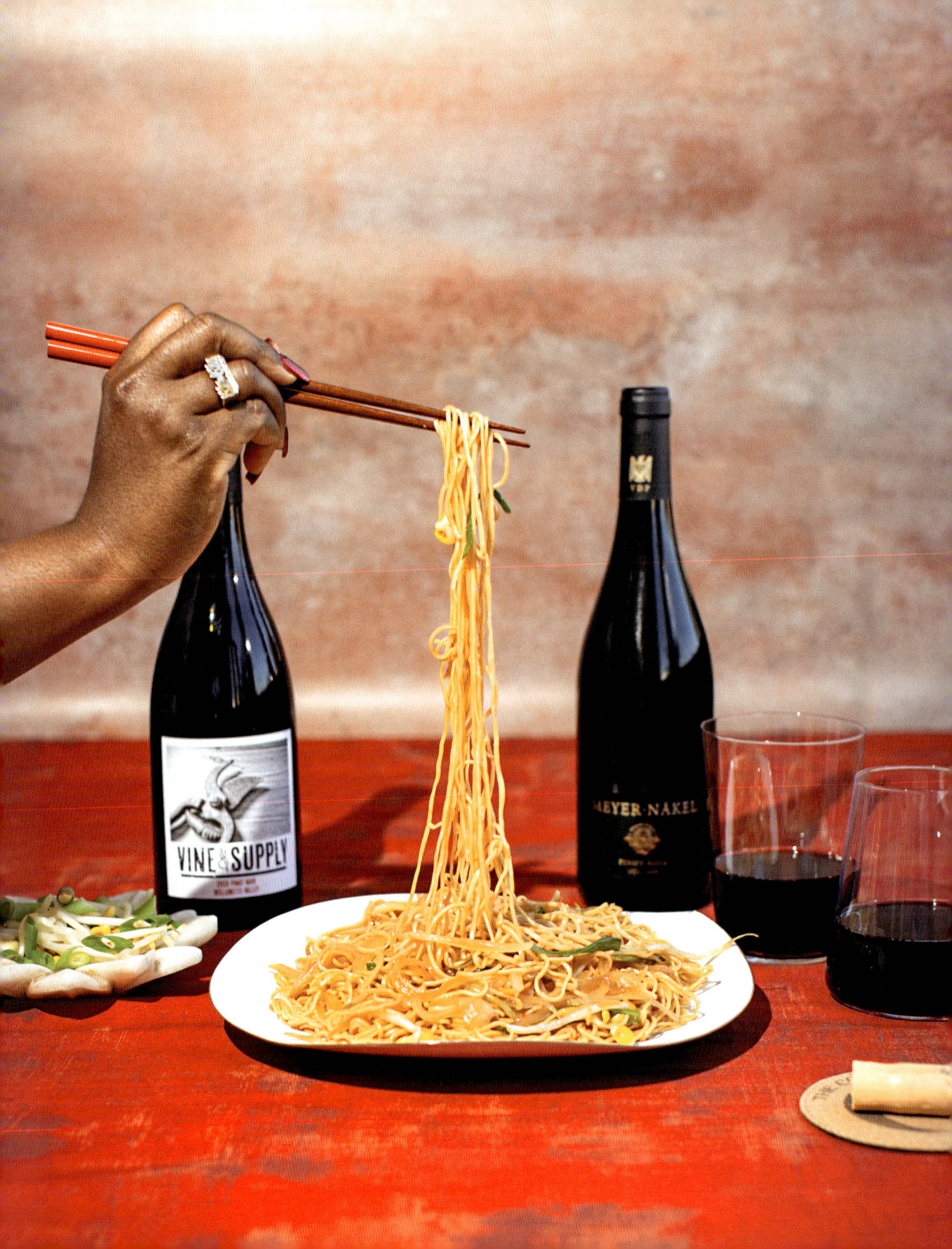
VINE&SUPPLY

ASIA

PAN-FRIED NOODLES IN SUPERIOR SOY SAUCE + PINOT NOIR, WILLAMETTE VALLEY, OREGON

Wilson Tang is the force behind one of New York City's institutions of Chinese food: Nom Wah Tea Parlor, which has been in business since 1920. In 2010, he took over the bakery and tearoom from his uncle Wally and started to transform it into a restaurant that could go from daytime dim sum into evening. He's opened new restaurants, started shipping frozen dumplings nationally, and written a cookbook, and he can still put together a good bowl of noodles. Use these as a side or a base for whatever you like, or enjoy them on their own.

Oregon Pinot Noir gets a cool climate influence from the Pacific Ocean, which provides a refreshingly bright red wine with notes of cherry, raspberry, and strawberry. Earthy notes of mushroom, dried herbs, and forest floor are the perfect complement to this light umami dish and can balance well with the addition of a protein.

1. Mix the soy sauces, toasted sesame oil, salt, sugar, wine, and white pepper in a small bowl, and set aside.
2. Bring a pot of water to a boil and add the noodles. Cook fresh noodles for about 1 minute (or dried for about 2 minutes). Drain, rinse under cold water, drain again very well, and then pat dry with a paper towel.
3. Heat a wok or large pan over high heat and add 1 tablespoon of neutral oil to coat. Add white parts of the scallion and onion to the pan. Stir fry for about 1 to 2 minutes. Add the noodles to the pan. Add the soy sauce mixture and toss continuously for 2 minutes or until the noodles are golden brown. Add the bean sprouts and the rest of the scallions and toss for 1 to 2 minutes, or until the bean sprouts are slightly transparent but still crunchy.

Used with permission from *The Nom Wah Cookbook: Recipes and Stories from 100 Years at New York City's Iconic Dim Sum Restaurant* by Wilson Tang and Joshua David Stein (Ecco, October 2020).

SERVES 4

4 teaspoons light soy sauce

2 teaspoons dark soy sauce

1 teaspoon toasted sesame oil

½ teaspoon salt

½ teaspoon sugar

1 tablespoon Shaoxing wine

¼ teaspoon ground white pepper

1 pound fresh thin HK-style egg noodles (we use the Twin Marquis brand)

4 scallions, cut in 2-inch long slices

1¼ cup white onion, thinly sliced

3 cups bean sprouts

WINE PAIRING FOR THE PEOPLE

Japan

Japan has been a bucket-list trip in the more recent years in my life. As I get acquainted with Japanese food and beverage culture, I find myself salivating for more, which is exactly the same feeling I had when I returned home after living in Italy. The art of gastronomy is very much part of both cultures, and the Japanese have definitely mastered the science and precision of it.

I was introduced to Japanese culture at my first wine job at The Winery. The shop was owned by Japanese native Nobu Otsu, who had also opened a second location in Tokyo. Everything from his love for hip-hop and streetwear to his tasting notes was eccentric, and I've remained curious about his culture ever since.

In 2012, on Fredrick Douglass Boulevard, walking distance from the shop, he opened Jado Sushi Wine Bar. Before the opening, he told a neighborhood blog *Harlem Bespoke*, "I love drinking a nice chilled white wine with sushi. But I've been very frustrated because there's no good sushi restaurant that has a good wine list, even in such a progressive city like New York, where anything is available. I have been even more frustrated by the fact that there is no real sushi restaurant in Harlem, my hood."

I was fortunate enough to be at the shop to support him during the opening process of the restaurant, and this experience exposed me to the diversity of Japanese food and profiles and endless pairings for wine and sake.

The closest I have been to experiencing the Japanese diasporic culture was during my trip to Brazil. The Liberdade neighborhood in the city of São Paulo is known as one of the largest Japan Towns in the world, easy to recognize by the distinctive red torii gates, traditional lanterns, and large anime wall murals. Japanese immigrants arrived in Brazil in the early 1900s as coffee farmers. For better opportunities, they moved to the city center, in the Liberdade neighborhood. In the 1920s, it started to transform from a Portuguese and Italian neighborhood to a Japanese one. Now the area has become a haven for other Asian immigrants, and you can find more of a fusion of cultures on most streets, but there are still some gems keeping this Japanese Brazilian community alive.

DRINK NOW: Japanese Brazilian Bars and Restaurants to Try in Brazil
- Izakaya Issa
- Bar Kintaro
- Lamen Kazu
- Kazu Cake

Sake Regions

According to Japan's National Tax Agency, Japan has fifteen Geographic Indications (GI) for sake. These factor in the regions' water, which has a huge impact on the finished sake, and regional styles, which tend to complement regional cuisines. But what might surprise those of us with a wine background is that the rice used is not regulated by GI.

Japan has about one hundred varieties of sake rice that are grown commercially. These have been bred to grow well in different regions. But sake makers can buy rice from anywhere in the country to make the style of sake they want to make. A few producers do use local grain rice and even make varietal sake, the way we see in wine. For the most part, though, when we're talking about regionality in sake, it's mostly about water and production styles.

Here's a look at Japan's protected sake regions, according to the National Tax Agency's GI registration information.

Hakusan: The regional sake here has a rich rice flavor with a bit of tartness. Water that's high in calcium and low in potassium helps emphasize the rice flavor. There is also a regional specialty of chrysanthemum sake.

Yamanashi: Sake here is delicate and fruit forward, made with soft water from Mount Fuji's rain and snow runoff.

Yamagata: This silky, delicate style comes from a region where a lot of fruit is grown, so the sake is also fruit forward.

Nadagogo: This region encompasses the cities of Nishigo, Mikagego, Uozakigo, Nishinomiyago, and Imazugo, as well as Higashinada Ward of Kobe City, Ashiya City, and the Nishinomiya City of Hyogo Prefecture. The sake is balanced, mild, and easy to drink.

Harima: The sake in this region in the Hyogo Prefecture tends to be rounder and less astringent than some other styles. It's made with Hyogo koji from Yamada Nishiki rice, which is considered one of the best sake rice varieties for high-end bottles.

Mie: Sake from this high-altitude inland region is described as having a warming characteristic, regardless of the temperature at which it's served. Mie is home to Ise Shrine.

Japan's Hybrid Grapes

Hybrid grapes are a growing area of interest in regions where the terroir might not be all that well suited to typical European *Vitis vinifera*. This isn't genetic modification—it's selectively breeding grapes so that they'll naturally be hardier in cold regions like Japan, more mildew resistant in damp regions, or less in need of water in drought-prone regions. Japan is ahead of the game, breeding native Japanese grapes with *Vitis vinifera*, different cold climate *Vitis vinifera* with each other, and sometimes throwing American hybrids in the mix. Here are a few examples:

Muscat Bailey A = Muscat Hamburg + Bailey
Riesling Lion = Koshu Sanjaku + Riesling
Riesling Forte = Koshu Sanjaku + Riesling
Shinano Riesling = Chardonnay + Riesling
Monde Briller = Chardonnay + Cayuga White
Kai Noir = Black Queen + Cabernet Sauvignon
Yama Sauvignon = Yama Budou + Cabernet Sauvignon
Kadaino R1 = Ryukyuganebu + Muscat of Alexandria

> **DRINK NOW: Sake Producers**
>
> The world of sake is vast, and even though it's steeped in tradition, it's also changing all the time and subject to trends. I'm also still tasting and learning, but here are some sake producers I'm enjoying right now.
> - Imada Brewery
> - Kokuryu
> - Dewazakura Sake Brewery
> - Brooklyn Kura

WINE PAIRING FOR THE PEOPLE

People pilgrimage to the shrine and are greeted with sake.

Tone Numata: Near the Sea of Japan, this region grows rice known for its high quality. Its sake is very fruity, but it has savory notes and ends with a bit of a bitter, vegetal characteristic.

Hagi: This volcanic region is known for sake with a fresh, green note. There's a delta of the Abu River here, and rice has been grown there since the seventeenth century, but sake making is newer to the area.

Saga: Sake brewing here dates back to the twelfth or thirteenth century. Today, the sake here is mellow and ripe, thanks in part to low-lying, warm plains where some of the rice is grown.

Nagano: This high-altitude region makes umami-rich, mouthcoating sake. Long winters here meant a diet with foods fermented for preservation, so the sake matches those flavors.

Niigata: A relatively mild climate here, without a huge diurnal swing, makes sake that's very delicate and light. It's got a hint of sweetness to it, and some umami. It's made from a blend of rices to achieve the desired style.

Shiga: This region spans a few different climates and contains Japan's oldest, largest lake, as well as mountains and rivers. It's important to know that this region has been making monks' sake since the Muromachi period in the 1300s. Today, the sake is tangy, but well balanced by umami and sweetness.

Omachi City: This subregion of Nagano earned GI status for the purity of its rice flavor. Rice has been cultivated here since the Yayoi period, which started in 10 BCE.

ASIA

Sip the Culture

Japan's wine region is growing, with lots of international investment and workaround hybrid grapes. But it's far from being Japan's only alcoholic beverage. Here are some of the others.

SHOCHU. Even though the name sounds similar to Korean soju, shochu is its own thing. It can be distilled from any number of things—sweet potato, barley, buckwheat, rice, even carrots or sesame seeds. It's typically around 20–35 percent alcohol. It can be distilled multiple times, so depending on what the producer is going for, it can be neutral and clean like vodka, or have a little more grain characteristic like whiskey, and even some sweetness like bourbon.

UMESHU. This is plum wine, made by steeping plums in shochu with sugar. Some artisan producers are using sake, and some may opt for a less sweet version. It's sweet, tart, and fruity. It can be sipped chilled on its own, but it's also become popular to use in cocktails.

WHISKY. In the United States, when we write about whiskey from Japan, we spell it without the e, the same way we spell Scotch whisky. That's because Japanese whisky can be sold in allocated single-malt bottlings at extremely high prices, just like Scotch. Two of Japan's most famous whisky distilleries, Nikka and Suntory, were founded before World War II. In the 1970s, Suntory started promoting the idea of drinking whisky with water, which helped it gain popularity in Japan. Due to its high quality and its similar production methods to Scotch, it didn't take long after that for the rest of the world to catch on. There's a range of quality, but for the most part, Japanese whisky tends to be dry, smoky, and sometimes peaty.

SAKE. Japan's signature rice wine has a lot fewer classifications and designations than grape wine. First, it's separated into two categories: junmai-shu, which is pure rice wine, and honjozo-shu, which can have alcohol added. Within these two categories, it's graded by how much of the rice grain is ground or milled away before brewing, with sake made from whole grains often being less rustic and inexpensive. There are also flavored sakes and sparkling sakes. This drink can range from crisp, delicate, and dry, to savory, funky, and viscous. Its flavor can be fruity or toasty or any number of other things. Basically, we'd need a whole other book to get into all the details and various styles. But it is worth noting that sake can pair with dishes well outside of Japanese food, the same way that grape wines can go beautifully with Japanese dishes.

Iwate: Described as soft and mellow but also intense, this sake is made with mineral-rich water from Paleozoic sediment mixing with underground water. Harsh winters here also help keep the water pure, because it gets too cold for microorganisms to grow.

Shizuoka: Clean, light, and low in acidity, this sake can have a banana aroma. The water here, too, is soft, clean spring water. This is an area that has historically had trade routes passing through, and then a lot of tourism. The sake style complements local seafood that would have been served to tourists.

MOMOTARO

MAKES 1 COCKTAIL

1½ ounces Toki Whisky

½ ounce pisco

½ ounce Mancino Sakura Vermouth

¼ ounce Monin White Peach Syrup

3 dashes orange bitters

3 dashes hinoki bitters

Edible flower, for garnish

Grapefruit peel

Christian Suzuki-Orellana, aka Suzu, made his mark on Netflix's *Drink Masters* by sharing his Japanese heritage through the cocktails he made. That's been a theme of his offscreen career, too. He started bartending in Tokyo before bringing his talents back stateside. This cocktail has a few Japanese elements: the Japanese whisky but also a vermouth made with botanicals that include cherry blossoms and bitters flavored with hinoki Japanese cedar.

1. Combine all the ingredients except the garnish in a mixing vessel. Stir for 20 seconds, strain into an Old-Fashioned glass with a large ice block.
2. Garnish with flower, and twist a grapefruit peel over the surface of the cocktail.

ASIA

+ PAIRED UP

SHOYU RAMEN + PINOT GRIS, ALSACE, FRANCE. This style of ramen has a soy broth with chashu roasted pork, garlic, and of course, noodles. Pinot Gris from Alsace has a juicy, apple-and-pear flavor that will counteract this dish's saltiness without clashing.

OKONOMIYAKI + FRIULANO, FRIULI, ITALY. The thick, savory pancake filled with cabbage and sometimes topped with meat or fish goes well with Friulano. The Italian white wine's aromatic herb and floral notes will act as a nice contrast.

AGEDASHI TOFU + PECORINO, UMBRIA, ITALY. Golden brown cubes of firm tofu are fried in potato starch to create a shatteringly crisp exterior. Pecorino is a clean and refreshing white wine, and its medium body makes it suitable for a fried dish like this one.

YASAI NO TEMPURA + MÜLLER-THURGAU, RHEINHESSEN, GERMANY. Vegetable tempura uses fresh vegetables from sweet potato, carrot, okra, green beans, eggplant, and even mushrooms. Müller-Thurgau, a German white wine with bright yet delicate acidity, is a nice way to cut through the airy fried batter of the tempura.

SUKIYAKI + PINOT NOIR, CENTRAL OTAGO, NEW ZEALAND. Pan-fried beef in sweet soy-sauce broth is usually cooked or simmered at the table and accompanied with the dipping sauce of a beaten egg. Pair it with a New Zealand Pinot Noir, which has a lot of bright fruit flavors but also a hint of woody spice to complement the sweetness of the dish.

TONKATSU CURRY + GRÜNER VELTLINER, WACHAU, AUSTRIA. A mild curry with strips of breaded pork cutlet, this works well with Grüner Veltliner. The Austrian white wine has plenty of acidity and a peppery character that is known to pair with schnitzel too.

KARAAGE + CRÉMANT DE LOIRE, ANJOU, FRANCE. Fried chicken pieces can benefit from the classic complement of bubbles. Try a Crémant de Loire for a refreshing option with minerality.

NEGIMA + AGLIANICO ROSÉ, CAMPANIA, ITALY. This dish of chicken breast or thighs with onions is one of Yakitori's most popular dishes. It's cooked over a charcoal fire with a sake-based basting sauce, tare. Pair it with Aglianico Rosé, which bursts with juicy red and pink fruit notes like strawberry and watermelon, to create a summer-barbecue vibe.

GYU DONBURI + JUNMAI SAKE, HYOGO PREFECTURE, JAPAN. A beef and rice bowl that's popular in fast-food restaurants, this pairs well with Junmai Sake. This rice wine is simple, with no alcohol added. It has an earthy, nutty flavor in which you can still taste the rice. This pairing is the epitome of comfort food.

The Sushi Menu

For people who love sushi, there's no replacement for it. Other cuisines have their own raw fish dishes, some even with rice, but for whatever reason, sushi has captivated Americans. I know people who love it so much that they pick it up at the grocery store, and others who hold out for beautiful, pricy omakase meals where they're presented with one piece of sushi at a time. Plus, there's a whole world of elaborate, sometimes Americanized, maki or handrolls.

Plenty of higher-end Japanese restaurants serving ramen, sushi, or both, also have great wine lists and talented, trained sommeliers to help you select something to drink with your meal. But there are also bring-your-own-bottle Japanese restaurants out there, a million takeout options, and home cooks creating delicious Japanese food in their own kitchens, so there's plenty of opportunity to explore pairing on your own. Here are some quick hits to inspire your pairing journey.

Sushi and Wine Pairings

Otoro (Fatty Tuna) + Gamay, BEAUJOLAIS, FRANCE

Salmon + Vermentino, SARDINIA, ITALY

Unagi (Eel) + Furmint, TOKAJ, HUNGARY

Uni + Marsanne, RHÔNE VALLEY, FRANCE

Yellowtail (Hamachi) + Verdicchio, MARCHE, ITALY

Shiromi (White Fish) + Melon de Bourgogne, MUSCADET SÈVRE ET MAINE, FRANCE

Vegetable Roll + Vinho Verde Branco, VINHO VERDE, PORTUGAL

California Roll + Sauvignon Blanc, CENTRAL COAST, CALIFORNIA

Philadelphia Roll + Aligoté, BURGUNDY, FRANCE

Spicy Tuna Roll + Brachetto, PIEDMONT, ITALY

Spider Roll + Sparkling Blanc de Noir, MENDOCINO, CALIFORNIA

Shrimp Tempura Roll + Prosecco Rosé, VALDOBBIADENE

ASIA

South Korea

Like many New Yorkers, my experience with Korean culture is thanks to Koreatown, or K-Town. It was and is perfectly situated as a refuge for young professionals cringing at their corporate desk jobs in Midtown all day. K-Town became a haven granting access to Korean barbecue, karaoke, K-pop, and happy hour soju on a Tuesday. It was a dangerous lifestyle, but those were my twenties. Steps away from a miracle on Thirty-Fourth Street there is immersion on Thirty-Second Street. Between Broadway and Fifth Avenue in Manhattan and now growing, there is a crossroads to the soul of Korean culture.

But this chapter would be remiss not to mention the link between the United States and South Korea. The United States played a major role on South Korea's side during the Korean War and currently still has troops stationed in the country. This alliance, which dates back to the 1950s, has reinforced everything from business development for brands like Samsung to the popularity of Korean Drama movies, and the increased appetite for Korean cuisine in America.

A great example of this link is Anju, a modern Korean restaurant in Washington, DC, led by Executive Chef Angel Barreto. Chef Angel was inspired to focus on Korean cuisine by his parents, who both served in the US military and were stationed in South Korea. He has reached the James Beard Foundation Award semifinals for Best Chef: Mid-Atlantic in both 2018 and 2019.

Sip the Culture

Korea has a lot of history with and a variety of alcoholic drinks made from grains. There are two major categories, but there a lot of options in each one:

MAKGEOLLI. This creamy, cloudy rice wine is a simple drink that tastes like candied melon. Steamed rice, yeast, and water are combined and fermented in a clay pot. The resulting drink is low alcohol, usually in the 6–8 percent range, with savory, toasty rice notes balanced with acidity. It was traditionally a cheap drink, but now in both South Korea and the United States, it's getting the small-batch, artisan treatment.

SOJU. This is a distilled spirit, traditionally made with rice. During World War II, when Japan was occupying Korea, the Japanese army requisitioned the majority of Korean rice. People started making soju with other things like tapioca, sweet potatoes, and barley. It was prohibited for rice to be used in soju until 1990—long enough for a soju tradition to be established with other grains. Make sure you try it, as well as yogurt flavored soju.

In addition to being made with a wide variety of grains, soju can be anywhere from around 12 percent alcohol to 40-plus percent. It's sometimes compared to vodka as a neutral grain spirit, but soju often has a bit of sweetness to it. The most common soju is what's called a "green bottle," which is inexpensive, lower in alcohol, and sometimes fruit flavored, but there are high-end bottles too, and everything in between. Soju's become popular in cocktails, but the traditional way to drink it is on its own, chilled.

Speaking of Anju, let's dive into the drinking culture of Korea. Anju is a Korean word that refers to food eaten with alcohol, and many Koreans have made a sport out of seeing who can last the longest throughout the night. It is said the society's only vice is drinking, since the country has such strict laws, and I now understand where K-Town energy gets its roots. Social drinking at various pojangmacha, or pocha for short, where rounds of soju are paired with various anju, or bar snacks, is what I understand to be a typical night for some in Seoul. There is an etiquette for drinking, like you shouldn't pour for yourself or sit with an empty glass. Games with the bottle cap will keep your group entertained while drinking. From what I hear, endless bar crawls can end with hangovers that can only be cured by piping hot soup.

While these bar crawls don't necessarily involve wine, that doesn't mean wine and Korean food don't belong together. A lot of times when foods are described as challenging or difficult to pair with wine, it's a shorthand for complex, flavorful, maybe spicy. That's the case with Korean food. A lot of meals come with banchan, an assortment of small side dishes like kimchi, cold marinated vegetables, and sauteed or steamed vegetables. So immediately you're mixing a lot of flavors. When you look at it from that perspective, it makes sense that the famous Korean fried chicken might have a diaspora connection too: It is said that Korean people learned how to fry chicken from US soldiers stationed there during the Korean War, naming it "the other KFC." Some New York City Korean restaurants like Atomix, Coqodac, and Cote Steakhouse (which also has a Miami location) prioritize their wine lists. I wanted to highlight more wine pairings for your next anju

ASIA

and inspire you to enjoy Korean food and wine magic at home.

Korean food has a lot of funky and spicy elements, and a lot of savory dishes include sweetness too. Many dishes are rich, hearty, and filling. It's almost like the food is so flavorful and well balanced on its own that it's hard to figure out what a drink can add. But wine can always add *something*. If you're reading this book, you probably agree.

> **DRINK NOW: Soju Producers**
>
> If you've never tried soju before, like any other drink it might be a little intimidating to jump in and pick a bottle at the store. Here are a few producers I'm enjoying lately.
>
> - West 32 Soju
> - The Han Seoul Night Plum Soju
> - Tokki Soju

+ PAIRED UP

DAK GALBI + DRY VIDAL, SHENANDOAH VALLEY, VIRGINIA. This spicy chicken stir-fry really sings with Dry Vidal Blanc. Stone fruits, green mango, and citrus, plus herbal characteristics, add refreshment and keep the spice at bay.

DOLSOT BIBIMBAP + SCHIAVA, ALTO ADIGE, ITALY. The classic rice dish served in a hot stone bowl and topped with meat, vegetables, and a fried egg, is fun to eat. Schiava, a light-bodied red wine from Italy, is fun to drink, with cotton candy notes and good acidity to keep you refreshed.

DOSIRAK + GAMAY ROSÉ, HUNTER VALLEY, AUSTRALIA. These Korean-style lunch boxes can be filled with rice and banchan—side dishes like kimchi, oi muchim cucumber salad, kongnamul bean sprout salad, and fish cakes. Sometimes, they're shaken to be mixed before being served. With all its options and flavors, dosirak pairs well with a down-for-whatever wine, Gamay Rosé, which is bright and fresh with just a hint of gaminess.

CHIKIN, AKA KOREAN FRIED CHICKEN (KFC) + CRÉMANT DE LIMOUX ROSÉ, LANGUEDOC-ROUSSILLON, FRANCE. Korean fried chicken has spices, sugar, and salt that make it a good candidate for a sparkling wine with a little bit of extra texture, like Crémant de Limoux Rosé, a blend of Chardonnay, Chenin Blanc, Mauzac, and Pinot Noir. Some will argue that sparkling wine originated in Limoux and not Champagne.

HAEMUL PAJEON + ARNEIS, PIEDMONT, ITALY. This is a Korean seafood pancake usually served with green onions and egg. Arneis, a white wine from northern Italy, has a lot of minerality that will accent the seafood in this dish.

SPAM KIMBAP + ROSÉ, PROVENCE, FRANCE. Spam rolled with rice and seaweed goes nicely with a pale, delicate Provence Rosé. The wine's strawberry notes give the Spam a high-class appeal, while the rosé's minerality complements the rice and seaweed.

A VERY GOOD KIMCHI JJIGAE + RAMATO PINOT GRIS, ALTO ADIGE, ITALY

SERVES 2

6 ounces boneless, skinless pork belly, cut into 1-inch pieces

2 large garlic cloves, fine-grated

1 tablespoon gochugaru, plus more to taste

Pinch of kosher salt, plus more to taste

1 tablespoon unsalted butter

1 cup rough-chopped Napa cabbage kimchi

½ cup kimchi juice

1 tablespoon gochujang

1 teaspoon fish sauce

½ medium yellow onion, thinly sliced

1 daepa or 2 large scallions, thinly sliced on the diagonal

Cooked white rice, for serving

DRINK NOW:
Ramato Pinot Gris

- Field Recordings Domo Arigato Mr. Ramato
- The Marigny Willamette Valley Carbonic Pinot Gris
- End of Nowhere Skin-Fermented Pinot Gris "Spaceboy"
- Channing Daughters Ramato Pinot Grigio

Eric Kim is an Atlanta-raised resident of New York City (where he's a *New York Times* staff writer) of Korean descent. His food writing and recipes embrace all three of these cultures and others with a real diasporic spirit. He's worked with Food Network, Saveur, Food 52, and more, and his first cookbook, *Korean American*, was a *New York Times* bestseller.

Here, he shares a kimchi and pork belly stew that's spicy, savory, and hearty.

Traditional to Italy's Alto Adige region, ramato-style Pinot Grigio wines take on a coppery color from skin contact. Pinot Gris is the French name for the same grape, and its wines are usually made in a softer, fruitier style than zippy, citrusy Pinot Grigio. In a ramato, the skin contact also gives them a grippy, savory quality that helps the fruit character stand up to the spicy stew.

1. In a small bowl, toss the pork belly with the garlic, gochugaru, and salt.
2. In a small pot, melt the butter over medium-low heat. Add the pork belly mixture and stir-fry until aromatic, just a few seconds, making sure the garlic and gochugaru don't burn. (The pork belly won't release a lot of fat at this stage.)
3. Add the kimchi, kimchi juice, gochujang, fish sauce, and 1 cup water. Raise the heat to high and bring liquid to a boil. Reduce the heat to medium-low. Cover the pot and gently boil until the kimchi has softened and the pork is cooked through, about 10 minutes.
4. Reduce the heat to low, add the onion, cover again, and simmer until the onion releases some of its juices and aroma, about 5 minutes. Taste for seasoning, and add more salt, gochugaru, or both, as desired. Garnish with the daepa or scallion and serve with the white rice.

Used with permission from *Korean American: Food That Tastes Like Home* by Eric Kim (Clarkson Potter, March 2022).

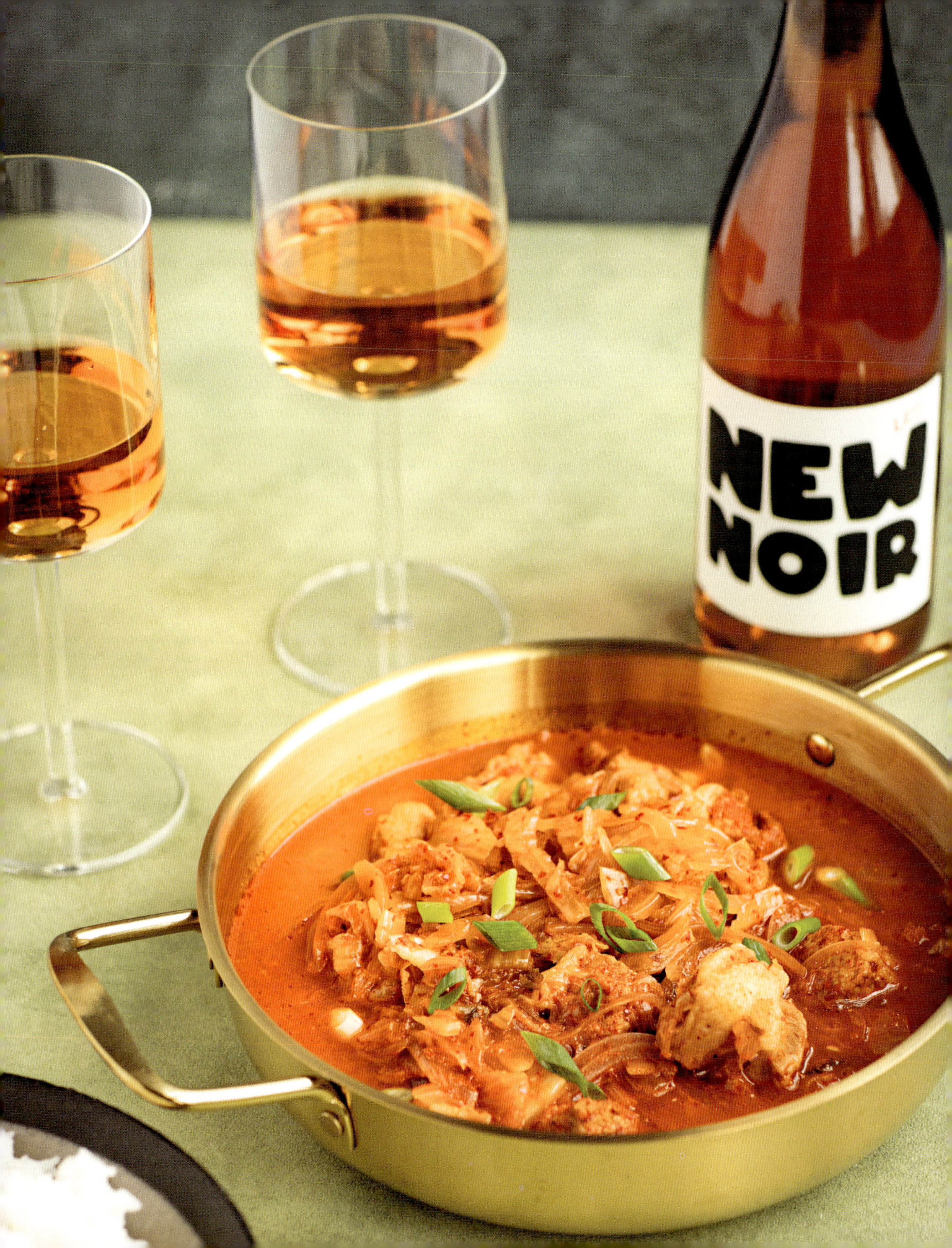
NEW
NOIR

Southeast Asia

B**eyond food, Southeast Asian culture may have** had its largest impact on me through American movies from *The Beach* to *Eat, Pray, Love* to *Tomb Raider*. And who can forget *The Hangover Part II*? For many millennials who don't have any cultural ties to Thailand, Vietnam, or the Philippines, these movies exposed us to pristine beaches, glamorous villas, enticing markets, vibrant nightlife, and spiritual temples.

The eleven countries that makeup Southeast Asia are Brunei, Cambodia, East Timor (Timor-Leste), Indonesia, Laos, Malaysia, Myanmar (Burma), Philippines, Singapore, Thailand, and Vietnam. But in this book, I am going to focus on Thai, Vietnamese, and Filipino cuisine, which have been taking over the food scene around the United States in my lifetime. I've gotten to travel to some parts of the country that have larger populations from these three countries, and let me tell you that short of going abroad, these areas are the best to get good Thai, Vietnamese, and Filipino cuisine.

The influx of Vietnamese immigrants can be traced back to the end of the Vietnam War, between the 1970s and '80s. During my visits to New Orleans, I was officially introduced to the country's cuisine through a strong Vietnamese community in New Orleans' East and West Bank, adjacent to where I stayed in Gretna. At first glance, it was hard for me to see the connection between Louisiana and Vietnamese cultures. However, through food you can see how easily Vietnamese Creole is a natural fit.

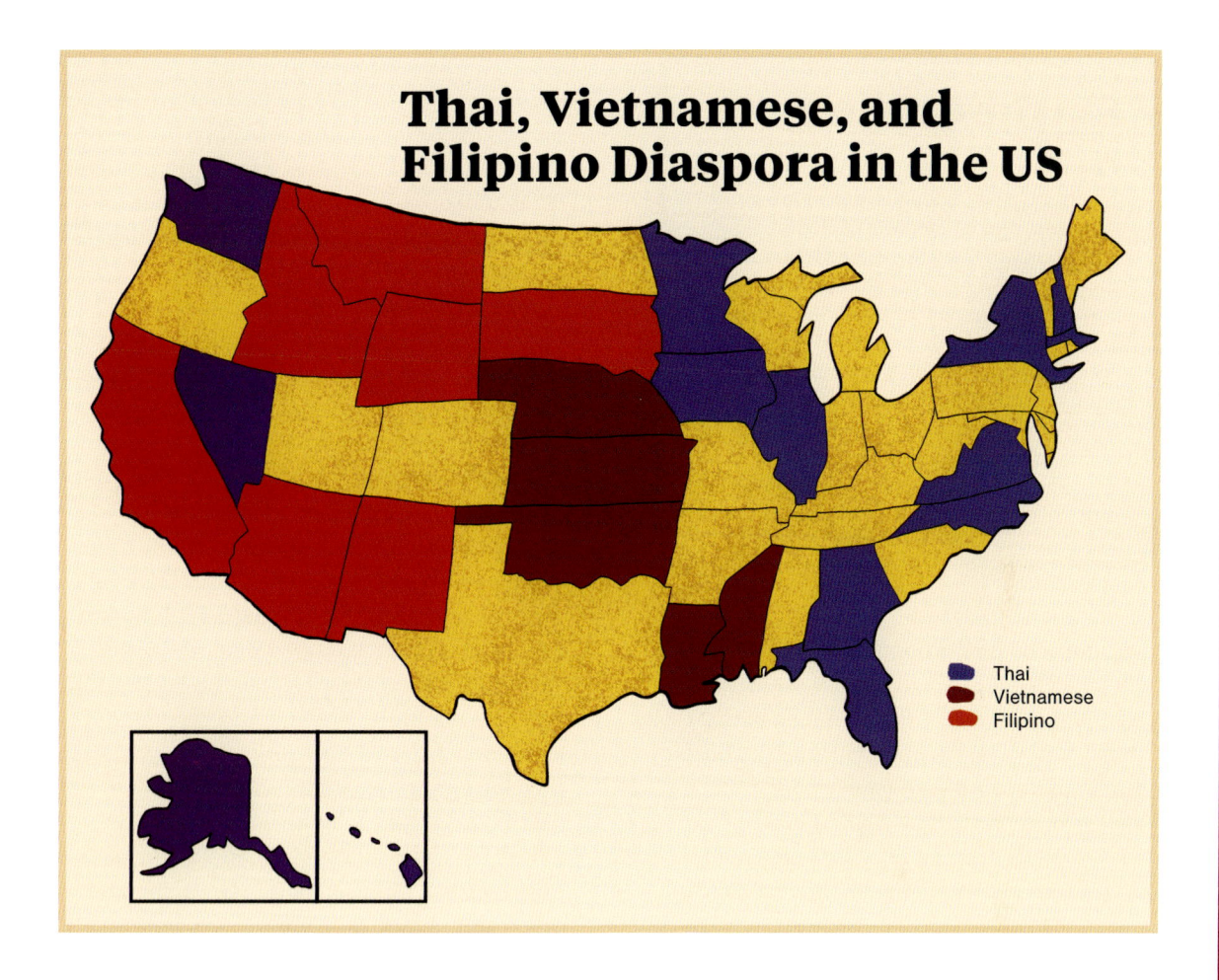

ASIA

Thai, Vietnamese, and Filipino Diaspora in the US

- Thai
- Vietnamese
- Filipino

Vietnamese food tends to use more raw vegetables, and the climate in New Orleans makes it easy to grow ingredients like cabbage, bean sprouts, radishes, cilantro, culantro, and basil. There is also the French connection in both cooking styles. Vietnam was occupied by France from 1887 to 1954. One Vietnamese dish that's become popular in the United States, the bánh mì, is an example of the French culinary influence. This sandwich of pâté, ham and/or roasted pork, pickled carrots, and daikon is served on a Vietnamese adaptation of a French baguette.

Some believe that bánh xèo, a savory, stuffed pancake made from rice flour, may have some relationship to a French crêpe, and that the broth for pho has roots in French technique, but those connections are up for debate. You can find a lot more Vietnamese-Creole fusion in New Orleans today, whether it's a bánh mì–po'boy mash-up or anything from Man Chu's takeout menu using traditional Vietnamese seasonings on Black American staple dishes.

The Thai community remains one of the smallest represented Asian groups in the United States, but Thai food has made

WINE PAIRING FOR THE PEOPLE

> ## Sip the Culture
>
> **TEA** is a popular drink throughout Southeast Asia. Some countries grow their own, and many parts of Southeast Asia cook with tea leaves (see map on page 232). Green and black tea are both popular. Vietnam might be better known for its coffee culture, another sign of French influence. One thing that makes both tea and coffee cultures distinct in much of Southeast Asia is the addition of sweetened condensed milk. Often, coffee or tea with sweetened condensed milk is served cold.

a big impact. I don't know when or where it happened, but at some point, it seems like pad thai became just as common in the United States as lo mein and spaghetti. Thai immigrants are predominately on the West Coast, where the majority settled in the cities of Los Angeles and San Francisco Bay Area following World War II, but another city out west is attracting Thai interest, and that's Las Vegas. Tourism and hospitality provide job opportunities for service work. History has proven that when a community moves to an area you can expect good authentic eateries will follow, and that is what is happening in Vegas.

Thai food has always been a staple for some people in this country, and for me, it's been cool to witness its growth. A few pieces may have contributed to this: more Asian restaurants became a gateway to new cuisines to Americans, or the more health-conscious eaters were attracted to the use of fresh ingredients and lean proteins for menu staples such as pad thai, tom yum soup, and green curry. Perhaps travel has been the most influential. For example, the Pok Pok restaurant empire was formed in Portland, Oregon, in 2005 by chef/owner Andy Ricker and got a ton of domestic press. Ricker's interest in the cuisine dates back to a mushroom curry dish he had during a backpacking trip to Thailand in 1987.

While I haven't yet had a chance to go to Vietnam or Thailand to be similarly inspired, I did almost make it to the Philippines. Life and work got in the way though, and I decided I'd rather wait until I could be fully prepared.

Since then, I have leaned into Filipino culture whenever there was an opportunity so that I'll be ready for my visit when the time comes. The West Coast of the United States is where you will find the HiFi (Historic Filipino) neighborhood in LA. Carson is known as the "heart of Filipino America." Beacon Hill in Seattle is another major hub, and here on the East Coast, Queens, New York, is home to a thriving Filipino community.

Filipino cuisine is another one from this part of the world that has influences from both China and a Western colonizer, but in the case of the Philippines, the colonizer was from Spain, who ruled for three hundred years. Like in Thai and Vietnamese cuisines, a lot of dishes are seasoned with garlic, ginger, chile peppers, star anise, and lemongrass. Some Spanish influence comes through in the cooking technique of braising meat with vinegar, which is most evident in dishes such as adobo (the national dish of the Philippines), stews mechado and caldereta, and arroz a la Valenciana, which is basically the Filipino version of paella, which originated in Valencia, Spain.

Through my role as the Charleston Wine + Food Festival head of beverage, I was excited to collaborate on an event for the festival with the James Beard finalist chef Nikko Cagalanan, executive chef and owner of Kultura Charleston. The event was named "Kamayan Nights." There is probably no better introduction to Filipino hospitality then enjoying a kamayan feast, or in my case, being part of the beverage team for one.

Kamayan, or boodle fight, as the Philippine Armed Forces call it, is a traditional feast. It's a communal-style dining that doesn't use any utensils and is typically enjoyed during celebrations and holidays. I was fortunate enough to enjoy a boodle fight at the GuGu Room in New York City to celebrate the birthday of my friend and the recipe tester for this book, Chef Shaquay Peacock.

There is an order to kamayan dining: first the table is covered with grilled banana leaves, then the starches, such as garlic fried rice and pancit noodles, a stir-fried noodle dish, are placed on top in various positions along the length of the table. Next, the protein dishes are set. These can include stews such as beef machado; inihaw na manok, which is grilled chicken; lechon roast pig; and grilled prawns. And don't forget the Spam. Lastly, grilled vegetables and fruits are added to the spread, and then a variety of sauces to top it off. The feast, with the colors of all the dishes on one long table against a green backdrop, is a feast for the eyes, and is a great gathering to get people to socialize.

For the Kamayan Nights event, I called in reinforcements, and Paula de Pano, sommelier and owner of Rocks & Acid in Chapel Hill, North Carolina, came up with the most epic pairings for this experience. Her background as the sommelier at fine-dining restaurants such as Eleven Madison Park and The Fearrington House, plus her Filipina upbringing in Manila, made her the right one for the job. I was excited to see the Riesling, red Burgundy, Champagne, and other wines she requested to pair with dinner. She told me very sarcastically, yet seriously, that the experience would not be complete without San Miguel, the national beer of the Philippines.

What Vietnamese, Thai, and Filipino cuisines share more than anything is a balance of spicy, sweet, salty, savory, and tangy flavors, and a lot of times, an intensity of flavor. When each bite of a dish is so complete, it can be hard to think about pairing in terms of what you want to add or balance. Defaulting to beer or a sweet wine to balance the heat would not be wrong, but I hope you explore further options.

A Deep Dive into German Wines

Why are we hopping from Southeast Asia to Germany? Sweet wines like Riesling and Gewürztraminer, which are common pairings for Thai and Vietnamese food, can come from several places. One of the biggest producers is Germany. I love drinking German wines, but they can be a bit confusing to buy. Here's a look at Germany's classification system, which is not like any other, to help you navigate.

QUALITY CLASSIFICATIONS

These tell you what measures a winemaker has taken in the vineyard and cellar to connect a wine with place and time.

Deutscher Wein: These are table wines. The grapes can be from anywhere in the country, the alcohol level can be between 8.5 percent and 15 percent, and there doesn't need to be a vintage or varietal on the label.

Landwein: These have a region named on the label, and at least 85 percent of the grapes must be from there.

Qualitätswein and Prädikatswein: All the grapes in these wines must be from the region on the label, which has to be one of Germany's thirteen designated regions. Within each region, only certain grapes are legally designated for use in Qualitätswein and Prädikatswein. And for Prädikatswein, the wine can't have any enhancing ingredients, like oak chips.

SWEETNESS CLASSIFICATIONS

Germany and other cold-climate regions produce a lot of sweet wines because the grapes ripen slowly and maintain good flavor and acidity even when they're very ripe. For all but Prädikatswein, there are two basic designations to know:

Trocken: Dry.

Halbtrocken: Literally, half dry. These are off-dry wines that can also be called Feinherb.

For Prädikatswein, there's a more complex system determined by how ripe the grapes are when they're picked. Here are the classifications, in order of earliest to latest picking.

Kabinett: These are dry to off-dry wines, usually with a light body and moderate alcohol.

Spätlese: Meaning "late harvest," Spätlese wines can be dry or sweet, with Spätlese Trocken indicating dry. They're richer than Kabinett wines, and have less sweetness than Auslese. Pairing options are versatile, from blue cheese to fruit or spicy dishes.

DECODING THE LABEL

- Winery Name
- Grape Varietal
- Soil Type
- Ripeness Level
- Wine Region

Auslese: These "select harvest" wines are made with hand-selected grapes, usually ones infected with botrytis, or noble rot, a mold that leads to wines with increased sweetness and flavors like honey, tropical fruit, and beeswax. Enjoy it alone or paired with dessert.

Beerenauslese: "Berry select wines" are only made in certain vintages, when the conditions are right. All grapes must be hand harvested. They're usually so ripe that they've started to shrivel up on the vine, like a raisin, and they almost always have botrytis.

Trockenbeerenauslese: This is a dry Beerenauslese.

Eiswein: In certain years, if the conditions are right, grapes will be allowed to freeze on the vine. To make Eiswein, they must be picked and pressed while frozen.

And now that you know, here's an all-German pairing for some of the dishes from these three countries.

ASIA

+ RIESLING PAIRED UP

TROCKENBEERENAUSLESE

Chè chuối: Vietnamese banana, coconut, and tapioca pudding

Biko: Filipino sticky rice cake

BEERENAUSLESE

Halo-halo: Filipino shaved ice with evaporated or coconut milk, topped with ube, coconut, and just about anything else sweet

Khao niao mamuang: Thai mango sticky rice dessert

AUSLESE

Drunken noodles: Thailand's spicy-sweet wide rice noodles

Bánh chưng: Vietnamese dish of sticky rice with mung beans and meat, wrapped in banana leaf and steamed

Chicken massaman curry: Thai curry made with peanuts

SPÄTLESE

Kare kare: Filipino stew made with peanut sauce and ox tails, pork hocks, tripe, and other cuts of meat that have been cheaper in the past

Green papaya salad: A tangy, spicy, refreshing Thai dish

Pad thai: Thailand's national dish of rice noodles with peanuts and fish sauce

Lumpia: Filipino fried egg rolls

KABINETT

Pho: Vietnamese noodle soup, in a rich broth and topped with fresh herbs

Thai green curry: Spicy coconut curry flavored with lemongrass

Bánh xèo: Stuffed Vietnamese crepe

Bánh mì: Vietnamese sandwich with pork and pickled vegetables.

TROCKEN

Bún chả: Vietnamese noodle dish with pork meatballs

Miến xào: Vietnamese dish of glass noodles stir fried with crab

BÚN THỊT NƯỚNG WITH EGG ROLLS + KABINETT RIESLING, GERMANY

SERVES 6

Noodle Salad

1 fresh lemongrass stalk, fine-sliced, or ⅓ cup frozen chopped lemongrass

8 garlic cloves

3 to 4 Thai chiles

½ cup oyster sauce

1½ pounds boneless chicken thighs or thin-sliced pork

¼ cup granulated sugar

¼ cup fish sauce*

¼ cup freshly squeezed lime juice

1 (16-ounce) pack vermicelli rice noodles, cooked and rinsed with cold water

1 head lettuce, cut into shreds

1 English cucumber, sliced in half moons

1 carrot, julienned

1 bunch fresh cilantro, rough-chopped

1 bunch fresh mint, leaves picked

1 pound bean sprouts

¼ cup crushed peanuts

Egg rolls, cut into 2-inch pieces, if using

---

*I prefer the Megachef brand of fish sauce. It has a lot of umami flavor. If you are at the store buying fish sauces, compare the sodium content and the protein. High protein and low sodium is what you are looking for. More protein means more umami from the fish, and less sodium means the fish sauce relies more on fish for flavor.

Chef Nini Nguyen is a two-time *Top Chef* competitor who's worked in New York City's Eleven Madison Park. Her first cookbook is called *Đặc Biệta*, which means "Something Special." It combines more traditional Vietnamese dishes with those influenced by her hometown, New Orleans, and all have a festive feel. In this recipe, egg rolls are a little extra razzle-dazzle to a noodle salad, but you can leave them out. The noodle salad, or bún thịt nướng, has plenty of flavor and texture on its own from grilled meat, fresh herbs, crunchy peanuts, and a dressing that uses chile, lime, and fish sauce.

Just barely sweet, Kabinett Riesling has beautiful peach and apricot notes that will really highlight the fresh herbs in this dish.

1. To make a marinade for the meat, crush the lemongrass with a mortar and pestle. Add 4 cloves of the garlic and 2 or 3 of the chiles, and crush. Add the oyster sauce and stir with a spoon. Rub the marinade onto the meat, and marinate for at least 30 minutes or up to overnight.
2. To make the sauce for the bowl, use a mortar and pestle to crush the remaining 4 cloves of garlic, the remaining chile, and a little bit of sugar, until they form a paste. Mix in the rest of the sugar, then add the fish sauce and lime juice. Place in a container and keep in the fridge until you're ready to serve.
3. Roast the meat or grill it on skewers if you have a grill.
4. To build the bowl, place the noodles in a bowl and distribute all the other ingredients on top. Dress with the sauce.

ASIA

EGG ROLLS

1 pound ground pork (the fattier the better)
1 pack cellophane noodles, rehydrated (optional)
¼ cup chopped mushrooms
1 medium onion, grated
1 carrot, grated
1 teaspoon sesame oil
1 tablespoon fish sauce
½ teaspoon salt
1 tablespoon sugar
2 quarts neutral oil, for frying
1 pack egg roll wrappers, such as Sweet Home brand

1. To make the filling, mix together everything except the neutral frying oil and the wrappers.
2. Add the neutral frying oil to a deep pan, and heat over medium-high heat.
3. Make a little patty of the mixture and fry it to see how it tastes. Adjust seasoning if you need to.
4. Wrap filling in wrappers and let sit for a few minutes before frying.
5. Fry until golden or freeze them to fry another time.

Used with permission from *Đặc Biệt: An Extra-Special Vietnamese Cookbook* by Nini Nguyen with Sarah Zorn (Knopf, August 2024).

WINE PAIRING FOR THE PEOPLE

Turkey

Latitude and Longitude: 38.9637° N, 35.2433° E
Capital: Ankara
Country/Continent: The majority of Turkey is in Asia, with the small part of the country that's in Europe bordering Greece to the west and Bulgaria to the northwest. The country is bordered by the Black Sea to the north; Georgia, Armenia, and Iran to the east; Iran and Syria to the southeast; the Mediterranean Sea to the south; and the Aegean Sea to the west.
Population: 84.8 million
National Drink: Raki, a brandy, and ayran, a yogurt drink
Top Exports: Cars, jewelry, refined petroleum
Official Language: Turkish
Independence Day: October 29, 1923
Independence from: The Allies of World War I

Everything is more electrifying in Istanbul: the vibrant colored tilework and intricate rugs; the resounding sound of the adhan; the intense aromas of saffron, anise, and Aleppo peppers in the bazaars. Tea lounges, mosques, and even a palace dot the city as they have for centuries. It was that sense of history that feels alive in Turkey that inspired my trip there—and my mom's love of the History Channel.

But as easy as it is to romanticize this ancient city with its surrounding sea views, it's also a bustling, cosmopolitan, international metropolis. Trendy restaurants perch up on roof decks to take advantage of the views of the Bosphorus Strait's turquoise waters. The food here was influenced by thousands of years of trade with Europe, Asia, and Africa, and this global fusion merged with spice blends that made my trip worthwhile.

To my surprise, though, some of those beautiful rooftops aren't just great restaurants but also refined cocktail bars. Turkey is 90–99 percent Muslim, depending on who you ask, but the government is technically secular. Only about 15–20 percent of Turkish people in the country drink alcohol, but Istanbul has been a center of trade and tourism for its entire existence, entertaining visitors from all over. According to Eurostar Monitor, it was the most visited city in the world in 2023. And so it's developed an exciting cocktail scene to accommodate locals who drink alcohol as well as visitors.

ASIA

The area that's now Istanbul has been occupied by humans since the Copper Age, around 6000 BCE. It's half in Europe, half in Asia, and separated by the Bosporus Strait, which runs from the Black Sea to the Sea of Marmara and the Mediterranean beyond it. Because it's a portal between Europe and Asia, the city has been appealing to the Byzantine Empire, the Persian Empire, the Roman Empire (which called it Constantinople, after Emperor Constantine), and the Ottoman Empire. The latter ruled Turkey for almost five hundred years, making it a Muslim country. Some Ottoman rulers supported tourism and technological progress, while others took a more seclusionist approach, inciting rebellions in the lead-up to World War I.

During World War I, the Ottoman Empire sided with the Central Powers of Germany, Austria-Hungary, and Bulgaria. Domestically, during World War I the empire also began the Armenian genocide in an effort toward what was called Turkification. When the Central Powers lost the war, Turkey was annexed by the Allies, a coalition of France, the UK, the United States, Italy, and Japan, from 1918 to 1923. When it regained its independence in 1923, the Turkish Republic made Ankara the national capital, but Istanbul has remained the cultural and financial hub.

All this history is important to understanding why Istanbul is such an international city, and also a glimpse into why and how there's a drinking tradition there. Some taverns, or meyhanes, remain that are more than a hundred years old.

The history also provides some context to why and how there's a seven-thousand-year-old wine making tradition. Grape seeds and evidence of wine making in Turkey date back to around the same time as in Georgia, which is considered the cradle of wine making (page 218). What's now Turkey was once the kingdoms of Thrace—the northern area around Istanbul—and Anatolia, the main land mass. It was the Phrygians in Anatolia who introduced the Greek Empire to wine, according to trade organization Wine Anatolia. Under the Muslim Ottoman Empire, wine making continued. It was carried out by non-Muslims, and most of the production was exported.

In the twentieth century, government support of the industry changed rapidly, depending on whether a more or less religious leader was in place. The wine industry fell under government control in 1923, when the Turkish Republic was established, but quality declined. Deregulation started in the 1980s, and the wine industry became fully privatized in 2003. Tourism became more important, and the

Wine Grapes of Turkey

Turkey has something like eight hundred indigenous grape varieties, and the country grows a huge number of table grapes and raisins.

Red

Öküzgözü
Kalecik Karasi
Boğazkere
Syrah

Cabernet Sauvignon
Merlot

White

Narince
Bornova Misketi
Emir

Semillon
Sauvignon Blanc
Chardonnay

country was becoming open to international trade, and so in the 1990s, wine making started taking off again and finding its footing.

Recep Tayyip Erdoğan, the prime minister of Turkey from 2004 to 2013, and the current president, is conservative. He's imposed a number of restrictions around how wine can be sold and marketed in the country. This has slowed the growth of the wine industry and made business harder for small and medium producers. At the same time, though, international recognition has been growing and wine making continues.

It's easy to see why wine making has persisted all these centuries in Turkey. The country has a wide variety of terrains, and so many of them are hospitable to wine making. Turkey has about five thousand miles of coastline with the same Mediterranean climate that's made Tuscany so famous.

Inland, in Cappadocia and other parts of Anatolia, a lot of the terroir is challenging for winegrowers, which usually means it's great for wine growing. I'm talking about high altitude, with volcanic soils that aren't good for agriculture. These areas have cold winters and hot, sunny summers. These are areas of extremes that typically make for wines with character. Some have slightly more fertile clay or limestone soils too. Most of the vineyards are planted on slopes, with good drainage, which helps with freshness in the wines.

It's worth noting that while a lot of the wine-growing regions are challenging, much of Turkey has historically been an agricultural hub of the world. Its southeastern corner is part of the Fertile Crescent, also known as the cradle of civilization, where agriculture and irrigation were first invented. The US Department of Trade's International Trade Administration stated in January 2024 that Turkey is one of the top ten agricultural economies in the world, with about half of the country's land area dedicated to farming wheat, sugar beets, milk, poultry, cotton, tomatoes, and other fruits and vegetables. The country has a number of fertile valleys and plains that make it well suited to growing a variety of produce. It remains to be seen if wine grapes will become a larger share of that production.

Turkey's Wine Regions

At the time of writing, Turkey has about 150 wineries producing around 80 million bottles of wine per year. Most of these are consumed domestically. Wine growing and wine making here is an ancient practice but also one that has ebbed and flowed. Like Georgia, the country has spent recent years rediscovering its wine identity. Turkey is a secular country, according to its constitution, but it's predominantly Muslim, so the wine industry doesn't have the same structural government support it has elsewhere.

That may be part of the reason why Turkey doesn't have official government-designated appellations or Geographic Indications like a lot of wine-producing countries do. Instead, most wineries identify themselves with one of the country's seven geographic regions—Aegean, Black Sea, Central Anatolia, Eastern Anatolia, Southeastern Anatolia, Marmara, and Mediterranean—with a few tweaks and exceptions. Here they are, from most wine produced to least.

Aegean Sea Region: Accounting for about half of Turkey's wine production, this region is on Turkey's west coast. Near the sea, it has a

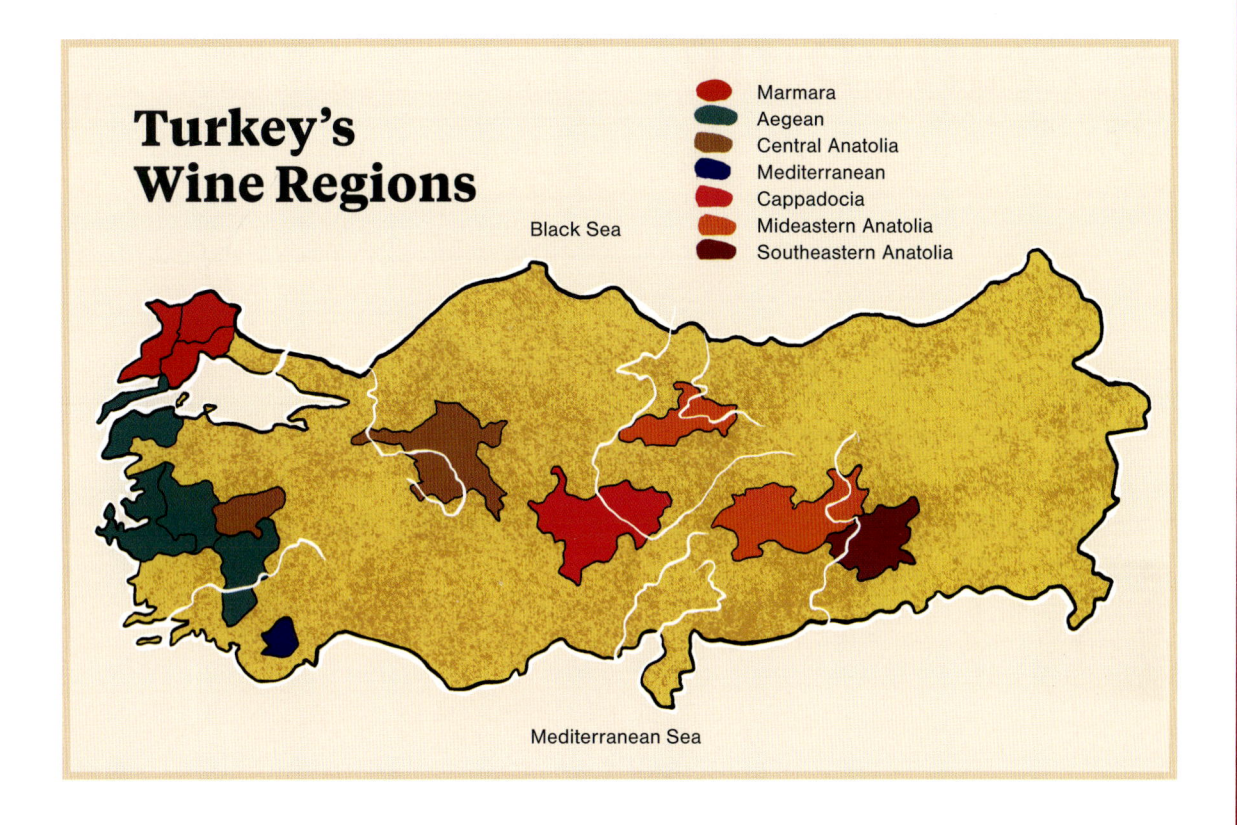

ASIA

Turkey's Wine Regions

Legend:
- Marmara
- Aegean
- Central Anatolia
- Mediterranean
- Cappadocia
- Mideastern Anatolia
- Southeastern Anatolia

Black Sea (north) • *Mediterranean Sea* (south)

Mediterranean climate, with cool winters and hot summers that benefit from sea breezes. Farther inland, the elevation climbs a bit and temperatures drop a little. A lot of grapes are grown here to be dried into raisins, but the region is also a mixed bag of wine grapes, with French varieties like Chardonnay, Sauvignon Blanc, and Syrah finding a home at higher altitudes, and Bordeaux varieties growing in lower areas. Indigenous grape Çalkarası is grown here to make rosé.

Marmara: This northwestern area is home to Istanbul and about 30–40 percent of Turkey's winemakers. With coasts along the Aegean, Black Sea, and Sea of Marmara, it has a lot of maritime influence to keep the climate cool. Away from the seas, mountains also have a cooling effect. Cabernet Sauvignon, Merlot, Gamay, and Semillon are the international varieties grown here. Local grapes include Papazkarası, Adakarası, Vasilaki, and Çavuş.

Black Sea: Stretching along Turkey's northern coast, the Black Sea region shares a border with another ancient wine country that's having a renaissance: Georgia. Several of the country's winemakers grow their grapes here, but not many producers are based in the Black Sea region. The subregion of Tokat is rugged, mountainous, and a center for growing the Narince white grape.

215

WINE PAIRING FOR THE PEOPLE

+ PAIRED UP

MANTI + MENCÍA, RIBEIRA SACRA, SPAIN. Little dumplings filled with ground beef or lamb and served with a yogurt sauce and a pepper oil go best with Spanish red Mencía. The wine's medium body, high acidity, and juiciness will cut through the richness of the meat and yogurt. Slight, subtle vegetal notes will pair well with the pepper oil.

KÖFTE + MOURVÈDRE, SWARTLAND, SOUTH AFRICA. These oval-shaped meatballs can be made from beef, lamb, or red lentils (these are called mercimek kofte) and bulgur, seasoned with onions, red pepper paste, and herbs. Pair them with South African Mourvèdre. Köfte have a bit of a kick to them, as well as lots of herbaceous characteristics, and the Mourvèdre will match it note for note.

LAHMACUN + SANGIOVESE, TUSCANY, ITALY. Flatbread topped with slightly spicy ground meat, tomatoes, peppers, and onions goes just as well with Sangiovese as a pizza would, thanks to its pepper notes. The Italian red wine is spicy and herbaceous, so anytime you've got tomatoes, meat, and a bit of heat, it's a safe bet.

HAMSILI PILAV + AVESSO, VINHO VERDE, PORTUGAL. From Turkey's Black Sea region, this is a rice dish made with anchovies. Try it with Avesso from Portugal. This seafood-friendly wine will act like a squeeze of lemon and a pinch of salt to accent this dish.

DÖNER KEBAB + BOBAL, REQUENA-UTIEL, SPAIN. Grilled on a vertical spit, döner kebab is usually served on flatbread, with a salad, or with rice. One of Spain's most-planted red grapes, Bobal, is a big wine to stand up to a rich, fatty dish. Savory notes complement meaty flavors, but black fruits add a juicy, refreshing component.

BAKLAVA + TOKAJI ASZÚ, TOKAJ, HUNGARY. The honey-soaked layered pastry goes beautifully with Hungary's sweet wine, Tokaji Aszú, which also has rich honeyed and nutty notes.

Central Anatolia: This region is mostly an arid plateau between two mountain ranges. Wine is grown along the Kızılırmak, Turkey's longest river. At the moment, this region is planted mostly to Kalecik Karası red grapes, but the white variety, Hasandede, is being revived. Some wines from here may be labeled from Cappadocia, a tourist-friendly region with volcanic soils and indigenous white grapes growing. Some orange wine is being produced here too.

Mideastern and Southeastern Anatolia: These are two separate regions, but their winegrowing areas are right next to each other. They're in the Fertile Crescent, an area that also covers what's now southern Iraq, Syria, Lebanon, Jordan, Palestine, Israel, Egypt, and parts of Iran, where agriculture is thought to have first developed. Vineyards here are about 3,000 feet above sea level, along the Euphrates River, and reds made from Öküzgözü and Boğazkere are the main wines here. Mideastern

ASIA

Anatolia also includes a northern area, Tokat, with a cooler climate. Narince is the main grape in Tokat.

Mediterranean: Turkey's southernmost wine region accounts for a very small portion of the country's production. The weather here is hot in the summer, and even the winters are mild. But some areas with elevation get enough cooling wind to grow wine grapes. Native grape Acıkara has shown promise here, and production is largely a mix of native and European grapes, as winegrowers get to know this little region better.

WINE PAIRING FOR THE PEOPLE

Georgia

Coordinates: 42.3154° N, 43.3569° E
Capital: Tbilisi
Country/Continent: Georgia is divided between Europe and Asia, with Russia to the north; Azerbaijan, Armenia, and Turkey to the south; and the Black Sea to the west.
Population: 3.7 million
National Drink: Chacha, a brandy
National Dish: Khachapuri stuffed bread
Top Exports: Metals, motor cars, nuts
Official Language: Georgian
Independence Day: May 26, 1918
Independence from: Russia

I first learned about Georgia from a speaker at the New York Travel Festival, a professional travel conference. Terrell Jermaine Starr, a foreign-policy journalist and former Fulbright Scholar who lived in Georgia, shared his experience on a Middle Eastern travel panel. Later, as my wine knowledge grew, so did my curiosity. As I researched the history of wine, Georgia, the country, became a bucket-list destination. I started seeing orange wine all over the place, and I learned that it was related to amber wine, a style that's traditional in Georgia. With the mental imagery of that beautiful country already in my head from that conference, I knew I had to learn more.

Just like Turkey, Georgia is considered to be in Europe and Asia. The Ural Mountains that separate the two continents stop north of Georgia, and at different times in the country's history, different rivers and depressions that run through it have been considered the dividing line between the two continents. The government has expressed a desire to join the European Union, but culturally Georgia draws from both continents.

I knew I had to include Georgia in this book because its historical wine culture is too important not to. Also, a lot of Georgian wines pair so well with diverse cuisines, so if we're here to talk about pairing, Georgia should be part of the conversation.

So the first thing that comes up when we talk about Georgian wine is the history. In 2015, archaeologists confirmed that wine making in Georgia dates back to 6000 BCE. There's evidence of wine being made in Turkey around that time, as we've seen—remember, the two share a border—but in Georgia, it's linked specifically to use of qvevri, a wine-making vessel that's still in use today and has been recognized as an important piece of cultural heritage by organizations like UNESCO. Qvevri are clay vessels used to ferment wine. They're egg-shaped, handmade, and always buried in the ground, both for temperature regulation and because, in less peaceful times, that made it easier to hide them. Sizes can range from one hundred to three thousand liters, with around one thousand liters the preferred size.

A big part of what makes qvevri different from amphorae used in other parts of Europe is the clay. Qvevri are always made from local clay, which is kiln fired. It comes out more porous than most amphorae, so the interiors of qvevri are coated in beeswax.

The traditional way to make wine in a qvevri is to crush the grapes and leave them in the qvevri with skins, seeds, and stems. They'll ferment using natural yeast for two or three weeks, and during that time, someone will stir or punch down the mixture inside. Once fermentation is finished, some winemakers will let the wine continue to age in the qvevri.

Others will transfer the wine to oak or stainless steel. The grape pomace left in the qvevri is distilled to make a strong, clear brandy, which some people refer to as a "grape vodka," called chacha. Only about 5 percent of Georgian wines are made using this ancient method. The other 95 percent of Georgian wines vary in style from dry or semisweet, and they can be made from red or white grapes. Those made with white grapes are an amber color. In Georgia, they're always called amber wines—never orange or skin-contact like in other parts of the world. There are also rosé wines made in Georgia, just not in qvevri. Modern Georgian wine making also includes sparkling wine made using both the traditional method and pet-nats, and a range of semisweet wines.

Qvevri wines are a living part of history. They're an important piece of a cultural legacy. They also have some characteristics that make them really versatile for pairing with food. The qvevri imparts tannins and texture, plus some minerality and sometimes a bit of funk, to make wines that stand up well to a cuisine that took some of the biggest and boldest flavors along the Silk Roads.

The Silk Roads were a network of trade routes that went from China to Greece, and from Portugal down through Iraq, Iran, and into India and East Africa. They went over land and sea, beginning when the Romans discovered silk from China about one century BCE. These became routes for trading spices, metals, books, music, ideas, you name it. And they passed through Georgia. So when you look at Georgian cuisine, you can see the influence of Chinese cooking in khinkali dumplings, the influence of Persia in the use of pomegranate and tart grape to season savory dishes, the fenugreek and chiles of Indian cooking. These come together in a cuisine that uses a lot of walnuts, cheeses, and kidney beans. It's food that's hearty and flavorful, but it can also be delicate and fresh.

One of the most important geographic

Georgia's Wine Regions

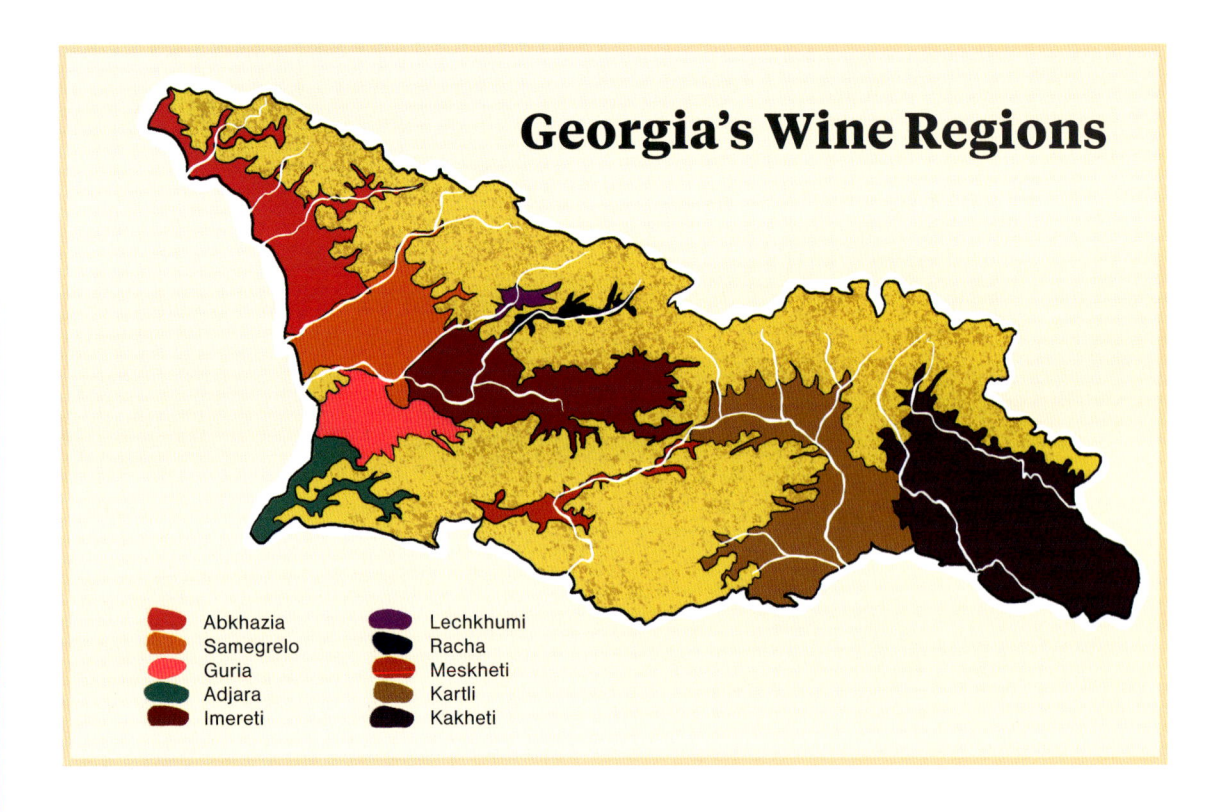

- Abkhazia
- Samegrelo
- Guria
- Adjara
- Imereti
- Lechkhumi
- Racha
- Meskheti
- Kartli
- Kakheti

features in Georgia, whether we're talking about cuisine, wine growing, or history, are its mountains. In the north, there is the Greater Caucasus range. The Lesser Caucasus range is in the south, along the border with Turkey and Armenia. Connecting those two ranges is the Surami Range. The Greater Caucasus blocks a lot of the cold air from the north, so much of the country has a continental climate.

The Black Sea brings a warm, moderating breeze inland, and so Western Georgia is pretty warm, rainy, and humid until you get to the mountains. The coastal region is subtropical in parts, with very fertile soil. It's one of the only parts of the country with low elevation.

Georgia also has lots of rivers and tributaries running through its lowlands. These create fertile basins that are great for agriculture.

Wine in the Soviet Era

Georgia was occupied twice. First, by the Russian Empire from 1801 to 1918, and then again by the USSR from 1921 to 1991. These are blips in a country where people have lived for at least eight thousand years, but they explain why Georgia's international reputation for wine is playing catch-up compared to the wine-making countries of Western Europe.

The government of the USSR treated wine the same way it did any other agricultural product. Farms of all sizes were nationalized, meaning farmers had to sell their harvest to the government for cheap. And at any time the government could decide some other product was more necessary than wine, which meant that vines could be uprooted to plant another crop.

The emphasis for wine growing was on quantity rather than quality. Wine was made in massive factories, where it was fermented in steel tanks. The cultural legacy of qvevri was considered unimportant by the government.

But Georgians were able to keep a bit of land to farm for themselves, and those qvevri that were buried in the ground stayed in the ground. Especially in rural areas, people could grow grapes and make wine for themselves. They could carry on the traditions of training vines up trees, fermenting in qvevri, and pouring a bit of wine on a piece of bread in memory of the dead. And now, in the post-Soviet era, they can share those traditions with the world too.

Georgia's Wine Regions

Georgia has six major viticultural zones and, at the time of writing, twenty-nine appellations with Protected Designation of Origin (PDO) status for specific styles of wine. Wine making in Georgia, although ancient, has changed a lot in the last decade or two, and that's probably not going to slow down anytime soon. Four new PDOs have been added in the last two years. Those are listed here, but there may be more on the way. For now, here's a look at Georgia's viticultural zones.

Kakheti: In the eastern part of Georgia, this is considered one of the country's most important wine regions, both for the amount of wine it produces and because of its use of traditional qvevri wine making. The mountainous region is home to two river basins, Alazani and Iori, with alluvial soils. Fifteen of Georgia's registered indigenous wine grapes grow here, and it's home to twenty PDOs:

- Akhasheni (semisweet red)
- Akhmeta (dry white, semidry white, semisweet white, dry amber)
- Akhoebi (dry red)
- Gurjaani (dry white)
- Kakheti (dry white, amber)
- Kardenakhi (fortified white, sweet amber)
- Kindzmarauli (semisweet red)
- Kisi Magraani (dry white, dry amber)
- Kotekhi (dry red, dry white)
- Kvareli (dry red)
- Manavi (dry white)
- Mukuzani (dry red)
- Napareuli (dry white, dry red)
- Saperavi Khashmi (dry red)
- Teliani (dry red)
- Tibaani (dry white, amber)
- Tsarapi (dry amber)
- Tsinandali (dry white)
- Vazisubani (dry white)
- Zegaani (dry red qvevri)

> **DRINK NOW: Georgian Wine Producers**
>
> There are so many incredible Georgian wines, but finding them in the United States can be a bit of a challenge. Here are some that are worth picking up if you see them around.
> - Baia's Wine
> - Gotsa
> - Ocho Wine
> - Gabriel's wine
> - Lapati Wines

DECODING THE LABEL

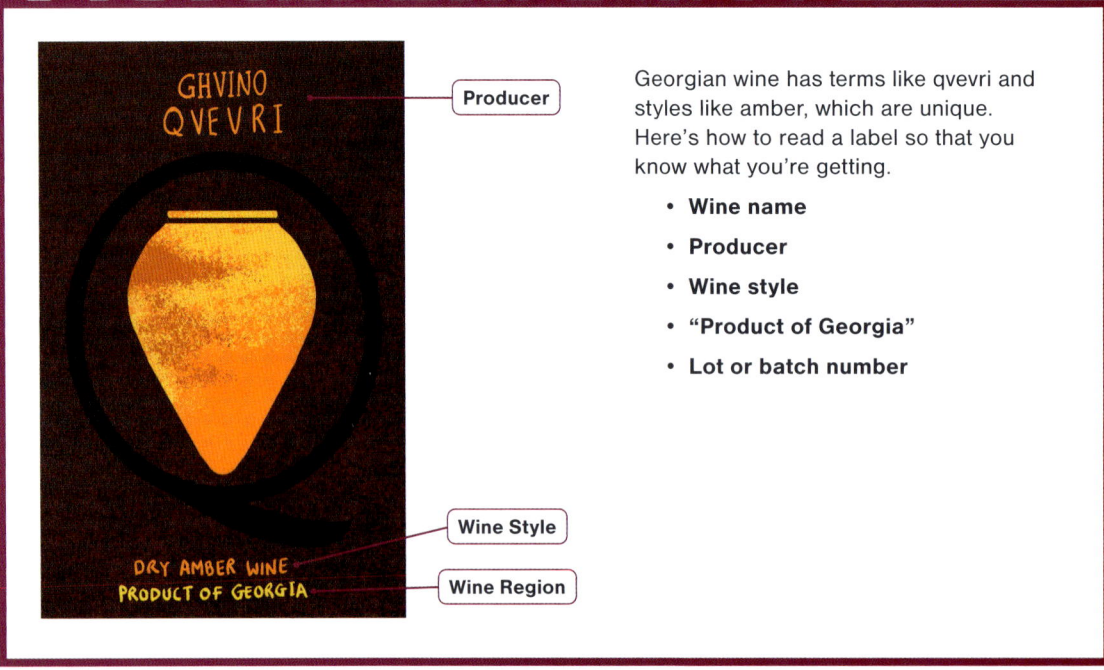

GHVINO QVEVRI — Producer

DRY AMBER WINE — Wine Style

PRODUCT OF GEORGIA — Wine Region

Georgian wine has terms like qvevri and styles like amber, which are unique. Here's how to read a label so that you know what you're getting.

- Wine name
- Producer
- Wine style
- "Product of Georgia"
- Lot or batch number

Kartli: In north-central Georgia, this mountainous region is known for sparkling wines in a crisp, European style, but it also produces amber wines and still, dry reds and whites. It grows indigenous grapes and European varieties like Aligote, Riesling, Sauvignon Blanc, and Chardonnay. Most vineyards are in the high-altitude river basins of the Mtkvari River and its tributaries. There's also been a growing movement to recognize microclimates that are conducive to specific native grapes, like the village of Asureti and the Okami PDOF. Kartli has four PDOs:
- Asuretuli Shala (dry red)
- Atenuri (sparkling white)
- Bolnisi (dry white, dry red, dry amber)
- Okami (dry white, dry red)

Imereti: This province is considered part of Western Georgia, but it's pretty close to the middle of the country. It has diverse terrains and soils that grow a range of native grapes. The use of qvevri in wine making is very common in this region, which has one PDO:
- Sviri (dry white wine)

Racha-Lechkhumi: In the northeastern part of Western Georgia, Racha is surrounded by the Caucasus Mountains to the north. It's small in terms of vineyard area but considered important for the distinct semisweet wines made there, three of which have PDO status:
- Khvanchkara (semisweet red)

ASIA

- Okureshis Usakhelouri (dry red, semidry red, semisweet red)
- Tvishi (dry to semisweet white)

Meskheti: This super-high-altitude region in the south borders Turkey. It's considered not just the country's highest wine-making area but also the oldest. Some scientists believe that Saperavi, Georgia's famous native red wine grapes, originated here. Vineyard areas are small, due to the elevation, but production continues.

Guria: Georgia's four regions around the Black Sea are lower in altitude, wetter, and warmer than the rest of the country's wine-growing area. Guria, near the south of the Black Sea coast, has fertile soils and a long growing season. Dry white, red, and rosé wines are made here.

Samagrelo: Part of a fabled, wealthy kingdom called Colchis during the Greco-Roman era, Samagrelo does have some high mountains sloping toward the Black Sea. Vineyards are planted on these slopes, mostly for red wine. Samagrelo is home to one PDO:

- Salkhino Ojaleshi (dry red)

Abkhazia: The region furthest north, on the Black Sea coast, Abkhazia is very historical. In the past, harvests have been wiped out by gray mold and powdery mildew. Now, vineyards are planted at slightly higher altitudes near the coast, to make red and white wines.

Wine Grapes of Georgia

Georgia has more than five hundred indigenous grape varieties that can be used for wine production. About forty-five are grown commercially for wine making, but a lot of those are grown in very small quantities. The same is true for the French grapes that have been brought in over the years.

About 75 percent of Georgia's vineyard acreage is white wine grapes, which are also used for amber wines. Here's a look at the most important wine grapes in Georgia.

Red

Saperavi	Chkhaveri
Aleksandrouli	Tavkveri
Ojaleshi	

White

Rkatsiteli	Chinuri
Mtsvane Kakhuri	Tsitska
Kisi	Tsolikouri

Adjara: An important tourism region at the south of the Black Sea Coast, Adjara borders Turkey. Wine grows along the the Acharistsqali and Chorokhi river basins, as well as near the coast. There's been a strong effort here to revive historic native grape varieties.

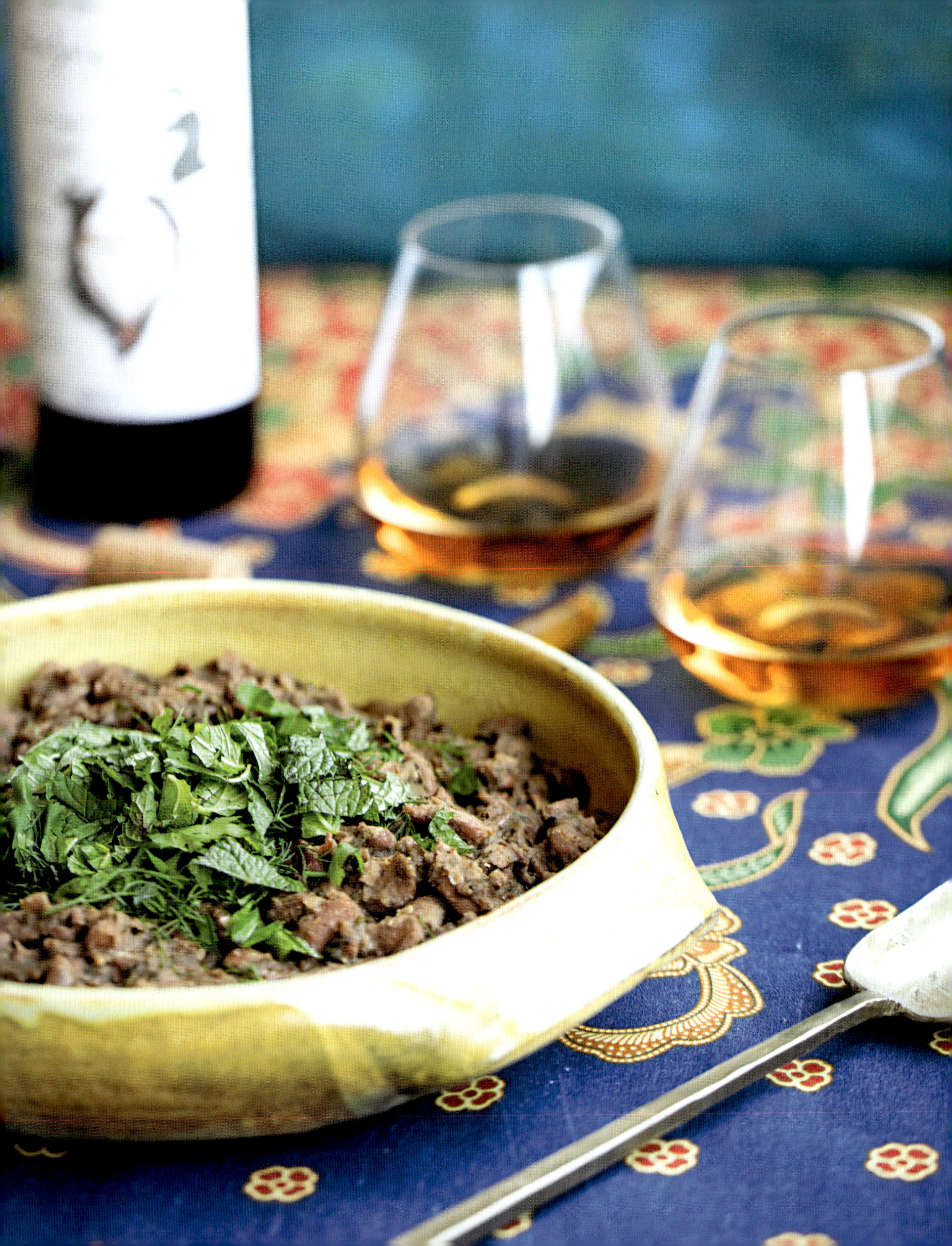

LOBIO MTSVANILIT + TAVKVERI, KARTLI, GEORGIA

Rose Previte became familiar with Georgian food when she was living in Russia while her husband worked as a foreign correspondent for NPR. It was during her time in Russia that she dreamed up Compass Rose, her Washington, DC, restaurant that is inspired by Georgian supras—festive multicourse meals. She went on to open two more restaurants, Maydan and Kirby Club, inspired by her travels, her mother's Lebanese cuisine, and her father's Sicilian food.

Lobio, or kidney beans, are common in Georgian cooking. Here, they're used in an herby salad that can be a side dish, starter, or main course with some bread.

Tavkveri, a light-bodied native red, has a soft mouthfeel that won't fight with the dish. Its sweet aromas and juicy red fruits will complement the herbs in this salad.

SERVES 6 TO 8

- 1 pound dried red kidney or other beans
- ¼ cup grapeseed or other neutral oil
- 1 large onion, fine-chopped
- 6 cloves garlic, thin-sliced
- 2 tablespoons ground blue fenugreek or ground fenugreek
- 2 teaspoons Aleppo pepper flakes or ground ancho chile
- 2 teaspoons ground coriander
- 2 teaspoons kosher salt, plus more as needed
- 1 cup chopped fresh cilantro leaves and tender stems, plus more for garnish
- ½ cup chopped fresh dill leaves, plus more for garnish
- ½ cup chopped fresh mint leaves, plus more for garnish
- Cornbread or flatbread, for serving (optional)

1. Rinse and drain the beans and place in a large pot. Add 2 quarts of water, and soak for 24 hours. (It's fine to skip this step; the beans will simply take longer to cook.)
2. In a large Dutch oven or other large pot with a lid, heat the oil over medium heat until it shimmers. Add the onion and garlic, and cook until very soft and lightly browned, about 8 minutes.
3. Stir in the fenugreek, Aleppo pepper, and coriander, and cook until fragrant, about 30 seconds.
4. Drain the beans and add them to the pot with 2 quarts of water. Bring to a boil over medium-high heat and boil gently for 10 minutes.
5. Reduce the heat and simmer, partially covered, until the beans are softened, adding more water if necessary to keep the beans covered, 1 to 3 hours. Stir in the salt.
6. Use a large fork or masher to mash about half the beans, adding water if needed to make the mixture very creamy but not soupy. Turn off the heat and stir in the cilantro, dill, and mint. Taste and add more salt, if desired. Serve hot, garnished with cilantro, dill, and mint, and with cornbread or flatbread, if desired.

Used with permission from *Maydan: Recipes from Lebanon and Beyond* by Rose Previte with Marah Stets (Abrams, November 2023).

+ PAIRED UP

KHACHAPURI + MTSVANE KHAKURI, KAKHETI, GEORGIA. Considered the national dish, this is a boat-shaped bread stuffed with egg and cheese. Pair it with Mtsvane Pét-nat. A native grape known for its floral aromas, this wine will add a light touch to the deliciously cheesy, starchy bread.

KHINKALI + TSOLIKOURI, IMERETI, GEORGIA. These dumplings are stuffed with meat, herbs, and broth. Pair them with Tsolikouri or Sauvignon Blanc from California's North Coast. The grassy, herbal notes of either wine will complement the herbs in the dish, and the high acidity will cleanse the palate with this rich dish.

LOBIO + SAPERAVI, KAKHETI, GEORGIA. The stewy kidney bean dish seasoned with chile, fried onions, and cilantro goes well with Georgia's most popular red wine, Saperavi. It has an earthy quality that will match the beans, but dark fruits and licorice notes add intrigue. Its high acidity will cut through the beans' starchiness.

MTSVADI + TAVKVERI, KARTLI, GEORGIA. Grilled meat skewers are usually made with lamb, beef, or pork, grilled over an open flame and served with raw onions and sour plum or pomegranate sauce. Tavkveri, a red grape, is native to Georgia. Its name means "hammerhead," but that's because the grape bunches are flat on top. Red wines made from this grape are medium in body, with red fruit notes—perfect for chilling and pouring with grilled meat.

LOBIANI + RKATSITELI, KAKHETI, GEORGIA. This flaky bread stuffed with kidney beans cooked in bacon fat and seasoned with paprika, pepper, and coriander has a couple of options. Rkatsiteli makes a good amber option with nutty notes and a bright squeeze of green apple. Chkhaveri is a light-bodied red with a juicy feel that will lighten up this dish.

United Arab Emirates

Just like my trip to Kenya, my trip to Dubai was partly inspired by a website flight glitch that opened up cheap tickets and sparked me to explore new destinations I never imagined I would be able to visit. It's impossible to visit Dubai without thinking about the newness of it. If you're visiting today, it's easy to stay within the version of Dubai that's a shiny, new luxury playground, with the food culture of Michelin-starred restaurants serving French and Italian cuisine, with wine lists to match. The city also has a creative, high-end cocktail scene to rival New York, London, or Tokyo. For a lot of people traveling to Dubai, there's a mystique around how this Muslim state under Sharia Law has so much great booze. The answer is that it's for tourists and the large number of expatriates who live there, a number which is growing continuously. Dubai has the largest population among the Emirates, with expatriates making up far more of the population than Emiratis; Indians account for the largest nationality, according to a 2023 article in the *Economic Times*. Today, anyone can drink in Dubai, as long as they're in a place that's licensed to serve alcohol, like a restaurant or hotel. Citizens of the United Arab Emirates still need a license to purchase alcohol in a licensed store, but foreigners don't.

All this drinking culture comes in tandem with the melting pot of international cuisines that I was able to experience while visiting, but you must search hard to find Emirati cuisine. It involves a lot of fish from the body of water known

Coordinates: 23.4241° N, 53.8478° E
Capital: Abu Dhabi
Country/Continent: The UAE is on the eastern end of the Arabian Peninsula. The Persian Gulf is north and northwest. To the southwest and south is Saudi Arabia, and Oman borders the UAE on the southeast and east.
Population: 9.4 million
National Drink: Karak spiced tea
National Dish: Khuzi roast lamb
Top Exports: Crude petroleum, refined petroleum, gold
Official Language: Arabic
Independence Day: December 2, 1971
Independence from: Known as National Day, the holiday recognizes when the emirates—territories ruled by emirs, or high-ranking officials—united and formed the UAE.

> ## Sip the Culture
> ### Arabic-Style Coffee or Gahwa
>
> This has been in Dubai for centuries, having spread from Ethiopia to Yemen and then across the Arabian Peninsula. Mioko Ueshima wrote in a September 2022 blog post for Smithsonian that gahwa is a welcoming drink in the United Arab Emirates. The drink is so ingrained in Emirati culture that a tahwah, or traditional coffee pot, is on one of its coins. In October 2014, the Dubai Coffee Museum opened to explore the drink's place in the culture there.
>
> While dark, strong, traditional Arabic-style coffee can still be found around the city, Dubai also has a thriving contemporary coffee scene. Shops and roasters here are sourcing sustainably grown beans from around the world to create single-variety and specialty coffee drinks. An increasing amount of coffee is also being grown in the Emirates. You can't taste the terroir of Dubai, but you can get a sense of its history and future through its coffee.

as both the Persian Gulf and the Arabian Gulf. It's influenced by the food of the Arabian Peninsula, as well as South Asian countries like India and Pakistan, Bedouin cuisine with its camel milk, and the Emirates' long agricultural history of growing dates and grains. Noodles, rice, and tomatoes have been incorporated into some dishes. Common spices and aromatics include dried lemon, saffron, turmeric, thyme, oregano, cinnamon, and cardamom.

People have been living in and trading with Dubai for thousands of years, and even as a tourist, you can catch glimpses of that Dubai.

By this point in the book, you should know that I'll always find a marketplace when I travel. Dubai Gold Souk market is located in the more traditional neighborhood of Deira and is famous for jewelry shopping, but there are also souks that specialize in textiles, perfumes, and of course, spices. These are smaller and more intimate than the Grand Bazaar in Istanbul, or even the spice market, but they're just as vibrant.

I was able to get a glimpse into the historic Emirates culture by taking a day trip to Al Lahbab Desert and spend a day camelback riding and tasting local delights. I would highly recommend spending some time outside the city life this way. Yes, technically this is also a tourist activity. Still, once I arrived at the desert campgrounds, it was very tranquil to take in the view of the desert at night with pitch-black skies and bright stars. I spent my time learning how to belly dance and play local games, which offered an opportunity to connect with their culture and with a less complicated time before technology. The food offered were straightforward items that can be transported easily and cooked over a fire—kebabs, tea, plus snacks and salads. It's simple food, and you get the feeling that eating these things in this place is something people have been doing for ages, which made it special.

A lot of dishes I ate in Dubai may have their birthplaces in Yemen, Oman, or Saudi Arabia, or even farther away, like Ethiopia, Somalia, or Sudan. But they are also considered traditional Emirati cuisine. With thousands of years of trade in the region, it can be hard to pinpoint what came from where, and when, so instead, I try to think of the cuisine as a celebration of shared history.

ASIA

✚ PAIRED UP

EMIRATI LAMB KABSA + SHIRAZ, BAROSSA VALLEY, AUSTRALIA. This is a dish of tender roasted lamb and rice seasoned with tomatoes, dried lemon, and warming spices. Shiraz from Barossa Valley region is a good match, jam-packed with spice notes, ripe blackberry, plum, and blueberry notes, plus a hint of menthol and eucalyptus.

MARRAG SAMAK + FRAPPATO, SICILY, ITALY. Emirati fish stew with a tomato base (I had no trouble finding seafood in the UAE, since much of it is on the water) will be enhanced by Frappato, a Mediterranean red wine with minerality and medium body that's perfect for fish dishes. It will deliver notes of white pepper, pomegranate, dried cranberries, and star anise.

HAREES + ROUSSANNE, RHÔNE VALLEY, FRANCE. Savory beef with wheat porridge is a good reason to break out a bottle of Roussanne from France's Rhône Valley. The wine is full-bodied with waxy brioche notes and fresh honeysuckle that make it just as soothing as this dish.

OMANI SHUWA + AIRÉN, LA MANCHA, SPAIN. Slow-cooked lamb marinated in spices and wrapped in banana leaves pairs well with a wine that has tropical fruit notes. Airén, a Spanish grape that's used a lot for blends and brandies, has those. It's relatively low in acidity, so it's got staying power on the palate alongside this dish.

JOOJEH KEBAB + COLOMBARD, RUSSIAN RIVER VALLEY, CALIFORNIA. A Persian dish of saffron-seasoned chicken deserves an equally aromatic wine. Colombard, used mostly for Armagnac brandy production and often blended with Sauvignon Blanc, is a more neutral wine with delicate floral aromas. On the palate you will find green apple, underripe peach, lemongrass, and nuts.

YEMENI SALTAH + FERNÃO PIRES, LISBOA, PORTUGAL. A meaty stew served in a hot stone dish was traditionally made to use up leftover pieces of meat, so it's exact ingredients can vary, but it's always flavored with fenugreek. Fernão Pires from Portugal is spicy with white pepper, and it has lime notes to act like a squeeze of lime on the stew.

PALESTINIAN MAQLUBA + BARBERA, BAROLO, ITALY. In this savory upside-down cake, lamb, vegetables, and rice are layered in a baking dish and then turned out to serve. Medium-bodied Nebbiolo, from the Barolo region, adds high acidity, smooth tannins, and notes of red cherry, blackberry, licorice, and black pepper.

IRANIAN FALOODEH + MOSCATO D'ASTI, PIEDMONT, ITALY. A frozen dessert made with vermicelli noodles and rosewater finds its sweet, floral match in Moscato d'Asti.

India

For my first trip to Europe, I visited college friends completing their junior year as a part of a study abroad program in London. This is not a typical destination for college students' spring break, but I was sold on the idea that I had somewhere to stay and a new place to explore, and I finally had a need for a passport, as my prior family trips on cruise ships did not require one. I have returned to London several times since then and every time I make sure to dine in the East End London neighborhood of Brick Lane, more popularly known as the "Curry Capital," deep diving into Indian regional cuisine.

These and other diasporic experiences make up my relationship with Indian food.

London has a unique connection with Indian food. There, getting a curry as a pub meal or curry sauce at the chip shop is as common as chicken tenders and fries with ketchup are in the United States. On this side of the pond, we also have our version of standard Indian takeout fare, and that's grounded in which parts of India people immigrated from and when. Some Indian restaurants outside of India may focus regionally or stick to a style like street food or Indo-Chinese food. Many Londoners of Indian descent have roots in Punjab, which is where the famous butter chicken and Tandoori chicken are from. These dishes are more commonly known as "Indian food" there.

During my time living in Portugal, I was introduced to

Goan cuisine. Portugal colonized Goa, which is in India's western region of Konkan, along the tropical coastline, from 1505 to 1961. Portuguese explorers brought foods like chile peppers and tomatoes from other colonies, and they were officially adopted as a part of Goa's local cuisine, which is heavy on fish, seafood, cashews, and coconut in all forms. As a colonizing force, Portugal also brought Catholicism and the Portuguese language to Goa. Both are still around, and they are prominent in the traditional Portuguese architecture of the churches.

Lots of Goans moved to Portugal too, in search of education and jobs. Some people from Goa also moved to Angola and São Tomé when those countries were under Portuguese occupation and then joined the groups of people from those countries who, after independence, moved to Portugal. Because Goa has its own regional cuisine, Indian food menus in Portugal might be different from what's in Brick Lane in London and Jackson Heights in New York. Goan cuisine is more of a fusion of local ingredients influenced by Portuguese traditions. When in Lisbon be sure to check out Jesus é Goês, Sabores de Goa, and Cantinho da Paz.

Indian cuisine is extremely regional and determined by geographical and cultural factors. What grows well in the Himalayan region you would not expect in coastal plains. Cultural exchange has also influenced some regional cuisines. Parts of India have traded with parts of the Levant, Arabian Peninsula, Southeast Asia, and the Himalayas for centuries. And of course, there's the effect of religion, which means some cuisines are vegetarian, some don't use pork, and some are heavier in meat of all types. For example, the Jain diet is vegan and avoids root vegetables, while Hinduism abstains from beef, and observant Muslims don't eat pork. But just like with Mexican or Chinese food, the Indian menu sold at your local takeout spot or Westernized modern restaurant is a cuisine of its own that reflects diaspora and colonialism, in addition to the history and culture of India.

For the purposes of this book, we're focusing on that classic menu with dishes like chicken tikka masala, butter chicken, tandoori chicken, palak paneer, vindaloo, rogan josh—you get the idea. And when we're thinking about pairing, there are a few things to keep in mind. One is that you might not just be eating one entree to yourself. Maybe you're bringing your own bottle to a buffet situation, or you're having thali or bhojanam, a "platter" or "full meal," respectively, with lots of different side dishes. Or maybe you're having chaat, with all of its vivid, contrasting chutneys and other toppings. These dishes will already complement each other with hot, sweet, tangy, and savory flavors, so you've got to think about what a wine can add. A lot of the spices used in a lot of Indian dishes pair really beautifully with wine. In addition to warming spices like cinnamon, cardamom, clove, ginger, nutmeg, and mace, you've got bright, citrusy coriander, earthy fenugreek and turmeric, and nutty mustard seeds. When you go to choose your wine, think about which flavors you want to uplift.

Here's the Tea

India is known for its tea, and especially its hot, milky, spiced chai. If you've heard of Darjeeling or Assam tea, those are named after regions in India. But tea probably isn't from India originally.

Tea might have been used medicinally in India back in the 1600s, but it was the English who made tea-growing an industry in India starting in the mid-1800s. When the British arrived in India, there was tea growing that's the same *Camellia sinensis* as all black and green teas, but it had thicker leaves than what was growing in China, and at the time, horticulturists thought it was a different plant.

So they introduced tea plants from China into Assam and then Darjeeling. These regions in the foothills of the Himalayas get heavy rainfalls. Assam has clay-rich soil, which makes for a robust, malty tea, while Darjeeling's soils are slightly more acidic, for a slightly brighter tea. Tea from both places tends to be more assertive than Chinese tea, which made them extremely popular back in the 1800s.

Something Else Brewing

The Asia section of the book does cover some wine-making regions and other alcohol brewed or distilled across the continent. But one ubiquitous drink across Asia gives us opportunities to talk about terroir, acidity, tannins, and aromas, and that's tea. Here's an overview of what's growing where.

Major Tea Regions

- Green Tea
- Oolong Tea
- Black Tea

ASIA

+ PAIRED UP

CHICKEN TIKKA + CARIGNAN, LANGUEDOC-ROUSSILLON, FRANCE. This dish of yogurt-marinated grilled chicken's attribution to India might go back to Partition, which is when England sort of arbitrarily drew a border between India and Pakistan. Mahira Rivers wrote for Whetstone about how chicken tikka is immensely popular in Pakistan, but that immigrants looking to open restaurants in the United States or the UK may have called themselves Indian because it would have been more familiar to diners. Rivers calls chicken tikka a Punjabi dish—from a region that spans the border of India and Pakistan. Pair it with Carignan from Languedoc-Roussillon in Southern France. Known as "the food wine," Carignan is medium in body with good acidity. Bright and fruit forward, it also has savory notes and a hint of baking spice that will complement this chicken.

CHICKEN TIKKA MASALA + CATAWBA, FINGER LAKES, NEW YORK. Considered the unofficial national dish of Great Britain, chicken tikka masala is said to have been created in Scotland in the 1960s by a chef named Ali Ahmed Aslam. The story goes that he served chicken tikka at his restaurant in Scotland, and people complained because in England at the time, the preference was to have meat served in some sort of sauce or gravy, so he created the creamy tomato sauce. Some have called him Pakistani and others Bangladeshi. It's hard to know because Bangladesh was part of Pakistan in the 1960s. Catawba, an indigenous American grape, is known for its bright, juicy wine, which works really nicely to freshen this creamy tomato sauce. The wine also has slightly strawberry jammy notes that will pair well with the chicken. With low tannins, medium to light body, and good acidity, Catawba's a very refreshing wine you can enjoy chilled.

VINDALOO + CASTELÃO, LISBOA, PORTUGAL. This hot, vinegary curry is a Goan dish descended from the Portuguese vinha d'alhos. The Portuguese dish had meat marinated in wine and garlic because the wine could help the meat keep for longer. In Goa, wine was replaced with vinegar, a lot more spices were added, and the name changed, making it a fully Indian dish. In Goa, pork is traditional, but elsewhere in the world, we can get it with all sorts of proteins. With this history, I'd pair it with a Portuguese wine: Castelão. It has plenty of body, so it can face the rich meat and vinegary sauce, and its savory, gamy notes will add an extra hint of umami.

WINE PAIRING FOR THE PEOPLE

SAAG PANEER, BUT WITH FETA + MALVASIA,
COLLIO, ITALY

SERVES 4

- ¼ cup plus 2 tablespoons ghee or extra-virgin olive oil
- 2 tablespoon coriander seeds
- ¼ teaspoon ground cardamom
- 1 small onion, chopped
- 1 garlic clove, fine-chopped
- 1½-inch piece ginger, peeled, chopped
- 1 pound baby spinach (about 12 cups)
- 1 small Indian green chile or serrano chile, coarsely chopped
- 1½ teaspoon fresh lime juice
- Kosher salt
- 6 ounces feta, cut into 1-inch pieces
- 1 teaspoon cumin seeds
- ¼ teaspoon asafetida (optional)
- ¼ teaspoon red chili powder
- Roti or rice (for serving)

New York Times food writer Priya Krishna made waves with her first cookbook, *Indian-ish*, which explored diasporic cuisine in her home kitchen, with her mother. Some of her dishes, like this one, make use of ingredients that would have been easier for her family to find when she was growing up. In this case, feta steps in for paneer and adds a bright saltiness.

Malvasia is a wonderfully aromatic white wine grape. Expressions from Colli in Northern Italy will have some lychee notes that add a playful edge to this dish, plus minerality that will pair nicely with the feta. You can expect ripe peach and green almonds with a distinct basil note and saline finish.

1. Heat ¼ cup of the ghee in a large skillet over medium. Cook the coriander seeds and cardamom, stirring constantly, until starting to brown, about 2 minutes. Add the onion and cook, stirring occasionally, until translucent and slightly browned, about 5 minutes. Mix in garlic and ginger and cook, stirring, 1 minute. Add spinach by the handful, letting it wilt slightly after each addition before adding more. Cook until all of the spinach is just wilted, about 3 minutes. Remove the pan from the heat and add the chile and lime juice; season to taste with salt. Let cool 5 minutes.

2. Transfer the spinach mixture to a blender and blend until a coarse paste forms, about 1 minute. Return the spinach mixture to the pan and set over low heat. Stir in ½ cup water, then gently fold in feta, being careful not to break up. Cook until the feta is slightly softened and has absorbed some of the sauce, 5 to 7 minutes.

3. Meanwhile, heat the remaining 2 tablespoons of ghee in a small saucepan over medium-high, 1 minute. Add cumin seeds. As soon as cumin seeds start to pop, sputter, and brown, remove the pan from the heat, 1 minute tops. Immediately add asafetida, if using, and chili powder. Pour ghee mixture over spinach mixture. Serve with roti or rice.

Used with permission from *Indian-Ish: Recipes and Antics from a Modern American Family* by Priya Krishna with Ritu Krishna (HarperCollins Publishers, April 2019).

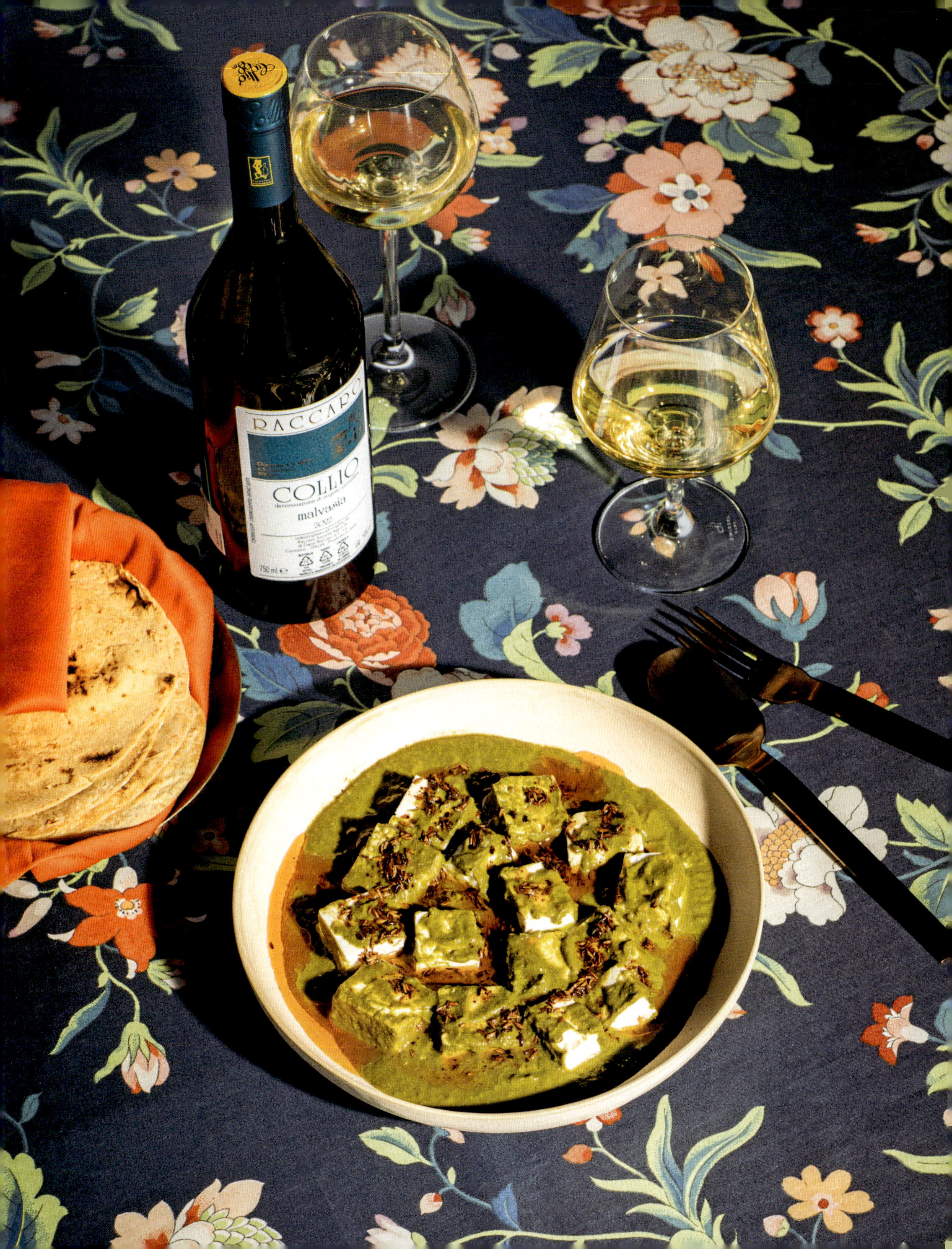
RACCARO
COLLIO
malvasia
2022
750 ml

THE WINE LIST
Asia

CHINA

Kung Pao Chicken + Gewürztraminer, ALSACE, FRANCE

Chairman Mao's Red-Braised Pork + Gamay, WILLAMETTE VALLEY, OREGON

Sweet-and-Sour Mandarin Fish + Auxerrois Blanc, ALSACE, FRANCE

Beggar's Chicken + Bordeaux Blanc, ENTRE-DEUX-MERS, FRANCE

Buddha Jumps Over the Wall + Skin-Contact Pinot Grigio, ŠTAJERSKA, SLOVENIA

Braised Intestines in Brown Sauce + Xinomavro, NAOUSSA, GREECE

Wang's Smelly Tofu + Spätburgunder, BADEN, GERMANY

Peking Duck + Viognier, CONDRIEU, FRANCE

General Tso's Chicken + Rosado, NAVARRA, SPAIN

Orange Chicken + Fiano, CAMPANIA, ITALY

Sweet-and-Sour Chicken + De Chaunac Pét-Nat, FINGER LAKES, NEW YORK

Fried Chicken Wings + Grenache Blanc, RHÔNE VALLEY, FRANCE

Beef and Broccoli + Trollinger, WÜRTTEMBERG, GERMANY

Pan-Fried Noodles in Superior Soy Sauce + Pinot Noir, WILLAMETTE VALLEY, OREGON

▼

JAPAN

Shoyu Ramen + Pinot Gris, ALSACE, FRANCE

Okonomiyaki + Friulano, FRIULI, ITALY

Agedashi Tofu + Pecorino, UMBRIA, ITALY

Yasai No Tempura + Müller-Thurgau, RHEINHESSEN, GERMANY

Sukiyaki + Pinot Noir, Central Otago, NEW ZEALAND

Tonkatsu Curry + Grüner Veltliner, WACHAU, AUSTRIA

Karaage + Crémant de Loire, ANJOU, FRANCE

Negima + Aglianico Rosé, CAMPANIA, ITALY

Gyu Donburi + Junmai Sake, HYOGO PREFECTURE, JAPAN

Otoro (Fatty Tuna) Sushi + Gamay, BEAUJOLAIS, FRANCE
Salmon Sushi + Vermentino, SARDINIA, ITALY
Unagi (Eel) Sushi + Furmint, TOKAJ, HUNGARY
Uni Sushi + Marsanne, RHÔNE VALLEY, FRANCE
Yellowtail (Hamachi) Sushi + Verdicchio, MARCHE, ITALY
Shiromi (White Fish) Sushi + Melon de Bourgogne, MUSCADET SÈVRE ET MAINE, FRANCe
Vegetable Roll + Vinho Verde Branco, VINHO VERDE, PORTUGAL
California Roll + Sauvignon Blanc, CENTRAL COAST, CALIFORNIA
Philadelphia Roll + Aligoté, BURGUNDY, FRANCE
Spicy Tuna Roll + Brachetto, PIEDMONT, ITALY
Spider Roll + Sparkling Blanc de Noir, MENDOCINO, CALIFORNIA
Shrimp Tempura Roll + Prosecco Rosé, VALDOBBIADENE, ITALY

▼

SOUTH KOREA

Dak Galbi + Dry Vidal, SHENANDOAH VALLEY, VIRGINIA
Dolsot Bibimbap + Schiava, ALTO ADIGE, ITALY
Dosirak + Gamay Rosé, HUNTER VALLEY, AUSTRALIA
Chikin + Crémant de Limoux Rosé, LANGUEDOC-ROUSSILLON, FRANCE
Haemul Pajeon + Arneis, PIEDMONT, ITALY
Spam Kimbap + Rosé, PROVENCE, FRANCE
A Very Good Kimchi Jjigae + Ramato Pinot Gris, ALTO ADIGE, ITALY

▼

SOUTHEAST ASIA

Chè Chuối + German Riesling Trockenbeerenauslese
Biko + German Riesling Trockenbeerenauslese
Halo-Halo + German Riesling Beerenauslese
Khao Niao Mamuang + German Riesling Beerenauslese
Drunken Noodles + German Riesling Auslese
Bánh Chưng + German Riesling Auslese
Chicken Massaman Curry + German Riesling Auslese
Kare Kare + German Riesling Spätlese
Green Papaya Salad + German Riesling Spätlese
Pad Thai + German Riesling Spätlese

Lumpia + German Riesling Spätlese
Pho + German Riesling Kabinett
Thai Green Curry + German Riesling Kabinett
Bánh Xèo + German Riesling Kabinett
Bánh Mì + German Riesling Kabinett
Bún Chả + German Riesling Trocken
Miến Xào + German Riesling Trocken
Bún Thịt Nướng + German Riesling Kabinett

▼

TURKEY

Manti + Mencía, RIBEIRA SACRA, SPAIN
Köfte + Mourvèdre, SWARTLAND, SOUTH AFRICA
Lahmacun + Sangiovese, TUSCANY, ITALY
Hamsili Pilav + Avesso, VINHO VERDE, PORTUGAL
Döner Kebab + Bobal, REQUENA-UTIEL, SPAIN
Baklava + Tokaji Aszú, TOKAJ, HUNGARY

▼

GEORGIA

Lobio Mtsvanilit + Tavkveri, KARTLI, GEORGIA
Khachapuri + Mtsvane Khakuri, KAKHETI, GEORGIA
Khinkali + Tsolikouri, IMERETI, GEORGIA
Lobio + Saperavi, KAKHETI, GEORGIA
Mtsvadi + Tavkveri, KARTLI, GEORGIA
Lobiani + Rkatsiteli, KAKHETI, GEORGIA

▼

UNITED ARAB EMIRATES

Emirati Lamb Kabsa + Shiraz, BAROSSA VALLEY, AUSTRALIA
Marrag Samak + Frappato, SICILY, ITALY
Harees + Roussanne, RHÔNE VALLEY, FRANCE
Omani Shuwa + Airén, LA MANCHA, SPAIN
Joojeh Kebab + Colombard, RUSSIAN RIVER VALLEY, CALIFORNIA
Yemeni Saltah + Fernão Pires, LISBOA, PORTUGAL
Palestinian Maqluba + Barbera, BAROLO, ITALY
Iranian Faloodeh + Moscato d'Asti, PIEDMONT, ITALY

▼

INDIA

Chicken Tikka + Carignan, LANGUEDOC-ROUSSILLON, FRANCE
Chicken Tikka Masala + Catawba, FINGER LAKES, NEW YORK
Vindaloo + Castelão, LISBOA, PORTUGAL
Sag Paneer, But with Feta + Malvasia, COLLIO, ITALY

▼

Acknowledgments

FROM CHA

"For I know the plans I have for you," declares the Lord, "plans to prosper you and not to harm you, plans to give you hope and a future."
—**Jeremiah 29:11**

Thank you, God, for your divine strategy over me.

Thank you to my mother, Gwen, for centering your life around protecting my future. Without your hard work, sacrifice, and dedication I would not have the privilege to become who I am today.

To my father, Tony, whose influence impacted me in more ways than he will ever know. Thank you for gifting me the power to dream big and for always believing I was more than special, I was *golden*.

To my brother, Chu, thanks for always being my best friend. During the two years of working on this book, life has changed drastically for the both of us, but your grace reminds me of God's promise, and I am thankful for the reminder that I am never alone on this journey.

To my extended family, the Champaynes, the McCoys, the Lesters, the Heartfields, the Smiths, and the Stiths, thank you for your prayers and support.

To my friends who have been holding me down from the '99 to the 2000s, Tiffanee and Sharday, I appreciate you for having the capacity for me and always showing me love. And to my Sorors of Alpha Kappa Alpha, and most specifically my line sister, Tamish, for always having my back during this process and embodying the meaning of sisterhood.

To my agent, Rica Allannic, for approaching me after I just delivered a speech to close to a thousand women, inspired by the future of the food and beverage industry and believing I had a book in me that could be that change. I appreciate your relentlessness through the years when I didn't know how to believe in myself. Thanks for being a constant reminder of what I am capable of as a writer during this journey.

To Layla Schlack, thank you for saying YES to this call. I knew the journey wouldn't be smooth, but I prayed for a partner who would weather storms with me. You have done just that and then some, and I am grateful for your support, your optimism, your flexibility, and your extended grace.

To the editors Stephanie Fletcher for seeing the vision and Sarah Kwak for executing it.

To the creative team who helped bring the words to life, illustrations by Joelle Avelino, and photography by Clay Williams, supported by Luciana Lamboy, Gerri Williager, stylist Erika Nunez, and MUA Marsha.

To my forever food friend and travel buddy Chef Shaquay Peacock, thank you for your input and contribution as the recipe tester for this book. I look forward to more adventures and projects with you.

To Stephen Satterfield, for the kind and inspiring words in the foreword, and to the

ACKNOWLEDGMENTS

chefs, mixologists, and restaurateurs featured in this book: Hawa Hassan, Jeny Sulemange, Pierre Thiam, Marcela Valladolid, Emme Ribeiro Collins, Pilar Hernandez, Alicia Kennedy, Lynnette Marrero, Paola Velez, Brittney Williams, Adrienne Cheatham, Amethyst Ganaway, Rodney Scott, Ed and Ryan Mitchells, Dominick Lee, Rose Previte, Wilson Tang, Christian Suzuki-Orellana (aka Suzu), Eric Kim, Priya Krishna, Nini Nguyen.

To Ivy Mix and the Leyanda team, Nilea Alexander and the Cafe Ru Dix team, Melba and Melba's Restaurant team, and Miss Lily's 7A Cafe.

To my Communion Community, if you ever worked for me virtually or at The Communion Wine & Spirits store, collaborated with me as a chef or restauranter for The Communion pop-up events, thank you for supporting the mission. Thank you to anyone who has ever attended an event, purchased wine from the shop, joined my wine club subscription, or tasted with me during your wine travels. Your purchases validate my mission that wine is for all of us, and I hope I have inspired you to embrace wine in a new way.

To New York, the city that raised me, and Harlem, the hood that blessed me.

FROM LAYLA

First and foremost, thank you to Cha for bringing me along on this journey. I appreciate your trust, your vast knowledge, and your work ethic.

Thanks as well to my agent, Kim Lindman, for your steadiness and encouragement, and to Cha's agent, Rica Allannic. I've learned so much from seeing you in action. Much appreciation to our editors—Stephanie Fletcher for getting us started and Sarah Kwak for helping us over the finish line. And, of course, to Clay Williams, Luciana Lamboy, and Joelle Avelino for making it beautiful, and Chef Shaquay Peacock for testing the recipes. Having such a good team has been invaluable.

To Jay, my husband and a very good friend to our dog, I couldn't have done it without you. Thanks for always being willing to get pizza for dinner (a true sacrifice!), for helping me work the knots out of my shoulders after I've been slouched over the computer in some godawful position, and for all the many silent refills of my water glass.

Working on a book can be isolating, but I'm lucky to have a whole crew of people who were happy to support me and understood that I couldn't see them or talk to them as much as I'd like: my parents, my sister, my incredible nieces; the aunts, the uncles, all the cousins; friends Meghan Foster, Danielle Sinkford, Jen Tremblay, Sarina Cass, Mekkin Lynch, Beca Grimm, and Max Acenowr; all the faculty and students of the Western Connecticut State University MFA program. Alicia Kennedy and Mayukh Sen, our chats saved my life. Emily Saladino, Lauren Buzzeo, and Stephen Satterfield, sharing wine with you all reminded me why I love it so much.

And, finally, a quick thank-you to every writer who told me my edits helped or that they were excited to work with me, who was kind and patient when I was slow to respond to email. Your faith in me, believe it or not, was one of the main things that made me feel competent to take on a project of this magnitude.

Bibliography

2023 Global Travel Trends Report. American Express, 2023. https://www.americanexpress.com/en-us/travel/discover/img/gtt2023/AmericanExpress2023GlobalTravelTrends.pdf.

Asimov, E. "Peruvian Cuisine Takes on the World." *New York Times*, May 26, 1999. https://www.nytimes.com/1999/05/26/dining/peruvian-cuisine-takes-on-the-world.html.

———. "From Chile, History in a Bottle." *New York Times*, October 17, 2007. https://www.nytimes.com/2007/10/17/dining/reviews/17wine.html.

———. "From the Itata Valley in Southern Chile, Old-Vine Cinsault."

New York Times, August 29, 2019. https://www.nytimes.com/2019/08/29/dining/drinks/wine-school-assignment-itata-valley-chile-cinsault.html.

Barnes, A. *The South American Wine Guide*. Self-published, May 31, 2021.

———. "Rediscovering Chilean Carmenère." Wine Enthusiast, September 13, 2022. https://www.wineenthusiast.com/basics/advanced-studies/rediscovering-chilean-carmenere/.

BBC News. "Soldier Confirms Chile Stadium Killings." June 27, 2022. http://news.bbc.co.uk/2/hi/americas/807599.stm.

Brummel, K. "Excelsa Coffee Beans: What You Need to Know." Home Grounds, May 18, 2022. https://www.homegrounds.co/excelsa-coffee-beans/.

"Classification and Labeling." Wines of Germany. https://germanwineusa.com/basics/classifications/.

DeJesus, E. "It's Not Easy Being Green: The Weird History of the Grasshopper." Eater, October 23, 2014. https://www.eater.com/2014/10/23/7036159/a-brief-history-of-the-grasshopper.

Economic Times. "Dubai and the UAE: Global Wealth Nexus." November 23, 2023. https://economictimes.indiatimes.com/news/international/uae/dubai-and-the-uae-a-global-wealth-nexus/articleshow/105355854.cms.

Garvin, D. "The Italian Coffee Triangle: From Brazilian *Colonos* to Ethiopian *Colonialisti*." *Modern Italy* 26, no. 3 (2021), 1–22. https://doi.org/10.1017/mit.2021.26.

Georgian Wine Guild. "Winemaking Regions." https://www.georgianwineguild.co.uk/georgian-wine/viticulture-and-wine making-regions.

Giliberti, B. "The South American Surprise." *Washington Post*, January 27, 2019. https://www.washingtonpost.com/archive/lifestyle/food/1999/0½7/the-south-american-surprise/4827e2ef-7feb-4ab0-a65a-67d628fcaaf7/.

"History of Japanese Whisky." Dekantā. https://dekanta.com/history-of-japanese-whisky/.

Japanese National Tax Agency. "Information on GIs Protected In Japan." https://www.nta.go.jp/english/taxes/liquor_administration/geographical/02.htm.

Johnson, C. "A Little Taste of Senegal in Harlem." NPR, August 12, 2008. https://www.npr.org/2008/08/12/93531100/a-little-taste-of-senegal-in-harlem.

Jones, A. "Kurt Evans on People Power and Black American Chinese Food." *Philadelphia*, April 25, 2023. https://www.phillymag.com/foobooz/2023/04/25/kurt-evans-last-dragon-takeout/.

Klein, M. "Chef Kurt Evans Is Raising Funds for Down North, His Pizza Shop with a Mission." *Philadelphia Inquirer*, October 20, 2020. https://www.inquirer.com/news/down-north-pizza-kurt-evans-black-restaurant-week-philadelphia-20201020.html.

La Competencia Imports. "About Us—Our Story." https://www.lacompetenciaimports.com/About-Us/Our-Story.

Lloyd, A. "What Does 'Fynbos' Mean in Wine?" Wine Enthusiast, May 11, 2021. https://www.winemag.com/2021/05/11/fynbos-definition-wine-south-africa/.

Lopes, J. *Vignette*. Hardie Grant Books, 2019.

Martins, C. "A Lisbon Chef's Life Was Changed by War as a Child. Her Story Became Her Restaurant." *Washington Post*, October 3, 2019. https://www.washingtonpost.com/travel/2019/10/03/batata-doces-cuisine-reflects-chef-whose-life-was-changed-forever-by-war/.

BIBLIOGRAPHY

McGunnigle, N. "The History of Cocktails in New Orleans." Thrillist, October 10, 2016. https://www.thrillist.com/drink/new-orleans/new-orleans-cocktails-drink-history-sazerac-vieux-carre-hurricane.

Migration Policy Institute. "The Nigerian Diaspora in the United States." June 2015. https://www.migrationpolicy.org/sites/default/files/publications/RAD-Nigeria.pdf.

Mix, I. *Spirits of Latin America: A Celebration of Culture & Cocktails, with 100 Recipes from Leyenda & Beyond*. Ten Speed Press, May 26, 2020.

National Research Institute of Brewing. "The Story of Japan Wine." March 2019. https://www.nrib.go.jp/English/sake/pdf/WineNo02_en.pdf.

Patel, M. "Sparkling Success: Wines of Brazil's Rise in the International Market." Sommeliers Choice Awards. https://sommelierschoiceawards.com/en/blog/interviews-3373/sparkling-success-wines-of-brazils-rise-in-the-international-market-962.htm.

Peartree, M. "The Difference Between Soul Food and Southern Food, According to a Pro." Delish, January 26, 2024. https://www.delish.com/food-news/a26356466/what-is-soul-food/.

Puckette, M. "South African Wine (with Maps)" Wine Folly. https://winefolly.com/deep-dive/south-african-wine-map/.

Reuters. "At Chile Wine Gala, Climate Change and Water Use in Focus." November 7, 2022. https://www.reuters.com/business/environment/chile-wine-gala-climate-change-water-use-focus-2022-11-07/.

Reynolds, M. (2023, January 16). "This Seriously Hipster Bean Is Coffee's Best Hope for Survival." *Wired*, January 16, 2023. https://www.wired.com/story/liberica-coffee-plants/.

Rivers, M. "Midnight Chicken and Rumination on Pakistani Cuisine." Whetstone, September 30, 2022. https://www.whetstonemagazine.com/journal/midnight-chicken-and-other-ruminations-about-pakistani-cuisine.

Robinson, Janice. "Brazil." JancisRobinson.com. https://www.jancisrobinson.com/learn/wine-regions/brazil.

——— "Turkey." JancisRobinson.com. https://www.jancisrobinson.com/learn/wine-regions/turkey.

Saayman, D. "South African Vineyard, Soils and Climate." Wines of South Africa, January 2013. https://www.wosa.co.za/The-Industry/Terroir/Related-Articles/Terroir-South-African-Vineyard-and-Soils-and-Climate/.

Saladino, E. "As Tastes and the Climate Change, Muscadine Wine 'Deserves Respect.'" Wine Enthusiast, last updated August 21, 2023. https://www.wineenthusiast.com/basics/grapes-101/muscadine-wine/?srsltid=AfmBOoq9iGAqPdd_vQ_gVKm4NjcZ_g2j-Yw6zVueYMFqv2vrWBNzl6n8.

Sciaudone, C. "Argentine Movement Tries to Make Black Heritage More Visible." AP News, November 26, 2021. https://apnews.com/article/immigration-entertainment-discrimination-migration-race-and-ethnicity-0d18920b22e0eab19f28202c591ef0ea.

Sloley, P. "Jollof Wars: Who Does West Africa's Iconic Rice Dish Best?" BBC, June 7, 2021. https://www.bbc.com/travel/article/20210607-jollof-wars-who-does-west-africas-iconic-rice-dish-best.

"Timeline: New Orleans." American Experience. PBS.org. https://www.pbs.org/wgbh/americanexperience/features/neworleans-timeline-new-orleans/.

Tipton-Martin, T. *Juke Joints, Jazz Clubs, and Juice: Cocktails from Two Centuries of African American Cookbooks*. Clarkson Potter, November 14, 2023.

"Turkey—Country Commercial Guide." International Trade Administration. https://www.trade.gov/country-commercial-guides/turkey-agriculture.

"Turkish Wine." The Quirky Cork. https://thequirkycork.com/turkish-wine/.

Wallace, N. "Photo Essay: Japanese Peruvian Lives Before World War II." Densho.org, April 18, 2022. https://densho.org/catalyst/photo-essay-japanese-peruvian-lives-before-world-war-ii/.

"Winegrowing Areas." Wines of South Africa. https://www.wosa.co.za/The-Industry/Winegrowing-Areas/Winelands-of-South-Africa/.

"With Millennia of History, Turkish Wine Continues to Evolve." Wine Enthusiast. https://www.wineenthusiast.com/basics/region-rundown/turkish-wine-guide/.

Yasuda, M. "Japan Adds Three Geographically Indicated Wine Regions." Vino Joy News, January 8, 2022. https://vino-joy.com/2022/01/08/japan-adds-three-geographically-indicated-wine-regions/.

Index

Note: Page references in *italics* indicate photographs.

A

Abkhazia, 223
acidity, defined, xxi
Aconcagua, 113
adhan (call to prayer), 6
Adjara, 223
Aegean Sea, 214–15
Africa, 1–53
    map, 2
    overview, 3
    popular beers, 32
    wine list, 52–53
Afrikaner, 48
AfroPunk music festival, 12
agave spirits, 95, 96
age of wine, defined, xxi
Agiorgitiko, 15, 161
Aglianico Rosato, 161
Aglianico Rosé, 197
Aguascalientes, 98
Airén, 229
Albariño, 133
alcohol, ABV, xxi
Alicante Bouschet, 75, 161
Aligoté, 198
Allende, Salvador, 110, 112
Alvarinho, 37, 76
Alvarinho Vinho Verde producers, 76
Anatolia, 214, 216–17
Andes Mountains, 107–8
Angola, 34–40
    facts and statistics, 34
    signature dishes and wine pairings, 37
    wine list, 53
Anhui cuisine, 188
anju (bar snacks), 200
Anju (restaurant), 199
apartheid, 43, 44, 46
appellation, xxi
Arabica coffee, 25
Argentina, 118–24
    bike tour, 121
    facts and statistics, 118
    signature dishes and wine pairings, 122
    wine grapes, 119

    wine list, 137
    wine regions, 120–24
Arneis, 155, 201
Asia, 180–239
    map of, 180–81
    wine list, 236–39
Aslina Wines, 48
Assyrtiko, 74
Asti Spumante, 146
Atacama, 112
Atlas Mountains, 5
Auslese, 208, 209
Austral, 113–15
Avesso, 75, 216
avocado smoothies, 6

B

bacanora, 95
Baga Rosé, 40
báhn mì, 205
báhn xèo, 205
Baja California, 97
balance, defined, xxi
Banks Beer, 83
Baraka, Amiri, 142
Barbados, 82–87
    Crop Over Festival, 86
    facts and statistics, 82
    rum, 83, 84–86
    signature dishes and wine pairings, 87
    signature drinks, 83
    wine list, 89
barbecue, 159–68
    crossover with soul food, 162
    origins of, 162
    recipes, 165, 168
    regional styles, 160, 162–63
    signature dishes and wine pairings, 161
    wine list, 177
barbecue belt map, 160
Barbera, 13, 229
Barreto, Angel, 199–200
Barriere, Tiffanie, 173
Batata Doce, 36–38
Bean Belt, 22–23

beans
    Lobio Mtsvanilit + Tavkveri, *224*, 225
beef
    Chilean Chacarero Sandwich + Carménère, *116*, 117
    Rainbow Pastelitos (Empanadas) + Petite Sirah, *78*, 79–80
    Stew, Somali, + Nerello Mascalese, 26, *27*
beer
    in Africa, 32
    in Barbados, 83
    in Chile, 108
Beerenauslese, 208, 209
berbere spice mix, 20–21
Berber people, 5
bike tour of Maipú wine region, 121
Biyela, Ntsiki, 48
Black Elephant Vintners & Co., 48
Black Sea, 215
Bobal, 100, 216
Bocanáriz, 109
Bodegas del Marques de Aguayo, 96
body, defined, xxi
Bonarda, 161
Bot River, 49
Botrytis/noble rot, xxi
braai, 49–51
Brachetto, 198
Brazil, 125–34
    facts and statistics, 125
    Japanese Brazilian community in, 193
    recipe, 133
    signature dishes and wine pairings, 132
    signature drinks, 126
    sparkling wines, 130, 132
    wine grapes, 128
    wine list, 137
    wine regions, 128–29
bright, defined, xxi
Buena Onda, 111
Buenos Aires, 119, 124
Bún Thịt Nướng with Egg Rolls + German Kabinett Riesling, 210–11
Butter, Strawberry, 149

INDEX

C

Cabernet Franc, 15, 168, 172
Cabernet Sauvignon, 50, 115, 165
cachaça, 126, 127
Cagalanan, Nikko, 207
caipirinhas, 126
Cake, Roasted Pineapple Cornmeal, + Sauternes, 151–52
Campanha, 129
Campbell, Maggie, 84–85
Campos do Cima da Serra, 129
Cannonau, 74
Cantinho do Aziz, 38, 40
Cantonese cuisine, 188
Cape Town, 43, 49, 51
Cape Verde, 34–40
    facts and statistics, 35
    signature dish and wine pairing, 37
    wine list, 53
Cappadocia, 214, 216
Caribbean, 56–89
    map, 56
    overview, 57
    rum, 84–86
    wine list, 88–89
Carignan, 174, 233
Cariñena Rosado, 66
Carménère grapes, 115
Carmen Stevens Wines, 48
Carnival, 125–26
Casa Madero, 96, 98
Castelão, 233
Catamarca, 121–22
Catawba, 233
Cava Rosé, 100
Central Anatolia, 216
Central Valley, 113
Chacarero Sandwich, Chilean, + Carménère, *116*, 117
chacha, 219
Champagne, 147
Champagne labels, 131
Chaouia-Ouardigha, 7
Chardonnay, 9, 63, 100, 114, 132
Charleston, 154
Charleston Wine + Food Festival, 154, 159–62, 206–7
Charmat method, 130
Cheatham, Adrienne, 151
cheese
    Saag Paneer, but with Feta + Malvasia, *234*, 235
chemical flavors, xvii
Chenin Blanc, 50
Chenin Blanc Pét-Nat, 100
chicha, 108, 110

chicken
    Barbecued Spatchcocked, + Cabernet Franc, 168
    Bún Thịt Nướng with Egg Rolls + German Kabitnett Riesling, 210–11
    and Eggnog Waffles, Melba's Signature, + Vintage Champagne Blanc de Noirs, 147–50, *148*
    and Sausage Gumbo + Carignan, 174–75, *175*
Chihuahua, 98
Chile, 104–17
    Carménère grapes, 115
    facts and statistics, 104
    politics, 110–12
    recipes, 111, 117
    signature dishes and wine pairings, 114–15
    signature drinks, 108
    wine grapes, 113, 115
    wine list, 136
    wine regions, 112–15
    wines, 106, 108–10
    wine traveler tip, 106
chile peppers
    peri peri, about, 38
    Peri Peri Sauce, 39
China, 182–91
    recipe, 191
    regional food styles and wine pairings, 187–88
    signature dishes and wine pairings, 189
    wine labels, 184
    wine list, 236
    wine regions, 185–87
Chinatown, NY, 183–85
Chubut, 124
cigars, Cuban, 70–71
Cinsault, 13
Cinsault Rosé, 155
Coahuila, 98
coconut
    Marrero Family Coquito, 62
coffee
    Arabic-style (gahwa), 228
    in Ethiopia, 19, 22–25
    in Italy, 19
    in Kenya and Tanzania, 30–31
    in Puerto Rico, 59
    in Southeast Asia, 206
cognac
    The Parish, 173
Collins, Emme Ribeiro, 133
Colombard, 229

comiteco, 95
Communion, The, wine dinner series, xiv, 12
Communion Wine & Spirits, The, xiv, 130
Constantia, 47
Coquimbo, 112–13
coquito, about, 60
Coquito, Marrero Family, 62
Cornmeal Roasted Pineapple Cake + Sauternes, 151–52
Corn 'n' Oil, 83
Côtes du Rhône–Red Blend, 9
crab
    Curry aka Ikala + Baga Rosé, 40, *41*
    Rice + Garganega, 158
Crémant de Bourgogne Brut Rosé, 172
Crémant de Limoux Rosé, 201
Crémant de Loire, 197
Creole, 169–75
    description of, 171
    New Orleans culture, 169–71
    in New York, 171–72
    recipes, 173, 174
    signature dishes and wine pairings, 172
    signature drinks, 170
    wine list, 177
Crianza Rioja, 63
Crop Over Festival, 86
Cuba, 67–71
    cigars, 70–71
    facts and statistics, 67
    signature dishes and wine pairings, 69
    wine list, 88
Cuyo, 122–23

D

Darling, 49
dawa, 30
De Chaunac Pét-Nat, 189
De Marco, Sylvie, 59
Demi-Sec Champagne, 172
Demi-Sec Chenin Blanc, 33
Dennis, BJ, 162
Deutscher Wein, 207
Dolcetto, 87, 172
Dominican Republic, 72–80
    facts and statistics, 72
    recipe, 79
    signature dishes and wine pairings, 74–75
    wine list, 89
Doukhala-Abda, 7
Dreamcatcher hotel, 59

INDEX

drinks
    Buena Onda, 111
    Marrero Family Coquito, 62
    Momotaro, 196
    The Parish, 173
dry, defined, xxi
Dry Vidal, 201
Dubai, 227–28
Dutch East India Company, 44

E
Eggnog, 149
Egg Rolls, Bún Thịt Nướng with, + German Kabinett Riesling, 210–11
Eiswein, 208
Elgin, 47
Encruzado, 37
Erdoğan, Recep Tayyip, 214
Essence Festival of Culture, 169
Ethiopia, 18–26
    coffee, 19, 22–25
    Ethiopian American population density, 21
    Ethiopian cuisine in the United States, 20–22
    facts and statistics, 18
    signature dishes and wine pairings, 23
    signature drinks, 22
    wine list, 52
Evans, Kurt, 182
Excelsa coffee, 25

F
Falanghina, 13
fermentation, xxi
Fernão Pires, 229
Fertile Crescent, 214, 216
Fes-Boulmane, 8
Fiano, 189
Figueira Rubaiyat, 127
finish, defined, xxi
Flavor Wheel, xviii
floral flavors, xvii
Foursquare Rum Distillery, 85–86
Franciacorta Extra Brut, 23
Franschhoek, 47–49
Frappato, 155, 229
Friulano, 155, 197
fruity flavors, xvii
Fujian cuisine, 188
Furmint, 198

G
Gahwa (Arabic-style coffee), 228
Gamay, 198
Gamay Rosé, 201
Ganaway, Amethyst, 158
Garganega, 75, 158
Garnacha, 75
Georgia, 218–26
    facts and statistics, 218
    recipe, 225
    signature dishes and wine pairings, 226
    in the Soviet Era, 220–21
    wine grapes, 223
    wine labels, 222
    wine list, 238
    wine producers, 221
    wines and wine regions, 219–23
German wines. *See also specific wines*
    labels, 208
    quality classifications, 207–8
    sweet classifications, 208
Gewürztraminer, 9
Ghana, 10–17
    facts and statistics, 11
    jollof rice, 15
    signature dishes and wine pairings, 13–14
    wine list, 52
Gharb-Chrarda-Beni Hssen, 8
gin and tonic, 30
Goan cuisine, 231
Godello, 69
Grand Kadooment, 86
Gran Reserva Cava Brut, 63
Grasshopper, 170
Grechetto, 75
Grenache, 99
Grenache Blanc, 189
Grillo, 33
Grüner Veltliner, 13, 197
Guanajuato, 98
Guinness, 32
Gumbo, Chicken and Sausage, + Carignan, 174–75, *175*
Guria, 223

H
Hagi sake, 194
Hakusan sake, 193
halal dietary standards, 144
Halbtrocken, 208
Harima sake, 193
Havana, 68
Hebei, 185–86
Hernandez, Pilar, 115
Highberry Farm, 48
Hispanics in Wine, 96
Hop Kee, 183–85
House of Mandela, 48
Humboldt Current, 107
Hunan cuisine, 187
Hurricane, 170

I
Ice Wine Vidal Blanc, 14
Imereti, 222
India, 230–34
    Indian cuisine, 231
    London connection with Indian food, 230
    recipe, 234
    signature dishes and wine pairings, 233
    tea culture, 231–32
    wine list, 239
Isabella, 132
Islamic culture, 6
Istanbul, 212–13
Iwate sake, 195

J
Jacinto, Isabel, 38
Jado Sushi Wine Bar, 192
Jaen, 37
Jamaica, 72–80
    facts and statistics, 73
    recipe, 76
    signature dishes and wine pairings, 74–75
    wine list, 89
Japan, 192–98
    hybrid grapes, 194
    recipe, 196
    sake producers, 194
    sake regions, 193–94
    signature dishes and wine pairings, 197
    signature drinks, 195
    sushi wine pairings, 198
    wine list, 236–37
Jiangsu cuisine, 187
Jjigae, A Very Good Kimchi, + Ramato Pinot Gris, 202, *203*
Johannesburg, 42–43
jollof rice styles and origins, 14–15
Jollof Rice + Zinfandel, *16*, 17
Junmai Sake, 197

K
Kabinett, 208, 209
Kakheti, 221
Kamayan dining, 207
Kartli, 222
Kenya, 28–33
    facts and statistics, 28

INDEX

signature beer, 32
signature dishes and wine pairings, 33
signature drinks, 30
wine industry, 29
wine list, 53
Kepley, Jenna, 159–60
khunjul, 6
Kim, Eric, 202
Kimchi Jjigae, A Very Good, + Ramato Pinot Gris, 202, *203*
Krishna, Priya, 234
Kumusha Wines, 48
KWV, 44–46

L
La Factoría, 59–60
Lambrusco di Sorbara, 145
Lambrusco di Sorbara Rosé, Extra Dry, 172
Landwein, 208
La Pampa, 123
La Rioja, 122
late-bottled vintage Port, 146
Latin America, 92–137
   map, 92
   overview, 93
   wine list, 136–37
Latinx Wine Summit, 96
Lee, Dominick, 174
lees, defined, xxi
Liberica coffee, 25
Lisbon, 35, 36–39
Lobio Mtsvanilit + Tavkveri, *224, 225*
Lobster Tails, Grilled Jerk, + Alvarinho, 76, *77*
Loíza, 61
London, 230
L'Oriental, 8
Loureiro, 75
Lowcountry, 153–58
   cuisine characteristics, 154
   geographic region, 153
   Madeira connection, 156–57
   recipe, 158
   signature dishes and wine pairings, 155
   wine list, 177

M
Maboneng, 42
Madeira, 156–57
Maghreb, 5
Maipo Valley, 106
Maipú wine region, 121
maize, 29–30
makgeolli, 200

Malbec, 99, 114
Malcolm X, 144
malolactic fermentation, xxi
Malvasia, 234
Mandela, Nelson, 43
Mardi Gras, 170–71
Marmara, 215
Marrakech, 6–8
Marrero, Lynnette, 111
Marsanne, 33, 198
Martinotti method, 130
mate tea, 108
mauby, 83
McCoy, Bill, 86
Mediterranean, 217
Meknes-Tafilalet, 8
Melba's Restaurant, 144, 147
Melon de Bourgogne, 198
Mencía, 69, 216
Mendoza, 119, 120, 123
Merlot, 69
Meskheti, 223
méthode cap classique (MCC), 46, 50
méthode champenoise, 130
Mexico, 94–102
   agave spirits, 95
   facts and statistics, 94
   Mexico City, 94–96, 99
   recipe, 102
   signature dishes and wine pairings, 100
   signature drinks, 95
   taco tour, 99
   wine grapes, 97
   wine list, 136
   wine producers, 96
   wine regions, 96–98
mezcal, 95
M'hudi Boutique Family Wines, 48
Mideastern and Southeastern Anatolia, 216–17
Mie sake, 193–94
Miller, Adrian, 142
mineral flavors, xvii
mint tea, 6
Mitchell, Ed and Ryan, 168
Mix, Ivy, 111
mofongo
   pairing with wine, 63
   Vegan, + Rioja Blanco, *64,* 65–66
mojito, 60
Mombasa, 31
Momotaro, 196
Monastrell, 33
moonshine
   The Parish, 173

Morocco, 4–9
   facts and statistics, 4
   signature dishes and wine pairings, 9
   signature drinks, 6
   wine list, 52
   wine regions, 7–8
Moscatel de Setúbal, 66
Moscato d'Asti, 75, 229
Mount Gay, 84–85
Mourvèdre, 216
mouthfeel, defined, xxi
Mozambique, 34–40
   facts and statistics, 34
   recipes, 39, 40
   signature dish and wine pairing, 37
   wine list, 53
Mtsvane Khakuri, 226
Müller-Thurgau, 197

N
Nadagogo sake, 193
Nagano sake, 194
Nairobi, 31
Negroamaro, 74
Nerello Mascalese, 26
Nero d'Avola, 100
Nero d'Avola Rosato, 9
Neuquén, 123
New Orleans
   culture, 169–72
   signature drinks, 170
   Vietnamese community in, 204–7
Nguyen, Nini, 210
Nigeria, 10–17
   facts and statistics, 11
   Guinness consumption, 32
   jollof rice, 15
   signature dishes and wine pairings, 13–14
   wine list, 52
Niigata sake, 194
Ningxia, 186
Nomadness Travel Tribe, 125
Nom Wah Tea Parlor, 191
noodles
   Bún Thịt Nướng with Egg Rolls + German Kabinett Riesling, 210–11
   Pan-Fried, in Superior Soy Sauce + Pinot Noir, *190,* 191

O
oak barrel aging, 70
Omachi City sake, 194
orange juice, 6
Otsu, Nobu, 192
oxidation, xxi

INDEX

P
PaardenKloof Estate, 48
Paarl, 49
País, 114
palm wine, 13
Pano, Paula de, 207
Partagás, 70
Parish, The, 173
Pastelitos (Empanadas), Rainbow, + Petite Sirah, *78*, 79–80
Patagonia and the Atlantic, 123–24
Peacock, Shaquay, 39
Peanut Sauce, Vatapá–Red Palm Oil, 134
pechuga, 95
Pecorino, 197
peri peri
  history of, 38
  Sauce, 39
Petite Sirah, 79
Petit Verdot, 161
pét-nat/pétillant nature/méthode ancestrale, 130
Philippines
  Filipino cuisine, 206–7
  Filipino diaspora in the United States, 204–7
  signature dishes and wine pairings, 209
Phylloxera, 110
Picpoul de Pinet, 87
piña colada, 60
pineapple
  The Parish, 173
  Roasted, Cornmeal Cake + Sauternes, 151–52
Pinochet, Augusto, 110–12
Pinotage, 44, 50
Pinot Gris, 74, 197, 202
Pinot Noir, 191, 197
Pinot Noir Rosé, 132
pisco
  about, 108
  Buena Onda, 111
  Momotaro, 196
  Yerba Mate–Infused, 111
Planalto Catarinense, 129
plantains. *See* mofongo
Pok Pok restaurant empire, 206
Polanco, 96
pork
  Bún Thịt Nướng with Egg Rolls + German Kabinett Riesling, 210–11
  Chicken and Sausage Gumbo + Carignan, 174–75, *175*
  dietary prohibitions against, 144

Rodney Scott's Spareribs + Cabernet Sauvignon, 165–67, *166*
A Very Good Kimchi Jjigae + Ramato Pinot Gris, 202, *203*
Portugal
  former colonies of, 35–39, 231
  Portuguese trade routes, 156
  Portuguese wines, 39
Prädikatswein, 208
Previte, Rose, 225
Primitivo, 99
Prosecco Rive di San Pietro di Barbozza Brut, 172
Prosecco Rosé, 198
Puerto Rico, 58–66
  coffee, 59
  facts and statistics, 58
  mofongo chronicles, 63
  recipes, 62, 65
  road tripping, 61
  rum, 60
  signature dishes and wine pairings, 66
  signature drinks, 60
  wine list, 88
pyrazines, xxi

Q
Qualitätswein, 208
Querétaro, 98
qvevri wines, 219

R
Rabat-Sale-Zemmour-Zaer, 8
Racha-Lechkhumi, 222–23
raicilla, 95
Ramato Pinot Gris, 202
ras el hanout, 7
Rastafari religion, 19–20
Real McCoy rum, 85–86
recipes
  Barbecued Spatchcocked Chicken + Cabernet Franc, 168
  Buena Onda, 111
  Bún Thịt Nướng with Egg Rolls + German Kabinett Riesling, 210–11
  Chicken and Sausage Gumbo + Carignan, 174–75, *175*
  Chilean Chacarero Sandwich + Carménère, *116*, 117
  Crab Curry aka Ikala + Baga Rosé, 40, *41*
  Crab Rice + Garganega, 158
  Eggnog, 149
  Grilled Jerk Lobster Tails + Alvarinho, 76, *77*

Jollof Rice + Zinfandel, *16*, 17
Lobio Mtsvanilit + Tavkveri, *224*, 225
Marrero Family Coquito, 62
Melba's Signature Chicken and Eggnog Waffles + Vintage Champagne Blanc de Noirs, 147–50, *148*
Momotaro, 196
Pan-Fried Noodles in Superior Soy Sauce + Pinot Noir, *190*, 191
The Parish, 173
Peri Peri Sauce, 39
Rainbow Pastelitos (Empanadas) + Petite Sirah, *78*, 79–80
Roasted Pineapple Cornmeal Cake + Sauternes, 151–52
Rodney Scott's Spareribs + Cabernet Sauvignon, 165–67, *166*
Rodney's Rib Rub, 167
Rodney's Sauce, 156, 167
Saag Paneer, but with Feta + Malvasia, *234*, 235
Somali Beef Stew + Nerello Mascalese, *26*, 27
Strawberry Butter, 149
Vatapá–Red Palm Oil Peanut Sauce, 134
Vegan Mofongo + Rioja Blanco, *64*, 65–66
Veracruz-Style Snapper + Rosé, 102, *103*
A Very Good Kimchi Jjigae + Ramato Pinot Gris, 202, *203*
Viera com Vatapá + Albariño, 133–34, *135*
residual sugar, xxi
Rib Rub, Rodney's, 167
rice
  Crab, + Garganega, 158
  Jollof Rice + Zinfandel, *16*, 17
  jollof styles and origins, 14–15
  in lowcountry, 153
Ricker, Andy, 206
Riesling, 209, 210
Rihanna, 86
Rioja Blanco, 65
Rioja Reserva, 69
Rioja Tempranillo Rosado, 74
Río Negro, 123–24
Rkatsiteli, 87, 226
robusta coffee, 25
Rosado, 189
rosé, 13, 102, 155, 201
Roussanne, 229
rum
  in Barbados, 83, 84–86

248

INDEX

bottle labels, 85
in the Caribbean, 84–86
Marrero Family Coquito, 62
The Parish, 173
in Puerto Rico, 60
Russian Empire, 220

S

Saag Paneer, but with Feta + Malvasia, 234, *235*
Saga sake, 194
Sahara, 5–6
sake
    categories of, 195
    Japanese regions, 193–95
    producers of, 194
Salazar, António de Oliveira, 36
Salta, 120
Salvador, 127
Samagrelo, 223
Sandwich, Chilean Chacarero, + Carménère, *116*, 117
Sangiovese, 23, 155, 216
San Juan, 59–61, 122–23
San Luis Potosí, 98
Santiago de Chile, 105–6, 109
Santurce, 59
São Paulo, 127–28, 193
São Tomé and Príncipe, 34–40
    facts and statistics, 34
    signature dish and wine pairing, 37
    wine list, 53
Saperavi, 226
sauces
    Peri Peri, 39
    Rodney's, 156, 167
    Vatapá–Red Palm Oil Peanut, 134
Sausage and Chicken Gumbo + Carignan, 174–75, *175*
Sauternes, 151
Sauvignon Blanc, 9, 114, *115*, 198
Savatiano, 69
Sazerac, 170
Schiavo, 201
Scott, Rodney, 162, 165
seafood
    in Barbados, 83
    Crab Curry aka Ikala + Baga Rosé, 40, *41*
    Crab Rice + Garganega, 158
    Veracruz-Style Snapper + Rosé, 102, *103*
    Viera com Vatapá + Albariño, 133–34, *135*
Selassie, Haile, 19–20
Sémillon, 87, 115

Senegal, 10–17
    facts and statistics, 10
    jollof rice (Thiéboudienne), 15
    recipe, 17
    signature dishes and wine pairings, 13–14
    wine list, 52
Serra do Sudeste, 129
Serra Gaúcha, 128
Ses'fikile Wines, 48
Seven Sisters Vineyards, 48
Shandong cuisine, 188
Shandong wine region, 185
Shanxi, 186–87
Shiga sake, 194
Shiraz, 75, 229
Shizuoka sake, 195
shochu, 195
Sichuan cuisine, 187
Silk Roads, 219
Skin-Contact Arinto, 37
Snapper, Veracruz-Style, + Rosé, 102, *103*
Sofrito, 65
soju, 200, 201
Somalia, 18–26
    facts and statistics, 19
    recipe, 26
    signature dishes and wine pairings, 23
    signature drinks, 22
    wine list, 52
Somali Beef Stew + Nerello Mascalese, 26, *27*
sotol, 95
souk (marketplace), 6
soul food, 142–52
    description of, 143
    history of, 142–43
    in New York City, 143–44
    recipes, 147, 151
    served with barbecue, 162
    signature menus and wine pairings, 145–46
    wine list, 176
South Africa, 42–51
    Black-owned wine brands, 48
    facts and statistics, 42
    lekker braai, 49–51
    signature dishes and wine pairings, 50
    sparkling wines, 46
    wine grapes, 44
    wine labels, 45
    wine list, 53
    wines and wine regions, 44–49
Southeast Asia, 204–11
    countries in, 204

Filipino food, 206–7
German wines for food, 207–9
kamayan dining, 207
recipe, 210
signature drinks, 206
Thai, Vietnamese, and Filipino diaspora in the United States, 204–7
Thai food, 205–7
Vietnamese food, 204–7
wine list, 237–38
South Korea, 199–202
    drinking culture, 200
    recipe, 202
    signature dishes and wine pairings, 201
    signature drinks, 200
    wine list, 237
Sparkling Blanc de Noir, 198
Sparkling Chardonnay, 114
sparkling wines. *See also specific types*
    Brazilian, 130
    Champagne, 131, 147
    methods for, 130
    pairing with soul food, 145
    South African, 46
Spätlese, 208, 209
spice flavors, xvii
spinach
    Saag Paneer, but with Feta + Malvasia, 234, *235*
Stellenbosch, 49
Stew, Somali Beef, + Nerello Mascalese, 26, *27*
St. Laurent, 66
Strawberry Butter, 149
Sulemange, Jeny, 38, 40
Super Tuscan, 69
Sur, 113
sushi, pairing with wine, 198
Suzuki-Orellana, Christian, 196
Swartland/Darling, 49
sweet potatoes, 30
Syrah, 50, 66, 99

T

Tacos, Mexican, 99
tacos and wine pairings, 99
Tang, Wilson, 191
tank method, 130
Tannat, 63, 132
tannins, xxi
Tanzania, 28–33
    facts and statistics, 29
    signature dishes and wine pairings, 33
    signature drinks, 30

249

INDEX

Tanzania (*continued*)
    wine industry, 29
    wine list, 53
Tastemakers Africa, 12, 42
Tavkveri, 225, 226
Tawny Port, 87
tea
    in Chile, 108
    in India, 231–32
    in Kenya and Tanzania, 30
    in Morocco, 6
    in Southeast Asia, 206
t'ej honey wine, 22, 23
Tempranillo, 161
tequila, 95
Terremoto, 108
terroir, xix, xxi
Tesselaarsdal Wines, 48
Texas wine producers, 162
Texas wine regions, 163
texture, defined, xxi
Thai cuisine, 205–7
Thailand
    signature dishes and wine pairings, 209
    Thai diaspora in the United States, 204–7
    Thai food, 205–7
Thiam, Pierre, 17
Tokaji Aszú, 216
Tokat, 215
Tone Numata sake, 194
Torontel, 114
Torrontés, 75
traditional method/méthode champenoise, 130
Trebbiano, 23
Trocken, 208, 209
Trockenbeerenauslese, 208, 209
Trollinger, 189
Trujillo, Rafael, 72
Tsolikouri, 226
Tucumán, 120–21
Turkey, 212–17
    facts and statistics, 212
    history, 213
    signature dishes and wine pairings, 216
    wine grapes, 213
    wine list, 238
    wine regions, 214–17
Tusker Beer, 32

U
umeshu, 195
United Arab Emirates, 227–29
    drinking culture, 227
    Emirati cuisine, 227–28
    facts and statistics, 227
    signature dishes and wine pairings, 229
    signature drinks, 228
    wine list, 239
United States of America, 140–77
    largest wine-making states, 163
    map, 140–41
    overview, 141
    up-and-coming wine-making states, 163
    wine label regulations, 164
    wine list, 176–77
USSR, 220–21

V
Vale de São Francisco, 128
Valpolicella Ripasso Doc Superiore, 23
Valpolicella Superiore, 87
varietal, defined, xxi
variety, defined, xxi
Vatapá–Red Palm Oil Peanut Sauce, 134
vegetal flavors, xvii
Velez, Paola, 79
Verdejo, 99, 132
Verdelho Madeira, 155
Verdicchio, 198
Vermentino, 87, 100, 198
vermouth
    Momotaro, 196
Vianda, 60–61
Viera com Vatapá + Albariño, 133–34, *135*
Vietnam
    signature dishes and wine pairings, 209
    Vietnamese cuisine, 204–6, 207
    Vietnamese diaspora in the United States, 204–7
Vieux Carré, 170
Viña del Mar, 107
Vin de Constance, 50
Vinho Verde, 37
Vinho Verde Alvarinho producers, 76
Vinho Verde Branco, 198
Vin Santo del Chianti Classico, 146
vintage, defined, xxi
Viognier, 33
Vitis vinifera, xxi

W
Waffles, Eggnog, and Chicken, Melba's Signature, + Vintage Champagne Blanc de Noirs, 147–50, *148*
Walker Bay, 49
Wells Supper Club, 144
whisky
    Japanese, 195
    in Momotaro, 196
Williams, Brittney "Stikxz," 76
Wilson, Melba, 147
wine
    approachable and easily paired, xx
    aromas and flavors, xvii–xix
    five S's tasting (deductive tasting), xvii
    Flavor Wheel, xviii
    serving rules, xx
    serving temperatures, xx
    terms and definitions, xxi
    terroir, xix
wineglasses, xx
wine pairings
    contrasting flavors, xx
    finding balance, xix
    matching flavors, xx
    Moroccan dishes, 9
    two approaches to, xix–xx
Winery, The (Harlem, NY), 10–11, 192
Woods, Sylvia, 143

X
xawaash spice mix, 22, 26
Xinjiang, 186
Xinomavro, 33

Y
Yamagato sake, 193
Yamanashi sake, 193
Yerba Mate–Infused Pisco, 111
Yunnan, 187

Z
Zacatecas, 98
Zanzibar, 31
Zhejiang cuisine, 187–88
Zinfandel, 15, 17